LONELY PLANET PUBLICATIONS

JOHN LEE

VANCOUVER
C I T Y   G U I D E

INTRODUCING VANCOUVER

Cameras at the ready for great sea-and-skyscraper city vistas

Kayakers bobble past, waving at friends on the beach. A floatplane shimmies over the park, diving to its watery landing strip. A chattery hubbub bounces off the gleaming glass towers that forest the city like latter-day totems.

When the Olympic and Paralympic Winter Games roll into town in 2010, there'll be no shortage of jaw-dropping visuals, instantly inspiring people around the world to check out Canada's immigration procedures. Vancouver is, after all, one of the cities that routinely tops those lists of the world's greatest places to live. But beyond the breathtaking snowcapped crags, city-hugging beaches and dense waterfront forests lies a comparatively young metropolis that's still trying to discover its true identity – less than 150 years after a 'gassy' Englishman rowed in and kicked it all off with a makeshift pub.

Covering the city's main outdoor, museum and gallery attractions will certainly keep you busy for a few days. After that it's highly advisable to start digging beneath the surface to find out what really makes this laid-back lotusland tick. You'll discover that the 'real Vancouver' is in the clamorous Commercial Dr coffee shops, the hipster hangouts of SoMa, the gay-friendly streets of the West End, the kaleidoscopic thoroughfares of Chinatown and the historic, re-invigorated old streets of Gastown, where that original pub once stood.

Of course, the rest of the world will know all about this in 2010. Why not beat them to it by dropping by for your own urban adventure – coupled with a giant doorstep of outdoor attractions.

CITY LIFE

Inspired by their stunning surroundings, Vancouverites have discovered more ways to interact with the outdoors than almost anyone – this really is a city where you can ski in the morning and hit the beach in the afternoon. But the locals are not just a bunch of rice-cake-noshing fitness freaks. The city is one of Canada's top dining towns, and is currently undergoing an Olympic-sized surge of new openings. The arts and nightlife scenes are similarly tasty – although you'll have to be a little adventurous to discover the highlights.

Wherever you end up rubbing shoulders with the residents, it won't be long before you've told them how much you love their city and they've replied that it's not all perfect. For every Vancouverite excited about the Olympics, you'll find another worried about how much it's going to cost. House prices have been rapidly rising in recent years, triggering angst among residents who can't afford to buy. And that's before you get onto the thorny topic of the Downtown Eastside, the destitute neighborhood that many feel should be a much more important funding priority than the Olympics.

'With its dozens of year-round annual events, the "city of glass" is more fun than it's ever been for visitors, who often come for the mountains and end up staying for the vibe'

But while the serious side of life is always bubbling beneath the surface, Vancouverites also know how to party. With its giant free fireworks displays, jazz, fringe and film festivals and dozens of year-round annual events, the 'city of glass' is more fun than it's ever been for visitors, who often come for the mountains and end up staying for the vibe.

Stanley Park (p52) – postcard-perfect in the fall – is a sea, sand and forest spectacular dear to the city's heart

HIGHLIGHTS

DINING, DRINKING & DISTRICTS

The lifeblood of the city is its distinctive districts, many worth a day of exploring. A rolling smorgasbord of great nosh will keep you fueled. While seafood is a good starting point, make sure you dip in to some finger-licking ethnic eateries and taste-trip at a night market.

❶ Commercial Drive
The Drive's coffee-fueled counterculture vibe keeps this area lively (p83)

❷ SoMa
South Main's eclectic designer shops are dripping with hipster fashions (p116)

❸ Gastown
Vancouver's once-grungy original 'hood is now alive with great bars (p152)

❹ Vij's
Fusion is a Vancouver dining trait, pioneered at this contemporary Indian restaurant (p140)

❺ Chinatown Night Market
Feasting at the alfresco market (p115) is the best way to dine and stroll

ACTIVE VANCOUVER

Vancouverites are born wearing Lycra, so you can expect to see plenty of muscle-stretching locals sweating their way around the city. Visitors can mix with the heavy-breathing fraternity on jogging and cycling trails, or at local ski, beach and kayaking hot spots.

❶ Grouse Mountain
Snowboarders and skiers hit the slopes at Vancouver's top winter playground (p183)

❷ Kayaking
Hop in a kayak and admire the cityscape from the water (p180)

❸ Stanley Park
Seawall cycling, jogging or blading is an ideal scenery-ogling activity (p178)

CITY STYLE

Set amid mountains, sea and forest, Vancouver is a visual treat for camera-wielding visitors. But it's not just about the natural surroundings here: the city is stuffed with non-natural sights that complement the appeal of those well-known outdoorsy vistas.

① City of Glass
Downtown's shimmering glass towers (p34) are Vancouver's modern-day forests

② Totem Poles
The handsome Stanley Park totems (p55) are stirring reminders of the region's first residents

③ Public Art
The city challenges with some wild and wacky public art displays (p27)

WATER, WATER EVERYWHERE!

Surrounded by water on three sides, Vancouver is a port city that will always have a little sea salt running through its veins. For visitors, there are plenty of ways to enjoy this coastal undercurrent.

❶ Second Beach
By day a sunbathing hot spot, but come dusk it's a sunset-viewing favorite (p54)

❷ Granville Island
A waterfront view is the ideal side dish for coffee or a meal of fish-and-chips (p138)

❸ False Creek
The city's colorful miniferries (p224) are the best way to hit the water

CONTENTS

Continued from previous page.

John Lee

Born in the southern UK city of St Albans, John made his first transatlantic trip to Vancouver for the Expo '86 world's fair, where he remembers an English-style pub and a levitating Japanese train. Returning home to plot a permanent move, he eventually finagled his way into British Columbia's University of Victoria, where he puzzled the Political Science profs with a determination to study utopian fiction. Finding an unexpected paucity of jobs in the utopian field upon graduation, he swapped his student visa for permanent citizenship and – after an inspirational trip on the Trans-Siberian Railway – jumped into a full-time freelance travel-writing career. John moved to Vancouver in 1999, and now lives just five minutes from Stanley Park. He has worked on 10 Lonely Planet books, and his journalism, recorded online at www .johnleewriter.com, has appeared in more than 120 publications, including the *Guardian, Los Angeles Times, Chicago Tribune* and *National Geographic Traveler*.

JOHN'S TOP VANCOUVER DAY

Even though I'm a tea-quaffing Brit, no day can really get rolling until a late-morning java, so I stroll to Caffè Artigiano (p149), snagging the last patio seat while I peruse the latest *Georgia Straight*. Nipping across the road, I duck into the shop at the Vancouver Art Gallery (p46) for a birthday card, then amble along Granville St and down toward Gastown for lunch with a friend. We decide on Six Acres (p152) and tuck into a shared plate of German sausage, sharp cheese and a couple of bottled brews from Vancouver Island. Walking back along Water St toward Granville St, I pick up a bus and make for Granville Island (p86). The artisan stores and public market keep me occupied for a couple of hours before I decide to head west for a seawall stroll. Watching the tiny sailboats and miniferries bobbing around in the waters under the Burrard Bridge, I eventually arrive in waterfront Vanier Park (p97). The summertime Bard on the Beach (p174) tents cover the area and I can hear an energetic matinee performance percolating the air with some familiar (and not-so-familiar) lines. After picking up some tickets for a show later in the week, I retrace my steps and head for an alfresco late-afternoon snack at Go Fish (p139), a seafood stand on the waterfront. Checking my watch, I stroll up South Granville and catch a bus to Commercial Dr. I'm meeting a couple of buddies for a few early-evening beers. We settle on the Charlatan (p153), managing to finagle a window seat where we can sip some Big Rock Ales and watch the lively streetscape, accompanied by some 'wacky backy' aromas wafting sweetly along from a nearby apartment block.

Outside Vancouver's peak summer season, you should have little trouble accessing hotels, restaurants, attractions and events, even if you roll into town without any advance notice. But if sleepover location, daily budget and catching specific events – sporting or artistic – are important to you, it's worth doing some homework before you pack your bags and head for the airport.

WHEN TO GO

Vancouver is definitely an all-season city but specific times of year are best suited to certain interests and pursuits. If you're determined to brush up on your snowsports before making a last-minute bid for Olympic glory, December to March is the ideal time to strap on your skis. If you want to bask on the beaches and stroll in shorts through the forests, you should bring your sunscreen to town in July or August. And if you're an arts buff and you just can't wait to get your next fix of live theater or classical music, the season kicks off in October and usually stretches to April. Summer is the hot season for festivals – especially outdoor ones – but the city stages large and small events throughout the year.

You can expect pleasant temperatures most of the time. In winter temperatures rarely drop below 0°C in the city and summer sees long, languid days with 25°C a common marker. It can rain here at any time, but the October to February period is the rainiest – remember that when it's raining here, it's often snowing in the hills. Peak season for hotels is midsummer, but there's good weather in late spring and early fall and these near-shoulder periods can be a good deal for budget-minded travelers.

FESTIVALS

While July and August remain the peak months for Vancouver festivals, the city has a year-round calendar of events that should give most visitors a couple of options whatever time of year they're arriving. Tourism Vancouver's website (www.tourismvancouver.com) has a round-up of the larger fests; check the free newspaper *Georgia Straight* for up-to-date listings covering smaller cultural happenings.

January
POLAR BEAR SWIM
☎ 604-665-3424; www.vancouver.ca/parks/events/polarbear

This chilly New Year's Day affair has been taking place on English Bay Beach (p65) annually since 1920, and it might just be the ultimate cure for a hangover. At around 2.30pm more than a thousand people charge into the ocean, the temperature of which hovers at a frosty 6.5°C.

PUSH FESTIVAL
☎ 604-605-8284; www.pushfestival.ca

A three-week season of innovative new theater, music, opera and dance from around the world or around the corner. Adventurous performance-art fans will love this unusual showcase, staged at venues around the city in mid-January.

DINE OUT VANCOUVER
www.tourismvancouver.com/visitors/dining

In mid-January the city's top restaurants offer two weeks of three-course tasting menus for $15, $20 or $25, plus a selection of British Columbia wines. Check the list of participating restaurants on Tourism Vancouver's website and book ahead – the top spots always sell out. See p134 for other local food fests.

February
CHINESE NEW YEAR
☎ 604-632-3808; www.vancouver-chinatown.com

Depending on the calendar, this multiday, highly festive celebration in and around Chinatown can take place in January or February, but it always includes plenty of color, dancing and great food. The highlights are the Dragon Parade and firecrackers.

VANCOUVER INTERNATIONAL STORYTELLING FESTIVAL
☎ 604-876-4272; www.vancouverstorytelling.org

A three-day celebration of the art of storytelling, usually with a different theme each year, held in early February. Expect public readings and associated events. Staged at

e VanDusen Botanical Garden (p90), this
s an ideal way to meet the local writerly
community.

WINTERRUPTION
☎ 604-666-5784; www.winterruption.com
Granville Island chases away the winter
blues with a warming weekend of live
music, theater and family-friendly events in
late February. Dress warmly – many of the
events are outside, and you'll enjoy the hot
chocolate more.

top picks
COMMUNITY FESTIVALS

- Powell Street Festival (p15)
- Commercial Drive Festival (p14)
- Greek Day (p14)
- Taiwanese Cultural Festival (p15)
- Caribbean Days Festival (p14)

March
VANCOUVER INTERNATIONAL DANCE FESTIVAL
☎ 604-662-7441; www.vidf.ca
Local, national and international contemporary dance artists come together for this
three-week-long spree of workshops and
performances, most of which take place at
the Roundhouse Community Arts &
Recreation Centre (p70).

CELTICFEST VANCOUVER
☎ 604-683-8331; www.celticfestvancouver.com
In mid-March downtown's annual St
Patrick's Day parade and five-day Irish
cultural fiesta attract those who like their
beer to be green-hued at least once a year.
Expect some shamrock-tinged shenanigans
and a chance to mix with local and visiting
Irish folk.

SPRING BREAK THEATRE FESTIVAL
☎ 604-687-1644; www.artsclub.com
A week-long run of shows and events
aimed at children. It's organized by the
Arts Club Theatre Company (p174) and
staged at venues around Granville Island in
mid-March.

VANCOUVER PLAYHOUSE INTERNATIONAL WINE FESTIVAL
☎ 604-872-6622; www.playhousewinefest.com
With more than 500 reds and whites to
sample, from 166 international vineyards,
this late-March event is one of the largest
wine shows in North America. There's a
strong educational element and several
events for neophytes. The main festival
venue is the Vancouver Convention &
Exhibition Centre.

April
SUN RUN
☎ 604-689-9441; www.sunrun.com
This is one of North America's largest street
races, attracting 55,000 runners and ambling
wannabes for a fun day out in late April. A
great way to see the city, the 10km route
winds though Stanley Park and along the
waterfront, and ends with a big party at BC
Place Stadium. See the boxed text, p182, for
more information.

May
VANCOUVER INTERNATIONAL MARATHON
☎ 604-872-2928; www.adidasvanmarathon.ca
Smaller than the Sun Run (above), this one's
for the serious hoofers. Strap on your
running shoes and race through the city's
streets in early May, along with hundreds of
local fitness fans and athletes from around
the world.

VANCOUVER INTERNATIONAL CHILDREN'S FESTIVAL
☎ 604-708-5655; www.childrensfestival.ca
The red-and-white tents go up in Vanier
Park (p97) on the third or fourth Monday
of May and stay up for eight days. During that time, almost 50,000 people enjoy
acts dedicated to keeping the young and
young-at-heart entertained. Expect plenty
of face painting.

NEW MUSIC WEST
☎ 604-689-2910; www.newmusicwest.com
A slew of new and emerging pop and rock
bands come to town and play live in various clubs over five days; you buy a wrist-
band and jump from place to place. The
festival's dates have been a bit erratic, but
mid-May is the current favored time frame.

June

PORTUGUESE HERITAGE MONTH
☎ 604-684-5876; www.portuguesemonth.com
This celebration of all things Portuguese brings the local expat community together for a month-long roster of arts and cultural happenings, including film, theater, dance, sport and culinary celebrations. The events are held at venues around the city.

FRANCOPHONE SUMMER FESTIVAL
☎ 604-736-9806; www.lecentreculturel.com
Held in mid-June, this is a week-long celebration of Francophonic music from French Canada and around the world. There are performances at venues throughout the city, plus a weekend festival at W 7th Ave and Granville St.

VANCOUVER INTERNATIONAL JAZZ FESTIVAL
☎ 604-872-5200; www.coastaljazz.com
Into its second decade, Vancouver's biggest music festival takes places at an eclectic array of venues over 10 days in mid-June. It combines superstar performances (Oscar Peterson and Diana Krall are past masters) with plenty of free outdoor shows – especially in Gastown and Yaletown, and on Granville Island.

GREEK DAY
☎ 604-738-7126; www.greekday.com
The local Hellenic community comes together for a rip-roaring showcase of Greek culture in mid-June. All are welcome to check out the one-day Kitsilano event (on W Broadway, between MacDonald and Blenheim Sts), complete with two performance stages, wandering street entertainers and lots of great food.

ALCAN DRAGON BOAT FESTIVAL
☎ 604-688-2382; www.adbf.com
During the third weekend of June, about 2000 competitors from around the world take part in dragon boat races on False Creek, accompanied by music, theater and food pavilions at the Plaza of Nations.

COMMERCIAL DRIVE FESTIVAL
www.commercialdrivefestival.org
Cars are barred from the Drive for two separate summer days (mid-June and mid-July),

enabling artists, street performers and food vendors – plus 35,000 locals – to wander in the sun and enjoy themselves.

July

CANADA DAY CELEBRATIONS
☎ 604-775-8025; www.canadadayatcanadaplace.com
Downtown's Canada Place (p46) is the main location for celebrations marking the country's July 1 birthday. Expect music, food and fireworks, plus lots of people wandering around with maple-leaf temporary tattoos. There's also a smaller event at Granville Island.

DANCING ON THE EDGE
☎ 604-689-0926; www.dancingontheedge.org
In early July top companies and dancers from across Canada gather for 10 days of world-leading contemporary dance. Expect some challenging but expertly executed performances, staged at venues around the city.

VANCOUVER FOLK MUSIC FESTIVAL
☎ 604-602-9798; www.thefestival.bc.ca
Jericho Beach (p96) is the venue for this weekend festival in mid-July, which attracts about 30,000 people and has musicians performing on seven stages. Past headliners have ranged from Billy Bragg to Bruce Cockburn.

TOUR DE GASTOWN
☎ 604-836-9993; www.tourdegastown.com
In mid-July the city's most elite cycling race attracts top pedal-pushers from across North America with its 1.2km course through Gastown. Men ride 50 laps, women ride 30 laps and the purse is $15,000.

CARIBBEAN DAYS FESTIVAL
☎ 604-515-2400; www.caribbeandaysfestival.com
Great music, dancing and food highlight these two days of fun held at Waterfront Park, Lonsdale Quay in North Vancouver in late July. One of North Van's most popular community events, it draws 15,000 locals.

ILLUMINARES LANTERN PROCESSION
☎ 604-879-8611; www.publicdreams.org
On a late-July Saturday, hundreds of people gather at dusk with shimmering

paper lanterns shaped like serpents, birds and other flights of fancy; participants walk around Trout Lake in East Vancouver amid fire sculptures, music and fireworks. Lantern-making workshops take place beforehand.

EARLY MUSIC FESTIVAL
☎ 604-732-1610; www.earlymusic.bc.ca
This celebration of medieval to baroque music stretches intermittently over three weeks in late July, as lute and harpsichord players roll into town to celebrate some of the world's most beautiful but lesser-known music. Expect plenty of chin-stroking musos listening intently to highly authentic performances, mostly held at UBC.

POWELL STREET FESTIVAL
☎ 604-739-9388; www.powellstreetfestival.com
This annual celebration of Japanese-Canadian culture is one of the city's most popular community festivals. Staged in East Vancouver's Oppenheimer Park in late July, it's a fascinating and colorful day of food, music, dance and theater.

CELEBRATION OF LIGHT
☎ 604-641-1193; www.hsbccelebrationoflight.com
The world's largest musical fireworks competition takes place at English Bay (p65) over four nights in late July and early August. Three competing countries (which change each year) put on their most spectacular displays of fireworks over three nights, then come together for a dazzling finale on the fourth night, when the winning country – chosen by popular vote – is also announced.

August
PRIDE WEEK
☎ 604-687-0955; www.vancouverpride.ca
A week-long kaleidoscope of gay-, lesbian- and bisexual-friendly fashion shows, gala parties and concerts that culminates in western Canada's largest pride parade. Typically held on the first Sunday of August, the saucy parade draws 200,000 people to its Denman and Davie Sts route.

FESTIVAL VANCOUVER
☎ 604-688-1152; www.festivalvancouver.bc.ca
In mid-August, more than 20,000 people come to hear national and international artists perform a huge variety of musical genres, including orchestral, choral, operatic, jazz, world and chamber music. The venues vary throughout the festival's two-week span, but there's usually a free outdoor stage on the Georgia St side of the Vancouver Art Gallery (p46).

ABBOTSFORD INTERNATIONAL AIR SHOW
☎ 604-852-8511; www.abbotsfordairshow.com
You'll need a car to get to this event – Abbotsford is 56km southeast of the city near the Canada–US border – but it will be worth it for what has become 'Canada's national air show.' The displays from world-leading aeronautical teams are thrilling; if you're in Vancouver during the mid-August event you'll likely see the Canadian Snowbirds team noisily buzzing the city before flying on to the skies above Abbotsford.

BARE BUNS FUN RUN
www.wreckbeach.org
The clothing-free Buns Run takes place – where else? – on Wreck Beach (p101). Among the prizes are those for 'best-decorated buns' and 'wackiest hat.' The run is usually held on a Sunday in mid-August and starts at 11.30am sharp, so get you buns in gear on time.

PACIFIC NATIONAL EXHIBITION
☎ 604-253-2311; www.pne.bc.ca
An old-school, two-week-long country fair that's evolved into a fairground with a kicking wooden roller coaster and an extensive program of family-friendly shows and music concerts from mid-August. Don't leave without downing a bag of mini donuts.

September
TAIWANESE CULTURAL FESTIVAL
☎ 604-263-9311; www.taiwanfest.ca
So successful it has now expanded to Toronto, this annual three-day event in early September allows the city's Taiwanese expats to celebrate the culture of their homeland. Food is a key delight at the festival, staged at venues around False Creek. Culinary displays (and plenty of samples) are offered, along with musical and theatrical displays.

top picks

QUIRKY FESTIVALS

- Bare Buns Fun Run (p15)
- Polar Bear Swim (p12)
- Push Festival (p12)
- Eastside Culture Crawl (right)
- Parade of the Lost Souls (right)

DAVIE DAY

☎ 604-696-0144; www.westendbia.com
The West End community along Davie St, between Broughton and Burrard Sts, invites the city (and visitors) to drop by for a day of live music, food and fun in early September. This is the center of the city's gay community, so you might notice a few drag queens added to the mix.

VANCOUVER INTERNATIONAL FRINGE FESTIVAL

☎ 604-257-0350; www.vancouverfringe.com
One of the city's biggest events, this lively 10-day roster of wild and wacky theatrics draws thousands to large, small and unconventional Granville Island venues in mid-September. Expect short plays, stand-up and comedy revues, and prepare to be adventurous.

GLOBAL COMEDY FEST

☎ 604-683-0883; www.vancouvercomedyfest.com
Nine days of rib-tickling mirth, with Canadian and international acts raising the roof at various venues around town in mid-September. Improv events feature heavily but there are tons of stand-up comedians doing their thing too.

VANCOUVER INTERNATIONAL FILM FESTIVAL

☎ 604-685-0260; www.viff.org
It lacks the star-studded glamour of its Toronto rival, but this film fest is much more of a Canadian affair. One of the city's most popular festivals, its 17-day calendar (beginning late September) covers hundreds of screenings of local, national and international movies, plus gala events and industry schmoozes. For other local film fests worthy of a look, see the boxed text, p170.

October

VANCOUVER INTERNATIONAL WRITERS & READERS FESTIVAL

☎ 604-681-6330; www.writersfest.bc.ca
Despite the mouthful of a name – with all those writers around, can't they think of something better? – this five-day mid-October literary event is highly popular. Local and international scribblers turn up for seminars, galas and public forums; past guests have included Salman Rushdie, Irvine Welsh and Douglas Coupland. Sign up early for an audience with the biggest scribes. It's held at venues around Granville Island.

NEW MUSIC FESTIVAL

☎ 604-633-0861; www.newmusic.org
Staged at downtown's Scotiabank Dance Centre, this three-day mid-October fest showcases an eclectic array of contemporary music that can range from indie guitar to free jazz. There are also workshops for visiting musos.

PARADE OF THE LOST SOULS

☎ 604-879-8611; www.publicdreams.org
A spectral Day of the Dead celebration in late October, in which a torch-lit procession of spookily dressed performers moves through the streets around Grandview Park, near Commercial Dr. Highly atmospheric, it's a Vancouver Halloween tradition.

November

EASTSIDE CULTURE CRAWL

www.eastsideculturecrawl.com
Dozens of eclectic local artists from Vancouver's Eastside area open their studios to visitors at this excellent three-day showcase in late November. A much better place to pick up a Vancouver memento than those tacky souvenir shops.

SANTA CLAUS PARADE

Slightly less naughty than Vancouver's other main street parade, this relatively recent addition to the Christmas scene has quickly become a firm family favorite. Wrap up warm, watch the colorful floats glide along W Georgia St and wait for the arrival of the big man himself. It's held in late November.

December

CHRISTMAS CAROLSHIP PARADE

☎ 604-878-8999; www.carolships.org

A Vancouver tradition, where 100 boats of all sizes are lit up like Christmas trees to take part in a flotilla that sails along False Creek, English Bay and beyond. Many boats feature singing carolers, while others play taped music.

FESTIVAL OF LIGHTS

☎ 604-878-9274; www.vandusengarden.org

VanDusen's (p90) enduring Yuletide tradition – and a clever way to keep the money coming in during the off-season – sees the botanical garden magically illuminated with thousands of fairy lights. Popular with families.

WINTER SOLSTICE LANTERN PROCESSION

☎ 604-878-9274; www.secretlantern.org

In mid-December, as winter takes hold, six Vancouver neighborhoods continue the age-old Winter Solstice tradition by staging mini lantern parades at the same time throughout the city. Expect to see the lights flicker on in Yaletown, Granville Island, Chinatown, Strathcona, East Vancouver and the West End.

COSTS & MONEY

While it's one of Canada's more expensive cities (Toronto is arguably the most damaging to the hip pocket), Vancouver will perhaps

HOW MUCH?

Liter of gasoline $1.05

Liter of bottled water $1

Pint of Granville Island Lager $5

Souvenir T-shirt $10

Salmon sushi roll $2

Movie ticket $12

Tim Hortons donut 80¢

Metered parking $2 per hour

Mt Seymour ski-lift ticket $40

Overseas postcard stamp $1.55

seem like a bargain to European visitors. No such luck for US travelers, whose currency was hovering at par during this book's production period.

Wherever you're visiting from, there are still some creative ways to keep your costs down. Families can take advantage of discounted admission at museums and attractions, and there are passes available that can save a considerable amount for those planning to see lots of attractions (see p229). For an even better deal, check the free attractions listed on p47.

It's also worth remembering that kids stay free at many Vancouver hotels. Some of these have kitchenettes where you can chef up your own nosh to keep your dining budget down. See p190 for hotel reviews.

If you're eating out, many restaurants will prepare half-orders for children, if they don't

ADVANCE PLANNING

If you'd like your Vancouver vacation to be as eco-friendly as possible, plan your trip using some of the accommodation, transportation and dining tips offered in the Green Vancouver section (p62).

Most regional sights and outdoor activities don't require much advance booking, but during the summer peak it's a good idea to book specialized guided tours (p232) as far in advance as possible. The Vancouver Art Gallery (p46) occasionally runs blockbuster exhibitions that require timed-entry tickets – you can book ahead on its website.

The city's main cultural festivals (p12) – especially the Film Festival, Jazz Festival and Fringe Festival – often require advance booking for many of their events. Visit their websites before you arrive in town for purchasing information. The same is true of many theaters (p173), especially if you are on a tight schedule and want to be sure of getting tickets for a specific day. The hottest ticket in town, where booking ahead is essential, is the annual summertime Bard on the Beach festival (p174). Most sporting events are easy to get into, but catching a Vancouver Canucks game (p187) is a different story: book as far in advance as possible.

To see what's on in the city before you arrive, visit the Georgia Straight (www.straight.com) website for comprehensive listings. Also check Tickets Tonight (www.ticketstonight.ca) for ticket booking and late-breaking discount seats to local theater and sporting events. Finally, if you want to dip into the hot local dining scene before you arrive, read the reviews at Urban Diner (www.urbandiner.ca).

already have a dedicated kids menu. You can also save your dine-out dosh by dropping by the city's three cooking-college restaurants (see the boxed text, p129). You'll get a similar good deal at area drama schools (see the boxed text, p176), where professional-level productions are staged by aspiring actors for a cut-price ticket fee.

The most expensive item in anyone's budget is likely to be their plane ticket and, after that, accommodations. Sleeping at mid-priced hotels or B&Bs, eating at neighborhood restaurants or shopping-mall food courts, and stretching your entertainment budget with a few freebies will mean that two people traveling together should be able to keep costs down to $100 or so each per day.

INTERNET RESOURCES

City of Vancouver (www.city.vancouver.bc.ca) Official city site with downloadable city maps.

CKNW (www.cknw.com) Frequently updated radio-station website with all the latest news from around the city.

Discover Vancouver (www.discovervancouver.com) General traveler website for info on hotels, restaurants, events and attractions.

Tourism Vancouver (www.tourismvancouver.com) Official city tourism site, stuffed with user-friendly trip-planning resources.

Urban Diner (www.urbandiner.ca) Up-to-the-minute listings and reviews of area restaurants.

Vancouver 2010 (www.vancouver2010.com) One-stop shop for official Olympics-related info.

BACKGROUND

HISTORY
LIVING OFF THE LAND

The ancestors of Vancouver's First Nations people began arriving in British Columbia at least 10,000 years ago, crossing via a land bridge at the Bering Strait near Alaska. They trickled southwards from here, with many setting up camp in coastal areas that are still regarded as important First Nations lands to this day. Those who traveled furthest eventually arrived at the warmer waters of what is now known as the Lower Mainland.

These first Vancouverites lived in villages comprising wood-plank houses arranged in rows, often surrounded by a stockade. Totem poles were set up nearby as an emblem of family or clan. It's not surprising these groups were attracted to this area – the local beaches and rivers teamed with seafood, the forests bristled with tasty wildlife including deer and elk, and fat silvery salmon were abundantly available to anyone who fancied outsmarting the odd bear for the privilege.

Several distinct communities formed. The Musqueam populated Burrard Inlet, English Bay and the mouth of the Fraser River, although they shared some of this area with the Squamish, who were largely based at the head of Howe Sound, but also had villages in North and West Vancouver, Kitsilano Point, Stanley Park and Jericho Beach. The Kwantlen controlled the area around New Westminster, while Delta and Richmond were home to the Tsawwassen. The Tsleil-Waututh occupied much of North Vancouver, while Coast Salish tribes, such as the Cowichan, Nanaimo and Saanich, set up seasonal camps along the Fraser River when the salmon were running.

Art and creativity were key features of everyday life at this time. Many homes were adorned with exterior carvings and totem poles – later examples of which are displayed at the Museum of Anthropology (p99). These exemplified a reverential regard for nature, suggesting that early First Nations people enjoyed a symbiotic relationship with their surroundings. In many ways, they were Vancouver's 'green' founding fathers.

Scant evidence exists about this intriguing period in Vancouver's history: most settlements have crumbled to dust and few have been rediscovered by archaeologists. In addition, these early settlers generally maintained oral records – they told each other (often in song) the stories of their ancestors, rather than writing things down for posterity. This method would have been highly successful until the disruptive arrival of the Europeans.

CAPTAIN VAN HITS TOWN

After centuries of unhindered First Nations occupation, Europeans began arriving in the late 18th century. The Spanish sent three expeditions between 1774 and 1779 in search of the fabled Northwest Passage. They ended up by the entrance to Nootka Sound on Vancouver Island and never ventured into the Strait of Georgia (but that didn't stop their influence from seeping into Vancouver, evidenced by latter-day street names like Cordova, Cardero and Valdez).

TIMELINE

AD 8000	1774	1791
The region's first inhabitants begin arriving from Asia, via the Bering Strait. Rather than head back after a quick look around, they decide to stay and enjoy the abundant food and temperate climate.	A little later than the First Nations settlers, the Spanish arrive in the area in search of the fabled Northwest Passage. They don't bother to venture any further than Nootka Sound on Vancouver Island.	A little more adventurous than his colleagues, Spanish explorer José María Narváez edges into the Strait of Georgia, perhaps looking for a Tim Hortons donut shop.

top picks

HISTORY SITES FOR VISITORS

- Museum of Anthropology (p99)
- Chinese Cultural Centre Museum & Archives (p77)
- Vancouver Museum (p95)
- Roedde House Museum (p65)
- Vancouver Police Centennial Museum (p73)

British explorer Captain James Cook e bowed in from the South Pacific in 1779. He had a similar Northwest Passage motive, and a similar result: he hit the west coast of Vancouver Island and believed it to be the mainland. It wasn't until 1791 that the Strait of Georgia was properly explored. Spanish navigator José María Narváez did the honors, sailing all the way into Burrard Inlet.

Next up was Captain George Vancouver, a British navigator who had previously sailed with Cook. In 1792 he glided into the inner harbor and spent one day here – a lucky day, as it turned out, though it didn't seem so at first. When he arrived, he discovered that the Spanish, in ships under the command of captains Valdez and Galiano, had already claimed the area. Meeting at what is today Spanish Banks, the men shared area navigational information. Vancouver made a note of the deep natural port, which he named Burrard after one of his crew. Then he sailed away, not thinking twice about a place that would eventually be named after him.

As Spanish influence in the area waned in favor of the more persistent British, explorers such as Simon Fraser and Alexander Mackenzie began mapping the region's interior, opening it up for overland travelers and the arrival of the legendary Hudson's Bay Company.

GOLD, FUR & TIMBER

The region's abundant natural resources spurred creeping development throughout the first half of the 19th century. In 1824 the Hudson's Bay Company, under James McMillan's leadership, launched a network of fur-trading posts. McMillan noted a particularly good location about 50km from the mouth of the Fraser River, building Fort Langley (p107) there in 1827. The region's first permanent European settlement, the fur-trading fort shipped more than 2000 beaver pelts in 1832. Today the Hudson's Bay Company has developed into the Bay, a cross-Canada chain of department stores. Its flagship downtown location is at the corner of Granville and Georgia Sts.

In 1858 an interesting tidbit of news began percolating around the region: gold had been discovered on the banks of the Fraser River. More than 25,000 American prospectors rapidly swept in with picks, pans and get-rich-quick dreams. Concerned that the influx might inspire a US northern push, the mainland – following the lead of Vancouver Island, which had declared its colony status in 1849 – announced it was officially becoming part of the British Empire. James Douglas was sworn in as the governor of the expanded region – officially named British Columbia – although BC and the island remained separate protectorates at this time. The proclamation was made at Fort Langley on November 19, 1858.

Douglas requested British support and the Royal Engineers, under the command of Colonel Richard Moody, arrived at the end of 1858. Alarmed by Fort Langley's poor strategic location, Moody selected another site on the Fraser River – closer to its mouth – and built New Westminster, which was declared BC's first capital. In 1859 Moody forged a trail (now called North Rd) from New Westminster to Burrard Inlet, providing the colony with an ice-free

1792	1827	1867
The Brits decide to join the party when the Royal Navy's Captain George Vancouver sails into Burrard Inlet. He stays 24 hours then turns tail and heads out, just like many latter-day cruise-ship passengers.	The Hudson's Bay Company builds Fort Langley, the first European settlement to grace the region. It would be several more decades before the Bay launches its first department-store sale.	'Gassy' Jack Deighton rows in with a barrel full of whiskey and a head full of big ideas. He opens a saloon, and a small, thirsty settlement – called Gastown – soon springs up near the entrance.

winter harbor. In 1860 he built another trail, more or less where Kingsway is today, linking New Westminster to False Creek. These trails were the foundation for moving the settlement to its present downtown location – although at this point it was a dense area of rainforest.

The sawmills soon changed all that. The first mills were set up along the Fraser River in 1860, and their logging operations cleared the land for farms across the region. It wasn't long before the companies began chewing northward through the trees toward Burrard Inlet. In 1867 Edward Stamp's British-financed Hastings Mill, on the south shore of the inlet, established the starting point of a town that would eventually become Vancouver.

In 1866 the protectorates of Vancouver Island and BC officially merged under the title of British Columbia. With the creation of a new country called Canada out east in 1867, the colony became concerned about its future, fearing US annexation. With the promise of access to a new national railway network, BC joined the Canadian Confederation in 1871. It would be another 16 years before the railway actually rolled into the region.

THE CITY'S BOOZY START

True, Hastings Mill was there first, but it was the demon drink that really launched Vancouver. In 1867 Englishman 'Gassy' Jack Deighton rowed into Burrard Inlet with his First Nations wife, a yellow dog and a barrel of whiskey. He knew the nearest drink for thirsty mill workers was 20km away in New Westminster. So he announced to the workers that if they helped him build a tavern, drinks were on him. Within 24 hours the Globe Saloon was in business, and when a village sprang up around the establishment it was dubbed 'Gastown.' In 1869 it became the town of Granville.

Another town thriving around a sawmill was Port Moody, at the eastern end of Burrard Inlet, which had been chosen as the western terminus of the Canadian Pacific Railway (CPR). However, a CPR official – who also happened to be an influential Granville landowner – 'discovered' that the eastern end of Burrard Inlet wasn't a practical harbor for large ships. Granville was suddenly selected as the new railway terminus location, much to the disgust of Port Moody residents.

The CPR negotiated with the provincial government for 2400 hectares in the area, making it Granville's largest property holder. The story goes that in 1884, while workers rowed the railway company's general manager, William Van Horne, around what would later be called Stanley Park, he commented that the new city needed a name to live up to its future as a great metropolis. Van Horne reasoned that since Granville was an unknown name, the city should be called 'Vancouver' after the man whom everyone knew was responsible for literally putting the area on the map. In April 1886 the town of Granville was incorporated as the City of Vancouver.

The first piece of business for the city's new council was to lease a 400-hectare military reserve from the federal government and establish it as the city's first park – and so Stanley Park was born. But the city faced a less enjoyable task at the tender age of two months: on June 13, 1886, CPR workers lit a fire to clear brush, and it rapidly spread out of control. The 'Great Fire,' as it came to be known, took 45 minutes to destroy Vancouver's 1000 wooden structures, kill as many as 28 people (the number remains disputed) and leave 3000 homeless.

Within hours, reconstruction was underway. But this time the buildings were constructed from stone and brick. By 1887, when the first CPR passenger train pulled into the city, Vancouver was back in business. Within four years the city grew to a population of 13,000, and between 1891 and 1901 the population skyrocketed to more than double that.

1886	1887	1901
The fledgling town is incorporated as the City of Vancouver, silencing those who wanted to bid for the 2010 Gastown Olympics. Within weeks, the new city burns to the ground in just 45 minutes.	The first transcontinental train pulls into rebuilt Vancouver, wondering exactly where it is. The residents of Port Moody, the originally proposed terminus for the major new service, decide never to speak to Vancouverites again.	First Nations communities, who have lived here for thousands of years, are displaced from their settlements in the Vanier Park area, as rapacious colonials sweep them and the forests away.

GROWING PAINS

The railway was responsible for shaping much of the city as it exists today. The CPR built Granville St from Burrard Inlet to False Creek, cleared and paved Pender and Hastings Sts, and developed the land around False Creek for railway yards and housing. The company also developed residential areas like the West End, Kitsilano and Shaughnessy Heights in South Vancouver. Shaughnessy Heights, once known as 'CPR Heaven,' was the home of Vancouver's new upper classes – just so long as they weren't Jewish or Asian, since both groups were forbidden from owning in the area.

Anti-Asian feeling was not new to Vancouver. Between 1881 and 1885 more than 11,000 Chinese arrived by ship to work on the construction of the railroad. In many respects they were treated as second-class citizens. They were paid $1 per day, half of what white workers were paid (but almost 20 times what they were paid at home). Government legislation denied all Asians the right to vote in federal elections, and did not allow Chinese women to immigrate unless they were married to a white man. In 1887 a white mob destroyed a Chinese camp in False Creek, and in 1907 an anti-Asian riot ripped through Chinatown and Japantown.

It was an issue the city would have to remedy, because by 1911 the census showed that Vancouver was a city of immigrants, with most people born outside of Canada. Indigenous rights were also taking a beating during this time. In 1901 the local government displaced a First Nations community from Vanier Park, sending some families to the Capilano Indian Reserve on the North Shore and others to Squamish.

During the first 30 years of the 20th century, all the suburbs around the city grew substantially. By 1928 the population outside the city was about 150,000. When Point Grey and South Vancouver amalgamated with the city in 1929, bringing in a combined population of more than 80,000, Vancouver became Canada's third-largest city – the ranking it retains today.

While the 1930s Great Depression saw the construction of several public works – the Marine Building, Vancouver City Hall, the third and present Hotel Vancouver, and Lions Gate Bridge, to name a few – many people were unemployed, as was the case throughout Canada. This marked a time of large demonstrations, violent riots and public discontent.

WWII helped to pull Vancouver out of the Depression by creating instant jobs at shipyards, aircraft-parts factories and canneries, and in construction with the building of rental units for the increased workforce. Japanese Canadians, however, didn't fare so well. In 1942, following the bombing of Pearl Harbor, they were shipped to internment camps in the province's interior, and had to endure the confiscation of all their land and property, much of which was never returned. Chinese, Japanese and First Nations people were finally given the provincial vote in 1949.

top picks

HISTORY BOOKS

- **The History of Metropolitan Vancouver**, Chuck Davis (2007) – comprehensive and highly readable exploration of city history from Vancouver's leading popular historian
- **Vancouver Remembered**, Michael Kluckner (2006) – colorful, image-heavy recollection of yesteryear Vancouver
- **Saltwater City**, Paul Yee (2006) – illuminating and well-illustrated retelling of the often tumultuous history of Vancouver's Chinese community
- **Wreck Beach**, Carellin Brooks (2007) – revealing history of Vancouver's famed naturist beach
- **The Ambitious City**, Warren Sommer (2007) – generously illustrated, glossy hardcover on the surprising and often overlooked history of North Vancouver

1949	1956	1977
The region's Chinese, Japanese and First Nations people are given the provincial right to vote in elections; a poor swap for losing their ancestral lands or their lives while building the railroad network.	The West End is rezoned for greater population density. The high-rise boom begins as hundreds of wooden homes are bulldozed to make way for apartment blocks and the annual Pride Parade that's due to kick off any decade now.	The SeaBus passenger ferry service launches between downtown Vancouver and the North Shore, sparking an immediate rush for the best seats at the front of the boat.

EXPO'S LASTING LEGACY

The event that launched a thousand condo towers, Vancouver's 1986 World Exposition on Transportation and Communication – or Expo '86 as it's remembered – had a profound impact on the development of modern-day Vancouver, triggering the regeneration of downtrodden city areas and showcasing the region on a global stage for the first time in its history. Coinciding with Vancouver's centennial, the summertime event (the first time this author visited Vancouver) was a colorful cavalcade of technological innovation and hokey homespun charm, unintentionally encapsulating a city at the crossroads between its past and future.

More than 50 nations had displays at the fair, ranging from an olde-worlde pub at the British pavilion to a working magnetically levitating train (a very smooth ride) at the Japanese pavilion. The 21 million visitors – including Princess Diana, Jaques Cousteau and Depeche Mode (this was the '80s, after all) – were won over by the city's laid-back charm, although the seemingly endless run of sunny days didn't hurt either.

The biggest event in BC history to date, Expo's legacy can still be seen throughout Vancouver: high-rise apartment towers line the old False Creek site, while infrastructure and venues built for the event and still in use include the original SkyTrain line, Canada Place, BC Place Stadium and Science World.

EXPO-SING THE CITY

By the start of the 1950s, Vancouver's population was 345,000 and the area was thriving. The high-rise craze hit in the middle of the decade, mostly in the West End. During the next 13 years 220 apartment buildings went up – and up – in this area alone.

In the 1960s and '70s, Vancouver was known for its counterculture community, centered on Kitsilano. Canada's gay-rights movement began here in 1964 when a group of feminists and academics started the Association for Social Knowledge, the country's first gay and lesbian discussion group. In 1969 the Don't Make a Wave Committee formed to stop US nuclear testing in Alaska; a few years later, the group morphed into the environmental organization Greenpeace.

But as the years passed, revolutionary fervor dissipated and economic development became the region's main pastime. Nothing was more important to Vancouver in the 1980s than Expo '86 (see the boxed text, above), the world's fair that many regard as the city's coming of age. The six-month event, which coincided with Vancouver's 100th birthday, brought millions to the city and kick-started a rash of regeneration in several tired neighborhoods. New facilities built for Expo included the 60,000-seat BC Place Stadium (p70), currently being spruced up for the opening and closing ceremonies of the 2010 Olympic and Paralympic Winter Games.

MULTICULTURAL MILESTONES

The brewing issue of First Nations land rights spilled over in the late 1980s, with a growing number of rallies, road blockades and court actions in the region. Aside from a few treaties covering a tiny portion of the province, land-claim agreements had not been signed and no clear definition of the scope and nature of First Nations rights existed. Until 1990 the provincial government refused to participate in treaty negotiations. That changed in December, when the BC Claims Task Force was formed among the governments of Canada, BC and the First Nations Summit with a mission to figure out how the three parties could solve land-rights matters. It's a slow-moving, ongoing process that in Vancouver's case involves the Tsawwassen, Tsleil-Waututh, Katzie, Squamish and Musqueam nations.

1979	1983	1985
Granville Island is developed from a grungy industrial wasteland, where tracking down artisan cheese was always a challenge, into one of the city's most popular hangouts. A cement factory stays behind to keep the faith.	BC Place Stadium inflates its Teflon roof and opens for business. Non–sports fans instead head to the old courthouse building, now transformed into the new Vancouver Art Gallery.	The first SkyTrain line opens, linking the communities of New Westminster and Vancouver. New Westminsterites flood into town and wonder what all the fuss was about.

Prior to the British handover of Hong Kong to China in 1997, tens of thousands of wealthy Hong Kong Chinese migrated to BC's Lower Mainland area, boosting the area's permanent Asian population by about 85% and creating the largest Asian population in any North American city. Real-estate prices rose, with Vancouver's cost-of-living figures suddenly rivaling those of London, Paris and Tokyo. Many of the new arrivals shunned the city proper in favor of the suburbs, especially Richmond. By 1998 immigration had tapered off but the city's transformation into a modern, multicultural mecca was already complete. By then, about 40% of Vancouver residents were foreign-born, and an ethnic smorgasbord of restaurants, stores and cultural activities had emerged, solidifying the worldly reputation the city earned by hosting Expo '86.

DOWNTOWN DESOLATION

An ever-present forest of cranes – plus the attendant soundscape of construction noise – shows that development is continuing at an extraordinary pace in Vancouver. Downtown is where much of the action is, but as space becomes scarce, new Yaletown, Coal Harbour and South Main (SoMa) developments are enticing the moneyed young to once bleak or nondescript neighborhoods. One area – just steps from these aforementioned successes – is a tougher nut for the developers to crack. Although a giant flagship housing, college and shopping complex is being developed on its old Woodwards department-store site, the Downtown Eastside (centered on Main and Hastings Sts) remains the black heart of the city.

Once a thriving business district, the area began its graceless decline in the 1940s, when city and provincial policies started concentrating the destitute here. It's since become a breeding ground for tragedy, exponentially increasing its population of poor, vulnerable and mentally disturbed residents. The area's squalid rooming houses reside above sketchy pawnshops and dodgy pubs, where the cheapest beer is always the most popular. Drugs are offered openly on the streets and prostitution is a way of life: bone-rack women with heavy make-up loiter in short skirts on the coldest nights. HIV is rampant (the neighborhood has North America's highest infection rate), while estimates of the junkie population here range from 5000 to 10,000 at any given time.

While a safe injection site initiative was introduced here in 2003 (see the boxed text, p38), its effectiveness is still being debated and the program is under threat from a conservative federal government. As the global spotlight turns on the city again in 2010, questions are increasingly being asked about how latter-day Vancouver will finally deal with its biggest social challenge.

GOING FOR GOLD

The turn of the millennium saw rapid development, as the transformation kick-started by Expo '86 saw the 'reforesting' of Vancouver with hundreds of glass-tower office and apartment buildings. For the first time in its history, the coastal metropolis began to be regularly recognized as one of the planet's 'most livable' cities. Seizing the initiative, the region again looked to the future. In 2003 GM Place stadium was packed to the rafters as the announcement that Vancouver had been awarded the 2010 Olympic and Paralympic Winter Games was made via satellite link from Prague.

While area developers are rubbing their hands in glee, not everyone is happy with the way the city is progressing. Older locals say its history as a counterculture leader is being forgotten, while many just moan that the boom times are making it too expensive to live here. Either way, Vancouver is again at a crossroads: young enough to change its identity and forge a leadership role on the world stage, yet old enough to have a past – complete with a few skeletons in the closet.

1986	1996	2003
The international spotlight shines on Vancouver as the Expo '86 world's fair dominates the summer, bringing Sheena Easton and Depeche Mode to local stages – although sadly not on the same bill.	With the Hong Kong handover to China imminent, Vancouver sees a massive influx of Asian immigrants into the city. Richmond is transformed from a farming backwater into the region's new Chinatown.	The city erupts into cheers – and a few rueful shrugs from those worried about the cost – as Vancouver is awarded the 2010 Olympic and Paralympic Winter Games. T-shirt sellers rub their hands in anticipation.

OLYMPICS COUNTDOWN

When the live announcement came through from Prague on July 2, 2003, the packed-to-capacity crowd waiting with their maple-leaf flags and ball caps in GM Place could be forgiven for cheering as if they had already won every gold medal on the table. After last hosting the event in Calgary in 1988, Canada had beaten its rival bidders to host the 2010 Olympic and Paralympic Winter Games, triggering a surge of Vancouver-wide pride that hadn't been seen since Expo '86, the world's fair that threw a global spotlight on the West Coast city for the first time in its history.

Once the hard part was over, the even harder part began. Hosting 17 days of Olympic events from February 12, 2010, followed by 10 days of Paralympic events one month later, takes several years of intense building, number-crunching and head-scratching from officials, who immediately gathered under the Vancouver Olympic Organizing Committee (Vanoc) banner to start work. The first order of business was venue selection.

While Vancouver is a sporty city with several stadiums and plenty of additional sporting facilities, few of these had been used to host international competitions and many were older and not exactly state-of-the-art. Dividing the events between the Lower Mainland and the winter resort town of Whistler (p211) was the initial task. Linked to Vancouver via the winding Hwy 99 coastal road that's being massively upgraded in time for the Games, Whistler received alpine skiing, biathlon, cross-country skiing, bobsleigh, luge and skeleton. Those hoping to see ski-jumping staged on the slopes of Vancouver's Canada Place were disappointed when the resort town was also awarded that plum event.

But that still leaves many sports planned for the city. Considered for demolition just a couple of years ago, BC Place Stadium (p70) will host the Olympic opening and closing ceremonies as well as nightly medal presentations. The venerable Pacific Coliseum in Hastings Park – more used to seeing pop concerts and minor hockey games (see p188) – received a $26 million renovation so that it can stage figure skating and speed skating. Out at UBC, the original ice-sheet facility is being expanded with a 7500-seat arena so that it can comfortably host hockey and Paralympic sledge hockey. And the city's old Hillcrest Curling Centre is being transformed (with the help of $50 million) into a state-of-the-art venue for curling and wheelchair curling.

Of course, the edge-of-the-city winter resorts were also keen for a slice of the Olympic pie. But while Grouse and Seymour have missed out (don't feel too sorry for them, they'll still see plenty of spin-off action), Cypress Mountain (p183) is sprucing itself up to host freestyle skiing and snowboard events. A brand-new venue that led to an unseemly tussle among some Greater Vancouver municipalities keen for a little Olympic gold is also being built in Richmond. The mammoth $178 million Speedskating Oval will revitalize an area of city-owned Fraser River waterfront, with additional new parks and plazas completing the area's restoration.

All of these projects are slated to have important legacy benefits for the Vancouver region. Popular facilities like the Hillcrest Curling Centre were long overdue for renovation and its rebuild will benefit the community for years to come. The same is being said of BC Place Stadium, which will be given a new lease on life for several years after its originally scheduled demise. In addition, the Olympic Village being built on the southeast corner of False Creek will be converted to social and market housing, creating homes for thousands, once the Games are over.

But while Vanoc has made much of these promised legacies, not all locals are convinced. The projects are underwritten by the BC government's fat checkbook – in other words, local taxpayers are on the hook for all costs not met by the private sector – and some Vancouverites are already accusing organizers of fudging the figures. The building budgets for some venues have doubled (tripled in the case of the Richmond Oval), while promised legacy projects appear to be sliding down the agenda. For example, the original ratio of social to market housing in the Olympic Village has already changed in favor of the higher-priced market homes – an important issue for those locals who thought some of the Games' giant budget might be used to address the city's paucity of housing for the poor. This led to an antipoverty campaigner throwing paint at the landmark digital countdown clock (it looks like a high-tech toast rack) that was placed on the Georgia St side of the Vancouver Art Gallery in 2006. A security guard was detailed to guard the clock day and night soon after. As well, local arts and culture groups were delighted when the Olympics were awarded to Vancouver, but the gravy train that might have been the Games' arts component seems to be less certain.

Other controversies have been on a lighter note. The official 2010 Olympic emblem – a multicolored Inukshuk figure – hasn't pleased everyone, although it's hard to recall an Olympic mascot or symbol that has. This one has been accused of looking like an overweight skateboarder tottering on his board. In fact, it's based on the famed stone sculptures used by Canada's Inuit people as directional landmarks across the north, and in later years adopted as a symbol of hope, friendship and hospitality throughout the country. Unveiled in April 2005, the emblem is named 'Ilanaaq,' the Inuit word for friend.

While some locals will continue to be vociferous in their complaints, the vast majority of Vancouverites view the upcoming Games in a hugely positive light. And it's clear that whatever happens during 2010, there's little doubt that, after years of planning and hard work, it will be over almost as soon as it began.

For the latest information on developments for the 2010 Olympic and Paralympic Winter Games, visit www .vancouver2010.com.

THE ARTS

Ask around and many locals will tell you that Vancouver doesn't even have an arts scene. It's the knee-jerk reaction from those who think that art only means blockbuster gallery shows, stadium-sized music concerts or visiting Broadway musicals that have absolutely nothing to do with the city. These are usually the kind of people who wouldn't know an artist from a hole in the ground (otherwise known as an installation).

In fact, Vancouver is crammed with galleries, authors, musical groups, film auteurs, theater companies and dance troupes. But reflecting a kind of citywide parochialism, these creative types often operate in isolation – rarely is Vancouver's true abundance of artists and activities counted together and regarded as a 'scene.'

For visitors, this means that if you want to tap into Vancouver's artistic side, you'll have to go looking for it. In the same way that exploring the separate, distinctive neighborhoods here reveals the city's true nature, so Vancouver's artistic soul is uncovered only if you scratch beneath the surface. If you're prepared to make the effort, you'll be rewarded with an artsy output that's authentically West Coast.

Luckily, you'll be spoilt for choice. Visual art – particularly photography – is a local specialty that attracts international recognition. The city's live-music scene is bursting with activity and ranges from hot local rock bands to an astonishing array of classical recital companies. Literature is another key area, with some world-renowned authors calling the city home (and often using it as a 'character' in their novels). Long regarded as 'Hollywood North,' Vancouver is also a major movie production site as well as a center for independent filmmaking. In performance arts – especially dance and theater – Vancouver has a depth and diversity that rivals much bigger cities.

And if you time your trip well, you can dip into festivals (p12) that cover film, music, fringe performance and just about everything in between. Check out the queues snaking around venues at these fests and then make up your own mind about whether Vancouver has an arts scene.

Flick to the Arts listings section (p166) for suggestions on what to see while you're here.

VISUAL ARTS

The region's artistic bent was sparked thousands of years ago when the First Nations arrived in the area and began adorning their homes with artsy reflections of the natural world. Later settlers continued to use nature as their muse, often adding images of the mysterious First Nations themselves to their canvases. In recent decades, the city's visual artists have moved successfully into provocative abstract painting and photography. A visit to the Vancouver Art Gallery (VAG; p46) will reveal some leading lights, while dropping by the Emily Carr Institute of Art & Design (p87) will point you to the rising stars. Visit www.art-bc.com for listings of area galleries and events.

Photography

Vancouver has an international, cutting-edge reputation for contemporary photography and is associated with a certain brand of photo-conceptual art now called the 'Vancouver School.' Stan Douglas, Roy Arden, Chris Gergley and Jeff Wall are among its most celebrated exponents and have exhibited at major galleries around the world. Douglas, a renowned urban streetscaper, photographed what has become the most famous Vancouver image in recent memory. Entitled *Every Building on 100 West Hastings*, it's a 3m-long panorama of mostly derelict but once-handsome buildings in the Downtown Eastside. Douglas photographed at night and lit the street like a movie set, but the image of pawnshops and crumbling bars is a heartbreaking encapsulation of the degradation of this once-vibrant area. The image is now part of the permanent collection at the VAG. It's also worth dropping by Yaletown's Contemporary Art Gallery (p50), which frequently exhibits work by top local photographers.

Painting & Sculpture

The natural beauty of Greater Vancouver, with its varied landscapes, colors, textures and ever-changing light, has long been an inspiration to painters and sculptors. In addition to the VAG and Emily Carr Institute, you can dip into the scene at the many private galleries in South Granville (p121).

Among the famous regional artists to look out for are Emily Carr and EJ Hughes. Regarded as Canada's first major female artist, Carr painted swirling nature-themed canvases that are moving tributes to the West Coast landscape. The VAG has a large permanent collection, as does the Art Gallery of Greater Victoria (p208) on Vancouver Island. In contrast, Hughes has only been rediscovered in recent years, with his stylized, often whimsical canvases of BC life – coastal communities feature heavily – now commanding million-dollar price tags. The VAG has the largest permanent collection of Hughes' work.

Other famed artists in the region include sculptors Gathie Falk and Alan Storey, whose brushed steel *Pendulum* is the permanent centerpiece to the Pendulum Gallery (p47), as well as Group of Seven painters Lawren Harris and Frederick Horsman Varley. Abstract painter Jack Shadbolt has an international reputation, while other celebrated contemporary artists include Chris Woods and Attila Richard Lukacs.

Public Art

Vancouver has a vigorous public-art program and you'll likely spot challenging installations, decorative apartment-building adornments and sometimes puzzling sculptures dotted throughout the city. Check www.city.vancouver.bc.ca/publicart for an online registry of works (there are more than 80 in the downtown peninsula alone) and a downloadable walking tour of shoreline-based installations.

Among the more popular artworks are *Device to Root Out Evil,* the large upturned church sculpture at the northeast foot of Bute St downtown; the towering granite Inukshuk figure on the beach at the foot of Bidwell St in the West End; *Footnotes,* a string of words that create a poem in the sidewalk along the 1300 block of Pacific Blvd in Yaletown; a kaleidoscopic Dale Chihuly glasswork installation abutting an apartment building at the corner of Bute and W Georgia Sts; and *Street Light* at the foot of Davie St in Yaletown, a series of 14m bronze girders from which hang city images either stamped in metal or etched in glass.

Entering into the spirit, the Vancouver International Airport increasingly lines its public spaces with artworks – check out the magnificent bronze *Spirit of Haida Gwaii* by Bill Reid and its ocean-themed *Great Wave Wall* backdrop by Lutz Hauschild. Both are in the atrium space between the US and international check-in areas.

First Nations Art

First Nations artists have contributed mightily to Vancouver's visual-arts scene, primarily through carving. Two carvers who preserved the past while fostering a new generation of First Nations artists were Charles Edenshaw, the first professional Haida artist, who worked in argillite, gold and silver, and Mungo Martin, a Kwakiutl master carver of totem poles. Martin passed on his skills to Bill Reid, the outstanding Haida artist of his generation and the first Haida artist to have a retrospective exhibition at the VAG. His work is permanently displayed at the Museum of Anthropology (p99).

Lawrence Paul Yuxweluptun is a well-known contemporary First Nations artist. He graduated from the Emily Carr Institute with a painting degree, and uses Coast Salish mythological images to comment on political, environmental and indigenous issues. Look out also for Roy Henry Vickers of Tofino, who expresses traditional themes through wildlife paintings, and Susan Point, a Coast Salish artist whose traditional themes show up in a variety of media.

One of the world's hottest First Nations artists, Brian Jungen disassembles well-known objects and recreates them in challenging new forms, usually fusing them with traditional arts-and-crafts visuals. His most famous works are the First Nations masks made from resewn sections of Nike running shoes, and his detailed whalebone sculptures created from humdrum plastic chairs.

MUSIC

Vancouver has a strong and diverse musical tradition founded on decades of homegrown talent and a wealth of concert venues. Sarah McLachlan, Nickelback, Matthew Good, Bif Naked, The New Pornographers and even Michael Bublé are based here, while jazz diva Diana Krall hails from across the water on Vancouver Island and Bryan Adams still drops by occasionally to check on his Gastown recording studio. If you miss your favorite performer, it's worth delving into one of Vancouver's pitch-perfect music festivals (p12), which cover genres from jazz to folk and from classical to new music.

Arch Vancouver group The New Pornographers electrifies stages here and abroad courtesy of its guitar-and-keyboard power pop and the vocals of Neko Case. When in town, the band is likely to turn up at the Commodore (p164). If you can't catch the band itself, Pornographers members have side projects that play locally on occasion: Carl Newman heads Zumpano and Neko Case solos as a Patsy Cline–like country singer.

The side-project concept is ubiquitous here. Jerk With a Bomb, a popular duo performing 'folk-noir' ballads, has splintered into both Black Mountain and Pink Mountaintops. NoMeansNo also performs as the punk Hanson Brothers. Speaking of which, punk does well in this city, hosted regularly at venues like the Cobalt (p163) and Pat's Pub (p164). In addition to NoMeansNo, legendary old-school punksters from the area include The Black Halos, The Dayglo Abortions (from Victoria) and Joey 'Shithead' Keithley's DOA.

The city developed a more mellow tone in the 1990s when local gal Sarah McLachlan burst onto the scene, eventually racking up sales of more than 25 million albums worldwide. Following her smash 1997 album *Surfacing*, she organized the women-only Lilith Fair tours before putting out the accomplished *Afterglow* in 2003.

From Nanaimo, jazz pianist and vocalist Diana Krall can almost be considered a local. Her albums post marriage to Elvis Costello took an experimental turn but she's returned to more trad territory in recent years. For more serious jazzsters, there's also François Houle, a clarinetist who likes to mix it with a little classical music. Many jazz aficionados spend their time in the city mooching at the subterranean Cellar Restaurant & Jazz Club (p162), where owner and saxophonist Cory Weeds releases celebrated CDs of the venue's most spine-tingling performances. Alternatively, blues fans will appreciate Jim Byrnes, local music royalty who frequently holds court at the Yale (p161).

But it's not all about kicking it here. Vancouver has one of North America's most vital classical-music scenes, with chamber and choral groups particularly well represented. Favorites include the Vancouver Bach Choir (p172), whose Messiah sing-along is a Christmastime legend; the internationally renowned Vancouver Chamber Choir (p172), which covers everything from jazz to avant-garde; and the Vancouver Symphony Orchestra (p167), which effortlessly draws serious

LOWDOWN ON THE LOCAL SCENE

An interview with Dave Gowans, lead singer and songwriter with The Buttless Chaps and owner of Red Cat Records (p117).

How would you rate Vancouver's live-music scene compared with other Canadian cities? I think Vancouver has a very strong music scene. We have lots of international touring acts playing here as well as a vibrant local scene.

What are the audiences like here? Audiences are very supportive, but it really depends on the venue and the show. The more comfortable and relaxed the venue is, the more I see audiences having a good time.

What is your favorite venue to play in the city and why? It would be the Railway Club (p164). It feels like a casual pub, with live music seven nights a week. There are lots of local and out-of-town bands and it serves a real pint of beer – in a mug with a handle!

Do you think the recent closure of old-school Vancouver venues like the Lamplighter and the Marine Club detrimentally affects the city's music scene? Yes I think so. Usually things will move around – a lot of the shows from the Marine Club now appear at Pat's Pub (p164) for example – but it definitely takes a while to recover when a venue closes.

For someone visiting the city for the first time, what is the best way to delve into the local music scene? Your best bet is always to visit an indie record store and listen to some music. Ask who is local and playing in town and where the good venues are located. You can come and visit me at Red Cat Records.

Which local bands do you like to check out when you're not performing? The Awkward Stage, The Parlour Steps, Veda Hille, The Fits, Swank, Eldorado, Fond of Tigers, Abernethy, Vonnegut Dollhouse, D Trevlon, Great Aunt Ida, Bison, Black Mountain, Lightning Dust, Destroyer…the list could go on for a while!

top picks

VANCOUVER CDS

- Challengers, The New Pornographers (2007) – the band's 'difficult' fourth album shifts the emphasis a little away from power pop to what some have called 'power folk,' which means a couple of lush ballads alongside the anthemic regulars
- Hello Love, The Be Good Tanyas (2006) – after a three-year hiatus, the all-female trio released its most addictive album to date, including a surprising cover of Prince's 'When Doves Cry'
- Vancouver Complication (2007) – an evocative '101' introduction to the local punk scene, recorded during its spittle-flecked late-1970s peak
- Hardcore 81, DOA (2002) – re-release of the 1981 punk classic, with tunes like 'I Don't Give a Shit' and '001 Losers' Club,' all yelled by Canada's godfather of punk, Joey 'Shithead' Keithley
- I Bificus, Bif Naked (1999) – the big single off the album, 'Lucky,' was part of the *Buffy* soundtrack, a clear indicator of the butt-kicking quality that multi-tattooed grrrl-rocker Bif brings to her music
- Hit Parade, Spirit of the West (1999) – many of the foot-stomping songs on the best-of compilation by this Celtic-influenced rock band make you want to chug beers, but there are also four lush tracks recorded with the Vancouver Symphony Orchestra

music fans and first-timers with a stirring mix of classics and pops.

For information on checking out Vancouver's music scene, see p161, p166 and p171.

LITERATURE

With an estimated 1500 professional authors living in the BC region, Vancouver is a center of Canadian literature. It's home to megapublishers like Raincoast Books (the Canadian publisher of the Harry Potter series released its weighty tomes on recycled paper here), while a cohort of smaller publishers, including Arsenal Pulp Press, annually releases around 250 titles. The region is said to boast the highest number of book readers anywhere in the country, which might explain the wild success of the Vancouver Public Library's One Book, One Vancouver campaign. Like a giant book club, the annual drive promotes a single book with a local tie, sparking mass reading, heated discussions, and literary events at the library and beyond.

Bookstores, from general to specialist, abound in the city, while regular literary events range from poetry slams to script readings (see p172). The city also hosts a couple of literary festivals that are among Vancouver's most popular events. These include Word on the Street (p172) and the Vancouver International Writers and Readers Festival (p16). For more information about Vancouver authors, read *Twigg's Directory of 1001 BC Writers* (1992) by Alan Twigg, who also publishes the free tabloid-format *BC Bookworld*, available at bookstores. The Saturday edition of the *Vancouver Sun* also has a book section covering local authors and events.

Fiction

While Vancouver has spurred the creative juices of thousands of novelists, many of its writers have focused on troubled times of their own. Hard-drinking Malcolm Lowry wrote his masterpiece *Under the Volcano* (about a day in the life of an alcoholic consul in central Mexico) when he lived in a cheap hovel in North Vancouver. Local author Michael Turner illuminated his teenage years in the city in *The Pornographer's Poem*, while the Chinese immigrant experience is explored in Wayson Choy's award-winning book *The Jade Peony*. Evelyn Lau shot to prominence at the age of 18 with *Runaway: Diary of a Street Kid*, which details her life as a prostitute on Vancouver's streets after she left her traditional Chinese home.

In fact, the darker side of Vancouver is often never far from the minds of city authors. In *Stanley Park* Timothy Taylor exposes the soft underbelly of the local foodie scene and the city's famed green space, while crime novelist Laurence Gough is one of Vancouver's most prolific writers, best known for his Willows and Parker crime novels about a detective duo on the Vancouver police force. The city always plays a prominent role in Gough's storylines: a body shows up in the Vancouver Aquarium whale tank in *Killers;* another is fished from Coal Harbour in *Karaoke Rap*.

Perhaps the city's most celebrated living novelist, Douglas Coupland reputedly coined the term 'Generation X' in his novel of the same name. His books frequently explore the slacker-flavored

top picks

VANCOUVER FICTION

- **Stanley Park**, Timothy Taylor (2002) – illuminating modern-day Vancouver through a story fusing the life of a local chef with the park's dark secrets
- **Runaway: Diary of a Street Kid**, Evelyn Lau (2001) – a 14-year-old honor student when she ran away from home, Lau makes her personal experience the basis for this novel about a dangerous life on the streets
- **The Jade Peony**, Wayson Choy (1995) – a searing portrayal of growing up in a Vancouver Chinese immigrant family in the 1930s
- **Generation X**, Douglas Coupland (1991) – the book that labeled a generation is the satirical story of three underemployed and overeducated escapees from yuppiedom
- **The Vancouver Stories** (2005) – an evocative series of shorts about the city by writers such as Douglas Coupland, Alice Munro, Ethel Wilson, Malcolm Lowry, William Gibson and Timothy Taylor

ennui of modern-day life and can give travelers a fascinating insight into the city's psyche before they arrive. Recommended Coupland tomes include *J-Pod*, *Eleanor Rigby* and *Girlfriend in a Coma*. Coupland is also an artist (although not many of his works have been displayed in recent years) and he sometimes appears at the Vancouver International Writers and Readers Festival, where he once copresented a fascinating Q&A with a visiting Chuck Palahniuk.

Science Fiction

Science-fiction author William Gibson, who was born in North Carolina but moved to Vancouver several years ago, is the godfather of 'cyberpunk.' His 1984 novel *Neuromancer* launched the genre of bleak, high-tech neoreality, which showed up in the mainstream in popular movies like *The Matrix*. *Neuromancer* won the sci-fi triple crown of Hugo, Nebula and Philip K Dick awards, an unheard-of feat. Gibson's subsequent novels include *Idoru*, *Mona Lisa Overdrive* and *Virtual Light*.

Speaking of Philip K Dick, how's this for a tenuous Vancouver tidbit: Dick, who wrote the story that eventually became *Blade Runner*, spent a few months in the city's Downtown Eastside in 1972, including time in a heroin rehab home. Some theorize that *Blade Runner*'s vision of non-stop rain and urban decay germinated there. Another well-known sci-fi writer who now calls Vancouver home is Spider Robinson, the author of *Stardance* and *Callahan's Crosstime Saloon*.

Poetry

Historically, E Pauline Johnson is Vancouver's most famous woman of poetic words. The daughter of a Mohawk chief and a middle-class Englishwoman, Johnson wrote poetry and recited it in public performances where she dressed in buckskin, rabbit pelts and metal jewelry, and carried a hunting knife and Huron scalp given to her by her great-grandfather. The 'Mohawk Princess' didn't come to Vancouver until later in her life, but she loved the city dearly and was quite prolific during her time here, which included the writing of *Legends of Vancouver*, a collection of Squamish myths.

Many area novelists also dabble in the dark arts of poetry. In 1992 Evelyn Lau became the youngest poet ever to be nominated for the Governor General's Award (one of Canada's most prestigious literary prizes) for her collection *Oedipal Dreams*. Canadian literary icon George Woodcock, the author of 150 books, was also a poet (*Tolstoy at Yasnaya Polyana* and *The Cherry Tree on Cherry Street*) – when he wasn't busy penning history, biography and travel tomes plus his seminal *Anarchism* text. *The Gentle Anarchist* is an excellent biography of this prolific author by Vancouverite George Fetherling, who's been known to pen a poem or two himself.

POETIC JUSTICE

In 2007 George McWhirter was unveiled as Vancouver's inaugural Poet Laureate. A professor in the UBC Creative Writing Program, McWhirter – originally from Belfast – is charged with championing poetry throughout the city, which means giving readings in his official capacity and appearing at city events (and council meetings) to recite his works. He's also expected to produce a few original verses that reflect the city and its people. The two-year position comes with a $5000 annual honorarium and applications are already being considered for the 2009 appointment. Time to sharpen your quill and search for your muse, methinks.

Nonfiction

There's a healthy and prestigious nonfiction edge to some of Vancouver's literary output. *Dead Man in Paradise,* by James Mackinnon, relates the gripping biographical story of his uncle's murder in the Dominican Republic. It won the Charles Taylor Prize for Literary Non-Fiction (Canada's top nonfiction prize) in 2006 – the year after his local writing buddy Charles Montgomery won it for *Ancestors in Melanesia.*

There's also a clutch of good nonfiction writing about Vancouver, including *Vancouver: Representing the Postmodern City,* edited by Paul Delany, and *Greenpeace: The Inside Story,* by Rex Wexler, which relates the development of the international movement from its early Vancouver days. One of the most colorful books about the city is Douglas Coupland's highly recommended *City of Glass,* a quirky, picture-packed alternative guidebook of musings and observations on contemporary Vancouver.

For a listing of great history books on the city, see p22; cooking fans should check p135 for some recommended books by famed local chefs.

CINEMA & TV

The film industry has a starring role in Vancouver's 'Hollywood North' economy, and the city ranks third in North American film production (behind the obvious hot spots, Los Angeles and New York). True, not many stories are set in Vancouver, and not many mainstream filmmakers are based here, but the industry was home to more than 200 productions in 2005, pumping more than $1.2 billion into the local economy and greasing the palms of 30,000 local workers. Although with the recent rise of the Canadian dollar, the local industry is holding its breath on the future of US-funded movie production.

Home of the influential Vancouver Film School, which serves up courses on moviemaking skills from makeup to directing and counts director/actor/screenwriter Kevin Smith (of *Clerks* and *Dogma* fame) as its most famed alumnus, the city is also a burgeoning center for animation. One of North America's largest fully computerized animation studios, Rainmaker, is based here, along with dozens of smaller operations and an equally impressive array of computer-game development companies.

You can mix with the local auteurs at screenings and industry events at the 17-day Vancouver International Film Festival (p16), held annually (beginning late September). It's even more grassroots at the many smaller movie showcases scheduled throughout the year – see the boxed text, p170.

But it's as a TV and movie set location that Vancouver has earned most of its cinematic brownie points. While the locally shot *X-Files* TV series was notorious for retaining Vancouver visuals in its supposedly US locations – watch for the SkyTrain sliding blithely past in some shots – recent shows such as *Smallville* and *Stargate SG-1* have made more of an effort to disguise their Vancouver backdrops. Canadian shows like *Da Vinci's Inquest* have also called the city home, although it's fair to say that US TV dominates almost all production here.

top picks

VANCOUVER INDIE FILMS

- On The Corner, directed by Nathaniel Geary (2003) – this gritty look at life in Vancouver's heroin-plagued Downtown Eastside follows a young man drawn into the worlds of addiction and prostitution after he comes to live with his sister
- Double Happiness, directed by Mina Shum (1994) – a comedy about 20-something Jade (Sandra Oh), who is trying to keep secret her modern career choice (actress) and boyfriend (he's white) from her traditional Chinese parents in the Vancouver suburbs
- That Cold Day in the Park, directed by Robert Altman (1969) – a lonely spinster (Sandy Dennis) invites a young hippie in from the Vancouver rain and then goes to drastic measures to make him stay; a bit dated, and odd, in retrospect
- The Delicate Art of Parking, directed by Trent Carlson (2003) – a mockumentary about a Vancouver parking officer and the hassles he encounters as he tickets irate motorists
- Mount Pleasant, directed by Ross Weber (2007) – three couples from Vancouver's Mount Pleasant (otherwise known as SoMa) find their lives fusing into a tangled mess of obsession and tragedy when a child finds a discarded needle in her garden; it's intense and disturbing

As for movies, with its mountain, ocean, forest and urban settings, Vancouver is a vast set for directors. It has stood in for everything from the North Pole in Will Ferrell's *Elf* to Tibet in director Martin Scorsese's *Kundun* and back-alley New York in Jackie Chan's *Rumble in the Bronx*. The area's mild climate allows for year-round filming, and with an army of skilled industry professionals and facilities, it's easy to see how the city slides so easily onto the silver screen.

BE PART OF THE ACTION

The website of the BC Film Commission (www.bcfilm commission.com) is the first stop for anyone interested in working in the industry. It gives the weekly lowdown on what's filming and who's in the cast and crew, and provides contact information for productions seeking extras.

Recent Hollywood titles shot in the area that you may have heard of (for better or worse) include *X-Men 2, Catwoman, Firewall, I Robot, Chronicles of Riddick, Scooby-Doo 2* and *Fantastic Four*. However, big-budget movies are more the exception than the rule. What are most commonly filmed here are Movies of the Week and B flicks that go straight to DVD. Keep your eyes peeled: wherever you wander in the city, it's common to come across lines of white trailers marking the latest shoot.

For information on Vancouver's movie theaters, see p168.

THEATER

Vancouver is home to one of Canada's most energetic independent theater scenes, with more than 30 professional performance groups. The Arts Club Theatre Company (p174) and the Playhouse Theatre Company (p175) hog the main spotlights. Both companies were formed in the 1960s, making them the city's oldest, and both stage classics and new works by Canadian playwrights, often starring a recognizable name or two from the national theater scene.

The real excitement lies in emerging companies and their creation of new works. A shortage of mid-sized venues (those in the 100- to 250-seat range) means groups have to be creative. The Firehall Arts Centre (p175) is in an old fire station, while Performance Works (p169) occupies an old machine shop. Smaller companies without a permanent home often use these spaces.

Veteran leading lights of the theater scene here include actors such as Christopher Gaze and Bernard Cuffling. You can also catch the up-and-coming next generation of thesps at several local colleges (see the boxed text, p176); each produces several full (and highly professional) stage productions every year.

One of the city's most popular annual events, the Vancouver International Fringe Festival (p16) attracts more than 100 smaller companies to the region each fall, many performing site-specific works everywhere from garages to dance clubs to a moving miniferry. This event is Canada's third-largest fringe fest, after Edmonton and Winnipeg.

Outdoor theater is also a hit in Vancouver, which is no wonder given the environs. Bard on the Beach (p174) is Shakespeare performed in a waterfront park against a backdrop of mountains and ocean. The outdoor Malkin Bowl in Stanley Park has been around since 1940 and is currently home to the Theatre Under the Stars (p175) troupe.

Amateur community theater groups, which come under the umbrella organization Theatre BC (☎ 250-714-0203; www.theatrebc .org), stage productions at venues around the region. In addition, the Playwrights Theatre Centre (☎ 604-685-6228; www.playwrightstheatre.com) chooses from about 250 scripts submitted by aspiring playwrights, and eight productions are staged annually.

For more information on Vancouver's theater scene, see p173.

HA BLOODY HA

Vancouver may not offer an overwhelming selection of comedy, but it does have the Vancouver TheatreSports League (p158), one of the largest nonprofit improv-based companies in the world. The TheatreSports concept, which was started by an acting teacher in Calgary and subsequently has been adopted by troupes across the globe, fuses the dramatic elements of comedy and tragedy with the excitement of sports. Vancouver's troupe gathered international interest in the concept after it held an improv tournament at Expo '86. The group earns its yuks four nights a week, 52 weeks a year, at Granville Island's New Revue Stage.

DANCE

Vancouver is second only to Montréal as a Canadian dance center. The city's dance scene is as eclectic as its cultural makeup, and ranges from traditional Japanese and Chinese dance to classical ballet and edgy contemporary. There are more than 30 professional dance companies and many more independent choreographers in the Vancouver area. The Scotiabank Dance Centre (p168) is the main resource for dance in the province and its range of activities is unparalleled in Canada, including support for professional dance artists, operation of Western Canada's flagship dance facility and presentation of programs and events for the public.

Until the 1960s Vancouver's dance scene was represented by those who trained in the city before leaving for greater things. The creation of the Pacific Ballet Theatre by Maria Lewis in 1969 saw the first permanent ballet company take hold in Vancouver and, now renamed Ballet British Columbia (p168), it has become one of the country's top ballet companies.

One of the first modern dance companies to emerge was the Western Dance Theatre in 1970. It inspired a generation of Vancouver dancers to form companies, including Karen Jamieson (p168). In contrast, Experimental Dance and Music (p168), founded in 1982, is an internationally respected company taking a multimedia-meets-improvisational approach. It inspired key dance companies such as Mascall Dance and Lola Dance.

Many of Vancouver's top dance companies converge at Vancouver's annual dance festivals, which help foster the city's reputation as a dance stronghold. The three-week Vancouver International Dance Festival (p13) is held during spring, and the 10-day Dancing on the Edge (p14) is in July.

For more information on Vancouver's dance companies and venues, see p167.

ARCHITECTURE
BUILT TO LAST

When the first version of Vancouver burned to the ground in just 45 minutes during the Great Fire of 1886, it seemed prudent to consider brick and stone for the new town that would emerge from the smoldering ashes. Some of the buildings from this era still survive and have been preserved as a reminder of a time when Vancouver's skyline was not just about glass towers.

While responsible for only a few of the Vancouver buildings created during this period, controversial turn-of-the-20th-century colonial Francis Rattenbury set the tone for the city's monumental rebuilding. Arriving from the UK in his early 20s with a modest background in architecture, he pumped up his credentials and impressed the locals with his grandiose ideas for city halls and courthouses across the province, at a time when BC was attempting to lay its foundations for the future. Those towns that didn't choose one of his turreted, multicolumned edifices usually chose designs that copied his grand confections.

Victoria was Rattenbury's main muse – the Parliament Buildings (p204) and the Empress Hotel (p204) were both his and both have design quirks that show his architectural deficiencies – but he also won a couple of commissions in Vancouver. He designed Roedde House (p65) in 1893, oversaw the facelift of the landmark Hotel Vancouver in 1901 and created the handsome Vancouver Courthouse (now the Vancouver Art Gallery, p46) in 1912.

Despite his role in shaping the look of early Vancouver and the wider province, Rattenbury is remembered today in rather less auspicious terms. As work dried up in the 1920s – there are only so many grand courthouses and city halls required in any given area – he was forced to return home to the UK, where he found his colonial designs were largely out of fashion. In March 1935 he was killed by his wife's young lover (the couple's chauffer), leading to a tawdry court case that gripped the nation's tabloid newspapers.

But Rattenbury's ideas had already become passé on the West Coast by the time of his demise. The buildings being fashioned in Vancouver in the 1920s and 1930s reflected influential international movements like Art Deco and Art Nouveau: sinuous streamlined designs that seemed far superior to the chunky monuments of the city's early days. The few elegant edifices that remain from this era are today among the city's favorite buildings, although their chequered histories make their existence almost miraculous.

These include the copper-colored Dominion Building at the corner of Hastings and Cambie Sts, built by the Dominion Trust Company in 1910. The company went bankrupt four years later and its manager committed suicide. The beloved Sylvia Hotel (p195) overlooking English Bay was built in 1912 but its owner had to sell up during WWI as a depression hit the city. When the green-domed World Tower (100 W Pender St) opened its doors in 1913, it claimed to be the tallest building in the British Empire – a claim already made by the Dominion two years earlier. Later renamed as the Sun Tower, it was home to the *Vancouver Sun* for decades. Take a look at the waterfront concrete monstrosity *Sun* staffers now work in – it's the one blighting your view from the towering Vancouver Lookout (p46).

The city's most beloved building from this era also has a colorful past. The Marine Building (p50) was started in 1929, just before the Great Depression. When the financial tsunami hit town, the builders decided to soldier on but couldn't find any tenants. When finished, they offered their $2.5 million tower to the city for $1 million. The city declined – a mistake, since it would have made an ideal city hall – and it was sold on to local developers at a massive loss. The no-expense-spared creation remains arguably the most attractive building in the city, complete with exterior aquatic friezes, interiors resembling a Mayan temple and elevators inlaid with 12 types of rare hardwood.

Of course, not all architecture of the time was quite so grandiose. In the early decades of the 20th century, Craftsman-style bungalows and large family homes sprouted up around the city, primarily in neighborhoods such as Kitsilano, Kerrisdale and Shaughnessy. Many of these were built for managers and senior workers in the burgeoning rail and port sectors and were the first wholesale attempts to colonize areas of the city that had previously been forest or traditional First Nations land.

These woodsy residences were distinguished by their brick chimneys, shingle exteriors, stained-glass flourishes and interior woodwork, often featuring built-in cupboards and shelves. While many of these oak-floored structures were cleared to make way for concrete towers and 'more efficient' developments from the 1950s onwards, the remaining homes are today the most sought-after in Vancouver, frequently fetching million-dollar price tags.

CONTEMPORARY CONSTRUCTIONS

By the 1950s the city's architecture had lost its flair. Nondescript but functional high-rises began foresting the West End and creeping across other parts of the city, often replacing cute housing developments and handsome business towers that seemed suddenly old-fashioned. The idea of heritage preservation was yet to take hold in Vancouver. By the time it eventually did, in the 1970s, huge swathes of architectural and social history had been lost and now only small pockets of it remain. The Architectural Institute of British Columbia (p233) offers excellent walking tours exploring this colorful heritage.

But the city's golden age of architecture was not just a flash in the pan. By the 1960s a new movement emerged that put the city back on the architectural map. Jumping on the modernist bandwagon that was sweeping the world at the time, Vancouver developed its own timber-framed version – called 'post and beam' – where horizontal lintels are supported by posts at either end. Attributes of this approach (considered novel at the time) included a flat roof and large windows to capitalize on scenery and natural light. The premier proponent was local architect and landscape designer Arthur Erickson. He took the idea to the next level, creating a look so specific to the city that it became known as 'Vancouver architecture.'

Erickson positioned his first project, Simon Fraser University, along the ridge of nearby Burnaby Mountain, using Douglas fir beams and steel tie-rods to support a glazed roof. The setup around a central mall encouraged student interaction, so much so that the design was blamed for prompting student unrest in the late 1960s. His most important contribution to the downtown core is Robson Square and the adjoining Provincial Law Courts – just across the street from the Vancouver Art Gallery building, Vancouver's original court.

VANCOUVER'S ENDANGERED BUILDINGS

Every year, Heritage Vancouver (☎ 604-254-9411; www.heritagevancouver.org) produces a list of 10 historic structures or neighborhoods it believes are under threat of destruction. The list has recently included St Paul's Hospital, the South Granville apartment district, Burrard Bridge, Malkin Bowl, Hastings Mill Store Museum and the houses around Yaletown. The nonprofit organization's motto is 'demolition is forever' and it advocates for heritage preservation across the city – before it's too late.

VANCOUVER'S LEADING SPANS

Often forgotten in Vancouver's architectural history, its all-important bridges are key city features. The stunning, postcard-hogging **Lions Gate Bridge** – likely the most beautiful in Canada – is the region's version of San Francisco's Golden Gate. Connecting downtown to the North Shore, it's named after a pair of snow-tipped regional peaks that resemble lion ears. Attractive in a less grandiose way, the Art Deco **Burrard Street Bridge** spans False Creek between downtown and Kitsilano and frames a spectacular view of the tree-covered North Shore mountains. Complete with nautical flourishes and 'flaming' sentry beacons, it was opened in 1932, when a Canadian air force seaplane flew under the bridge to mark the occasion. Less stylish than both – but certainly no less important – is East Vancouver's **Iron-workers Memorial Bridge** (known by most locals as the Second Narrows), an ever-busy span that has a more troubled past. Midway through construction in June 1958, the bridge's north anchor arm buckled, killing 18 workers. It took $19 million, five more lives and two more years before it was completed. In 1994 the Second Narrows was officially renamed the Ironworkers Memorial Bridge to commemorate those killed during its construction.

The giant Provincial Law Courts building, envisaged like a structure encased in a cool glass wrapper, was opened back in 1979 but Erickson has remained active and prolific in the city ever since – despite now being revered as one of Canada's greatest living architects. His work can be seen in diverse projects around Vancouver, including the Museum of Anthropology (p99), the Sikh Temple (p80) and the Scotiabank Dance Centre (p168). Among his most striking – and controversial – downtown blocks is the MacMillan Bloedel Building (1075 W Georgia St), perhaps the epitome of 'Vancouver architecture.' Coloquially known as the 'waffle building,' it combines a flared base (like tapering tree trunks) with a multifloored tower of uniform concrete squares, each a deeply recessed window.

Expo '86 delivered more new forms to the local cityscape. Canada Place (p46), with its five great sails of fiberglass fabric, rose on the site of an old cargo pier. Credited to designers Eberhard Zeidler (architect of Toronto's Eaton Centre), Musson Cattell Mackey Partnership and Archambault Architects, the building was intended to rival Australia's Sydney Opera House. Science World (p76) is renowned for its golf-ball-like geodesic dome. Local boy and UBC grad Bruno Freschi created it from 766 vinyl-covered aluminum triangles yielding a volume of 36,790 cubic meters. The best part? It lights up at night.

International architect Moshe Safdie has said there's no connection between his $100 million Vancouver Public Library (p47) built in 1995 and Rome's Colosseum, but everyone else disagrees. The library drew criticism from the design community as an out-of-place eyesore, but its shop-filled piazza and bright spaces for reading, studying and hanging out are well used by Vancouverites. In fact, its glass-enclosed atrium is a reflection of latter-day Vancouver's main architectural moniker, 'City of Glass' – a label that continues to apply to the latest construction projects here. The Shangri-La hotel and condo tower at the corner of W Georgia and Bute Sts is a soaring glass block that will be the city's tallest tower on completion in 2008. Across the street, Erickson is back to design what aims to be the second-tallest tower: a twisting triangular glass spike that will house a Ritz-Carlton hotel when it opens in 2011. Kick-started by the Asian immigration wave of the 1990s, this forest of glass towers has rapidly grown in recent years as developers have sought to maximize their build on the increasingly limited number of available downtown lots. Small parcels of land that once hosted a couple of clapboard pioneer homes can now be used for soaring 20-floor condo towers. And with the Olympics just around the corner, everyone wants to build before the city is showcased to potential homebuyers around the world.

ENVIRONMENT & PLANNING
THE LAND

Greater Vancouver straddles the lowlands of the Fraser River and the Coast Mountains of southwest BC. The Coast range, at only 20 million years of age, is one of North America's youngest mountain groups. The Coast's North Shore Range stretches from the Black Mountain in the west to Mt Seymour in the east. It is separated by Burrard Inlet's Indian Arm fjord from the Golden Ears mountain group, which dominates the Fraser Valley.

HERE COMES THE BIG ONE

Supposedly ever-ready with their 'emergency earthquake kits,' Vancouverites reside in one of North America's most active quake zones. Of the 300 or so tremors that hit every year, most go unnoticed by all except seismologists. The rest of the region is reminded of the danger every 20 to 50 years, when a larger quake strikes the area – such as the one that hit north of Courtenay on Vancouver Island in 1946 and measured 7.3 on the Richter scale.

Every 300 to 600 years, the region has been hit by a major quake measuring 8.5 – that's the 'big one' that may be due any day now, since the last one of this magnitude was in 1700. In the worst-case scenario, an 8.5+ quake would result in landslides and tsunamis along the coast, and damage up to 30% of Greater Vancouver's homes and 15% of its high-rises.

About $300 million has been spent to reinforce bridges, tunnels, buildings and other structures in the region, while an emergency operations center has been built at Rupert and Hastings Sts. Three saltwater pumping stations with earthquake-resistant piping have been built around town to act as backups in case the main water supply fails or is shut down, and other waterlines are gradually being upgraded.

The Fraser River, which cuts through the center of the Lower Mainland, has its source in the Rocky Mountains and travels 1375km to its delta on the Strait of Georgia. The Fraser's tributaries include the Coquitlam, Chilcotin, Nechako, Pitt and Thompson Rivers. Not only is this Canada's third-largest river, it is also the country's fifth-largest river system and the richest salmon river in North America. The many bays, inlets and river branches that lap the coastline are distinctive features.

The region's original First Nations inhabitants occupied many of the best waterfront stretches here, favoring areas that offered inlet shelter, access to hunting grounds and proximity to rivers. The later colonials also stayed close to the shoreline in their first few years, gradually clearing the dense forests and moving into the interior as far as the baseline of local mountains. Latter-day Vancouverites are lucky if they can afford to live on the waterfront, although mountain views are a cheaper and more ubiquitous substitute.

URBAN PLANNING & DEVELOPMENT

Much of the city's current urban planning is being driven by the 2010 Olympic and Paralympic Winter Games. The Olympic Village being built on the southeast corner of False Creek aims to be a model for sustainable development, mixing market and social housing with eco-friendly construction approaches. BC Place Stadium, Hastings Park's Agrodome and the Pacific Coliseum buildings are also up for Olympic-sized renovations. The third leg of the SkyTrain (known as the Canada Line) is being built from downtown to Richmond and is scheduled to open in 2009.

The grungy Downtown Eastside area around Main and Hastings Sts has long been the subject of revitalization buzz. Lo and behold, a developer was hired in late 2004 to transform the old Woodward's department-store building. The giant structure will comprise market and social housing, a university satellite campus and a clutch of shops. Desolate since 1993, the site has been the subject of numerous failed proposals as well as protests from locals determined to have a say in how it's used. Complete with a refurbished 'W' neon sign on its roof, the new Woodwards building may yet prove the catalyst that sparks the area's long-overdue recovery.

Tower blocks continue to sprout across the downtown area and beyond as the city rides the current boom in the provincial economy. Luxury condo housing is the common denominator in most of these developments, with prices soaring in the years leading up to 2010. Not surprisingly, many locals are complaining about being priced out of their own city.

See p59 for more on sustainable development.

GOVERNMENT & POLITICS

Under the terms of its Vancouver Charter, the city (www.city.vancouver.bc.ca) has a mayor – its chief administrative official – plus nine city councillors. Each is elected every three years and serves at the imposing City Hall located at the intersection of W 12th Ave and Cambie

St. The officials all represent the entire city, although this has been the subject of ongoing debate, with some locals believing the city should be split into wards again, as it was until the mid-1900s.

Provincial party politics do not have a direct bearing on city government, although there are affiliations. When it comes time for elections, there are civic political parties, including the Committee of Progressive Electors (COPE) and the Non-Partisan Association (NPA), that put forward candidates, although many individuals run and have been elected as independents. However, these political parties don't seem to have much bearing on the actual policies implemented by the mayor or councillors during their tenure.

For several years Vancouver maintained a fairly conservative-leaning city council, but the new millennium brought a more progressive group to office, including Mayor Larry Campbell, an affable former coroner who championed safe injection sites (see the boxed text, p38). Campbell's ideas divided the city, though, and many see his tenure as a time of political gridlock.

Campbell declined to stand in the following election, and his chosen COPE successor lost, returning the NPA to power. With high hopes from the locals, Sam Sullivan, a veteran city-hall politician, became the next mayor. But his honeymoon period didn't last long and Sullivan – Canada's only wheelchair-bound mayor – soon became embroiled in controversies of his own. Some blamed his bluff manor for fueling the civic workers strike that gripped the city in 2007.

Including the city itself, Greater Vancouver consists of 21 Lower Mainland municipalities, each with its own elected mayor and councillors. Metro Vancouver (www.gvrd.bc.ca), as it calls itself – replacing the old Greater Vancouver Regional District moniker – oversees the joint interests of these municipalities. This is a voluntary federation designed to deliver essential services more economically and equitably. In addition, the Government of BC (www .gov.bc.ca) has jurisdiction over Vancouver and the rest of the province from its Victoria base, while the Government of Canada (www.canada.gc.ca), located across the country in Ottawa, is responsible for federal political issues.

Although the provincial capital is Victoria, Vancouver is the center of the region's economy, with head offices and financial institutions crowding the downtown area. While the tourism and film industries are among the most important here, the older resource sectors continue to dominate. Forestry and mining are the major industries in BC, which is one of the main reasons why environmental organizations are so strong here. Logging has particularly drawn the ire of local environmentalists over the years, sparking protests against clear-cutting and nonsustainable forestry practices by locals across the region. These protests have clearly affected the way logging companies operate in BC – and not only the amount of money they now spend on public relations.

As logging and mining slowly diminish, newer industries are taking hold in Vancouver's economy. These include high-tech and biotech: the city is home to dozens of upstart biotech companies, many clustered around UBC, and has also become a key international player in computer animation and game development – both offshoots of the city's veteran film-industry role. Finally, with its geographical role as a gateway to Asia, the city's port is the biggest and busiest in Canada, hence the continual movement of freight containers at the bustling waterfront east of town.

HAPPILY EVER AFTER

Following the kind of ugly, multiyear tussle usually associated with the end of a marriage rather than the beginning, Canada's Equal Marriage Act finally became law throughout the country in July 2005, two years after British Columbia had passed its own legislation officially recognizing same-sex unions. Anyone over the age of 19 can now marry in BC, once a marriage license has been issued by the province. With a simple one-page application form, and costing $100, the required license is valid for three months. After pioneering the idea of gay marriage, BC – and particularly Vancouver, with its large gay population – has since become a destination of choice for travelers who want to tie the knot on their West Coast visit: don't be surprised to find beaming same-sex couples having their wedding photos taken in summertime Stanley Park. For handy information and resources on gay marriage, visit www.queermarriage.com and www.vs.gov.bc.ca/marriage.

SAFE INJECTION SITES

In September 2003 Vancouver opened North America's first safe injection site (also called a supervised injection site), a 12-seat room where users come in to inject drugs under the supervision of trained health-care staff, who issue clean needles, spoons, tourniquets and water.

The site is located in the Downtown Eastside, which has one of the largest concentrations of injection drug users on the continent. With AIDS and hepatitis beginning to reach epidemic proportions, the controversial program is part of a 'four pillars' approach (harm reduction, prevention, treatment and enforcement) pioneered in Switzerland and Germany. The idea is to reduce disease, infections, overdose deaths and drug-related crime.

After injecting, clients move to a 'chill-out' room, where staff can connect them with on-site services, such as medical care and counseling, or off-site services like withdrawal management. In the site's first year, an average of 588 injections took place daily, 107 overdose incidents were successfully prevented and two to four clients per day were referred to addiction treatment.

The experimental facility has remained controversial since it opened – locals are divided on whether they want it in their city and the conservative federal government has threatened several times to pull the plug, noting that its pioneering approach has yet to prove itself fully effective at 'solving' the problem of drug use.

MEDIA

Vancouverites like to read, which explains the presence of two daily newspapers – the *Vancouver Sun* and the *Province* – plus Canada's largest alternative weekly, the *Georgia Straight*. There are also dozens of freebie community and specialty rags, and a raft of locally focused magazines, ranging from *Vancouver Magazine* to a sustainability glossy called *Granville*.

Some locals will tell you that quantity does not always equal quality, however, and they point to the city's two dailies as evidence of this. Vancouver's two main newspapers are owned by Canadian media corporation Canwest; the company also owns most of the the main radio and TV stations in the city. While Canwest would term this convergence – you're likely to see *Vancouver Sun* reporters appearing on Global news shows and large ads running in the *Province* for upcoming TV shows – some locals call it media bias.

One result of this growing feeling was the creation of an online city newspaper by a former *Sun* editor. Established by David Beers in 2004, the *Tyee* (www.thetyee.ca) – named after a 'feisty fish' – features some of the city's best non-Canwest journalists. While it breaks stories missed by the mainstream media, its main strength is in its in-depth analysis of pertinent local issues, which can range from street racing in Richmond to the green building claims of local developers. Predominantly a listings paper, the *Georgia Straight* often fulfills a similar investigative role in its feature stories.

For a comprehensive listing of the city's main media publications, see p232.

top picks

VANCOUVER BLOGS

- Urban Diner (www.urbandiner.ca) – the city's best restaurant news and reviews site (see p138)
- Vitamin V (www.vitaminv.ca) – covering local fashion, trends and lifestyle (see p113)
- Urban Vancouver (www.urbanvancouver.com) – a community of local bloggers offering the inside track on the city
- Beyond Robson (www.beyondrobson.com) – excellent local arts, music, film and culture site
- General Manager's Blog (www.opushotel.com/blog) – highly readable insider take on the local hotel industry (see p197)

BLUELIST[1] (blu,list) *v.*
to recommend a travel experience.
What's your recommendation? www.lonelyplanet.com/bluelist

NEIGHBORHOODS

top picks

- Capilano Suspension Bridge (p103)
- Vancouver Aquarium (p52)
- Museum of Anthropology (p99)
- Grouse Mountain (p103)
- Vancouver Art Gallery (p46)
- Vancouver Police Centennial Museum (p73)
- Granville Island Brewing (p86)
- English Bay Beach (p65)
- Lighthouse Park (p105)
- Gulf of Georgia Cannery National Historic Site (p106)

NEIGHBORHOODS

While 'outsiders' frequently label Vancouver as one the planet's best places to live, hand-wringing locals often ask themselves whether or not this really is a world-class city. The answer lies not in making futile comparisons with older, larger and denser metropolises like London or New York but in searching for what really makes this area tick.

That's where Vancouver's varied neighborhoods come in. Unlike some cities, there's more than one heart here – no one calls the downtown area the 'city center' – and travelers can have a distinctively different day out depending on where they head. Luckily, with the city's on-foot suitability and user-friendly transit system, these neighborhoods are ideal for a spot of urban exploration.

'Unlike some cities, there's more than one heart here – no one calls the downtown area the "city center" – and travelers can have a distinctively different day out depending on where they head'

Since it's where most of the hotels are, many visitors start among the towers and shops of downtown. The gridlike road system makes it easy to find your way around here, and you'll get frequent glimpses of snowcapped mountains grinning at you between the buildings. If you like to mix a little greenery with your concrete, head west along the seawall from Canada Place and you'll arrive at Stanley Park, where you can circumnavigate the forest and drink in the sea-to-sky vistas. In contrast, the adjoining West End is a densely packed residential district with plenty of life, lots of restaurants and some enticing historic enclaves. It's a gay-friendly neighborhood with a buzzing nightlife scene too.

There's also history to the east in Yaletown, a former industrial area reinvented as a 'little Soho' stretch of yuppie apartments, lounge bars and excellent restaurants. You can stroll north from here to historic Gastown, the city's founding area. Another district reclaimed from a grungy past, it's Vancouver's main old-town neighborhood and has some great bars and characterful brick buildings. There's even more character in the adjoining Chinatown, where brightly painted, clammy-windowed restaurants lure visitors with aromas both sweet and savory.

A different crowd haunts the streets of South Main (SoMa), an edgy, student-chic district where the shabby hovels and mom-and-pop shops have been refreshed with cool coffeeshops, unusual new restaurants and stores hawking hipster duds from bright local designers. Coffee is even more important on Commercial Dr, where generations of Italian immigrants serve the city's best java. It's not only about caffeine, though: this bohemian neighborhood is lined with convivial bars and restaurants.

The city's favorite half-day hangout for visitors, Granville Island is a strollable smorgasbord of artisan studios, galleries and the Granville Island Public Market. You can continue exploring in the nearby Fairview area, then take in the window-shopping delights of South Granville.

To the west of South Granville, Kitsilano enjoys some of the province's best urban beaches plus three of the city's main museums – bookstores are an additional shopping specialty here. The bookish might also enjoy the University of British Columbia (UBC). Western Canada's largest uni, it combines a city-best museum, landscaped gardens and rugged parkland.

Exploring Greater Vancouver, many visitors will be lured by North Van's mountainous charms and the coastal promise of West Vancouver. Both are located across Burrard Inlet – this is your excuse to cross the stunning Lions Gate Bridge. In contrast, a trip south of the city will bring you to Richmond, the region's latter-day 'Asia town' that still has a pocket of old fishing-village charm.

Now that you know where to go, it's time to hit the road. There are some handy walking tours in this chapter, but don't be afraid to wander off the beaten path to see what's just around the corner.

STANLEY PARK (p52)

WEST END (p65)

DOWNTOWN (p46)

GASTOWN (p73)

CHINATOWN (p76)

YALETOWN (p70)

GRANVILLE ISLAND (p86)

FAIRVIEW & SOUTH GRANVILLE (p90)

SOUTH MAIN (SOMA) (p80)

COMMERCIAL DRIVE (p83)

KITSILANO (p94)

UNIVERSITY OF BRITISH COLUMBIA (UBC) (p99)

GREATER VANCOUVER (p103)

GREATER VANCOUVER (p103)

North Vancouver

Queensdale

Strathcona

Renfrew

Renfrew Heights

Collingwood

Vancouver Harbour

Mount Pleasant

Main

Knight Road

Cambie

Shaughnessy

Quilchena

Fairview

Kitsilano

Arbutus

Mackenzie Heights

Point Grey

Dunbar

English Bay

Burrard Inlet

0   1 mile
0   2 km

ITINERARY BUILDER

Vancouver's not a difficult city to explore, but to really get under its skin you'll need to check out its distinctive districts, the lifeblood of the city. This tool should help you find a range of treats in all of the featured neighborhoods, from the beaches and bookshops of Kitsilano to the coffee shops and bars of Commercial Dr.

AREA	ACTIVITIES Sights	Shopping	Eating
Downtown	Vancouver Art Galley (p46) Canada Place (p46) Contemporary Art Gallery (p50)	John Fluevog (p112) Mink Chocolates (p111) Holt Renfrew (p111)	C Restaurant (p127) Nu (p128) Templeton (p128)
West End & Stanley Park	Vancouver Aquarium (p52) Roedde House Museum (p65) English Bay Beach (p65)	Rubber Rainbow Condom Company (p113) Little Sisters Book & Art Emporium (p113) Lululemon Athletica (p113)	Raincity Grill (p131) Fish House in Stanley Park (p130) Hapa Izakaya (p132)
Yaletown	Roundhouse Community Arts & Recreation Centre (p70) BC Sports Hall of Fame & Museum (p70)	Coastal Peoples Fine Arts Gallery (p114) Lola Home & Apparel (p114) Bionic Footwear (p114)	Blue Water Café (p132) Glowbal Grill & Satay Bar (p133) Rodney's Oyster Bar (p133)
Gastown & Chinatown	Vancouver Police Centennial Museum (p73) Science World (p76) Dr Sun Yat-Sen Classical Chinese Garden (p76)	Wanted – Lost Found Canadian (p116) Goon Pack (p115) Chinatown Night Market (p115)	Salt Tasting Room (p135) Chill Winston (p134) Hon's Wun-Tun House (p135)
SoMa & Commercial Drive	Punjabi Market (p80)	Smoking Lily (p117) Regional Assembly of Text (p118) HT Naturals (p118)	Aurora Bistro (p136) Havana (p138) Nyala (p136)
Granville Island	Granville Island Public Market (p86) Granville Island Brewing (p86) Emily Carr Institute of Art & Design (p87)	Wood Co-op (p120) Paper-Ya (p120) Circle Craft (p120)	Go Fish (p139) Sandbar (p139) Bridges (p139)
Fairview & South Granville	VanDusen Botanical Garden (p90) Bloedel Floral Conservatory (p92)	Equinox Gallery (p121) Restoration Hardware (p122) Meinhardt Fine Foods (p121)	Tojo's (p140) Vij's (p140) West (p139)
Kitsilano & University of British Columbia (UBC)	Museum of Anthropology (p99) Kitsilano Beach (p96) UBC Botanical Garden (p99)	Travel Bug (p122) Gravity Pope (p123) Zulu Records (p123)	Bishops (p141) Bistrot Bistro (p142) Lumiere (p141)

HOW TO USE THIS TABLE

The table below allows you to plan a day's worth of activities in any area of the city. Simply select which area you wish to explore, and then mix and match from the corresponding listings to build your day. The first item in each cell represents a well-known highlight of the area, while the other items are more off-the-beaten-track gems.

Drinking	Nightlife	Sports & Activities
Chambar (p149) Fountainhead Pub (p148) Bacchus (p149)	Railway Club (p164) Commodore (p164) Caprice (p159)	Hockey: Vancouver Canucks (p187) Spa Utopia (p187) YWCA Health & Wellness Centre (p184)
The Calling (p151) Cardero's Marine Pub (p150) Mill Marine (p150)	Balthazar's House of Comedy (p158) O'Doul's (p163)	Second Beach Pool (p185) Spokes Bicycle Rental (p179) Vancouver Aquatic Centre (p185)
Yaletown Brewing Company (p152) Afterglow (p151) George Ultra Lounge (p151)	Bar None (p159) Capones Restaurant & Live Jazz Club (p162)	Yaletown Yoga (p186) Skoah (p187)
Six Acres (p152) Irish Heather (p152) Steamworks Brewing Company (p152)	Honey (p160) Shine (p161) Pat's Pub (p164)	
Stella's Tap & Tapas Bar (p154) Whip (p153) Café Calabria (p154)	Main on Main (p162) Café deux Soleils (p162) Rime (p163)	Cliffhanger Vancouver (p181)
Dockside Brewing Company (p154) Granville Island Brewing Taproom (p154)	Vancouver Theatresports League (p158) Backstage Lounge (p163)	Reckless Bike Stores (p179) Ecomarine Ocean Kayak Centre (p181)
		Baseball: Vancouver Canadians (p187)
Bimini Public House (p155) Nevermind (p155) Galley Patio & Grill (p155)	Cellar Restaurant & Jazz Club (p162) Jericho Folk Club (p162)	UBC Aquatic Centre (p185) Windsure Adventure Watersports (p182) University Golf Club (p179)

GREATER VANCOUVER

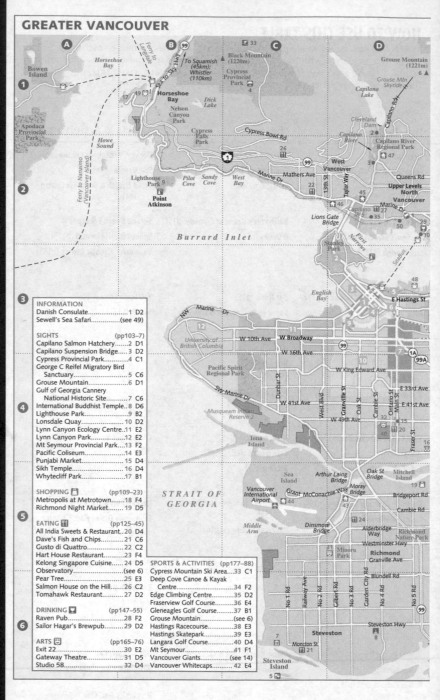

INFORMATION
Danish Consulate....................1 D2
Sewell's Sea Safari...............(see 49)

SIGHTS (pp103–7)
Capilano Salmon Hatchery......2 D1
Capilano Suspension Bridge.....3 D2
Cypress Provincial Park...........4 C1
George C Reifel Migratory Bird
  Sanctuary.........................5 C6
Grouse Mountain....................6 D1
Gulf of Georgia Cannery
  National Historic Site.........7 C6
International Buddhist Temple..8 D6
Lighthouse Park......................9 B2
Lonsdale Quay.......................10 D2
Lynn Canyon Ecology Centre..11 E2
Lynn Canyon Park.................12 E2
Mt Seymour Provincial Park...13 F2
Pacific Coliseum....................14 E3
Punjabi Market......................15 D4
Sikh Temple..........................16 D4
Whytecliff Park.....................17 B1

SHOPPING (pp109–23)
Metropolis at Metrotown.......18 F4
Richmond Night Market.........19 D5

EATING (pp125–45)
All India Sweets & Restaurant..20 D4
Dave's Fish and Chips............21 C6
Gusto di Quattro....................22 C2
Hart House Restaurant...........23 F4
Kelong Singapore Cuisine.....24 D5
Observatory..........................(see 6)
Pear Tree.............................25 E3
Salmon House on the Hill....26 C2
Tomahawk Restaurant...........27 D2

DRINKING (pp147–55)
Raven Pub............................28 F2
Sailor Hagar's Brewpub.........29 D2

ARTS (pp165–76)
Exit 22.................................30 E2
Gateway Theatre...................31 D5
Studio 58..............................32 D4

SPORTS & ACTIVITIES (pp177–88)
Cypress Mountain Ski Area....33 C1
Deep Cove Canoe & Kayak
  Centre..............................34 F2
Edge Climbing Centre...........35 D2
Fraserview Golf Course..........36 E4
Gleneagles Golf Course.........37 B1
Grouse Mountain...................(see 6)
Hastings Racecourse..............38 E3
Hastings Skatepark................39 E3
Langara Golf Course..............40 D4
Mt Seymour..........................41 F1
Vancouver Giants...................(see 14)
Vancouver Whitecaps............42 E4

44

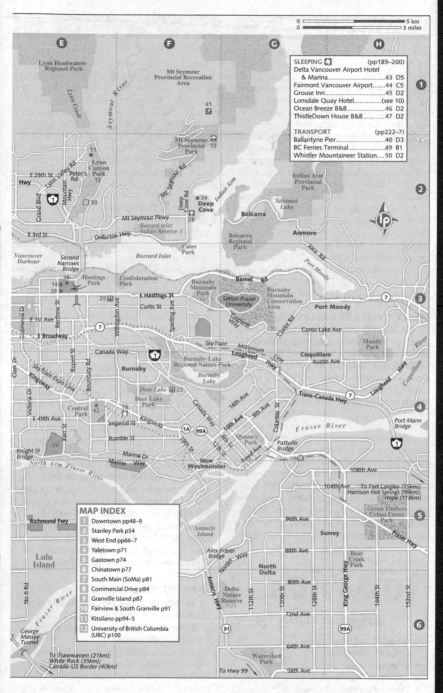

SLEEPING 🛏 (pp189–200)
Delta Vancouver Airport Hotel
& Marina..............................43 D5
Fairmont Vancouver Airport.......44 C5
Grouse Inn...............................45 D2
Lonsdale Quay Hotel..............(see 10)
Ocean Breeze B&B....................46 D2
ThistleDown House B&B.............47 D2

TRANSPORT (pp222–7)
Ballantyne Pier.........................40 D3
BC Ferries Terminal....................49 B1
Whistler Mountaineer Station....50 D2

MAP INDEX

To Tsawwassen (21km);
White Rock (35km);
Canada-US Border (40km)

To Fort Langley (15km);
Harrison Hot Springs (98km);
Hope (118km)

To Hwy 99

0 — 5 km
0 — 3 miles

Drinking p148; Eating p127; Shopping p110; Sleeping p191

Bordered by water to the north and south and the West End to the west, downtown Vancouver combines shimmering glass apartment and business towers with clamorous, shop-lined streets and malls. It's the city's main hub and most visitors spend plenty of wandering time here – you can see them on every street corner clutching their maps, facing in opposite directions and looking puzzled. But while you'll soon get your bearings – the streets are on a grid system here – there are several key areas that encourage a little unplanned exploration.

The intersection of Granville and Georgia Sts is the center of the action in modern-day Vancouver, and it's a good place to stop and watch the world go by for a few moments. It's even better to head to the grassy expanse on the Georgia St side of the Vancouver Art Gallery, where you can recline in the sun, close your eyes and take in the sounds (and hotdog smells) of the area. On the opposite Robson St side of the building, you'll find a large flight of steps that make for another great people-watching perch.

At night, the downtown action is centered on Granville St. This has been Vancouver's neon-lit entertainment strip for decades, although the cinemas and music halls that lined the area in the 1950s have mostly been replaced by nightclubs and bars. Check the sidewalk here: it's studded with plaques recalling the famous (and not-so-famous) entertainers who have played the strip over the years.

Main transit access to downtown includes the Granville and Burrard SkyTrain stations, plus Burrard St's buses 2, 22 and 44 and Granville St's 4, 10 and 50. Canada Line construction has temporarily rerouted some of these buses, so check before you travel.

VANCOUVER ART GALLERY Map pp48–9
☎ 604-662-4719; www.vanartgallery.bc.ca; 750 Hornby St; adult/child/student/senior $15/6/10/11, admission by donation 5-9pm Tue; ☯ 10am-5:30pm Fri-Mon & Wed, 10am-9pm Tue & Thu; Ⓜ Granville
Once a disappointing regional gallery with nothing more than a clutch of Emily Carr canvases to recommend it, the VAG – housed in an old courthouse but rumored to be moving to a new downtown location soon – has dramatically transformed in recent years, becoming a vital part of the city's cultural scene. Edgy contemporary exhibitions, often showcasing Vancouver's wealth of internationally renowned photographers, are combined with blockbuster traveling shows. The gallery comes into its own on select Fridays for FUSE (admission $15), a late-night party where you can hang out with the city's arty types.

top picks

BEHIND-THE-SCENES TOURS
- Granville Island Brewing (p86)
- BC Place Stadium (p70)
- GM Place (opposite)
- Vancouver Aquarium (p52)
- University of British Columbia (p99)

In summer the mezzanine-level café (p149) is among downtown's best sunny haunts.

CANADA PLACE Map pp48–9
☎ 604-647-7390; www.canadaplace.ca; 999 Canada Place Way; Ⓜ Waterfront; ♿
Built for Expo '86, this iconic, postcard-friendly landmark is shaped like a series of sails that jut into the sky over the harbor. Now a cruise-ship terminal and convention center (a large convention-center expansion will open on the building's west side before the Olympics), it's also a pier where you can stroll out over the waterfront, watch the splashing floatplanes and catch some spectacular sea-to-mountain views. If it's raining, duck inside for the CN IMAX Theatre (p169) and the Port Authority Interpretation Centre (☎ 604-665-9179; admission free; ☯ 8am-5pm Mon-Fri), a hands-on, kid-friendly showcase illuminating the city's maritime trade.

VANCOUVER LOOKOUT Map pp48–9
☎ 604-689-0421; www.vancouverlookout.com; 555 W Hastings St; adult/child/youth $13/6/9; ☯ 8:30am-10:30pm May–mid-Oct, 9am-9pm mid-Oct–Apr; Ⓜ Waterfront
Expect your lurching stomach to make a bid for freedom as one of the two glass elevators here whisks you 169m to the apex of this needle-like viewing area. Once

up top, there's not much to do but wander around and check out the truly awesome 360-degree vistas of city, sea and mountain panoramas unfurling around you. If you want to know what you're looking at, join one of the free tours or just peruse the recently added historic photo panels showing just how much the landscape around here has changed. Tickets are pricey but are valid all day – consider coming back for a soaring sunset view of the city to get your money's worth.

CHRIST CHURCH CATHEDRAL Map pp48–9

☎ 604-682-3848; www.cathedral.vancouver.bc.ca; 690 Burrard St; ☷ 10am-4pm; Ⓜ Burrard
Completed in 1895 and designated as a cathedral in 1929, the biggest and best Gothic-style church in the city is nestled incongruously among Vancouver's looming glass towers. Undergoing extensive renovations in recent years, it's a busy site and is home to a wide range of cultural events, including regular choir and chamber music recitals and the occasional Shakespeare reading. Self-guided tours of the 32 stained-glass windows are available, but if you're short of time just head down to the basement for the highlight: a colorful William Morris beauty. It's a working church, so visiting hours may be cut when services are scheduled.

GM PLACE Map pp48–9

☎ 604-899-7440; www.generalmotorsplace.com; 800 Griffiths Way; Ⓜ Stadium
Also known as 'the Garage,' the newer of Vancouver's two downtown stadiums hosts the Vancouver Canucks of the National Hockey League (see p187). Game nights, when the 20,000-capacity venue heaves with fervent fans, are the city's most exciting sporting events – you'll enjoy the atmosphere even if the rules are a mystery. The main hockey venue for the 2010 Winter Olympics, this is also a favored arena for money-spinning stadium rock acts. Behind-the-scenes tours (☎ 604-899-7440; Gate 6; adult/child/student & senior $10/5/7; ☷ 10:30am, noon & 1:30pm Wed & Fri) take you into the hospitality suites and the nosebleed press box up in the rafters.

PENDULUM GALLERY Map pp48–9

☎ 604-250-9682; www.pendulumgallery.bc.ca; HSBC Bank Bldg, 885 W Georgia St; admission free; ☷ 9am-6pm Mon-Wed, 9am-9pm Thu-Fri, 9am-5pm Sat; Ⓜ Burrard

top picks

IT'S FREE

- Dr Sun Yat-Sen Park (p76)
- Pendulum Gallery (left)
- Lost Lagoon Nature House (p55)
- Canada Place (opposite)
- Port Authority Interpretation Centre (opposite)
- Christ Church Cathedral (left)
- Stanley Park Totem Poles (p55)
- Contemporary Art Gallery (p50)
- Wreck Beach (p101)
- Stanley Park Seawall (p55)
- Capilano Salmon Hatchery (p104)
- Lynn Canyon Park Suspension Bridge & Ecology Centre (p104)

A creative use for the cavernous atrium of the city's main HSBC Bank Building – you'll be overlooking the cash machines and smiling bank tellers – this gallery offers an ever-changing roster of temporary exhibitions. It's mostly new art, and can range from striking paintings to challenging photographs and quirky arts and crafts. The space also houses one permanent exhibit: a gargantuan 27m-long buffed aluminum pendulum that will be swinging over your head throughout your visit. Designed by Alan Storey, it weighs 1600kg and moves about 6m (the swing is assisted by a hydraulic mechanical system at the top).

VANCOUVER PUBLIC LIBRARY Map pp48–9

☎ 604-331-3600; www.vpl.ca; 350 W Georgia St; ☷ 10am-9pm Mon-Thu, 10am-6pm Fri & Sat, 1-5pm Sun; Ⓜ Stadium
This spectacular, Roman Colosseum–like building must be a temple to the great god of libraries. If not, it's certainly one of the world's most magnificent public library facilities. Built in 1995, it contains 1.2 million books and other items spread out over seven levels, all of them seemingly populated by language students silently learning English from textbooks. The awesome glass atrium curving around the entrance is filled with tables and cafés, making it an ideal spot to hang out on a rainy day and check your home-country newspapers (found on level five). If you're traveling with kids, the library's downstairs children's section is tons of fun.

DOWNTOWN

INFORMATION
American Express....................1 E2
Australian Consulate................2 E2
Berlitz...................................3 F2
Canada Post Main Outlet......4 F4
Dutch Consulate....................5 E2
Electric Internet Café............6 F3
German Consulate..............(see 17)
Howe St Postal Outlet...........7 C5
Indian Consulate....................8 F2
Italian Consulate....................9 G3
New Zealand Consulate......(see 2)
Pharmasave..........................10 F2
St Paul's Hospital.................11 C4
Stein Medical Clinic..............12 E2
Touristinfo Centre................13 F1
Ultima Medicentre Plus..........14 E2
Travelex Currency Services...(see 93)
Vancouver Bullion & Currency
  Exchange...........................15 F2
Vancouver Convention &
  Exhibition Centre...............16 G1
Vancouver Public Library......(see 25)

SIGHTS (pp46–51)
Canada Place........................17 G1
Christ Church Cathedral........18 E3
Contemporary Art Gallery.....19 E4
GM Place..............................20 G5
Marine Building....................21 F2
Pendulum Gallery.................22 E3
Vancouver Art Gallery...........23 E3
Vancouver Lookout...............24 G3
Vancouver Public Library.......25 F4
Waterfront Station................26 G2

SHOPPING (pp109–23)
a&b sound...........................27 F3
Canadian Maple Delights.....28 E3
Golden Age..........................29 F3
Heavens Playground.............30 F3
Henry Birks & Sons..............31 F2
Holt Renfrew.......................32 F3
John Fluevog.......................33 E4
Mink Chocolates..................34 F2
Momentum..........................35 C4
Pacific Centre......................36 E3
Roots..................................37 D3

Scratch Records....................38 F4
Sikora's Classical Records......39 G3
Sophia Books........................40 G3
True Value Vintage...............41 E3

EATING (pp125–45)
Bin 941..............................42 C4
C Restaurant.......................43 B6
Culinaria Restaurant............44 F3
Elbow Room........................45 D5
Gorilla Food........................46 G3
JJ's Fine Dining...................47 G3
La Bodega...........................48 C5
Le Crocodile.......................49 D3
Metro.................................50 F2
Nu.....................................51 B6
Nuba.................................52 D5
Sanafir...............................53 D4
Templeton...........................54 D4

DRINKING (pp147–55)
Bacchus...........................(see 98)
Caffè Artigiano....................55 E3
Chambar.............................56 G4
Fountainhead Pub................57 C4
Gallery Café......................(see 23)
Ginger 62............................58 C5
Lennox Pub..........................59 E4
Mario's...............................60 E2
Railway Club........................61 F3

NIGHTLIFE (pp157–64)
AuBar.................................62 F3
Caprice...............................63 D4
Celebrities...........................64 C4
Commodore..........................65 E4
Media Club...........................66 F4
Odyssey...............................67 C5
Plaza Club............................68 E4
Railway Club......................(see 61)
Republic...............................69 D4
Roxy...................................70 D4
St Andrew's Wesley United
  Church...............................71 C4
Yale....................................72 C5
Yuk Yuk's...........................(see 86)

See West End Map pp66–7

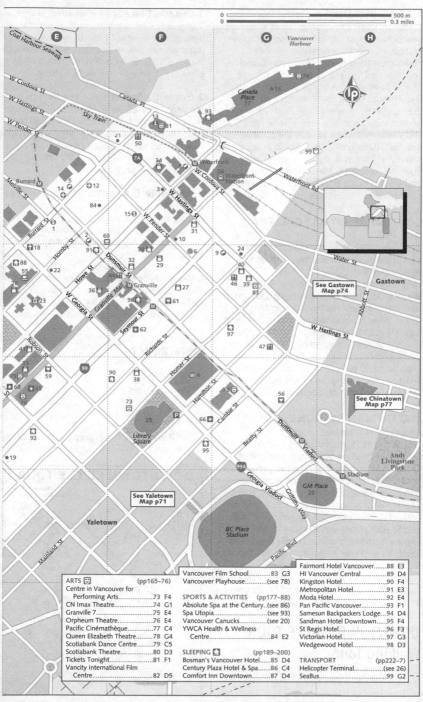

0 ____ 500 m
0 ____ 0.3 miles

See Gastown
Map p74

Gastown

See Chinatown
Map p77

See Yaletown
Map p71

Yaletown

Andy
Livingstone
Park

GM Place

BC Place
Stadium

ARTS	(pp165–76)
Centre in Vancouver for	
Performing Arts	73 F4
CN Imax Theatre	74 G1
Granville 7	75 E4
Orpheum Theatre	76 E4
Pacific Cinémathèque	77 C4
Queen Elizabeth Theatre	78 G4
Scotiabank Dance Centre	79 C5
Scotiabank Theatre	80 D3
Tickets Tonight	81 F1
Vancity International Film	
Centre	82 D5

Vancouver Film School	83	G3
Vancouver Playhouse	(see 78)	
SPORTS & ACTIVITIES	**(pp177–88)**	
Absolute Spa at the Century	(see 86)	
Spa Utopia	(see 93)	
Vancouver Canucks	(see 20)	
YWCA Health & Wellness		
Centre	84	E2
SLEEPING	**(pp189–200)**	
Bosman's Vancouver Hotel	85	D4
Century Plaza Hotel & Spa	86	C4
Comfort Inn Downtown	87	D4

Fairmont Hotel Vancouver	88	E3
HI Vancouver Central	89	D4
Kingston Hotel	90	F4
Metropolitan Hotel	91	E3
Moda Hotel	92	E4
Pan Pacific Vancouver	93	F1
Samesun Backpackers Lodge	94	D4
Sandman Hotel Downtown	95	F4
St Regis Hotel	96	F3
Victorian Hotel	97	G3
Wedgewood Hotel	98	D3
TRANSPORT	**(pp222–7)**	
Helicopter Terminal	(see 26)	
SeaBus	99	G2

MARINE BUILDING Map pp48–9

355 Burrard St; 🕑 **8am-6pm Mon-Fri;** Ⓜ **Waterfront**
Vancouver's most romantic old-school tower block is an evocative reminder of what skyscrapers used to look like before bland concrete and faceless glass caught the eye of area developers. A graceful, 22-story, Art Deco tribute to the city's maritime past, its grand entranceway resembles a ship's prow while a salty frieze of waves, marine flora and sea horses wraps around the building's exterior. The interior lobby, awash in aqua-green and blue, is designed to resemble a huge, treasure-filled Mayan temple. The tallest building in the British Empire when it was completed in 1930, it now houses offices.

CONTEMPORARY ART GALLERY
Map pp48–9

☎ **604-681-2700; www.contemporaryartgallery .ca; 555 Nelson St; admission free;** 🕑 **noon-6pm Wed-Sun;** 🚌 **4**
Originally the Greater Vancouver Artists' Gallery, this small, off-the-beaten-path art space transformed itself into an independent gallery in 1996, moving to a crisp, purpose-built facility in 2001. It focuses on a wide range of modern art, but photography is particularly well represented here. Exhibitions are ever-changing and include local and international artists – check the gallery's website for artist events and exhibition openings.

WATERFRONT STATION Map pp48–9
Cordova St; Ⓜ **Waterfront**
Opened in 1915, this handsome, multi-columned heritage building at the foot of Granville St was originally the old Canadian Pacific Railway station and the western terminus for transcontinental passenger trains. These days it houses offices, cafés and shops, and acts as the main link between SkyTrain and SeaBus transit services (the West Coast Express commuter train also rolls into town here). It's well worth boarding the SeaBus for the short hop across Burrard Inlet – you'll have a lovely duck's-eye view of the city as well as some bustling port life. Aim for a seat at the front of the boat for the best views.

DOWNTOWN CIRCLE TOUR
Walking Tour
This looping stroll will take you around the main streets and give you a handy overview of the downtown core.

1 Canada Place Start your stroll at one of Vancouver's most photographed landmarks (p46), giving yourself time to walk along its outer promenade so you can watch the floatplanes diving onto the water. There's often a giant cruise ship or two parked alongside.

2 Granville Street Head southwest along Howe St, turn left on W Hastings St and then right on Granville St. Follow this uphill thoroughfare; it's one of the city's most important commercial streets. You'll pass coffee shops, clothing stores and the Pacific Centre (p110), downtown's biggest mall.

3 Granville & Georgia Sreets Get your bearings at this busy street corner, the center of the downtown core. You can check out the department stores here or nip across one block to the Vancouver Art Gallery (p46) for a culture fix.

4 Vancouver Public Library Stroll southeast a couple of blocks to the magnificent, Colosseum-like library (p47). Here, the glass-enclosed atrium is a perfect place to grab a

WALK FACTS

Start Canada Place

End Canada Place

Distance 3km

Duration One hour

Fuel stop Vancouver Public Library

DOWNTOWN CIRCLE TOUR

coffee, or you can nip inside and check your email for free.

5 Robson Street Head northwest along Robson St, the city's main shopping promenade, where you can wander to your credit card's content at boutiques, bookstores and shoe shops. There are restaurants (p127) here too if it's time to eat.

6 Robson & Burrard Streets Take a breather at this clamorous intersection, then turn right and head along Burrard St toward the mountain vista glinting ahead of you. You can duck into the **Fairmont Hotel Vancouver** (p191) for a stroll through the elegant lobby or continue downhill past **Christ Church Cathedral** (p47). Within minutes, you'll be back at the waterfront Canada Place.

STANLEY PARK

Eating p129

Adjoining the West End, Vancouver's magnificent Stanley Park (☎ 604-257-8400; http://vancouver.ca/parks; admission free; ⏱ 24hr) is one of the largest urban parks in North America and certainly enjoys one of the world's most breathtaking settings: it's surrounded on three sides by the ocean and loomed over by the snowcapped North Shore mountains. The park's perimeter seawall stroll is one of the best ways to spend your time here – and it's a great introduction to the expansive 'Beautiful BC' wilderness encircling the region.

Originally home to the Musqueam and Squamish First Nations, Vancouver's first park was opened in 1889 by Canada's governor general, Lord Stanley. His opening speech announced that the park was for 'the use and enjoyment of people of all colors, creeds and customs for all time.' It's a motto that still stands: more than eight million visitors are drawn here every year.

Within its 404 hectares you'll find forests of cedar, hemlock and fir, mingled with meadows, lakes and cricket pitches. On a sunny day it seems all of Vancouver is here hiking, cycling and jogging along the seawall or through the woods. There are also a couple of excellent beaches – ideal spots to perch on a driftwood log with a picnic and catch a kaleidoscopic sunset over the water.

But the park isn't just for dewy-eyed nature lovers; other highlights include the Vancouver Aquarium and the Second Beach Swimming Pool. Not surprisingly, there's plenty for kids to do here, and there's also a good selection of eateries if it's time for lunch.

The park's information center is 500m from the Georgia St entrance, along the seawall. The free shuttle bus that travels around the park stops just 100m further along the seawall; alternatively, you can hop on a plodding horse-drawn carriage (see p234). Transit access to the park is via bus 19.

VANCOUVER AQUARIUM Map p54
☎ 604-659-3474; www.vanaqua.org; adult/child/youth, student & senior $20/12/15; ⏱ 9:30am-5pm Sep-Jun, 9:30am-7pm Jul & Aug; ⎍ shuttle bus; ♿

Stanley Park's biggest draw, the aquarium is home to 9000 water-loving creatures – including sharks, dolphins, Amazonian caimans and a somewhat shy octopus. There's also a small, walk-through rainforest area full of birds, butterflies and turtles.

Check out the iridescent jellyfish tank and the two sea otters who eat the way everyone should: lying on their backs using their chests as plates. If you feel like treating your offspring, consider a behind-the-scenes tour (from $25), where you'll learn how to be a trainer. The aquarium has repositioned itself as a conservation center in recent years (see the boxed text, p131) and plans are afoot to expand its facilities before 2010.

MINIATURE RAILWAY & CHILDREN'S FARMYARD Map p54
☎ 604-257-8531; railway adult/child/youth $5.50/2.75/4, farmyard $5.50/2.75/4; ⏱ railway 10:30am-5pm daily mid-May–Aug, Sat & Sun Feb–mid-May & Sep, plus special Halloween & Christmas services; ⏱ farmyard 11am-4pm daily mid-May–Aug, Sat & Sun Feb–mid-May & Sep; ⎍ shuttle bus; ♿

Near the aquarium, these twin, kid-friendly attractions are a big draw in summer. The farmyard allows youngsters to interact with llamas, sheep, goats, cows, hens and other small animals in a way that will make you wonder why you bother spending money on much pricier zoos back home. In contrast, the railway offers a 15-minute train ride that kids of all ages can enjoy. The engines are replicas of actual locomo-

top picks
PICNIC SPOTS
- Third Beach (p54) – spectacular sea and sunset views in Stanley Park
- Vanier Park (p97) – laid-back grassy knoll with languid sea and mountain vistas
- Lumberman's Arch (p55) – Stanley Park's other great picnic spot, with views of passing cruise ships
- Kitsilano Beach (p96) – giant sandy expanse with a nearby swimming pool to help you work up an appetite
- Wreck Beach (p101) – UBC's naturist enclave, complete with its own wandering food vendors

AQUARIUM ANTICS

An interview with Troy Neale, Senior Marine Mammal Trainer, Vancouver Aquarium (opposite).

In your experience, which marine animals are the easiest and the hardest to train? I don't think that any of the animals are particularly easy to train; however, most of our new trainers start off working with the beluga whales. It is usually only the most experienced trainers that work with orca whales, so I would say they would be considered the most challenging marine animal to work with. We take the most precautions when working with our male Steller sea lion. They are known to be potentially aggressive animals so that's something you have to consider when interacting with him.

In general terms, what is the process for training a marine animal? Most importantly, you have to build trust; without that you won't get anywhere. The first thing you train is what is known as a target. We can use either our hand or a target pole (a long pole with a white float on the end). The target pole is used as an extension of our arms so we can position the animals out in the water. Once the animals understand to focus on the target, we can have them follow it and then mold the behavior. When they do the behavior we are asking for we either blow a whistle or use our voices to tell them they have done the correct behavior. Then we give them some kind of reinforcement – sometimes fish and sometimes rubs and scratches or a toy to play with.

What do the animals eat? For the beluga whales, dolphins, sea lions and seals we feed them mainly fish – herring and capelin – and squid, and we supplement with multivitamins designed specifically for marine mammals. The sea otters are the smallest marine mammals in our care but they are the most expensive animals to feed. They eat clams, squid, cod, crabs and prawns – all of which are restaurant quality.

Who are the star performers and what are some of their favorite tricks? I think all the animals are fantastic but as a trainer I'm a bit biased. The majority of our visitors come to see the dolphins leaping in the air. They are such amazing, acrobatic animals and to be able to see them this close up is something people remember.

Are some animals more interested in performing than others? Some of the animals really seem to get excited when the music starts up before the shows – the louder the crowds are, the more energy they seem to put into their behaviors. This might result in the belugas jumping a little higher or the dolphins doing splashy leaps and breaches on their own before the presentation even gets started.

What naughty things do some of the animals do when they don't want to perform on a particular day? All of the animals have distinct personalities and have their good and bad days. Probably the most difficult time is during their mating seasons, as they often have other things on their minds! I remember doing a show one summer with two of our dolphins, one male and one female. About halfway through the show they stopped paying attention to us and went off together. They spent the rest of the show mating and putting on their own show for the visitors.

How do you become a trainer? The most important things you need are education and experience. We look for people with degrees in the field of biology, either a marine biology or a zoology degree. We also have a few trainers with Animal Health Technician degrees. Volunteering is a great way to gain experience with animals, whether it's at the aquarium or at a zoo or animal shelter.

What do visitors experience if they take your behind-the-scenes trainer tours? They make up a bucket of food to feed to the animals, then we take them up to the habitat and teach them about how we work with the animals and they get to feed them. This allows us the opportunity to share with people the way we see the animals and they get to learn some of the funny little characteristics that each animal has.

tives, including No 374, which pulled the first passenger train into Vancouver. At Halloween the railway rises from the dead of the off-season to become a ghost train, while at Christmastime its carriages and route are adorned with fairy lights.

PROSPECT POINT Map p54

🚌 shuttle bus

One of Vancouver's most glorious lookouts, this lofty spot is located at the park's north ern tip. In summer you'll be jostling for elbow room with the tour groups as you angle for a view of the passing cruise ships – heading down the steep stairs to the viewing platform usually shakes some of them off. Look out for scavenging raccoons here and remember that it's never a good idea to try to pet these semi-tame, rabies-carrying critters. The cairn here commemorates the 1888 wreck of the SS *Beaver*, a Hudson's Bay Company steamship

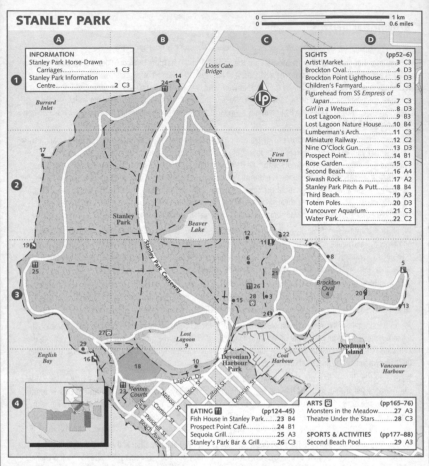

STANLEY PARK

0   1 km
0   0.6 miles

INFORMATION
Stanley Park Horse-Drawn
   Carriages...........................1 C3
Stanley Park Information
   Centre...............................2 C3

SIGHTS (pp52–6)
Artist Market.............................3 C3
Brockton Oval...........................4 D3
Brockton Point Lighthouse.....5 D3
Children's Farmyard.................6 C3
Figurehead from SS Empress of
   Japan.....................................7 C3
Girl in a Wetsuit.......................8 D3
Lost Lagoon..............................9 B3
Lost Lagoon Nature House......10 B4
Lumberman's Arch...................11 C3
Miniature Railway....................12 C2
Nine O'Clock Gun....................13 D3
Prospect Point..........................14 B1
Rose Garden.............................15 C3
Second Beach...........................16 A4
Siwash Rock.............................17 A2
Stanley Park Pitch & Putt.........18 B4
Third Beach..............................19 A3
Totem Poles..............................20 D3
Vancouver Aquarium...............21 C3
Water Park................................22 C2

Burrard
Inlet

Lions Gate
Bridge

First
Narrows

Stanley
Park

Beaver
Lake

Stanley Park Causeway

Brockton
Oval
4

Lost
Lagoon
9

Deadman's
Island

English
Bay

Devonian
Harbour
Park

Coal
Harbour

Vancouver
Harbour

Lagoon Dr
Nelson St
Chilco St
Gifford St
Denman St
Comox St
Beach Ave
Pendrell St

Tennis
Courts

EATING (pp124–45)
Fish House in Stanley Park.......23 B4
Prospect Point Café..................24 B1
Sequoia Grill............................25 A3
Stanley's Park Bar & Grill.........26 C3

ARTS (pp165–76)
Monsters in the Meadow.........27 A3
Theatre Under the Stars...........28 C3

SPORTS & ACTIVITIES (pp177–88)
Second Beach Pool...................29 A3

---

that was the first to travel the entire west coast of North America. **Prospect Point Café** (p130) offers refreshments – aim for a table on the deck.

SECOND BEACH & THIRD BEACH
Map p54

🚌 shuttle bus; 🚴

Second Beach is an ever-busy, family-friendly area on the park's western side, with a large, grassy playground, a greasy-spoon snack bar that also serves ice cream, and the **Stanley Park Pitch & Putt** golf course. Its main attraction, though, is the seasonal outdoor **swimming pool** (p185) that sits on the waterfront overlooking the distant UBC peninsula.

Third Beach is recommended if you're looking for a more peaceful visit. A lovely

sandy expanse with plenty of large logs to sit against, this is Vancouver's best sunset-viewing spot, hence the locals who drop by every summer evening with barbecues and coolers.

LOST LAGOON Map p54

🚌 shuttle bus

This area near the park's entrance was originally an extension of Coal Harbour, but by 1916 the bridge was replaced with a causeway, and in 1922 the new body of water was named, transforming itself into a freshwater lake a few years later. Today it's a wild-bird sanctuary and its perimeter path makes for a wonderful nature-bound walk. The lagoon's **Jubilee Fountain**, originally at the Chicago World's Fair, was installed here in 1936 to commemorate Vancouver's 50th anniversary. The friendly folk at the excellent **Lost Lagoon Nature House** (☎ 604-257-6908; www.stanleyparkecology.ca; admission free; 🕐 10am-7pm Tue-Sun May-Sep) provide exhibits and illumination on the park's wildlife, history and ecology.

BROCKTON POINT Map p54
🚌 **shuttle bus**

The name refers to the eastern end of the park as well as the eastern tip of the peninsula. It contains **Brockton Oval** playing field and cricket pitch, a colorful clutch of **totem poles** from several different First Nations people (the adjacent information center explains their origins), and the **Nine O'Clock Gun** on Hallelujah Point – an electrically fired cannon that sounds at 9pm nightly and was originally used by ships' captains to set their chronometers. The squat **Brockton Point Lighthouse** was completed in 1915. It's not too far from here to the summertime **artist market**, where you can pick up a painterly souvenir of your visit.

LUMBERMAN'S ARCH Map p54
🚌 **shuttle bus**

Once the site of a Coast Salish village, Lumberman's Arch received its modern name from the beefy, rough-hewn archway donated by the Lumberman's and Shingleman's Society. If your kids have overheated themselves by running wild in the sun, cool them off here at the giggle-inducing seafront **Water Park**. Just east along the seawall from here is the **Girl in a Wetsuit** bronze statue by Elek Imredy – sometimes wearing a sweater to preserve her modesty – and the colorful **ship's figurehead** of the SS *Empress of Japan,* which commemorates Vancouver's early trade with Asia.

STANLEY PARK OUTDOOR EXPLORER
Walking Tour

This invigorating walk (or bike ride) will take you right around the park, passing totem poles, inviting beaches and towering trees.

1 Coal Harbour Start your stroll at the park's Georgia St entrance, heading north around the curving seawall toward the Tudoresque boat-club building. Continue

on to the park's info center, where you can pick-up a route map and an ice cream for the trek.

2 Totem Poles Follow the route until you reach the totems (left), a highly colorful array of carvings that attract plenty of camera-wielding visitors. There's a gift shop here if you want to grab a postcard and write an evocative line or two about the scenery.

3 Brockton Point There's an uphill incline from here – grab onto a passing bike for extra help – but you'll be rewarded at the point (left) with a view across the water from the little lighthouse. Cruise ships pass this way as they head toward the Lions Gate Bridge, which you'll pass under as you continue.

4 Third Beach After rounding Prospect Point (p53) you'll find that the trail gets a bit wilder: fewer people make it this far and the walkway is usually buffeted by fresh winds whipping in off the water. It's a nature-lover's delight however, and a reminder of the city's coastal location. Continue on to

STANLEY PARK (sidebar)
NEIGHBORHOODS (sidebar)

WALK FACTS

Start Coal Harbour

End English Bay

Distance 9.5km

Duration Two to three hours

Fuel stop Bring a picnic and stop anywhere you like

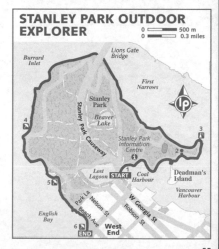

STANLEY PARK OUTDOOR EXPLORER

0 ━━━ 500 m
0 ━━━ 0.3 miles

PARK TAKES A HIT

In the early hours of December 15, 2006, a shattering windstorm smashed into Vancouver's favorite park, causing massive devastation. At least 45 hectares of the park's 243 forested hectares were leveled in a matter or hours – an estimated 10,000 trees were uprooted or snapped beyond repair, leaving windswept piles of debris and upturned root networks that were often many metres high. For the first time in its history, the park was entirely closed to the public, as officials struggled to assess the destruction. The storm had destabilized the park's western slope, causing structural damage to the popular seawall, and had blocked most of the interior trails. The $9 million restoration program began almost immediately (a swift public appeal quickly raised a hefty chunk of this). Once the major repairs were complete, the seawall was finally reopened to visitors in late 2007 – nearly a year after the catastrophic storm swept through. Consider buying *Stanley Park: A Special Place* – it's complete with 50 pages of photography and a donation to the restoration fund is included in every purchase.

Third Beach (p54), where you can rest on a log and enjoy the view.

5 Second Beach Head on to Second Beach (p54) and, suitably informed, decide which strand is your favorite. You can grab a drink at the concession stand here if you're feeling parched after your long trek.

6 English Bay You'll start to see a lot more people as you reach the end of your nature-hugger's marathon at English Bay (p65). The beach here is often teeming with sun-worshipping locals and there are frequently buskers and street artists to keep things interesting. If it's time to dine, there are dozens of restaurants in this area (see p130).

GREEN VANCOUVER

Enjoy the rich autumnal colors of Stanley Park (p52), the lungs of the city

VanDusen Botanical Garden (p90)

top picks

VANCOUVER'S GREEN BOOKS

- **Greater Vancouver Green Guide**, UBC Design Centre for Sustainability (2007) – a showcase of green buildings, projects and initiatives around the city
- **100-Mile Diet: A Year of Local Eating**, Alisa Smith and JB Mackinnon (2007) – fascinating autobiographical story of what happened to a local couple when they tried to source their entire diet from their Vancouver doorstep
- **Tree: A Life Story**, David Suzuki and Wayne Grady (2004) – sweeping yet highly readable 'biography' of a 700-year-old Douglas Fir tree that anchors each stage of its life to an aspect of human history
- **Guerilla Gardening: A Manualfesto**, David Tracey (2007) – tips for greening our urban space, including where to find cheap or free plants and how to plant them without permission
- **Earth's Blanket: Traditional Teachings for Sustainable Living**, Nancy J Turner (2007) – illuminating the ecological wisdom and environmental stewardship ideas within the cultures of the region's First Nations people

It's hard to see Vancouver as anything but a green city. Its dense, majestic forests and verdant, rain-fed plant life make nature an ever-present fact of life here. But beyond the breathtaking visuals, how does the city measure up to its environmental responsibilities? And – just as importantly – what can a visitor do to reduce their eco-footprint in the region without turning their vacation into a monastic, fun-free zone?

Wandering the city, you'll notice an active, outdoorsy populace that likes to celebrate the natural surroundings on foot, blade or bike whenever possible (and in all weathers). Many of these grinning, superfit locals are members of one of Vancouver's dozens of eco-active lobby groups. Their widespread concern for the environment means that large developments – whether improvements to Hwy 99 or new housing blocks at the University of British Columbia – are usually accompanied by plenty of hand-wringing and, more often than not, some determined protests.

As environmental issues become more pressing, Vancouver is rising to prominence as an important think tank for ideas such as livability, sustainability and urban density. City and provincial governments have gradually accepted that the area's green agenda has moved from the periphery to the political mainstream. In 2003 Vancouver's city council instituted a Climate Change Action Plan designed to reduce greenhouse-gas emissions by 20% before 2010, while in 2007 the provincial government committed to an even bigger, across-BC reduction of 33%. The birthplace of Greenpeace and the home of David Suzuki may finally be ready for its long-touted green leadership role on the world stage.

The 'green roof' installation at Robson Square

Activists aboard the Greenpeace ship Arctic Sunrise

PAINTING THE TOWN GREEN

Vancouver has an international reputation for being a green city, but that doesn't mean everyone here wears biodegradable socks and eats only elderly vegetables that have died of natural causes. In fact, if you stroll the Robson St boutiques or dip into a take-out coffee shop, it's easy to think that 'green Vancouver' doesn't exist at all. As with many of the city's best features – think arts and neighborhoods – you have to do a little digging to find the meat (or at least the tofu) of the issue.

Given the city's breathtaking natural surroundings, it was just a matter of time before Vancouver's residents were inspired to protect the planet, which explains why a few of them began gathering in a Kitsilano basement in 1969 to plan the fledgling Don't Make a Wave Committee's first protest against nuclear testing in Alaska. By the time their campaign boat entered the Gulf of Alaska in 1971, they had renamed themselves Greenpeace and sailed into environmental history.

Greenpeace set the tone and the city has since become a headquarters for environmental groups (see p63), from the Western Canada Wilderness Committee to the Raincoast Conservation Foundation and the David Suzuki Foundation – the eponymous organization headed by Canada's most celebrated environmental scientist (see p64).

Actions speak louder than words, though, and Vancouver's green scene is not just about protest and discussion. The city is home to dozens of large and small eco-initiatives, enabling many locals to color their lives as green as they choose. Vancouver has one of the largest

A blader cruises along the seawall promenade in Stanley Park (p52)

Eat your greens – and make them organic and locally grown

top picks

SUSTAINABLE SHOPPING OPTIONS

- Wanted – Lost Found Canadian (p116)
- Dream Designs (p119)
- HT Naturals (p118)
- Hope Unlimited (p122)
- Highend Organics (p123)

hybrid-vehicle taxi fleets in North America and has a commitment to mass public transport, including electric trolley buses and a light-rail train system that, at the time of research, was being expanded to the airport. Carpooling is also big in the city, with the Jack Bell Foundation's rideshare scheme (www .ride-share.com) matching travelers with shared vehicle trips throughout the region.

In construction, the green potential of any design project is always part of the plan here. And while developers often tout their green credentials as if they're saving their planet single-handedly, few of the new towers currently reforesting the city are built without environmental considerations – this includes the 2010 Olympic village, currently being created on the southeast edge of False Creek. Vancouver is also a leader in 'green roofs' – planted rooftops that curb wasted energy through natural evaporation in summer and natural insulation in winter. The law courts and the Vancouver Public Library (p47) have these, while the giant new extension to the convention centre at Canada Place (p46) will also have one.

Inspired by a surging demand for locally sourced food and the popular 100-Mile Diet movement (www.100milediet.org) established by two local writers (see the boxed text, p58), many city restaurants and food stores are now bringing BC seafood, meat, vegetables and fruit to the tables and kitchens of city diners from just a few kilometers away – rather than the thousands of 'food miles' that used to be attached to the dishes in many city eateries.

SUSTAINABLE VANCOUVER

You're gnawing on a rubbery sandwich at 35,000ft, marveling that your flight to Vancouver is taking just a few hours, when a wave of regret hits you like a burst of unexpected turbulence. It's not that your meal tastes like an old beach sandal, or that the legroom on the plane seems designed for a height-challenged five-year-old. What really raises your hackles is the question of just how green your trip is.

Pedal power – a great way to sightsee (p178)

BACKYARD FARMS TAKE ROOT

Taking the burgeoning local-food movement one step further, Vancouver's **City Farm Boy** (☎ 604-812-7848; www.city farmboy.com) is colonizing the area's tiny, often forgotten green spaces to grow fruit and vegetables right on people's doorsteps. Founded by Saskatchewan transplant Ward Teulon, City Farm Boy works by turning urban residents' unloved and unused garden plots into mini produce-growing areas for everything from carrots, lettuce and beans to chard, rhubarb and garlic. Usually the owners of the plots, happy to see their unkempt garden corners being put to good use, ask only for a few kilos of produce in payment. Teulon, who deploys pesticide-free organic growing methods, harvests the produce and sells it at local farmers markets (see the boxed text, p142) the day after it's picked – the produce travels less than 5km from garden to shopping bag. Dedicated to urban agriculture as a way of improving the city landscape and enhancing local lifestyles, the fledgling operation started with four plots and aims to have a network of 20 more within a couple of years.

Fall pumpkins, fresh for Halloween

A leafy backyard bonanza

Luckily, there are lots of ways to make your Vancouver vacation a little more enviro-friendly. Travelers from North America can ditch the plane completely and take options that reduce their greenhouse-gas footprint. Trains (p226) from across Canada and south of the border arrive throughout the day, while buses (p224) – still a better option than flying – trundle in from similar locales. If you have to fly, consider a carbon-offsetting scheme (see the boxed text, p222).

Vancouver has an extensive transit network (p226) as well as more than 200km of designated bike lanes (p223), so you can get around the city without burning up the planet. Bike rentals are easy to come by here and there are many operators that can get you on two wheels for a citywide pedal (see p178). If you're a die-hard driver and you're here for more than a few days, consider joining the Zipcar rental network of smaller, often hybrid cars as an alternative to traditional car hire (see p225). Keep in mind that the downtown core is eminently walkable

The Zipcar rental network (p225) provides a cool, green alternative to car ownership

Enjoy the Japanese flavor of Nitobe Memorial Garden (p100)

top picks

GREEN SPACES

- **Stanley Park** (p52) – a sea, sand and forest spectacular just minutes from downtown
- **Mt Seymour Provincial Park** (p104) – trails, trees and wintertime snow: a great nature-hugger's day out
- **Dr Sun Yat-Sen Classical Chinese Garden** (p76) – harmonious natural haven in the city (love those bobbing turtles)
- **UBC Botanical Garden** (p99) – fascinating, educational and evocative landscaped gardens
- **VanDusen Botanical Garden** (p90) – gardens, pathways and a cool Elizabethan maze

Plants for sale in the garden-rich UBC (p99)

and there are many green spaces and businesses that will help to keep your trip on the right eco track.

Pick up a copy of Vancouver's sustainable city mag, *Granville* (www.granvillemagazine .com), to tap into additional local initiatives and inspirational green ideas.

ON THE GROUND

Once you're in Vancouver (or before you arrive), consider selecting accommodation that has some kind of environmental program. The Opus Hotel (p195), for example, has a water and energy conservation scheme. Going several steps further, the Pacific Palisades Hotel (p193) has a paperless check-in system, energy-efficient lighting and organic in-room snacks. The hotel also donates unused toiletries as well as all refundable drinks containers to local charities and uses eco-friendly cleaning products in all its rooms.

Dining is also firmly on the green vacation agenda here. Spearheaded by the Vancouver Aquarium and a growing menu of city restaurants, Ocean Wise (www.oceanwisecanada .org) encourages sustainable fish and shellfish supplies that minimize environmental impact (see the boxed text, p131). Visit its website for a list of participating restaurants and check local menus for symbols indicating Ocean

A-maze-ing VanDusen Botanical Garden (p90)

Dr Sun Yat-Sen Classical Chinese Garden (p76)

Wise dishes. A similar, fledgling movement called the Green Table Network (www.greentable.net) can help you identify area restaurants that try to source all their supplies – not just seafood – from sustainable, mostly local sources.

If you'd like to rub shoulders with some local greenies, consider taking an escorted tour with the friendly folk at North Van Green Tours (p233). They operate regional sightseeing excursions in a Toyota Land Cruiser that runs on vegetable oil collected from local restaurants. Sustainability also has a social side with Green Drinks (www.greendrinks.org), a monthly drop-in gathering for anyone interested in environmental issues. The meetings take place at Steamworks Brewing Company (p152) and usually attract more than 50 regulars for beer-fueled discussions on alternative energy, global warming and the sky-high price of tickets to Al Gore events.

HELPFUL ORGANIZATIONS

Local organizations that can help green your Vancouver vacation:

David Suzuki Foundation (☎ 604-732-4228; www.davidsuzuki.org) Working with individuals, industry and government stakeholders, this 40,000-member organization researches the root scientific causes of environmental destruction and searches for sustainable alternatives.

Green My Flight (☎ 604-681-9192; www.greenmyflight.com) This Vancouver-based carbon-offsetting company calculates the greenhouse-gas emissions from your flight and uses the offset fees it collects to fund alternative-energy projects across Canada, including a wind farm in Alberta.

Raincoast Conservation Foundation (☎ 877-655-1229; www.raincoast.org) A regional nonprofit grassroots organization that partners with scientists, local communities and First Nations groups to help preserve BC's Great Bear Rainforest.

Western Canada Wilderness Committee (☎ 604-683-8229; www.wildernesscommittee.org) One of Canada's largest wilderness preservation organizations, the 30,000-member WCWC has successfully campaigned to save millions of hectares of natural lands across the country, much of it from logging practices.

DAVID SUZUKI'S GREEN TRAVEL TIPS

An interview with David Suzuki, co-founder of the Vancouver-based David Suzuki Foundation and an award-winning scientist, environmentalist and broadcaster.

What are some of the biggest issues facing the environment today? Global warming is clearly the number-one issue, since it affects the entire planet. It is also the one that has galvanized public opinion because the evidence that it is happening is now obvious. But looking deeper, I think the problem lies in the beliefs and values that we cling to. We have forgotten that we are biological beings as dependent on nature's services – clean air, clean water, clean food and soil, clean energy, biodiversity – as any other creature. So we 'exploit' the very life-support systems of the planet while failing to recognize it jeopardizes the quality of our own lives.

What can readers of this book do to participate in solutions? They can get involved at every level of their lives. They can start making sustainable decisions by eating locally grown organic food, reducing emissions by using public transit, and making decisions at work that reflect their environmental values. Most importantly, they need to get involved politically and tell their elected leaders to make the environment a priority so that it's easier for us all to make better environmental choices and punish those who do not, like industrial polluters.

How 'green' is Vancouver? While there are some groundbreaking ideas about sustainability taking place here, Vancouver could be doing much more to make itself greener. For example, free public transportation would reduce air pollution and greenhouse-gas emissions and make it easier for people to get around. And considering that it is such a young city, more buildings and developments could be built with better energy efficiency in mind.

What can travelers to Vancouver do to make their vacations as green as possible? They can use public transit instead of renting a car. Most travelers find it a fascinating way to see the city. Vancouver also has lots of natural beauty that is best seen on foot, such as Stanley Park and the beaches around the city. They can also reduce their impact by staying in green hotels, purchase carbon-neutral credits to offset the emissions that come from traveling, and avoid buying things they don't need like tacky souvenirs for their friends back home.

Are you optimistic about our environmental future? Rationally, I can see we are headed down a very dangerous road, undermining the life-support systems in the name of economic growth. But I have grandchildren and I have hope that we can turn the corner and move to a truly sustainable way of living. The need for change is urgent and I don't see the alarm being sounded in the political or corporate sphere. But I plug away because I have hope and I am inspired by Nelson Mandela, who in 27 years of prison must have despaired but never wavered. I just want to be able to look my grandchildren in the eye and tell them 'Grandpa did the best he could for you.'

The voice of Vancouver's eco-conscience, David Suzuki

Eco-friendly public transit – Vancouver SkyTrain (p227)

WEST END

Drinking p150; Eating p130; Shopping p112; Sleeping p193

With its main Denman St and Davie St thoroughfares, the lively West End area borders downtown and Stanley Park and stretches languidly from Coal Harbour to English Bay. Characterized by tree-lined boulevards, diverse midrange restaurants and streets of boutique shops, it serves a population of young people and seniors in a largely adult-focused area of the city. It's also home to western Canada's largest gay population – which explains why the mammoth, carnivalesque Pride Week (p15) winds through the streets here every August, attracting 200,000 visitors to party with the Dykes on Bikes and oil-covered Speedo-wearers.

But despite the pink bus shelters and rainbow-flagged businesses lining the area, the West End isn't just one big 'gayborhood.' In fact, it's among Vancouver's oldest residential districts and still has pockets of highly attractive heritage buildings for visitors of a historic bent. Although most of these were cleared in a mid-1950s housing boom that saw more than 200 apartment blocks added to the area (some are now heritage buildings in their own right), you can still get a taste of how the rich locals used to live in Barclay Heritage Sq. Lined with handsome old homes, its highlight is the fascinating Roedde House Museum, complete with antique-lined rooms and an English country garden.

The West End's main transit routes are bus 5, which travels along Robson and Denman Sts, and bus 6, running along Davie St.

ENGLISH BAY BEACH Map pp66–7

southwest foot of Davie St; ☐ 6; ⑤

Whether it's a languid early evening in August with buskers, sunbathers and volleyballers sharing the beach, or a cold, blustery day in November with just you and a dog-walker staring at the waves, English Bay is a top West End highlight. A great place to picnic, gaze at the freighters moored offshore and view golden sunsets – Stanley Park beckons next door if you fancy adding a seawall hike – this is also the home of the annual Celebration of Light (p15) fireworks festival. Check out the 6m stone Inukshuk here; an Inuit sign of welcome, it's been co-opted as a symbol for the 2010 Winter Olympics.

ROBSON STREET Map pp66–7

btwn Thurlow & Denman Sts; ☐ 5

Locals, international tourists and recent immigrants – count the number of accents you catch as you stroll along here – throng the hotels, eateries and shops of Robson St, Vancouver's de facto promenade. While most shops are of the ubiquitous chain-store variety, it's also worth heading to the Stanley Park end of the strip, where you'll find a modern 'mini-Asia' of subterranean internet cafés, hole-in-the-wall noodle eateries and discreet karaoke bars populated by homesick Japanese and Korean language students. It's a great area for a cheap-and-cheerful, authentically south Asian lunch (see p130).

ROEDDE HOUSE MUSEUM & BARCLAY HERITAGE SQUARE Map pp66–7

☎ 604-684-7040; www.roeddehouse.org; 1415 Barclay St; admission $5; ⊙ 10am-5pm Tue-Sat, 2-5pm Sun May-Sep, 1.30-4pm Tue-Fri, 2-4pm Sun Oct-Apr; ☐ 5

For a glimpse of what pioneer-town Vancouver looked like before the glass towers, drop by this handsome 1893 Queen Anne–style mansion, now a lovingly preserved museum. Designed by infamous BC architect Francis Rattenbury, the house is packed with period antiques and the surrounding gardens are planted in period style. Sunday entry, including tea and cookies in the garden, costs $1 extra. The abode is the showpiece of Barclay Heritage Square, a one-block site containing nine historic West End houses dating from 1890 to 1908. If you don your top hat, monocle and twirly waxed moustache, you'll fit right in.

top picks

ATTRACTION GIFT SHOPS

- Vancouver Art Gallery (p46)
- Capilano Suspension Bridge (p103)
- Museum of Anthropology (p99)
- Vancouver Aquarium (p52)
- Vancouver Public Library (p47)

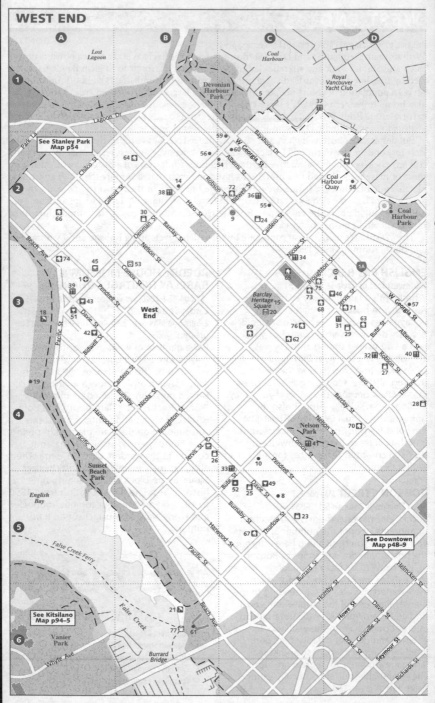

lonelyplanet.com

WEST END

A   **B**   **C**   **D**

NEIGHBORHOODS WEST END

Lost Lagoon

Coal Harbour

Royal Vancouver Yacht Club

Devonian Harbour Park

See Stanley Park Map p54

Lagoon Dr

Park La

Chilco St

Gilford St

Denman St

Barclay St

Nelson St

Comox St

Haro St

Robson St

Bidwell St

W Georgia St

Alberni St

Cardero St

Bayshore Dr

Coal Harbour Quay

Coal Harbour Park

Beach Ave

Pacific St

Bidwell St

Davie St

Pendrell St

Cardero St

Burnaby St

Nicola St

Broughton St

Jervis St

Harwood St

West End

Barclay Heritage Square

Broughton St

Jervis St

Bute St

Thurlow St

Haro St

Robson St

Alberni St

W Georgia St

Nelson Park

Nelson St

Comox St

Barclay St

Sunset Beach Park

English Bay

See Downtown Map p48–9

Burrard St

Hornby St

Howe St

Davie St

Granville St

Seymour St

Drake St

Richards St

Helmcken St

See Kitsilano Map p94–5

False Creek Ferry

False Creek

Vanier Park

Whyte Ave

Burrard Bridge

Pacific St

Beach Ave

Harwood St

Burnaby St

Thurlow St

Pendrell St

Davie St

Bute St

66

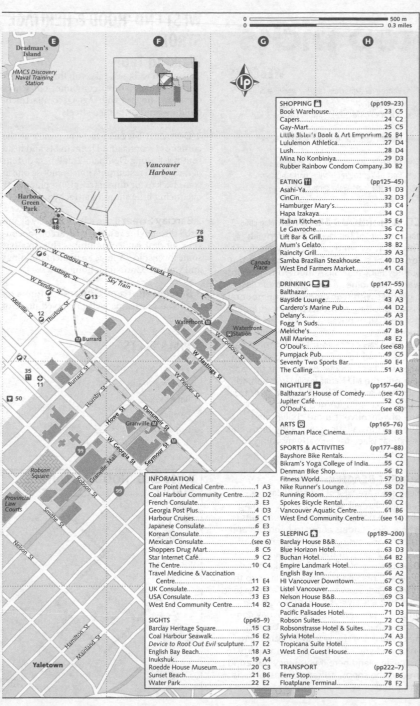

NEIGHBORHOODS WEST END

| 0 | 500 m |
| 0 | 0.3 miles |

Deadman's Island

HMCS Discovery Naval Training Station

Vancouver Harbour

Harbour Green Park

W Cordova St
W Hastings St
W Pender St

Sky Train

Canada Pl

Canada Place

Melville St
Thurlow St

Waterfront M

Waterfront Station

W Cordova St

M Burrard

W Pender St

W Hastings St

Burrard St
Hornby St
Howe St
Granville
Dunsmuir St
Seymour St

W Georgia St

Robson Square

Robson St

Granville Mall

99

Smithe St

Nelson St

Provincial Law Courts

Yaletown

Hamilton St
Mainland St

SHOPPING (pp109–23)
Book Warehouse.....................23 C5
Capers....................................24 C2
Gay-Mart.................................25 C5
Little Sister's Book & Art Emporium.26 B4
Lululemon Athletica................27 D4
Lush.......................................28 D4
Mina No Konbiniya.................29 D3
Rubber Rainbow Condom Company.30 B2

EATING (pp125–45)
Asahi-Ya..................................31 D3
CinCin......................................32 D3
Hamburger Mary's..................33 C4
Hapa Izakaya...........................34 C3
Italian Kitchen.........................35 E3
Le Gavroche............................36 C2
Lift Bar & Grill.........................37 C1
Mum's Gelato..........................38 B2
Raincity Grill............................39 A3
Samba Brazilian Steakhouse....40 D3
West End Farmers Market........41 C4

DRINKING (pp147–55)
Balthazar.................................42 A3
Bayside Lounge........................43 A3
Cardero's Marine Pub..............44 D2
Delany's...................................45 A3
Fogg 'n Suds............................46 D3
Melriche's.................................47 B4
Mill Marine..............................48 E2
O'Doul's...............................(see 68)
Pumpjack Pub..........................49 C5
Seventy Two Sports Bar...........50 E4
The Calling...............................51 A3

NIGHTLIFE (pp157–64)
Balthazar's House of Comedy.(see 42)
Jupiter Café.............................52 C5
O'Doul's...............................(see 68)

ARTS (pp165–76)
Denman Place Cinema..............53 B3

SPORTS & ACTIVITIES (pp177–88)
Bayshore Bike Rentals..............54 C2
Bikram's Yoga College of India..55 C2
Denman Bike Shop..................56 B2
Fitness World...........................57 D3
Nike Runner's Lounge..............58 D2
Running Room..........................59 C2
Spokes Bicycle Rental..............60 C2
Vancouver Aquatic Centre........61 B6
West End Community Centre..(see 14)

SLEEPING (pp189–200)
Barclay House B&B..................62 C3
Blue Horizon Hotel..................63 D3
Buchan Hotel...........................64 B2
Empire Landmark Hotel............65 C3
English Bay Inn........................66 A2
HI Vancouver Downtown...........67 C5
Listel Vancouver......................68 C3
Nelson House B&B...................69 C3
O Canada House......................70 D4
Pacific Palisades Hotel.............71 D3
Robson Suites..........................72 C3
Robsonstrasse Hotel & Suites..73 C3
Sylvia Hotel.............................74 A3
Tropicana Suite Hotel..............75 C3
West End Guest House.............76 C3

TRANSPORT (pp222–7)
Ferry Stop................................77 B6
Floatplane Terminal.................78 F2

INFORMATION
Care Point Medical Centre..............1 A3
Coal Harbour Community Centre......2 D2
French Consulate.............................3 E3
Georgia Post Plus............................4 D3
Harbour Cruises..............................5 C1
Japanese Consulate.........................6 E3
Korean Consulate............................7 E3
Mexican Consulate.....................(see 6)
Shoppers Drug Mart........................8 C5
Star Internet Café............................9 C2
The Centre....................................10 C4
Travel Medicine & Vaccination
   Centre.......................................11 E4
UK Consulate.................................12 E3
USA Consulate................................13 E3
West End Community Centre..........14 B2

SIGHTS (pp65–9)
Barclay Heritage Square..............15 C3
Coal Harbour Seawalk................16 E2
Device to Root Out Evil sculpture..17 E2
English Bay Beach.......................18 A3
Inukshuk....................................19 A4
Roedde House Museum...............20 C3
Sunset Beach..............................21 B6
Water Park.................................22 E2

67

top picks

WEBCAMS

- **Vancouver Aquarium** (p52) – www.vanaqua .org/ottercam
- **Science World** (p76) – http://198.162.3.42/view /view.shtml
- **Jericho Beach** (p96) – www.jericho.bc.ca /webcam/webcam.html
- **Vanier Park** (p97) – www.katkam.ca
- **Port of Vancouver** – www.portvancouver .com/the_port/web_cams.html

COAL HARBOUR SEAWALK Map pp66–7

northeast foot of Thurlow St; Ⓜ Waterfront; ⓐ
This pathway winds along the waterfront for 2km or so before hooking up with the Stanley Park seawall. A modern-day boardwalk, it combines a background of glassy high-rises with twinkling sea and mountain vistas, bobbing sailboats and the dramatic rise and fall of buzzing floatplanes. Relax and spread out on the grassy slopes of Harbour Green Park or let your kids hit the area's free water park to cool off – you can grab a beer and keep an eye on them at the popular pub the Mill Marine (p150). Just behind is Device to Root Out Evil, a dramatic sculpture shaped like an upturned church – one of Vancouver's more challenging public art installations. For early birds, this is a great place for an early-morning sunrise stroll.

SUNSET BEACH Map pp66–7

along Beach Ave, west of Burrard Bridge; 🚍 6
A chain of small, sandy beaches running along the north side of False Creek, this is where West Enders come to hang out and catch some rays on sunny days, many of them lounging on the grassy banks overlooking the waterfront. The walking, cycling and blading trail here – it links to the Stanley Park seawall trail if you want extend your trek – is always packed in summer, often with members of the local gay community checking each other out. Swimmers will enjoy the Vancouver Aquatic Centre (p185), and you can also catch a miniferry to Granville Island here if you fancy puttering around the shops, artisan studios, galleries and cafés.

WEST END 'HOOD & HERITAGE STROLL
Walking Tour

This urban walk will take you through an attractive residential area, combining old-school clapboard houses with Art Deco apartment buildings and café-lined streets.

1 Denman Street Start your walk at the corner of Georgia and Denman Sts and head southwest along Denman. You'll pass dozens of midpriced restaurants here – choose one to come back to for dinner (see p130) – plus plenty of enticing little shops to attract your wallet.

2 Barclay Street Turn left on Barclay St and stroll through the residential heart of Vancouver's vibrant gay community. This area has some lovely old heritage apartment buildings and wooden Craftsman homes.

3 Barclay Heritage Square Continue on until you reach this well-preserved plaza of

WALK FACTS

Start Corner of Georgia and Denman Sts

End Sunset Beach

Distance 2km

Duration 1½ hours

Fuel stop Melriche's

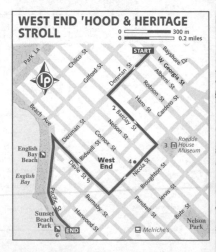

WEST END 'HOOD & HERITAGE STROLL

heritage houses, a reminder of how yesteryear Vancouverites used to live. Duck into the antique-lined **Roedde House Museum** (p65) and you'll have an even better idea.

4 Firehall No 6 Head southwest along Nicola St and you'll come across this lovely red-brick 1907 firehall. It's still in use but has the feel (and look) of a museum.

5 Davie Street Continue on Nicola St and turn right into Davie St, a teeming shop and café area that's also the commercial hub of the gay community. It's a popular place at night, with plenty of bars and clubs. If you need a coffee break, **Melriche's** (p151) is nearby.

6 Sunset Beach When you reach the end of Davie St at **English Bay Beach** (p65), turn left and stroll along Beach Ave. After a few minutes this becomes the main promenade for **Sunset Beach** (opposite), where you can sit on a grassy bank and watch the locals jog and blade by or catch a miniferry to **Granville Island** (p88).

YALETOWN

Drinking p151; Eating p132; Shopping p113; Sleeping p195

Pedestrian-friendly Yaletown is Vancouver's 'little Soho,' a red-brick rail terminal and warehouse district transformed in the early 1990s into swanky condo towers and chichi boutiques. Roughly bounded by Nelson St, Homer St, Drake St and Pacific Blvd, the focal point of this modern-day yuppie enclave has a hip and inviting atmosphere – especially at night, when its swanky drink and dine spots are packed to the rafters with the city's beautiful people checking each other out.

The area has certainly come a long way since Canadian Pacific Railway workers settled here in the late 19th century to be close to the rail yards that merged at nearby False Creek. Many of them had worked at the CPR yards in Yale, about 180km northeast of Vancouver, hence the neighborhood moniker. Yaletown thrived as the city's industrial core until the 1940s, when highways replaced rail for goods transport. By the 1970s it was a dodgy 'hood known more for its rough bars and derelict warehouses, where getting beaten up was part of a regular night out.

Vancouver's Expo '86 world's fair changed all that, as planners designated the district a historic area. The first settlers to arrive were artists seeking studio space, then came bohemian coffee shops and a smattering of stores and galleries. The transformation was complete when high-tech paper millionaires moved in during the 1990s.

Yaletown has since developed into an increasingly attractive area for visitors. It has plenty of pricey boutiques to window shop and lots of places to stop for lunch, coffee or a splurge-worthy dinner. You'll still see plenty of shiny Hummers parked on the streets here, while your fellow shoppers will likely have handbag-dwelling Chihuahuas as fashion accessories. If you're curious about the area's almost-forgotten, rough-and-ready past, follow the old rail lines still embedded in many of the streets and amble over to the Roundhouse Community Arts & Recreation Centre. You'll find a mothballed steam train that recalls the area's original raison d'etre.

Transit access to Yaletown is via buses C21 and C23 and the nearby Cambie St bus 15.

ROUNDHOUSE COMMUNITY ARTS & RECREATION CENTRE Map p71

☎ 604-713-1800; www.roundhouse.ca; 181 Roundhouse Mews, cnr Davie St & Pacific Blvd; ☺ hours vary; ☒ C21

Those interested in the history of the Canadian Pacific Railway should visit the Roundhouse, formerly a CPR repair shed. It now houses handsome Engine No 374 (www.wcra.org/engine374), which brought the first passenger train into the city in 1887. Yaletown was once a busy locomotive hub, and rail lines are still embedded in the streets around the area. This is a busy community facility, so you can rub shoulders with the locals here at a wide array of educational classes, eclectic theater productions and ever-changing cultural events.

BC PLACE STADIUM Map p71

☎ 604-669-2300; www.bcplacestadium.com; 777 Pacific Blvd; ☒ Stadium

Home of the BC Lions Canadian Football League team (see p187), this 60,000-seat Teflon-domed sports stadium was rumored to be on its last legs until it was named as a 2010 Olympic and Paralympic Winter Games venue and resuscitated with a makeover. The dome's quilted appearance is due to the crisscrossing steel wires holding down the air-supported roof – it deflated spectacularly in 2007 and had to be given the kiss of life by engineers. The stadium is also used for rock concerts and shows that range from indoor fairs to an annual food festival (see the boxed text, p134), and there's a popular tour (☎ 604-661-7362; Gate H; adult/child/student & senior $8/5/7; ☺ 11am & 1pm Tue mid-Jun–Aug) offering a glimpse behind the scenes.

BC SPORTS HALL OF FAME & MUSEUM Map p71

☎ 604-687-5520; www.bcsportshalloffame.com; Gate A, BC Place Stadium; adult/child, student & senior $10/8; ☺ 10am-5pm; ☒ Stadium; ♿

Located inside BC Place Stadium, the small but perfectly formed Sports Hall of Fame showcases top BC athletes, both amateur and professional, with special galleries devoted to each decade in sports. There's

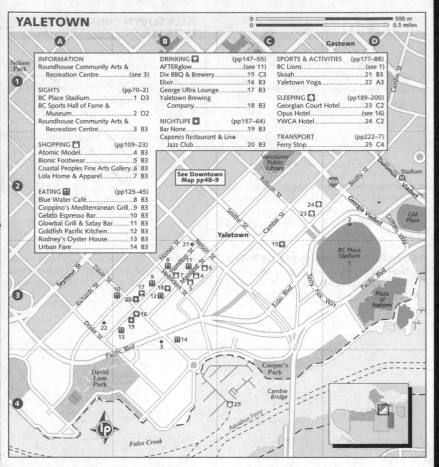

YALETOWN

0 — 500 m
0 — 0.3 miles

INFORMATION	
Roundhouse Community Arts & Recreation Centre...............(see 3)	
SIGHTS	(pp70–2)
BC Place Stadium......................1 D3	
BC Sports Hall of Fame & Museum.............................2 D2	
Roundhouse Community Arts & Recreation Centre.................3 B3	
SHOPPING	(pp109–23)
Atomic Model..........................4 B3	
Bionic Footwear.......................5 B3	
Coastal Peoples Fine Arts Gallery.6 B3	
Lola Home & Apparel................7 B3	
EATING	(pp125–45)
Blue Water Café.......................8 B3	
Cioppino's Mediterranean Grill...9 B3	
Gelato Espresso Bar.................10 B3	
Glowbal Grill & Satay Bar........11 B3	
Goldfish Pacific Kitchen...........12 B3	
Rodney's Oyster House............13 B3	
Urban Fare..............................14 B3	

DRINKING	(pp147–55)
AFTERglow..........................(see 11)	
Dix BBQ & Brewery...............15 C3	
Elixir....................................16 B3	
George Ultra Lounge.............17 B3	
Yaletown Brewing Company.........................18 B3	
NIGHTLIFE	(pp157–64)
Bar None..............................19 B3	
Capones Restaurant & Live Jazz Club.........................20 B3	

SPORTS & ACTIVITIES	(pp177–88)
BC Lions...........................(see 1)	
Skoah.................................21 B3	
Yaletown Yoga....................22 A3	
SLEEPING	(pp189–200)
Georgian Court Hotel.............23 C2	
Opus Hotel......................(see 16)	
YWCA Hotel........................24 C2	
TRANSPORT	(pp222–7)
Ferry Stop..........................25 C4	

a wealth of medals, trophies and sporting memorabilia on display (judging by the size of their shirts, hockey players were much smaller in the old days) and there are tons of hands-on activities to tire the kids out. Check out the stirring exhibits on Terry Fox and his 'Marathon of Hope' run across Canada, plus Rick Hanson and his 'Man-in-Motion' worldwide wheelchair journey.

YALETOWN DRINK, DINE & DASH
Walking Tour
This short stroll – rounded off with a culture stop – is a good way to see what's on offer before you commit to a place for dinner.

1 Hamilton Street One of the city's favourite eat streets, Hamilton St is lined with excellent restaurants (see p132), and high-end seafood eateries are a particular specialty here. There's also Capones Restaurant & Live Jazz Club (p162), a good jazz restaurant, if you fancy a musical accompaniment to your meal.

2 Opus Hotel Turn left and head down Davie St and you'll hit the Opus (p195), Vancouver's favorite boutique sleepover. You can nip in here for a coffee or a beer at Elixir (p151) – keep an eye open for visiting celebs.

3 Mainland Street Turn left onto Mainland St and you'll find another selection of swish eateries, including the excellent Glowbal Grill & Satay Bar (p133). You can dine here – lunch and

NEIGHBORHOODS YALETOWN

WALK FACTS

Start Hamilton St

End Roundhouse Community Arts & Recreation Centre

Distance 1km

Duration One hour

Fuel stop Elixir

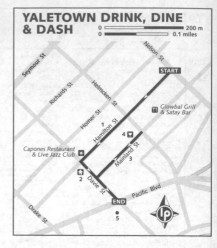

brunch are recommended – or drop by later for a cocktail in the intimate back bar.

4 Yaletown Brewing Company Continue along Mainland St until you reach this popular brewpub (p152). It's a great place to grab an afternoon beer and decamp to the patio to watch the city go by.

5 Roundhouse Community Arts & Recreation Centre Double back a couple of blocks along Mainland St and turn left onto Davie St. Check to see if there are any shows or events at the community center (p70) or just content yourself with a view of the preserved steam engine – it brought the first passenger train to the city in 1887.

GASTOWN

Drinking p152; Eating p133; Shopping p114

Centered on Water St and its intersection with Carrall and Alexander Sts, Gastown is the city's most historic district. It's named after a talkative, Yorkshire-born colonial called 'Gassy' Jack Deighton and is the area where modern-day Vancouver began (see p21). An enormous fire in 1886 wiped out most of the fledgling settlement here but it was soon back in business thanks to the arrival of the transcontinental Canadian Pacific Railway, which rumbled into town along the nearby waterfront. Eventually the center of Vancouver moved westward to its current location and Gastown hit hard times, becoming a rough skid row area by the 1970s.

Just as the city was preparing to bulldoze its problems and start over, a group of history-loving locals – mindful of Gastown's key role in the city's foundation – successfully lobbied for a heritage preservation order. Thus began a concerted effort to restore the district, pushing its seedier characters further east toward Main and Hastings Sts.

It's been a long process, though, and only in recent years has the effort really begun to work. Now a highly evocative neighborhood of excellent character bars and a smattering of good restaurants, Gastown is Vancouver's best old-town area – the cobbled streets and antique street lamps only add to its distinctive ambience.

The area has also become a hotbed for local designer-owned shops, drawing a new crowd of regulars to the area and – it seems – marking its permanent reclamation. Gassy Jack would likely be proud of the area's resurgence: you can salute him yourself at the statue (complete with whiskey barrel) erected to his honor at the north end of Carrall St.

For more information on the area, visit www.gastown.org. Transit access to Gastown is via Waterfront SkyTrain station and buses 4, 7 and 50.

VANCOUVER POLICE CENTENNIAL MUSEUM Map p74

☎ 604-665-3346; www.vancouverpolicemuseum.ca; 240 E Cordova St; adult/child, student & senior $7/5; ☼ 9am-5pm Mon-Sat; ☒ 7

Colorfully charting the city's murky criminal past, displays at this excellent little museum include an autopsy room with pieces of damaged body parts posted on the wall (note the brain with a .22 caliber bullet in it) and an exhibit describing how to determine a corpse's age via insects (blowflies appear in 15 days, cheese-skippers in 40 days). Visitors can see what a 1oz lump of heroin looks like or peruse bad-ass weaponry, including a gangster-era Thompson submachine gun. Also consider the gripping Sins of the City walking tour ($12), which escorts curious visitors through the dodgy Downtown Eastside's eye-popping vice and crime-fighting history.

STEAM CLOCK Map p74

cnr Water & Cambie Sts; Ⓜ Waterfront

The much ballyhooed steam clock halfway along Water St is a silly little landmark, though its charm is that it's the only one of its kind in the world. Misleadingly historic looking, it was built in 1977 to resemble London's Big Ben. Join the camera-wielding hordes waiting for it to belch steam and sound the quarter-hour like a train whistle, but keep this secret to yourself: the 'steam clock' is actually powered by electricity. Check out its clunking ball bearings and interior workings through the side glass panels.

MAPLE TREE SQUARE Map p74

cnr Alexander, Powell & Carrall Sts; ☒ 7

Still the heart of Gastown, this old cobbled area is now lined with convivial bars (p152) and restaurants (p133) but it's still dripping with historic charm and has an almost European feel. The jaunty statue of Gassy Jack, perched atop a whiskey barrel, rests in about the same place where his Globe Saloon once stood. The Byrnes Block (2 Water St), built shortly after the 1886 fire, was one of the city's first brick buildings and stands on the site of Gassy's second saloon. Behind is Gaolers Mews

top picks

PLACES TO ESCAPE THE CROWDS

- Dr Sun Yat-Sen Classical Chinese Garden (p76)
- Spanish Banks (p101)
- Roedde House Museum (p65)
- Lighthouse Park (p105)
- Nitobe Memorial Garden (p100)

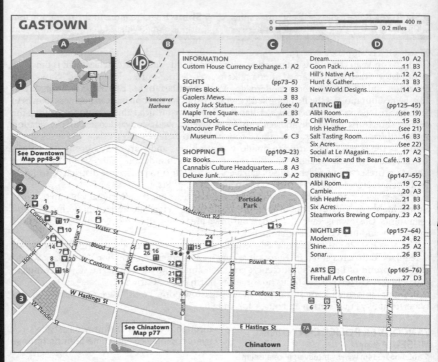

GASTOWN

INFORMATION
Custom House Currency Exchange..1 A2

SIGHTS (pp73–5)
Byrnes Block................................2 B3
Gaolers Mews..............................3 B3
Gassy Jack Statue.....................(see 4)
Maple Tree Square.......................4 B3
Steam Clock................................5 A2
Vancouver Police Centennial
 Museum...................................6 C3

SHOPPING (pp109–23)
Biz Books....................................7 A3
Cannabis Culture Headquarters.....8 A3
Deluxe Junk................................9 A3

Dream......................................10 A2
Goon Pack................................11 B3
Hill's Native Art.........................12 A2
Hunt & Gather...........................13 B3
New World Designs....................14 A3

EATING (pp125–45)
Alibi Room............................(see 19)
Chill Winston............................15 B3
Irish Heather.........................(see 21)
Salt Tasting Room......................16 B3
Six Acres.............................(see 22)
Social at Le Magasin..................17 A2
The Mouse and the Bean Café...18 A3

DRINKING (pp147–55)
Alibi Room................................19 C2
Cambie.....................................20 A3
Irish Heather.............................21 B3
Six Acres..................................22 B3
Steamworks Brewing Company..23 A2

NIGHTLIFE (pp157–64)
Modern....................................24 B2
Shine.......................................25 A2
Sonar.......................................26 B3

ARTS (pp165–76)
Firehall Arts Centre...................27 D3

(12 Water St), the location of the city's first jail and customs house, and home to Gastown's first constable, Jonathan Miller.

GASTOWN NIGHT OUT
Walking Tour
This short walk will take you to Gastown's best bars and nightclubs.

1 Irish Heather The city's best and most authentic Irish pub, the brick-lined Heather (p152) is convivial enough to make you want to stay all night. The food is also good if you want to line your stomach for the debauchery ahead. Whiskey fans should drop by the Shebeen Whiskey House out back.

2 Statue of Gassy Jack Turn left after exiting the Heather and pay your respects to the bronze statue saluting the square. Englishman 'Gassy' Jack Deighton was one of the city's founding fathers, building a bar in this area that developed into the forerunner of the modern-day city.

WALK FACTS
Start Irish Heather
End Steamworks Brewing Company
Distance 1km
Duration Depends on how fast you drink
Fuel stop Anywhere you like

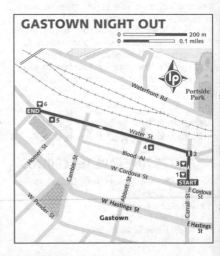

GASTOWN NIGHT OUT

3 Six Acres Raise a glass to Deighton's spirit at the nearby Six Acres (p152). It's one of the city's best bars, complete with a bewildering array of choice ales and a great menu of shareable food.

4 Sonar Turn left at the end of Carrall St and head along Water St to this ultracool, attitude-heavy nightclub (p161), which takes an experimental, progressive approach to its DJ selection.

5 Shine If you're more in the mood for fun, continue along Water St to the highly popular subterranean Shine (p161). Saturday is the big night here and you can rest your dance muscles in the calming, cavelike back room.

6 Steamworks Brewing Company If you're all danced out, nip across the street for a nightcap at this chatty brewpub (p152), where you can compare notes on the evening's best beers and hottest clubs.

CHINATOWN

Eating p135; Shopping p115

Exotic sights, sounds and aromas pervade North America's third-largest Chinatown, predominantly occupying the East Vancouver thoroughfares around Main, Pender and Keefer Sts. You'll find families bargaining over durian fruit in a flurry of Cantonese; shops redolent of sweet-and-sour fish; and street vendors selling silk, jade and Hello Kitty footstools. The steamy-windowed wonton restaurants, butchers with splayed barbecued pigs, and ubiquitous firecracker-red awnings will make you think for a moment that you're in Hong Kong.

Chinatown has been around since before the City of Vancouver was incorporated in 1886. At that time Shanghai Alley (close to what is now the intersection of Carrall and Pender Sts) housed a small Chinese settlement. Ironically, it was the Great Fire that helped Chinatown develop further. In an attempt to rebuild the city, 60 hectares of forested land were leased to Chinese immigrants, who were given a 10-year rent-free agreement on the condition they clear and farm the land. By the end of 1886 almost 90 Chinese lived in the area on farms yielding pigs and produce.

It wasn't long before brightly painted, two-story wooden buildings sprang up along Pender and Carrall Sts, which became a gathering place for socializing and banking (to wire money home). Many Chinese were enticed by the opportunity to earn hard cash working in sawmills, lumber camps, fish canneries and mines and on railroad construction gangs. In 1883 alone, of the nearly 2000 gold miners in BC, 1500 were Chinese, and during the period from 1881 to 1885 more than 11,000 Chinese arrived by ship to work on the construction of the CPR. They were paid $1 a day – half of what white workers were paid.

Many locals will tell you that Chinatown isn't what it used to be, and that the 'real' Chinatown is now located in Richmond (p106), where many of BC's new Asian immigrants have landed in the last 10 years. But this evocative old area is still worth a visit. If you only have time for one trip, drop by for the summertime weekend night market (p115).

For more information on the area and its regular special events visit www.vancouverchinatown.ca. Transit access to Chinatown is via the Stadium and Main St–Science World SkyTrain stations and buses 3, 8 and 19.

SCIENCE WORLD & ALCAN OMNIMAX THEATRE Map p77

☎ 604-443-7443; www.scienceworld.bc.ca; 1455 Quebec St; adult/child/youth & senior $16/11/13; ☼ 10am-6pm; Ⓜ Main St-Science World; ♿ Nestled under the city's gleaming geodesic dome (or 'silver golf ball' as the locals often call it) are two levels of hands-on science, technology and natural-history exhibits aimed at satisfying the most enquiring of minds. It's an ideal place to bring kids – the gallery that explores sustainability issues is recommended, along with the water course of ball cannons and bridges. Expect

to spend at least a few hours here. Level 3 holds the 400-seat Omnimax Theatre (tickets $10), showing large-format documentary movies to those who need a sit down.

DR SUN YAT-SEN CLASSICAL CHINESE GARDEN & PARK Map p77

☎ 604-662-3207; www.vancouverchinesegarden .com; 578 Carrall St; garden adult/child, senior & student $8.75/7, park free; ☼ 10am-6pm May–mid-Jun & Sep, 9:30am-7pm mid-Jun–Aug, 10am-4:30pm Oct-Apr; Ⓜ Stadium A tranquil break from clamorous Chinatown, this intimate 'garden of ease'

NEON CAPITAL

In the 1950s Vancouver was home to the largest neon-production company in the world and was second only to Shanghai in number of neon signs per capita – 18,000 signs (one for every 19 residents) flashed, crackled and illuminated buildings throughout the city. While only a few of these evocative displays remain, neon is making a comeback in downtown's Granville St entertainment district, where new businesses are being encouraged to add bold exterior lighting that echoes the city's colorful, neon-lit past. Among the old signs still visible from the previous neon age – many of them in the Chinatown and Gastown districts – are those of the Ovaltine Cafe (251 E Hastings St), Save On Meats (43 W Hastings St), Only Seafood Restaurant (20 E Hastings St) and the 2400 Court Motel (2400 Kingsway) in Burnaby.

exhibits the Taoist symbolism behind the placing of gnarled pine trees, winding covered pathways and ancient limestone formations. Entry includes a fascinating 45-minute guided tour – look out for the lazy turtles bobbing in the jade-colored water – where you'll learn that everything in the garden reflects balance and harmony, and the placement of each item has a considered purpose. Check the garden's website for its summer schedule of Friday-evening concerts. Adjacent is the free-entry Dr Sun Yat-Sen Park. Dowdier than

its neighbor, it's still a pleasant oasis of whispering grasses, a large fishpond and a small pagoda.

CHINESE CULTURAL CENTRE MUSEUM & ARCHIVES Map p77

☎ 604-658-8880; www.cccvan.com; 555 Columbia St; adult/child, student & senior $4/2.50, admission free Tue; 🕑 11am-5pm Tue-Sun; Ⓜ Stadium
Check out this museum for a deeper understanding of the often turbulent history of Vancouver's Chinese immigrants. Changing exhibits are on the main floor,

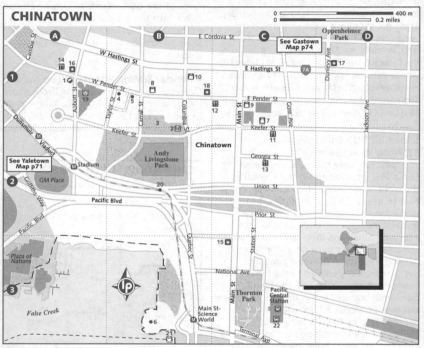

CHINATOWN

top picks

GARDENS

- Dr Sun Yat-Sen Classical Chinese Garden (p76)
- VanDusen Botanical Garden (p90)
- UBC Botanical Garden (p99)
- Bloedel Floral Conservatory (p92)
- Nitobe Memorial Garden (p100)

while the 2nd floor's permanent collection highlights Gold Rush history and Chinatown settlement. It also houses the Military Museum, showcasing the sometimes unsung role of Chinese-Canadian soldiers in both world wars. The museum is linked to the Cultural Centre (☎ 604-658-8883; 50 E Pender St), where you can sign up for short workshops in calligraphy, t'ai chi and Chinese music. The centre also offers museum tours (adult/child $4/3) and Chinatown walking tours (adult/child $8/5).

SAM KEE BUILDING Map p77
8 W Pender St; Ⓜ Stadium
This structure near the corner of Carrall St made it into *Guinness World Records* as the world's narrowest office building. It's easy to miss because it looks like the front of the larger building behind, to which it is attached. It's currently an insurance-company office and there isn't much to see inside, but it's still a nifty stop if you're passing this way. A businessman's vendetta against city hall led to the building's anorexic shape. Chang Toy, the Sam Kee Co owner, bought land at this site in 1906, but in 1926 all but a 1.8m-wide strip was expropriated by the city to widen Pender St. Toy's way of thumbing his nose at city officials was to build anyway, and up sprang the unusual 'Slender on Pender' dwelling.

CHINATOWN CULTURE CRAWL
Walking Tour
Dip into the historic streets of one of North America's biggest Chinatown districts and you'll immerse yourself in some fascinating culture and heritage.

1 Millennium Gate Start your trek at this magnificent – and fairly recent – addition to

the Chinatown cityscape, at the intersection of W Pender and Taylor Sts. Built in 2000, it's a fitting reminder that the area is still a vibrant community.

2 Dr Sun Yat-Sen Classical Chinese Garden Head under the gate and turn right onto Carrall St. This magnificent landscaped garden (p76) is right in front of you, complete with tranquil pools, intriguing limestone formations and gnarly pine trees.

3 Chinese Cultural Centre Museum & Archives After strolling the garden, nip next door to the Cultural Centre (p77) and you can delve into the long and turbulent history of the area's Chinese immigrants – the 2nd floor covers the role of Chinese-Canadian soldiers.

4 Pender & Main Streets Exit the Cultural Centre and continue east along Pender until the intersection with Main St. You're right in the heart of Chinatown here – check out the dragon-covered lampposts and red phone booths.

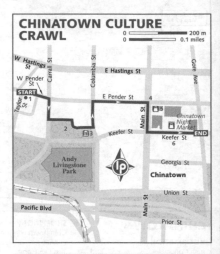

CHINATOWN CULTURE CRAWL

WALK FACTS

Start Millennium Gate

End Keefer St

Distance 1km

Duration One hour

Fuel stop Ten Lee Hong Enterprises

5 Ten Lee Hong Enterprises Peruse the ancient apothecaries and trinket stores around Main and Pender, then cross the street to this renowned tea shop (p116), where you can sample some of the wares and choose your favorite tipples to take back home. Hungry? There are several good restaurants (p135) in the vicinity.

6 Keefer Street Continue south along Main St for one block and turn left on Keefer St. This is the area's grocery-store hub and a great place to browse the live catches and barbecued pigs. On weekend evenings from mid-May to mid-September, this is where you'll find the clamorous night market (p115) that will taste-trip you to Hong Kong.

SOUTH MAIN (SOMA)

Drinking p153; Eating p136; Shopping p116

Known as Mt Pleasant to anyone over 40 and SoMa (South Main) to everyone else, the section of S Main St from around 6th to 29th Aves has been the city's up-and-coming beatnik-chic area for several years now. The cool shops and restaurants cluster between 6th and 10th, taper off between 11th and 19th, then pick up again at 20th.

The area was a haven for hookers and crack addicts until the early 1990s, but the pace of gentrification has picked up considerably since 2000 and SoMa is now home to dozens of indie shops, bohemian bars and coffee shops, adventurous eateries and bold little artist-run galleries. It's still a little rough around the edges for visitors: if you get off the bus too early, you'll find yourself speed-walking past lame eateries and generic mom-and-pop stores and wondering why you bothered to come here in the first place. Then you'll burst upon an area of grunge-cool calm, lined with quirky and exciting clothing stores stocked with creations from the city's best young designers. Suddenly, everyone walking the streets here will look cool. If you want to meet them, just drop by a local coffee shop and crack open an old Eastern European novel (make sure it's the right way up).

Further south, starting at 49th Ave, is the Punjabi Market district. Also known as 'Little India,' it's a colorful strip that hosts several annual cultural events and is an alternative spot for an afternoon of gentle browsing.

Transit access to SoMa is via bus 3.

PUNJABI MARKET Map pp44–5
Main St btwn 48th & 51st Aves; Ⓜ Main St-Science World then bus 3

You won't find cows wandering the streets, or bicycle rickshaws weaving between the traffic, but some of the sounds, smells and colors of the subcontinent are condensed into this short Main St strip. This enclave of sari stores, Bangra music shops, jewelry emporiums and some of the region's best-value curry restaurants has seen better days – as in Chinatown, the younger people have dispersed around the region because they don't feel compelled to live in a neighborhood together – but it's still a good spot for a spicy all-you-can-eat lunch followed by a restorative walkabout.

SIKH TEMPLE Map pp44–5
☎ 604-324-2010; 8000 Ross St; ☼ 8am-8pm; 🚌 22

Not in the market, but close enough to be worth the extra trip, is the Sikh Temple. Designed by revered local architect Arthur Erickson, the building has the hallmarks of traditional Indian architecture. Visitors are welcome to look inside as long as they follow the prescribed customs: women need to bring a scarf to cover their head, and you'll be asked to leave your shoes at the entrance. It's off SE Marine Dr, near Knight St.

SOMA HIPSTER STROLL
Walking Tour

Vancouver's newly hip strip is ideal for those who like to browse in cool indie stores stocked with fashions created by the city's bright young designers. Spicy food is just up the street at the Punjabi Market area.

1 Smoking Lily Start your Main St trek by hopping on bus 3 at the Main St–Science World SkyTrain station, then hopping off at the Main St intersection with 20th Ave (save your transit ticket). Nip into this smashing little designer shop (p117) that's aimed at intellectual clotheshorses.

2 Eugene Choo Cross the street and increase your coolness quotient at this stalwart of the SoMa clothing scene (p117). You'll be able to unleash your credit card on a whole new look.

3 Regional Assembly of Text Continue three blocks south along Main St and cross the road to one of the city's most eclectic stores. The Assembly (p118) is where you can indulge your fetish for sumptuous writing paper, old-fashioned typewriters and all manner of naughty stationary items.

4 Grind Gallery Café If you need to sit down after all that excitement, continue south for a couple more blocks to this laid-back,

SOUTH MAIN (SOMA)

See Chinatown
Map p77

See Fairview
& South
Granville
Map p91

To Red Cat
Records
(2km)

SOMA HIPSTER STROLL

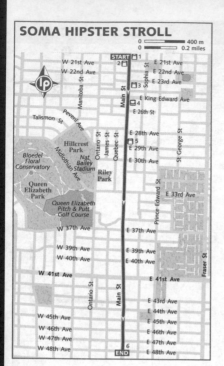

WALK FACTS

Start Smoking Lily
End Punjabi Market
Distance 3km
Duration Two hours (including bus ride)
Fuel stop Grind Gallery Café

art-lined coffee shop (p153). It's a good place to flop for an hour and write postcards.

5 Legends Retro Fashion Two blocks further, on the same side of Main St, drop by this long-established vintage-clothing store (p118), where you can pick up an old-school concert T-shirt – a much more useful souvenir than maple-syrup cookies.

6 Punjabi Market If you still have some time left on your transit ticket, hop back on bus 3 and get off at the intersection with 48th Ave. Stroll around the 'Little India' stores here and stop for a meal: there are some cheap-and-cheerful all-you-can-eat curry joints here.

COMMERCIAL DRIVE

Drinking p153; Eating p137; Shopping p118

Commercial Dr is like Robson St's far more interesting evil twin. Old-world bakery aromas mingle with the smell of patchouli and wafting pot. Skateboarders glide down the sidewalk alongside dainty girls with monstrous tattoos. And this may be the only place in town where you can shop for soy wax candles, belly-dancing supplies and a Che Guevara backpack in one fell swoop.

The centerpiece of the sprawling East Vancouver district, Commercial Dr (everyone calls it 'the Drive' here) is a microcosm of the city's diversity. Focused mainly on the 17-block strip between Broadway and Venables St, it's traditionally melded Italian, Portuguese, Latin American, Caribbean and Southeast Asian immigrant communities. Stir the pot some more by adding the artist, student and lesbian communities who also call this area home and you've got easily the city's most diverse cultural quarter.

But the Drive's history goes further back than most locals know. The street was named in the early 1900s, when it was the first road built along the interurban rail line from New Westminster to Vancouver (constructed in 1891), triggering a wave of development that transformed it into a major shopping thoroughfare. From the 1950s to the 1970s the Italian community settled here, and it became known as 'Little Italy.' You'll still find plenty of family-owned coffee shops from this era, many lined with chatty old Italian men debating the fortunes of their favorite soccer teams 'back home.'

For visitors there's no better street to hang out with the locals (rather than fellow tourists) and enjoy some excellent and highly convivial dining – make sure you wander along the strip for a few blocks before you settle on a place that truly whets your appetite. The same goes for the chatty bars here, where you'll meet everyone from pixie-chick bohemians to chin-stroking poets and old-school dope smokers. The Drive is also 'patio central,' making it the best place in Vancouver to drink and dine al fresco on languid summer evenings. And it's the best spot in town to watch a soccer game with the locals – call it football and they'll be really impressed.

For more information on Commercial Dr, visit www.thedrive.ca. Transit access is via the Commercial Dr and Broadway SkyTrain stations and bus 20.

COMMERCIAL DRIVE INDULGENCE
Walking Tour

You don't have to hit all these recommended drink and dine spots, but it's a good idea to see what's on offer before you make a decision.

1 Café Calabria From the Commercial Dr SkyTrain station, walk north past the counterculture stores to drop by this legendary coffeeshop (p154), one of several celebrated Italian java joints lining the strip.

2 Charlatan Not that you should usually mix your drinks, but continue north three more blocks to this friendly corner bar (p153), where there's a good selection of local tipples. Ask if they have Storm: it's brewed on Commercial.

3 Havana If it feels like time to eat and you'd like to sit outside, walk two more blocks and aim for a table on the usually heaving patio

of this ever-popular Afro-Cuban restaurant (p138). It's the kind of vibey place where you end up staying all night.

4 Stella's Tap & Tapas Bar Peel yourself from Havana's patio and continue on to the next block for a nightcap at this Euro-style

top picks
LATE-OPENING ATTRACTIONS
- Vancouver Art Gallery (p46) – until 9pm Tuesday and Thursday
- Vancouver Lookout (p46) – until 10.30pm May to mid-October
- Museum of Anthropology (p99) – until 9pm Tuesday
- Vancouver Museum (p95) – until 9pm Thursday
- Bloedel Floral Conservatory (p92) – until 9pm Saturday and Sunday, April to September

lonelyplanet.com

NEIGHBORHOODS COMMERCIAL DRIVE

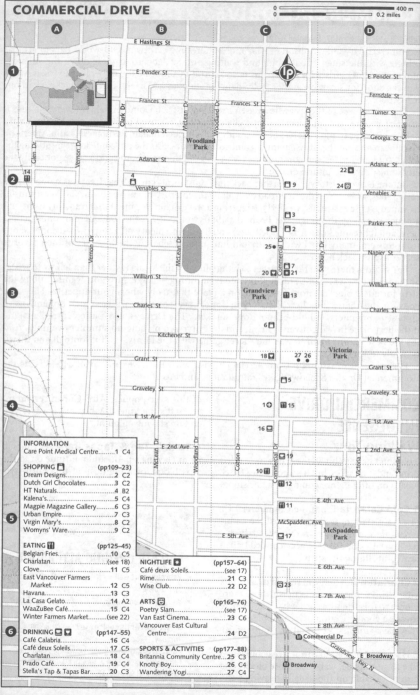

COMMERCIAL DRIVE

INFORMATION
Care Point Medical Centre........1 C4

SHOPPING (pp109–23)
Dream Designs...........................2 C2
Dutch Girl Chocolates.............3 C2
HT Naturals...............................4 B2
Kalena's....................................5 C4
Magpie Magazine Gallery........6 C3
Urban Empire............................7 C3
Virgin Mary's............................8 C2
Womyns' Ware..........................9 C2

EATING (pp125–45)
Belgian Fries...........................10 C5
Charlatan.............................(see 18)
Clove......................................11 C5
East Vancouver Farmers
   Market.................................12 C5
Havana....................................13 C3
La Casa Gelato.......................14 A2
WaaZuBee Café......................15 C4
Winter Farmers Market........(see 22)

DRINKING (pp147–55)
Café Calabria..........................16 C4
Café deux Soleils....................17 C5
Charlatan................................18 C4
Prado Café..............................19 C4
Stella's Tap & Tapas Bar........20 C3

NIGHTLIFE (pp157–64)
Café deux Soleils.................(see 17)
Rime.......................................21 C3
Wise Club...............................22 D2

ARTS (pp165–76)
Poetry Slam.........................(see 17)
Van East Cinema....................23 C6
Vancouver East Cultural
   Centre.................................24 D2

SPORTS & ACTIVITIES (pp177–88)
Britannia Community Centre...25 C3
Knotty Boy.............................26 C4
Wandering Yogi......................27 C4

84

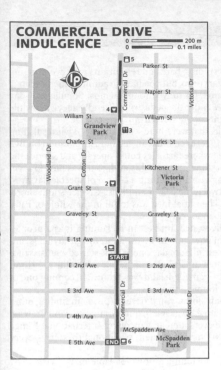

WALK FACTS

Start Café Calabria
End Café deux Soleils
Distance 1km
Duration How fast can you drink?
Fuel stop Pick one!

bistro-pub (p154). Play it safe with a whiskey or work your way down the amazing menu of imported Belgian microbrews.

5 Dutch Girl Chocolates If it's still open or you just want somewhere to walk off your booze, stroll to the end of the next block and cross the road to salivate through the window of this eclectic little chocolate shop (p118).

6 Café deux Soleils Weave back south toward the SkyTrain station and drop by this bohemian café (p154) for a final, sobering coffee. Check to see what's on stage here: there's almost always some folk music or spoken-word performances to keep the java drinkers entertained.

GRANVILLE ISLAND

Drinking p154; Eating p138; Shopping p119; Sleeping p196

Fifteen hectares brimming with arts and crafts studios, bars and restaurants with eye-popping views, and even a hotel: it may have taken 100 years or so, but you have to admit formerly grungy Granville Island has finally hit upon the right mix. It's now among the most popular half-day destinations in town for visitors, who come to wander the pedestrian-friendly alleyways while enjoying the sounds of the buskers and the sights of the waterfront.

In the beginning, the original two sandbanks that were here were a favorite winter fishing ground for the Squamish First Nations. But by 1916, as colonial-fueled industrialization hit BC, planners transformed the sandbars into an area where factories could operate and service the sawmills and rail yards emerging along the coastline. Industrial Island, as it was now known, underwent many ups and downs in the ensuing years, including a couple of spectacular fires. At one stage the city dumped dredging fill between the island and False Creek's south shore, transforming it into the peninsula it is today. The initial idea was to fill in the whole of False Creek, but due to cost overruns the plan was abandoned.

As the 'island's' industrial fortunes gradually waned, interest in reclaiming it as a people-friendly area took hold and, after major federal government investment, the Granville Island Public Market opened for business in 1979. Successful from day one, it kick-started a renaissance that saw the crumbling factory buildings patched up and given a new lease on life as artisan studios and gallery-style arts and crafts shops. Granville Island was reborn, becoming one of North America's most successful urban redevelopment projects.

Once you've exhausted the market and artisan stores, you'll have no problem finding other things to do here. You can paddle False Creek with a kayak (p181), tour Granville Island Brewing (below) or catch an evening show (p173). And the ever-popular Vancouver International Fringe Festival (p16) colonizes Granville Island venues – not all of them traditional theaters – every September.

For more information on Granville Island – including a downloadable map – visit www.granvilleisland.com. Main access to the area is via transit bus 50 or miniferry (p224) from the north side of False Creek.

GRANVILLE ISLAND PUBLIC MARKET

Map p87

☎ 604-666-6477; www.granvilleisland.com; Johnston St, near cnr of Duranleau St; ☉ 9am-7pm; ☐ 50

A multisensory deli specialising in gourmet fish, cheese, fruit and bakery treats, the covered market is a chatty, visceral place to mix with the locals. It's a great place to pick up picnic fixings (Vanier Park is a short seawall stroll away if you're looking for a spot) and buskers are a regular fixture around the market's exterior. There's a small but good international food court here (eat lunch early or late to avoid the rush) as well as a regular clutch of arts and crafts stalls. Consider a guided foodie tour of the market with Edible BC (see the boxed text, p131). See p120 for more info, including details of specific stalls.

GRANVILLE ISLAND BREWING

Map p87

☎ 604-687-2739; www.gib.ca; 1441 Cartwright St; tours $9.75; ☉ tours noon, 2pm & 4pm; ☐ 50

Canada's oldest microbrewery offers half-hour tours where the smiling guides will walk you through the tiny brewing room (production has mostly shifted to larger premises) before depositing you in the Taproom for samples, including Cypress Honey Lager and the recommended Kitsilano Maple Cream Ale. You'll spot many of these brews in bars and restaurants around the city. You can also buy some takeout in the adjoining store – look out for any seasonal or special-batch tipples that might be worth a try.

top picks

STROLL-WORTHY STREETS

- Commercial Drive (p83)
- SoMa (p80)
- W 4th Avenue (p96)
- Robson Street (p65)
- South Granville (p92)

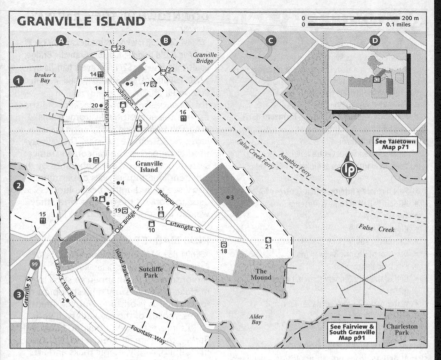

GRANVILLE ISLAND

EMILY CARR INSTITUTE OF ART & DESIGN Map p87

☎ 604-844-3800; www.eciad.ca; 1399 Johnston St; admission free; ☼ 10am-6pm; 🚌 50

Named after BC's most famous historic painter (Emily Carr, 1871–1945), the institute is well regarded for its visual-arts and media-arts programs. Housed in a corru-

gated metal factory building near a cement plant, it has a gritty, angst-worthy vibe that matches that of its creative young students. The school presents a range of free exhibits in its three galleries: two showcase the work of the school's up-and-coming students, while the Charles H Scott Gallery (☎ 604-844-3811; www.chscott.eciad.ca; ☼ noon-5pm Mon-Fri,

top picks

FOR CHILDREN

- Capilano Suspension Bridge (p103)
- Vancouver Aquarium (p52)
- Miniature Railway & Children's Farmyard (p52)
- Second Beach Pool (p185)
- Science World (p76)
- HR MacMillan Space Centre (p96)
- Vancouver International Children's Festival (p13)
- Port Authority Interpretation Centre (p46)
- BC Sports Hall of Fame & Museum (p70)
- SeaBus (p226)
- Kidsbooks (p122)
- Vancouver Public Library (p47)
- Downtown Historic Railway (right)
- Kitsilano Beach (p96)
- Gulf of Georgia Cannery National Historic Site (p106)
- Water parks at Granville Island (right) and Lumberman's Arch (p55).

10am–5pm Sat & Sun) hosts shows by professional artists. If you're an art lover, you'll also enjoy the offerings of the school's excellent arty bookstore.

MODEL TRAINS MUSEUM & MODEL SHIPS MUSEUM Map p87

☎ 604-683-1939; www.modeltrainsmuseum .ca, www.modelshipsmuseum.ca; 1502 Duranleau St; dual entry adult/child/youth, student & senior $7.50/4/6; ☙ 10am-5:30pm Tue-Sun; 🚌 50; ♿ Of the twin museums discreetly housed here under one roof, the train museum wins hands down. With one of the world's largest toy locomotive collections – there are so many that only a lucky few get to rattle around the giant BC railway layout – it will be rare if you don't spot a reminder or two from your childhood. There are no similarly exciting moving displays in the downstairs ship museum, but there are still some intriguing, highly detailed model freighters, frigates and submarines – check out that Nautilus. Expect to see several excited fathers trying unsuccessfully to interest their kids in schooner rigging and double-O gauges here.

DOWNTOWN HISTORIC RAILWAY Map p87

☎ 604-665-3903; www.trams.bc.ca; near cnr W 2nd Ave & Old Bridge St, below Granville Bridge; adult/child & senior $2/1; ☙ every half-hour, 12:30-4:30pm Sat, Sun & holidays mid-May–mid-Oct; 🚌 50; ♿ This beautifully restored, clackety old streetcar hits the ancient tracks from Granville Island to Science World (p76) during a smile-inducing 15-minute journey. The railway used to be part of the Vancouver tramcar system, and today it's still operated by the city's Engineering Services department – you'll see retired uniformed volunteers, who used to work on the old cars when they were in full service, staffing the line.

KIDS MARKET Map p87

☎ 604-689-8447; www.kidsmarket.ca; 1496 Cartwright St; ☙ 10am-6pm; 🚌 50; ♿ A nightmare if you happen to stroll in by mistake, this two-story mini shopping mall for under-10s is bristling with kid-friendly stores, mostly of the toy variety. If your child's interests extend beyond Lego and Barbie, there are also retailers specializing in clothing, candy, magic tricks and arts and crafts. If it all gets a bit too much, you might try enticing your kids away from the shops to the huge Granville Island Water Park (admission free; ☙ 10am-6pm mid-May–mid-Sep) just behind the market (or perhaps sneaking to the nearby Granville Island Brewing for a swift libation).

GRANVILLE ISLAND ARTISAN TRAWL
Walking Tour

This stroll will take you around some of Vancouver's favorite artisan studios and arts and crafts galleries.

1 Crafthouse If you're entering the area from the main entrance on Anderson St, take the first right onto Cartwright St and dip into this shiny gallery (p120) of regional arts and crafts.

2 Railspur Alley Head back down Cartwright St and turn right onto Old Bridge St. Take the next right onto Railspur Alley, where you'll find several excellent artisan stores and a couple of coffee shops to keep you occupied.

3 Wood Co-op Rejoin Old Bridge St and turn left at Johnston St, where you'll find the Wood Co-op (p120), an airy gallery of fantastic wood-crafted furniture and knick-knacks that's enough to turn anyone into a tree hugger.

4 Net Loft Continue along Johnson St to the next building. The popular Net Loft is lined with arts and crafts stores, including Circle Craft (p120) and Paper-Ya (p120), where you can pick up a journal to record your travels.

5 Granville Island Public Market Facing you diagonally across the street is the entrance to the public market (p120). It specializes in deli-style food stalls but always has additional artisan stands that are well worth a look. There's also a food court here if it's time for a snack.

6 Granville Island Brewing To experience a different kind of artistry, end your visit with a guided tour of this famed local brewery (p86), where you'll be able to taste the creativity with a lip-smacking complement of beer samples.

GRANVILLE ISLAND ARTISAN TRAWL

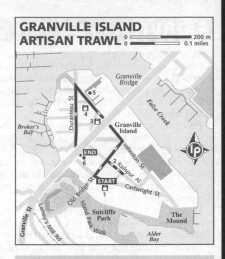

WALK FACTS

Start Crafthouse
End Granville Island Brewing
Distance 1km
Duration One hour
Fuel stop Granville Island Public Market

FAIRVIEW & SOUTH GRANVILLE

Eating p139; Shopping p121; Sleeping p196

Fairview (to the east) and South Granville (to the west) are part of the sprawling West Side district that covers the long-established residential neighborhoods and bustling commercial centers south of downtown and across False Creek. Further west, Kitsilano (p94) and UBC (p99) are also part of the West Side but have developed as their own distinct neighborhoods in recent years.

Predominantly residential, Fairview lies to the south of False Creek, roughly between Granville and Main Sts. Broadway and Cambie St are its main thoroughfares – the former is home to many brawny outfitter shops, including the legendary Mountain Equipment Co-op. Just taking a look around these stores can make you feel like you've recently climbed a mountain or paddled through rapids. Luckily, you can bulk up for your next trek at a plethora of restaurants serving everything from Jamaican to Fijian cuisine. This is also where you'll find Tojo's, perhaps North America's best sushi joint.

If you have a more sedentary approach to nature, pull up a bench among the trees and flowers of Queen Elizabeth Park or dip into VanDusen Botanical Garden, a Vancouver favorite. Alternatively, you can spend a sunny afternoon at a Nat Bailey Stadium ball game.

South Granville (the strip of Granville St running south of the Granville Bridge as far as W 16th Ave) has been a popular shopping and dining district for years. Recently it's also become a destination for gallery hoppers – particularly on the uphill area before Broadway that's become known as 'South Granville Rise,' which houses some of the city's best contemporary art galleries. They mainly feature leading local contemporary artists: it's a good place to drop a few thousand dollars on an up-and-coming auteur of the Vancouver School.

The entire South Granville area is a manageable afternoon excursion from the downtown core, and is especially good if you like shopping but hate malls: the retailing thoroughfare here is reminiscent of a bustling high street in a mid-sized European town and is home to some of the city's best boutique, food and gift shops. You'll find fashion stores, interiors outlets and the kind of tempting knickknack joints where you can easily drop $50 without even thinking about it. Save some money for dinner, though: some of Vancouver's best restaurants, including Vij's and West, line the street (or nestle just off the main drag) here.

For more information on South Granville, visit www.southgranville.org. Transit access to Fairview is via buses 9, 15 and 17; take bus 10 for South Granville.

VANDUSEN BOTANICAL GARDEN
Map p91

☎ 604-878-9274; www.vandusengarden.org; 5251 Oak St; adult/child/senior/youth Apr-Sep $8.25/4.25/6/6.25, Oct-Mar $6/3/4.25/4.50; 10am-4pm Nov-Feb, 10am-5pm Mar & Oct, 10am-6pm Apr, 10am-8pm May, 10am-9pm Jun-Aug, 10am-7pm Sep; 17

Vancouver's favorite ornamental green space, this 22-hectare idyll is a web of paths weaving through 40 small, specialized gardens: the Rhododendron Walk blazes with color in spring, while the nearby Korean Pavilion is a focal point for a fascinating Asian plant collection. There's also a fun Elizabethan maze, walled by 1000 pyramidal cedars, and an intriguing menagerie of marble sculptures. Free tours are offered daily at 2pm. The gardens are a Christmastime magnet, with thousands of fairy lights illuminating the dormant plant life. Check the website to see what's in bloom seasonally and consider dropping by the bustling June Garden Show (www.vancouvergardenshow.com).

QUEEN ELIZABETH PARK Map p91
☎ 604-257-8584; http://vancouver.ca/parks; cnr W 33rd Ave & Cambie St; admission free; 24hr; 15

The city's highest point – it's 167m above sea level and has smashing views of the mountain-framed downtown skyscrapers – this 52-hectare park claims to house specimens of every tree native to Canada. Sports fields, manicured lawns, formal gardens and pitch-and-putt golf keep the locals happy, and you'll likely see wide-eyed couples posing for their wedding photos. If you want to be taken out to the ball game, the recently restored Nat Bailey Stadium (p187) is a popular summer-afternoon haven for baseball lovers. Seasons in the Park (p140) is a good fine-dining restaurant that makes full use of the vistas.

FAIRVIEW & SOUTH GRANVILLE

0 — 500 m
0 — 0.3 miles

See Granville Island Map p87

See South Main (SoMa) Map p81

lonelyplanet.com

INFORMATION
BC Children's Hospital	1 C5
Broadway Ballroom	2 B2
Chinese Consulate	3 A3
Cookshop & Cookschool	4 C2
Le Centre Culturel Francophone de Vancouver	(see 20)
Vancouver General Hospital	5 C2

SIGHTS (pp90–3)
Bloedel Floral Conservatory	6 D5
Queen Elizabeth Park	7 D5
VanDusen Botanical Garden	8 B5

SHOPPING (pp109–123)
Bau-Xi Gallery	9 A3
Equinox Gallery	10 A2
International Travel Maps & Books	11 C2
Meinhardt Fine Foods	12 A3
Purdy's Chocolates	13 A2
Restoration Hardware	14 A2
Riley Park Farmers Market	15 D5
Zonda Nellis	(see 19)

EATING (pp125–45)
Bin 942	16 A2
Figmint	(see 32)
Go Fish	17 A1
Ouisi Bistro	18 A3
Paul's Place Omelettery	19 A2
Salade de Fruits Café Bistro	20 A2
Seasons in the Park	21 D5
Tojo's	22 B2
Vij's	23 A2
West	24 A2

NIGHTLIFE (pp157–64)
Fairview Pub	25 C2

ARTS (pp165–76)
Cold Reading Series	26 D1
Stanley Theatre	27 A2

SPORTS & ACTIVITIES (pp177–88)
Miraj Hammam Spa	28 A1
Reckless Bike Stores	29 A1
Suki's International	30 A3
Vancouver Canadians	(see 15)

SLEEPING (pp189–200)
Douglas Guest House	31 D2
Plaza 500 Hotel	32 C2
Shaughnessy Village	33 B2
Windsor Guest House	34 D2

91

TOP 10 THINGS TO DO WHEN IT RAINS (WHICH IT WILL)

- Take a tour of **BC Place Stadium** (p70) and listen out for the tempest drumming on the Teflon roof.
- Dry off and caffeinate in comfort at a **Commercial Drive coffee shop** (p154).
- Run like mad between the market and the artisan shops on **Granville Island** (p88).
- Grab some protection at the **Umbrella Shop** (p121).
- Catch a big-screen matinee movie at the **CN IMAX Theatre** (p169).
- Embrace the misery amid the mortuary room and the confiscated weapons at the **Vancouver Police Centennial Museum** (p73).
- Bask in the tropical heat of the glass-domed **Bloedel Floral Conservatory** (below) at Queen Elizabeth Park.
- Take a tour through the brewing process and then sample the wares in the Taproom at **Granville Island Brewing** (p86).
- Snag a front seat on the **SkyTrain** (p227) for a tour through the region's rainy sights. Take a Millennium Line train from Waterfront and stay on until it reaches Commercial Dr, then switch to the Expo Line at the adjoining Broadway station to return to your starting point.
- Be like a Vancouverite: put on your Gore-tex and your shorts and pretend everything's just fine.

BLOEDEL FLORAL CONSERVATORY
Map p91

☎ 604-257-8584; http://vancouver.ca/parks; Queen Elizabeth Park; adult/child/senior/youth $4.50/2.25/3.15/3.40; ⏰ 9am-8pm Mon-Fri, 10am-9pm Sat & Sun Apr-Sep, 10am-5pm daily Oct-Mar; 🚌 15

Cresting the hill in Queen Elizabeth Park, this popular Plexiglas conservatory – an ideal indoor warm-up spot on a rainy day – is the area's green-fingered centerpiece. It has three climate-controlled zones with 400 plant species, dozens of koi carp and 100 free-flying tropical birds – expect Charlie the cockatiel to harangue you with his verbal dexterity. Ask at the front desk for a free brochure to help you identify the exotic flora and fauna. Locals like to get married here, presumably because it's cheaper than flying to Hawaii.

SOUTH GRANVILLE STROLL
Walking Tour

Artsy types can scratch their gallery itch along Granville St – most galleries occupy the compact uphill stretch known as South Granville Rise – while mall-avoiding shopping fans will enjoy perusing the many stores and boutiques here.

1 South Granville Rise Start your stroll at the intersection of Granville St and W 6th Ave (bus 10 from downtown stops right here) and walk uphill past the many contemporary galleries lining the street, including the **Equinox Gallery** (p121).

2 Granville Street & Broadway Continue along Granville St until your reach the intersection with Broadway. This is the neighborhood's bustling heart and you can head in any direction to explore the shops and restaurants that abound here.

WALK FACTS

Start South Granville Rise

End Stanley Theatre

Distance 1km

Duration One hour

Fuel stop Coffee shops dot the intersection between Broadway and Granville St

SOUTH GRANVILLE STROLL

3 Restoration Hardware If you've decided to continue along Granville St, cross over Broadway and you'll soon hit this popular interior and homewares store (p122), where you can pick up some design tips for your apartment.

4 Vij's Cross the street and continue walking a couple more blocks until you reach the intersection with W 11th Ave. Just in from the corner, you'll see Vij's (p140), the city's favorite Indian restaurant. If you don't have time for dinner, it has a great takeout café next door.

5 Meinhardt Fine Foods There's also a takeout adjoining this popular fine-food store (p121), located several blocks further along Granville.

6 Stanley Theatre Amble back along either side of the street, crisscrossing when you see a store or coffee shop that takes your fancy. If you're a theater fan, consider booking a show at the Stanley (p174). Cross the street to the purple building on the corner and you'll find Purdy's Chocolates (p121), the city's favorite homegrown chocolate purveyor.

KITSILANO

Drinking p155; Eating p141; Shopping p122; Sleeping p198

One of Vancouver's most attractive and established neighborhoods, Kitsilano – or 'Kits' as every local calls it – is a former hippie enclave where the counterculture flower children grew up to reap large mortgages and professional jobs. They still practice yoga and advocate organics, of course, but they're more than willing to pay top dollar for the privilege. The hybrid SUV was invented for the kind of people who now live here.

The area was named after Chief Khahtsahlanough, leader of the First Nations village of Sun'ahk, which occupied the seafront stretch now designated as Vanier Park. In 1901 the local government displaced the entire community, sending some families to the Capilano Indian Reserve on the North Shore and others to Squamish. The colonials replaced them with a vengeance.

The first Kits streetcar service in 1905 triggered an explosion of housing construction, from the 'Vancouver Box' (two-story wood-framed homes) to low-rise apartment buildings and expansive, fully fledged estates. During the 1950s and '60s many of these airy heritage mansions were converted into rooming houses popular with university students, sparking the 'beatnik ghetto' feel that transformed the district. Fueled by pungent BC bud, counterculture political

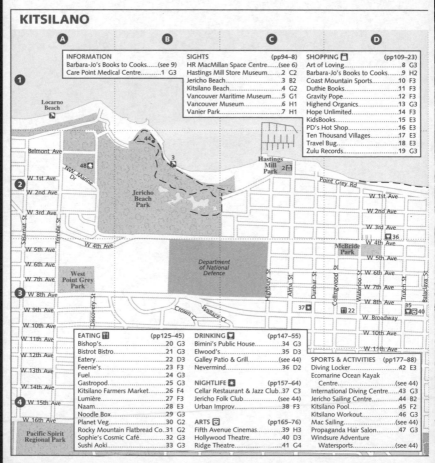

KITSILANO

INFORMATION
Barbara-Jo's Books to Cooks......(see 9)
Care Point Medical Centre............1 G3

SIGHTS (pp94–8)
HR MacMillan Space Centre......(see 6)
Hastings Mill Store Museum......2 C2
Jericho Beach......3 B2
Kitsilano Beach......4 G2
Vancouver Maritime Museum......5 G1
Vancouver Museum......6 H1
Vanier Park......7 H1

SHOPPING (pp109–23)
Art of Loving......8 G3
Barbara-Jo's Books to Cooks......9 H2
Coast Mountain Sports......10 F3
Duthie Books......11 F3
Gravity Pope......12 F3
Highend Organics......13 G3
Hope Unlimited......14 F3
KidsBooks......15 E3
PD's Hot Shop......16 E3
Ten Thousand Villages......17 E3
Travel Bug......18 E3
Zulu Records......19 G3

EATING (pp125–45)
Bishop's......20 G3
Bistrot Bistro......21 G3
Eatery......22 D3
Feenie's......23 F3
Fuel......24 G3
Gastropod......25 G3
Kitsilano Farmers Market......26 F4
Lumière......27 F3
Naam......28 E3
Noodle Box......29 G3
Planet Veg......30 G2
Rocky Mountain Flatbread Co..31 G2
Sophie's Cosmic Café......32 G3
Sushi Aoki......33 G3

DRINKING (pp147–55)
Bimini's Public House......34 G3
Elwood's......35 D3
Galley Patio & Grill......(see 44)
Nevermind......36 D2

NIGHTLIFE (pp157–64)
Cellar Restaurant & Jazz Club...37 C3
Jericho Folk Club......(see 44)
Urban Improv......38 F3

ARTS (pp165–76)
Fifth Avenue Cinemas......39 H3
Hollywood Theatre......40 D3
Ridge Theatre......41 G4

SPORTS & ACTIVITIES (pp177–88)
Diving Locker......42 E3
Ecomarine Ocean Kayak
  Centre......(see 44)
International Diving Centre......43 G3
Jericho Sailing Centre......44 B2
Kitsilano Pool......45 F2
Kitsilano Workout......46 G3
Mac Sailing......(see 44)
Propaganda Hair Salon......47 G3
Windsurf Adventure
  Watersports......(see 44)

Locarno Beach

Belmont Ave

NW Marine Dr

W 1st Ave
W 2nd Ave
W 3rd Ave
W 4th Ave
W 5th Ave
W 6th Ave
W 7th Ave
W 8th Ave
W 9th Ave
W 10th Ave
W 11th Ave
W 12th Ave
W 13th Ave
W 14th Ave
W 15th Ave
W 16th Ave

Sasamat St
Trimble St
Discovery St

West Point Grey Park

Pacific Spirit Regional Park

Jericho Beach Park

Department of National Defence

Crown C
Wallace Cr

Hastings Mill Park

Point Grey Rd

W 1st Ave
W 2nd Ave
W 3rd Ave
W 4th Ave
W 5th Ave
W 6th Ave
W 7th Ave
W 8th Ave
W Broadway
W 10th Ave
W 11th Ave

Highbury St
Alma St
Dunbar St
Collingwood St
Waterloo St
Trutch St
Balaclava St

McBride Park

movements and edgy newspapers mushroomed here, a drive that created the *Georgia Straight,* Vancouver's leading latter-day listings newspaper.

Kits today is a fun fusion of groovy patchouli and slick retail therapy, particularly along W 4th Ave and Broadway. These two primary commercial strips are lined with distinctive, sometimes quirky shops and a full menu of excellent restaurants. Also, the neighborhood's beaches and museums rank among the best in the city. The area's top annual event is the ever-popular Bard on the Beach Shakespeare run (p174).

For more information on the area, visit www.kitsilano4thavenue.com. Transit access to Kits is via buses 2, 4 and 9.

VANCOUVER MUSEUM Map pp94–5
☎ 604-736-4431; www.vanmuseum.bc.ca;
1100 Chestnut St; adult/child/student & senior
$10/6.50/8; ☼ 10am-5pm Fri-Wed, 10am-9pm Thu
Jul-Aug, 10am-5pm Tue-Wed & Fri-Sun, 10am-9pm
Thu Sep-Jun; ☐ 22; ♿
One of the three well-established educational attractions clustered together

in Vanier Park, the Vancouver Museum recounts both distant and recent city history. It includes some colorful displays on 1950s pop culture and 1960s hippie counterculture – a reminder that Kits was once the grass-smoking center of Vancouver's flower-power movement. Permanent exhibits include a look at the everyday life

of First Nations people; passenger quarters on a groaning life-sized immigrant ship; and a full-scale sawmill wheel. The temporary exhibits are usually intriguing – check the museum's website to see what's coming up.

HR MACMILLAN SPACE CENTRE
Map pp94–5

☎ 604-738-7827; www.hrmacmillanspacecentre .com; 1100 Chestnut St; adult/child/youth, student & senior $15/10.75/10.75; ✆ 10am-5pm, closed Mon Sep-Jun; 🚍 22; ♿

Popular with packs of marauding school kids – expect to have to elbow them out of the way to push the flashing buttons – this high-tech science center illuminates the eye-opening world of space. There's plenty of fun to be had battling aliens, designing a spacecraft or strapping yourself in for a simulator ride to Mars, and there are also movie presentations on all manner of spacey themes. There's a free-entry stand-alone observatory (open weekends, weather permitting) across from the main entrance, and a popular planetarium that runs weekend laser shows (tickets $10.75) with music by the likes of Jimi Hendrix and Pink Floyd.

VANCOUVER MARITIME MUSEUM
Map pp94–5

☎ 604-257-8300; www.vancouvermaritime museum.com; 1905 Ogden Ave; adult/child & senior $10/7.50; ✆ 10am-5pm daily May-Aug, 10am-5pm Tue-Sat, noon-5pm Sun Sep-Apr; 🚍 22; ♿

The final member of the triumvirate – it's a five-minute walk west of the Vancouver Museum – this library-quiet attraction combines dozens of intricate model ships with some detailed re-created boat sections and a few historic vessels. The main draw is the St Roch, a 1928 Royal Canadian Mounted Police Arctic patrol sailing ship that was the first vessel to navigate the legendary Northwest Passage in both directions. The A-frame museum building was actually built around this ship and evocative free tours of the vessel are offered. The Children's Maritime Discovery Centre has hands-on displays where kids can dress up and pretend to be pirates.

KITSILANO BEACH
Map pp94–5

cnr Cornwall Ave & Arbutus St; 🚍 22; ♿

Mega-popular Kits Beach faces English Bay and has a strong claim to being the city's favorite summer hangout. The wide, sandy expanse flanking the water here attracts buff Frisbee tossers and giggling volleyball players, as well as those who just like to preen while they're catching the rays. The beach is fine for a dip, though serious swimmers should dive into the heated 137m Kitsilano Pool (p185), one of the world's largest outdoor saltwater pools. For refreshments, check out the cafés and restaurants along Cornwall Ave or south up Yew St.

WEST 4TH AVENUE
Map pp94–5

🚍 4

A strollable smorgasbord of stores (p122) and restaurants (p141) may have your credit card whimpering for mercy after a couple of hours here. Since Kits is now a bit of a middle-class utopia, shops where you could once buy cheap groceries or grow-op paraphernalia are now more likely to be hawking designer yoga gear, hundred-dollar hiking socks and exotic (and unfamiliar) fruits from around the world. It's nice to look – although your resolve may buckle at some of the excellent themed bookshops and clothing stores. It's also a great place for a coffee stop, and some of the city's most exciting new restaurants have opened here in recent years. You're also never far from the beach if you want to tote a picnic instead.

JERICHO BEACH
Map pp94–5

north foot of Alma St; 🚍 4

An activity-lovers idyll – see p182 for ideas – Jericho is also great if you just want to putter along the beach, clamber over driftwood logs and catch stunning panoramic vistas of downtown Vancouver sandwiched between the water and the looming North Shore mountains. It's also popular with

top picks

BEACHES

- Third Beach (p54)
- Kitsilano Beach (left)
- English Bay Beach (p65)
- Jericho Beach (above)
- Wreck Beach (p101)

top picks

ATTRACTION DINING

- Vancouver Art Gallery (p46)
- Vancouver Aquarium (p52)
- Grouse Mountain (p103)
- Capilano Suspension Bridge (p103)
- Queen Elizabeth Park (p90)

sunset fans. Check out the nearby Hastings Mill Store Museum (☎ 604-734-1212; 1575 Alma St; admission by donation; ⏰ 11am-4pm Tue-Sun mid-Jun–mid-Sep, 1-4pm Sat & Sun mid-Sep–mid-Jun). Built in Gastown in 1865, this ancient shop is the city's oldest building and was one of the few structures to survive the 1886 Great Fire. It was floated over here in 1930.

VANIER PARK Map pp94–5
west of Burrard Bridge; 🚌 22; ♿
Winding around Kitsilano Point and eventually connecting with Kits Beach, waterfront Vanier Park is more a host site than a destination. Home to three museums (see p95), it's also the evocative venue for the tents of the annual Vancouver International Children's Festival (p13) and the summertime Bard on the Beach (p174) Shakespeare extravaganza. If you want to avoid the sweaty crush in English Bay on fireworks night (p15), bring your blanket and spread out here; you'll have great views of the aerial shenanigans among a

convivial and family-friendly crowd. The park is also a good picnic spot – bring some takeout from nearby Granville Island and watch the kite flyers strut their stuff.

KITSILANO FOOD-FOR-THOUGHT HOP
Walking Tour
This walk will introduce you to the Kitsilano neighborhood and two of its main obsessions: culture and dining.

1 Barbara-Jo's Books to Cooks Kick things off on 2nd Ave (near the intersection with Burrard St) at this great cook-themed bookshop (p122), where you can pick up a tome or two from famed local chefs (see p135 for some recommendations).

2 Zulu Records Stroll west to Burrard St, turn left and walk two blocks south until you reach W 4th Ave. Cross over and head up W 4th for two blocks until you come to the city's favorite indie record store (p123).

WALK FACTS

Start Barbara-Jo's Books to Cooks

End Feenie's

Distance 2.5km

Duration Two hours

Fuel stop Sophie's Cosmic Café

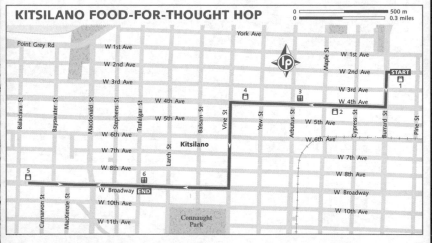

KITSILANO FOOD-FOR-THOUGHT HOP

3 Sophie's Cosmic Café You're in the heart of the Kits shopping district here, so spend some time checking out what's on offer. Once you've had you fill, drop by Sophie's (p143), a retro diner with a great line in heaping brunches and hearty comfort-food lunches.

4 Duthie Books Fortified for the walk ahead, cross the street and head two blocks along W 4th to this popular generalist bookstore (p122). It's an ideal place to pick up some holiday reading.

5 Travel Bug Continuing along W 4th, turn left at Vine St and walk five blocks until you reach Broadway, the neighborhood's second main shopping street. Turn right onto Broadway – there are specialty kids and used bookstores here – until you reach this popular travel bookshop (p122).

6 Feenie's Once you've exhausted the shopping on both sides of the street here, head back along Broadway to this popular West Coast lounge restaurant (p142), where you can sit back and peruse your purchases.

UNIVERSITY OF BRITISH COLUMBIA (UBC)

Sleeping p198

The giant University of British Columbia (UBC; ☎ 604-822-2211; www.ubc.ca) is more than just your average college campus. Its 402-hectare grounds are part of an area called the University Endowment Lands, and are set amid rugged forest. Three of the city's most treasured and wild beaches – Locarno, Spanish Banks and Wreck – are located around this area. The tranquil Nitobe Memorial Garden and sweeping UBC Botanical Garden flourish nearby. And one of the world's foremost First Nations museums nestles along the clifftop: the Museum of Anthropology, with its fantastical totem poles.

Although UBC is often referred to locally as being in Point Grey, technically it's not part of the City of Vancouver. The provincial government's ministry of municipal affairs administers the area, which harks back to the 1908 University Loan Act, when the government set up the site for the province's first university.

Even though the area was heavily logged from 1861 to 1891, it wasn't clear-cut, mainly because many of the trees were too difficult to reach. This allowed the remaining trees to generate substantial regrowth, hence the remarkable forests standing today. With the creation of the Pacific Spirit Regional Park in 1988 (administered by MetroVancouver), an area almost twice the size of Stanley Park has been preserved for future generations to use and enjoy.

For visitors, the campus is a tranquil break from the busy downtown core, and even if you're not studying here there's enough to keep you occupied for a half-day or so. There's also an array of accommodation. And if you feel like running free with nature, consider dropping your pants and joining the crowd at Wreck Beach, Vancouver's popular naturist hangout.

Transit access to UBC is via the 99 B-Line express bus or regular buses 4, 9, 17 and 41.

MUSEUM OF ANTHROPOLOGY Map p100

☎ 604-822-3825; www.moa.ubc.ca; 6393 NW Marine Dr; adult/child, student & senior $9/7, by donation after 5pm Tue; ☽ 10am-5pm Wed-Mon, 10am-9pm Tue mid-May–mid-Oct, 11am-5pm Wed-Sun, 11am-9pm Tue mid-Oct–mid-May; ☒ 41
With Canada's best display of northwest-coast First Nations artifacts in a spectacular waterfront setting, this is Vancouver's best museum. The totem poles alone – displayed against a wall of glass overlooking the coastline – are worth the admission. Technically speaking, the focus is global cultures – you'll be able to dip into Asian, African and Pacific artifacts – but the best exhibits showcase the intricacies of BC's coastal First Nations, including many works by legendary Haida artist Bill Reid. Take one of the free tours to get the most from your visit, and save time for the Haida village, an outdoor re-creation of a traditional settlement, complete with a longhouse and totem poles.

UBC BOTANICAL GARDEN Map p100

☎ 604-822-9666; www.ubcbotanicalgarden.org; 6804 SW Marine Dr; adult/child $7/free mid-Mar–mid-Oct, admission by donation mid-Oct–mid-Mar, combination pass with Nitobe Memorial Garden $10; ☽ 10am-6pm mid-Mar–mid-Oct, 10am-4:30pm mid-Oct–mid-Mar; ☒ 41

A haven for green-fingered visitors, this 10,000-tree, 28-hectare plot near the corner of West 16th Ave comprises eight separate gardens, including Canada's largest collection of rhododendrons (plus some lovely blue poppies), a 16th-century-style apothecary garden and a winter garden of plants that bloom outside springtime. A recommended highlight is the BC Native Garden, which has around 3500 specimens from dunes, bogs and more. Drop by for the annual weekend Apple Festival (see the boxed text, p134) held here in mid-October, where you can salivate and select from more than 60 lip-smacking popular, heritage and lesser-known varieties.

top picks

ATTRACTIONS WITH TOURS

- Museum of Anthropology (left)
- Vancouver Art Gallery (p46)
- Vancouver Lookout (p46)
- Vancouver Maritime Museum (p96)
- VanDusen Botanical Garden (p90)

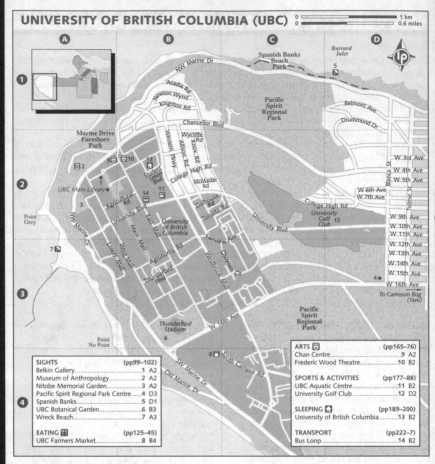

UNIVERSITY OF BRITISH COLUMBIA (UBC)

SIGHTS (pp99–102)
Belkin Gallery...............................1 A2
Museum of Anthropology.............2 A2
Nitobe Memorial Garden..............3 A2
Pacific Spirit Regional Park Centre....4 D3
Spanish Banks...............................5 D1
UBC Botanical Garden...................6 B3
Wreck Beach.................................7 A3

EATING (pp125–45)
UBC Farmers Market.....................8 B4

ARTS (pp165–76)
Chan Centre..................................9 A2
Frederic Wood Theatre.................10 B2

SPORTS & ACTIVITIES (pp177–88)
UBC Aquatic Centre......................11 B2
University Golf Club......................12 D2

SLEEPING (pp189–200)
University of British Columbia........13 B2

TRANSPORT (pp222–7)
Bus Loop......................................14 B2

NITOBE MEMORIAL GARDEN Map p100

☎ 604-822-6038; www.nitobe.org; 1895 Lower Mall; adult/child $5/free mid-Mar–mid-Oct, admission by donation mid-Oct–mid-Mar, combination pass with UBC Botanical Garden $10; 10am-6pm daily mid-Mar–mid-Oct, 10am-2:30pm Mon-Fri mid-Oct–mid-Mar; 41

This lovely garden is a perfect example of Japan's symbolic horticultural art form. Aside from some traffic noise, it's a tranquil retreat, ideal for quiet meditation. Considered one of North America's most authentic Japanese gardens, it's divided into a Tea Garden – complete with ceremonial teahouse – and a Stroll Garden, where the layout reflects a symbolic journey through life following the principles of yin and yang. You can take part in a teahouse tea ceremony (☎ 604-224-1560; admission $5) on select days

throughout the summer here – reservations are recommended. The garden is named after Dr Inazo Nitobe, a Japanese scholar whose mug appears on Japan's ¥5000 note.

PACIFIC SPIRIT REGIONAL PARK
Map p100

☎ 604-224-5739; cnr Blanca St & W 16th Ave; 8am-10pm Jun-Aug, 8am-dusk Sep-May; 41

This stunning 763-hectare park – the city's largest – cuts a wide swathe across the peninsula. Stretching from Burrard Inlet on one side to the North Arm of the Fraser River on the other, it's a green buffer zone between the campus and the city. It's a smashing spot to hug some trees and explore (there are 54km of walking, jogging and cycling trails) – you'll marvel at the giant cedars and firs that will be towering over you here. You'll also find the 12,000-year-old Camosun Bog (accessed by a boardwalk at 19th Ave and Camosun St), a unique wetland home of native bird and plant species. Visit the Park Centre for maps and info on the park's many features.

SPANISH BANKS Map p100
cnr NW Marine Dr & Blanca St; 🚍 4
There are some stunning views from this beach on the north side of the peninsula: you can wave at the giant freighters moored in Burrard Inlet or just sit back and watch the city and distant West Vancouver slowly fade in the setting sun. Recalling the early arrival of Spanish explorers in the region, the British – who arrived later but eventually won control of the area – named the waterfront after them. Nowadays, it's one of the city's least crowded beaches, populated mostly by homework-avoiding UBC students and skimming connoisseurs – Spanish Banks is renowned for its ideal skimboarding conditions (see the boxed text, p183).

UNIVERSITY TOWN Map p100
www.ubc.ca; 🚍 99 B-Line
Although surrounded by undeveloped waterfront and enjoying a verdant, tree-lined location, the UBC campus – complete with 44,000 students – is a bustling, building-packed minicity. If you have the time, it's worth a day out from downtown since there's plenty to do here and lots of easy-to-find lunch and coffee spots. Consider a free walking tour (☎ 604-822-8687; www.ceremonies .ubc.ca/tours; departs Brock Hall; ⏰ 10am & 1pm Mon-Fri mid-May–mid-Aug) to get your bearings. If you fancy a swim, the UBC Aquatic Centre (p185) is open to the public. The free-entry Belkin Gallery (☎ 604-822-2759; www.belkin-gallery.ubc.ca; 1825 Main Mall), which focuses on contemporary art, and the popular Chan Centre (☎ 604-822-9197; www.chancentre.com; UBC, 6265 Crescent Rd) concert venue will keep visiting arties occupied.

WRECK BEACH Map p100
www.wreckbeach.org; 🚍 41
From the intersection of NW Marine Dr and University Blvd, follow Trail 6 into the woods then head down the steps to the waterfront for Wreck Beach, a microcosm taste of what makes Vancouver unlike almost any other North American city. You'll find an undeveloped, log-strewn, 7.8km beach sur-

rounded by a hulking forest that makes you feel worlds away from the city, yet downtown is only 20 minutes away. Reflecting Vancouver's former hippie days, this is the city's only nudist beach (although as long as you're respectful, you don't have to be completely in the buff) and it's your chance to meet and greet the counterculture locals, most wearing little more than a smile and the occasional piercing.

'Undeveloped' doesn't mean you'll want for creature comforts, though. Soon after you drop your pants, you'll be offered a massage or haircut by one of the wandering vendors who stroll the sand. Or, if you're feeling peckish, you can amble over to one of the ever-smiling food vendors for some sustenance – try Stormin' Norman's buffalo burgers or Marco's organic fruit juices.

Beach regulars are in a continuing battle with the university over the building of residential towers that threaten their privacy, so be sure to offer your support as you peel off. For further information on the campaign, visit the Wreck Beach website. And if you fancy connecting with other local naturists during your stay in town, check in with the Van Tan Nudist Club (☎ 604-980-2400; www.vantan.ca) for events, including regular swimming meets at local pools.

UBC CAMPUS & GARDENS WALK
Walking Tour
This walk will introduce you to the UBC campus, combining its leading cultural attractions with its celebrated gardens.

1 Museum of Anthropology Start your visit at Vancouver's best museum (p99), where you'll gain a deep appreciation for the culture and artistry of the region's original First Nations residents.

2 Belkin Gallery Cross NW Marine Dr and head down West Mall, turning left on Crescent Rd. You'll soon come to this free-entry gallery (left), which houses an impressive art collection.

3 Chan Centre While you're in the area, continue along Crescent Rd and see if there's anything on this evening at this state-of-the-art classical-music venue.

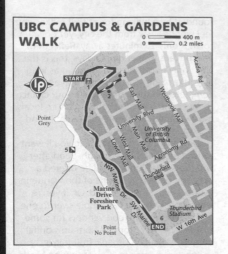

UBC CAMPUS & GARDENS WALK

5 Wreck Beach Return to NW Marine Dr and, if you're feeling adventurous, look for the signs through the forest that indicate Trail 6. Follow the trail until your reach the waterfront, where you can disrobe – you're on Vancouver's official naturist beach (p101).

4 Nitobe Memorial Garden Retrace your steps along Crescent Rd and rejoin NW Marine Dr, turning left and following the curving road to this tranquil landscaped Japanese garden (p100). Traditional tea ceremonies are staged here on select summer days.

6 UBC Botanical Garden Continue your walk (don't forget to put your clothes back on first) along NW Marine Dr until it becomes SW Marine Dr. Near the intersection with W 16th Ave, you'll find the lovely botanical garden (p99), complete with a series of fascinating minigardens.

GREATER VANCOUVER

Drinking p155; Eating p144; Sleeping p199

Greater Vancouver – sometimes referred to as the Lower Mainland – is chock full of looming mountains, crenulated coastal parks, wildlife sanctuaries, historic attractions and characterful communities, all within a 45-minute drive of downtown Vancouver. North Vancouver and West Vancouver together make up the North Shore, located across Burrard Inlet from Vancouver proper. Richmond lies directly south of Vancouver via Hwy 99.

NORTH VANCOUVER

'North Van' in localese, this nature-bordered community is the place to hike (p180) or ski (p183), visit a salmon farm, teeter across a suspension bridge or learn to kayak in a stunning fjorded area (p180). It's the easiest area to reach if you want to hit the mountains framing your photos of downtown.

Like so much of the Lower Mainland, North Van had industrial beginnings as a logging and sawmilling center. Transportation across the inlet started in 1866 when Navvy Jack Thomas, a gravel merchant, fired up his rowboat and charged a small fee to get mill workers over to Gassy Jack's Globe Saloon in Gastown. In 1873 Thomas moved to the area that is now West Vancouver with his wife, Row'i'a (the granddaughter of Chief Ki'ep'i'lan'o, after whom the Capilano River is named). He became the first white resident on the North Shore.

Life in the area remained quiet until the Lions Gate Bridge opened in 1938, sparking a rash of house building throughout the North Shore. The district further boomed after the opening of the Second Narrows Bridge (now also known as the Ironworkers Memorial Bridge) in 1960, which cut the total travel time to Vancouver to about 20 minutes.

For more information on North Van, visit www.cnv.org. Transit access to the community is via the handy SeaBus (p226) service from Vancouver's Waterfront Station.

CAPILANO SUSPENSION BRIDGE
Map pp44–5

☎ 604-985-7474; www.capbridge.com; 3735 Capilano Rd; adult/child/youth/student/senior May-Oct $26.95/8.30/15.65/20.75/24.95, Nov-Apr $23.95/7.40/13.90/18.45/21.95; ☼ 9am-5pm Nov-Mar, 9am-6:30pm Apr, 9am-7:30pm May, 8:30am-8pm Jun & Sep, 8:30am-9pm Jul & Aug, 9am-6pm Oct; ☒ 236 from Lonsdale Quay; ☷

As you walk gingerly out onto the world's longest (140m) and highest (70m) suspension bridge, swaying gently over the roiling waters of tree-lined Capilano Canyon, remember that the thick steel cables you are gripping are safely embedded in huge concrete blocks on either side. That should steady your feet – unless the teenagers are stamping across to scare the oldsters. It's the region's most popular attraction – hence the summertime crowds and relentless tour buses. The grounds here also include rainforest walks, totem poles and a swinging network of smaller bridges strung between the trees, called Treetops Adventure (see the boxed text, p104). Drop by the souvenir shop, one of BC's biggest, for First Nations artworks and 'moose dropping' choccies.

GROUSE MOUNTAIN Map pp44–5

☎ 604-980-9311; www.grousemountain.com; 6400 Nancy Greene Way; Skyride adult/child/youth/senior $33/12/19/31; ☒ 236 from Lonsdale Quay; ☷

Calling itself the 'Peak of Vancouver,' this mountaintop perch offers smashing views of the downtown towers, shimmering in the water below you. In summer, Skyride gondola passengers can access restaurants, lumberjack shows, alpine hiking trails and a grizzly-bear refuge. You can also avoid the gondola and harden your calf muscles on the Grouse Grind, a steep 2.9km wilderness trek that takes most people around 90 minutes. In winter, Grouse becomes the locals' favorite snowy playground (see p183).

top picks

FREE VIEWS

- Canada Place (p46)
- Lonsdale Quay (p104)
- English Bay (p65)
- Prospect Point (p53)
- Harbour Green Park (p68)

GREENING VANCOUVER'S BIGGEST ATTRACTION

Visitors to the Capilano Suspension Bridge (p103) have more than one bridge to cross if they want to make full use of the attraction's facilities. In addition to its giant famed walkway, a series of five minibridges, called Treetops Adventure, was added in 2005. But while the original bridge is anchored in concrete, the new attraction aimed for a 'greener' approach.

Offering an educational, squirrel's-eye view of the West Coast rainforest, the series of short, gently swaying suspension bridges link eight towering Douglas fir trees. At heights of up to 25m above the forest floor – still far from the top of many of these 300-year-old trees – the bridges have viewing platforms where Capilano's naturalists hold court on the area's ecological attributes.

Respecting the park's rich ecological heritage, the new attraction was designed to have as little impact as possible on the area's fragile environment. Bridge cables and steel tubing were painted a tree-blending brown, while natural hemp netting and recycled wood was used throughout. A treehouse that serves as a two-story access point to the course was constructed from antique beams salvaged from a defunct Hudson's Bay store.

But it's the delicate spider's web of engineering itself that attracts most interest. A team of arborists, bridge specialists and environmental consultants drafted plans for the course, agreeing that their main challenge was to protect the eight Douglas fir 'anchors.' They ultimately devised a system that attaches cables and platforms to a collar around each tree – a solution that barely touches the trunk and enables the trees to continue growing. The collars subject each tree to around 20 pounds of force per square inch – about the same amount of pressure exerted by pressing a thumb on a tabletop.

Treetops Adventure is included in the regular admission fee to Capilano Suspension Bridge.

MT SEYMOUR PROVINCIAL PARK
Map pp44–5
☎ 604-986-2261; www.bcparks.ca; 1700 Mt Seymour Rd; ☽ 24hr
A popular, rustic retreat from the downtown clamour, this giant, tree-lined park is suffused with more than a dozen summertime hiking trails that suit walkers of most abilities (the easiest path is the 2km Goldie Lake Trail). Many trails wind past lakes and centuries-old Douglas firs and offer a true break from the city. This is also one of the city's three main winter playgrounds (see p183). Drivers can take Hwy 1 to the Mt Seymour Pkwy (near the Second Narrows Bridge) and follow it east to Mt Seymour Rd.

LYNN CANYON PARK Map pp44–5
☎ 604-984-3149; Peter's Rd; admission free; ☽ 7am-9pm May-Aug, 7am-7pm Sep-Apr; 🚌 229 from Lonsdale Quay
Set amid a dense bristling of ancient trees, the main feature of this provincial park is its swinging suspension bridge, a free alternative to Capilano. Not quite as long or high as its tourist-magnet rival, it provokes the same jelly-legged reaction as you sway over the river 50m below – and it's also far less crowded and commercialized. There are hiking trails, swimming areas and picnic spots around the park to keep you busy once you've done the bridge. The free-entry

Ecology Centre (☎ 604-981-3103; www.dnv.org /ecology; 3663 Park Rd; admission by donation; ☽ 10am-5pm daily Jun-Sep, 10am-5pm Mon-Fri & noon-4pm Sat & Sun Oct-May) houses interesting displays on the area's rich biodiversity, complete with dioramas and video presentations.

LONSDALE QUAY Map pp44–5
☎ 604-985-6261; 123 Carrie Cates Court; ☽ market 9:30am-6:30pm; SeaBus from Waterfront Station
As well as being a transportation hub – this is where the SeaBus from downtown docks and you pick up transit buses to Capilano, Grouse and beyond – this waterfront facility built for Expo '86 houses a colorful indoor market. The region's second-best market (after Granville Island), this one is a popular spot for fresh fruit and glassy-eyed whole fish on the main floor and books and clothing on the 2nd floor. There's also a cheap-and-cheerful food court and a couple of sit-down restaurants. It's a nice afternoon jaunt from the city, with many visitors scooping up an ice cream and lingering over the boardwalk vistas of downtown.

CAPILANO SALMON HATCHERY
Map pp44–5
☎ 604-666-1790; 4500 Capilano Park Rd; admission free; ☽ 8am-4pm Nov-Mar, 9am-4.45pm Apr & Oct, 8am-7pm May & Sep, 8am-8pm Jun-Aug; ♿

Located in Capilano River Regional Park, about 2km north of the Capilano Suspension Bridge, this fish farm is run by the Federal Department of Fisheries and Oceans to protect valuable Coho, Chinook and Steelhead salmon stocks. Visit from July to November – October, when the Chinooks return, is the optimum month – and you'll catch adult salmon swimming through fish ladders past the rapids in a heroic effort to reach their spawning grounds upstream, after which they promptly die in a scripted lifecycle that must have been written by Samuel Beckett. Eye-level tanks display the creatures and enlightening exhibits help explain the entire mysterious process.

WEST VANCOUVER

West Vancouver, the kissing cousin of North Vancouver, is one of the region's poshest neighborhoods, a place where sprawling waterfront homes snuggle into the cliffs above Burrard Inlet, and rocky beaches and small coves lie hidden away from the road. Residents of West Van earn a higher per capita income (and read more library books) than any other group of Canadians. They're also the proud developers of Canada's first shopping mall, Park Royal.

West Van stretches west from the Capilano River to Horseshoe Bay. Marine Dr is its main east–west thoroughfare: it hugs the shore while passing through Ambleside and Dundarave, collectively known as 'the Village' – the commercial center of West Van, where you'll find designer shops, cafés and restaurants. Park Royal mall sits just west of the Lions Gate Bridge, straddling Marine Dr.

While the area's attractions aren't the biggest must-sees around, the neighborhood does accommodate some truly lovely and inviting green spaces, such as Lighthouse Park and Whytecliff Park. It's also home to Cypress Provincial Park, Greater Vancouver's best skiing mountain (see p183) and the host of several events at the 2010 Olympic and Paralympic Winter Games.

Transit access to West Vancouver from downtown is via bus 240, 250, 251, 252 or 257.

CYPRESS PROVINCIAL PARK Map pp44–5
☎ 604-924-2200; www.bcparks.ca; Cypress Bowl Rd; ☼ 24hr
Around 8km north of West Van via Hwy 99, Cypress offers some great summertime

hikes, including the Baden-Powell, Yew Lake and Howe Sound Crest trails, which plunge through forests of cedar, yellow cypress and Douglas fir and wind past little lakes and alpine meadows. In winter, the park's Cypress Mountain (p183) resort area makes this one of the city's favorite snowbound playgrounds.

LIGHTHOUSE PARK Map pp44–5
☎ 604-925-7200; cnr Beacon Lane & Marine Dr; admission free; ☼ dawn-dusk; ☒ 250
Some of the region's oldest and most spectacular trees live within this accessible 75-hectare park, including a rare stand of original coastal forest and plenty of those gnarly, copper-trunked arbutus trees. It's ideal for a romantic picnic, and you'll find plenty of doe-eyed couples hogging the grass here. About 13km of hiking trails crisscross the area, including a recommended trek that leads to the rocky perch of the Point Atkinson Lighthouse, where you'll come across some shimmering, camera-worthy views over Burrard Inlet and the nearby tree-covered islands. If you're driving from downtown, turn left on Marine Dr after crossing the Lions Gate Bridge to reach the park.

HORSESHOE BAY Map pp44–5
☒ 257
The small coastal community of Horseshoe Bay marks the end of West Vancouver and the start of trips to Whistler, via the Sea to Sky Hwy (Hwy 99), or Vancouver Island, Bowen Island and the Sunshine Coast via the BC Ferries (p224) network. It's a pretty village, with great views across the bay and up Howe Sound to distant glacial peaks. Cutesy places to eat and shop line the waterfront on Bay St, near the marina, where you can also take a whale-watching boat trek with Sewell's Sea Safari (p234).

WHYTECLIFF PARK Map pp44–5
☎ 604-925-7200; 7100 block, Marine Dr; admission free; ☼ dawn-dusk; ☒ 250
Just west of Horseshoe Bay, this is an exceptional little park right on the water. Trails lead to vistas and a gazebo, from where you can watch the boat traffic in Burrard Inlet. The rocky beach is a great place to play, go for a swim or scamper over the large rocks protruding from the beach. The park is also popular with scuba divers – see p182 for details.

WORTH THE TRIP: DEEP COVE

Take the Dollarton Hwy exit off Hwy 1 and go east – right if you just crossed Second Narrows Bridge, left if you're driving toward it. Stop in Cates Park to enjoy the views of Belcarra Regional Park across the waters of Burrard Inlet, or follow the road as it turns left and becomes Deep Cove Rd.

The road will pass close to some ultrarich homes before making a right turn, leading you down through the quaint hamlet of Deep Cove and the protected waters of...Deep Cove (Map pp44–5). A strip of galleries, gift shops, and pizza and gelato cafés leads down to the rocky beach, which is one of the most deeply relaxing parts of the Lower Mainland. Fuel up with a scrummy yeast-free donut at Honey's (☎ 604-929-4988; 4373 Gallant Ave; mains $4-8), then take part in the region's leading activity and the main reason many keep coming back here.

An ideal spot for kayak virgins, the waters of Deep Cove are glassy calm and the setting, around North America's southernmost fjord, couldn't be more tranquil. Deep Cove Canoe & Kayak Centre (p180) will show you how to paddle and take you around the lovely Indian Arm area on a guided tour.

Nearby Cates Park provides another vantage point from which to see Indian Arm. It's best known as the place where novelist Malcolm Lowry, author of *Under the Volcano*, lived with his wife from 1940 to 1954: a walk dedicated to him meanders past the spot where his squatter's shack once stood. The park also shelters the remains of the Dollar Lumber Mill (in operation from 1916 to 1942), a 15m First Nations war canoe, forest walks and a sandy beach.

Deep Cove can be accessed via buses 211 and 212.

RICHMOND & BEYOND

What started as a sleepy agricultural and fishing community at the turn of the 20th century has become a mini Hong Kong, populated by new-generation immigrants who flocked to the area in the mid-1990s prior to Britain's 1997 territorial handover to China. Perhaps Richmond's geography reminded the immigrants of home, for, like Hong Kong, it's an island city.

Today the area is a bit of a dichotomy. It's a place for nature lovers, who can get their fill at the George C Reifel Migratory Bird Sanctuary, and history fans, who can drop by waterfront Steveston for the excellent Gulf of Georgia Cannery, as well as some great fish-and-chips (see p145). But it's the urban shopping experience that attracts most visitors. Strung along No 3 Rd south from Bridgeport Rd to Granville Ave are malls and more malls. These Asian shopping centers can be an interesting diversion if you have time on your hands: they're filled almost exclusively with Chinese stores, Chinese products and Chinese shoppers, and most of the signs are in Chinese. You'll also find excellent Asian food here at very reasonable prices. For a true taste of Hong Kong–style shopping, it's hard to beat the summertime night market (p117), the area's best attraction.

Richmond comprises a group of islands sandwiched between the North Arm of the Fraser River on one side and its main channel on the other. One of the main islands – Sea Island – houses the city's airport. No 3 Rd is the main north–south thoroughfare, while Westminster Hwy is the main east–west road. Coastal Steveston is southwest of central Richmond.

For more information on the area, visit www.tourismrichmond.com. Transit access to Richmond from Vancouver is via bus 98 (B-Line), 401, 402 or 403 (the 402 will get you to Steveston).

INTERNATIONAL BUDDHIST TEMPLE

Map pp44–5

☎ 604-274-2822; www.buddhisttemple.ca; 9160 Steveston Hwy; admission free; ☺ 9:30am-5:30pm; ☒ 98 B-Line from Burrard Station, transfer to bus 403 at Richmond Centre

Reflecting the classical architecture of Beijing's Forbidden City, a highlight of this fascinating, two-tiered temple complex (also known as Kuan Yin Temple) is its sumptuous Gracious Hall, complete with deep-red exterior walls and a gently flaring orange porcelain roof. Check out the colorful 100m Buddha mural and the golden, multi-armed Bodhisattva figure here. The surrounding landscaped garden with its sculptures and bonsai trees is another highlight, but save time for a lip-smacking veggie lunch in the ground-floor cafeteria. You don't have to be a Buddhist to visit and the monks are highly welcoming if you just want to have a look around.

GULF OF GEORGIA CANNERY NATIONAL HISTORIC SITE Map pp44–5

☎ 604-664-9009; www.gulfofgeorgiacannery .com; 12138 4th Ave, Steveston; adult/child/senior $7.15/3.45/5.90; ☺ 10am-5pm Thu-Mon May & Sep, 10am-5pm daily Jun-Aug; ☒ 98 B-Line from Burrard Station, transfer to bus 402 at Richmond Centre

Once you've perused the boats hawking the day's fresh catch, Steveston's main attraction is the old-school cannery, now transformed into an excellent industrial heritage museum that explores the sights and sounds (and smells) of the region's bygone era of labour-intensive fish processing. Most of the machinery remains – polished and cleaned of its permanent film of blood and fish oil – and there's an evocative focus on the people who used to work here before the plant closed in 1979. You'll hear recorded testimonies from old workers percolating through the air like ghosts and see large black-and-white blow-ups of some of the staff who spent their days immersed in entrails in order to roll thousands of cans down the production line.

GEORGE C REIFEL MIGRATORY BIRD SANCTUARY

☎ 604-946-6980; www.reifelbirdsanctuary.com; 5191 Robertson Rd, Delta; adult/child & senior $4/2; ◷ 9am-4pm; ♿

Across the South Arm of the Fraser River, this smashing 300-hectare sanctuary attracts feathered fowl and curious visitors in almost equal measure. Bald eagles, Siberian swans, peregrine falcons, blue herons and 264 other species choose to roost here and there are plenty of opportunities for viewing.

Undoubtedly the most spectacular sight is when up to 80,000 snow geese drop by in the fall en route to Wrangel Island, off Siberia's eastern coast. October is the best time to catch the early arrival of these birds, when they move around the area in huge, surging flocks of up to 20,000 in search of tasty marsh plants.

In contrast, springtime brings millions of Western Sandpipers to the site, as well as beady-eyed hawks, eagles, cormorants, ospreys and other fish-eating wildlife (including seals). All are hungrily following the migratory salmon – a roiling aquatic buffet – to the Fraser River's mouth.

The sanctuary has an observation tower, plenty of wooden hides, 3km of winding paths and a smattering of picnic tables, but keep in mind that there is very little activity here in summer: October to April is the best time to visit. This is not a park, so dress as if you're heading out on a soft hike and bring some bottled water along to keep you hydrated, plus sunscreen if necessary.

A 40-minute drive from Vancouver, the sanctuary is 13km west of Ladner in the Municipality of Delta. From downtown Vancouver, take Hwy 99 south through Richmond and the George Massy Tunnel and follow the signs toward Ladner. From Ladner, follow Ladner Trunk Rd west to 47A Ave and on to River Rd. Follow River Rd for 3km and cross the bridge to Westham Island. Follow the main road to where it ends in front of some large black gates. The driveway to the left leads to the sanctuary's parking lot.

WORTH THE TRIP: FORT LANGLEY NATIONAL HISTORIC SITE

Little Fort Langley's tree-lined streets and 19th-century storefronts make it one of the Lower Mainland's most picturesque historic villages, ideal for an afternoon away from Vancouver. Its main historic highlight is the colorful Fort Langley National Historic Site (☎ 604-513-4777; www.pc.gc.ca/langley; 23433 Mavis Ave; adult/child/senior $7.15/3.45/5.90; ◷ 9am-8pm Jul & Aug, 10am-5pm Sep-Jun; ♿), perhaps the region's most important old-school landmark.

A fortified trading post since 1827, this is where James Douglas announced the creation of BC in 1858, giving the site a legitimate claim to being the province's birthplace. With costumed re-enacters, re-created artisan workshops and a gold-panning area that's very popular with kids – they also enjoy charging around the wooden battlements – this is an ideal place for families who want to add a little education to their trips.

If you need an introduction before you start wading into the buildings here, there's a surprisingly entertaining time-travel-themed movie presentation on offer. And make sure you check the website before you arrive: there's a wide array of events that bring the past evocatively back to life, including a summertime evening campfire program that will take you right back to the pioneer days of the 1800s.

If you're driving from Vancouver, take Hwy 1 east for 40km, then take the 232nd St exit north. Follow the signs along 232nd St until you reach the stop sign at Glover Rd. Turn right here, and continue into the village. Turn right again on Mavis Ave, just before the railway tracks. The fort's parking lot is at the end of the street.

If traveling by transit, take the SkyTrain to Surrey Central Station, then transfer to bus 501, 502 or 320 to Langley. Transfer in Langley to the C62 and alight at the intersection of 96 Ave and Glover Rd. The fort is a signposted 400m walk from here.

BLUELIST[1] (blu list) *v.*
to recommend a travel experience.
What's your recommendation? www.lonelyplanet.com/bluelist

SHOPPING

top picks

- Richmond Night Market (p117)
- Mountain Equipment Co-op (p118)
- Wanted – Lost Found Canadian (p116)
- Holt Renfrew (p111)
- Regional Assembly of Text (p118)
- Smoking Lily (p117)
- Granville Island Public Market (p120)
- Zulu Records (p123)
- John Fluevog (p112)
- KidsBooks (p122)

SHOPPING

Shopping in Vancouver used to involve little more than selecting a thick winter coat or picking up some maple-sugar cookies for overseas visitors, but the city's retail experience has changed dramatically in recent years. While familiar chain outlets and department stores are still the mainstay in the city center, there are some highly browseworthy shopping enclaves that require a little traveling to get to, but they're trips well worth making.

You'll find hot independent fashion designers that can transform you into a pale and interesting muse; record stores where you can delve into the undiscovered pantheon of great local music; galleries where you can splash some cash on established Canadian artists; arts and crafts emporiums where unique artisan creations will provide you with a suitcase full of unusual souvenirs for everyone back home; and specialist bookshops that cater to every interest, selling everything from gay-lit to travel guides and kids' books.

Keep in mind that the strong Canadian dollar means Vancouver is not the bargain-hunter's paradise it once was, especially when you factor in the added taxes (see below). Also remember that museum shops are another place to buy something out of the ordinary, if you haven't already blown your budget; see p112 for more.

OPENING HOURS

Typical retail shopping hours are 10am to 6pm Monday to Saturday, noon to 5pm Sunday – some shops close on Sundays, though. Prime shopping areas and malls may stay open until 9pm, especially from Thursday onward. Most shops and malls extend their hours in the month before Christmas. In the reviews following, only shop opening hours that deviate from these standard times are noted.

CONSUMER TAXES

The prices on most goods in shops do not include tax, which is added when you take the item to the cash register to pay. GST (5%) and PST (7%) taxes are usually added. See p235 for more information on these taxes and for tips on how you can claim a refund.

DOWNTOWN

Centered on clamorous Robson St – Vancouver's main shopping promenade and the home of most major clothing chains – the city's downtown core is a strollable outdoor mall of grazing shoppers moving between their favorite stores with an ever-growing clutch of shopping bags. High fashion, shoes and jewelry are the mainstays here, and there are also plenty of coffee shops if you need to stop and count your money. Head southwest along Granville Mall from the intersection with Robson St and you'll find an emerging enclave of highly fashionable urban streetwear shops: this is

where you can pick up those hand-painted or limited-edition Adidas or Puma runners you've always wanted.

For top-rank labels such as Tiffany, Hermes and Gucci, head to the area around the Burrard and Alberni Sts intersection; for urban fashions aimed at moneyed under-30s, make for the 800-block of Granville St. If rain stops play, head inside to the Pacific Centre (Map pp48–9; ☎ 604-688-7235; cnr Howe & W Georgia Sts; ♥ 10am-7pm Mon-Wed, 10am-9pm Thu & Fri, 9:30am-6pm Sat, 11am-6pm Sun; M Granville), a large mall with a good food court and all the shops you'll ever need.

top picks

SHOPPING STRIPS

- Robson Street (left)
- Commercial Drive (p118)
- SoMa (p116)
- W 4th Avenue (p122)
- South Granville (p121)

SOPHIA BOOKS Map pp48–9   Bookshop
☎ 604-684-0484; 450 W Hastings St; M Waterfront
This multilingual bookstore serves ESL students, homesick francophones and Japanese manga fans, as well as just about everyone else interested in reading in another language. Shelves devoted to comics, *anime*, foreign magazines, language-learning tapes and Japanese origami fill the cramped aisles.

MINK CHOCOLATES Map pp48–9 Candy
☎ 604-633-2451; 863 W Hastings St; Ⓜ Waterfront
If chocolate is a food group in your book, follow your candy-primed nose to this decadent designer choccy shop in the downtown core. Select a handful of souvenir bonbons – little edible artworks embossed with prints of trees and coffee cups – then hit the drinks bar for the best velvety hot choc you've ever tasted.

ROOTS Map pp48–9 Clothing
☎ 604-683-4305; 1001 Robson St; 🚌 5
Basically a maple leaf–emblazoned version of the Gap, Roots designs athletic streetwear that's unmistakably Canadian; its retro-styled Olympic jogging pants and hoodies are ever-popular. If you can't find this one, there are additional outlets – usually in malls – dotted throughout the city.

GOLDEN AGE Map pp48–9 Comics & Collectibles
☎ 604-683-2819; 852 Granville St; 🚌 4
If you're missing your regular dose of *Emily the Strange* or you just want to blow your vacation budget on a highly detailed life-size model of Ultra Man, head straight to this Aladdin's cave of the comic-book world. While the clientele is unsurprisingly dominated by spotty males of a certain age, the staff are friendly and welcoming – especially to wide-eyed kids buying their first *Archie*.

HOLT RENFREW Map pp48–9 Department Store
☎ 604-681-3121; 737 Dunsmuir St; Ⓜ Granville
Not far from the Bay and Sears, Canada's ubiquitous chain department stores, Holt's is where it's really at for designer shopping. You'll need a healthy credit-card limit to swan through the sumptuously loungey departments, but you can expect to run into old friends such as Armani, Gucci and Tiffany. The end-of-season sales here are awesome, and hotly anticipated by the locals.

HEAVENS PLAYGROUND
Map pp48–9 Fashion
☎ 604-646-4787; 850 Granville St; 🚌 4
Nestled in a new ministrip of urban fashion boutiques including Puma, Adidas and American Apparel, this is the first North American outlet for this ultra-cool Dutch chain that kits out people who want to look hip without looking like they're trying. The hot item here is the Gsus and the Seven Deadly Sins T-shirt

top picks
CANDY
- **Mink Chocolates** (left)
- **Mina No Konbiniya** (p113)
- **Dutch Girl Chocolates** (p118)
- **Purdy's** (p121)

HENRY BIRKS & SONS Map pp48–9 Jewelry
☎ 604-669-3333; 698 W Hastings St; Ⓜ Waterfront
A Vancouver institution since 1879 – hence the landmark freestanding clock outside – Birks crafts exquisite heirloom jewelry and its signature line of timepieces. It's an upscale place, similar to Tiffany's in the USA, and ideal for picking up that special something in a classy, blue embossed box for a deserving someone back home.

A&B SOUND Map pp48–9 Music
☎ 604-687-5837; 556 Seymour St; Ⓜ Granville
With several other outlets around the Lower Mainland, purple-painted a&b sells all types of music, DVDs and electronic equipment. Taken over by a new owner in recent years, its selection can be a bit patchy but its prices – especially on new-release CDs – are generally still the best in town. Check the local press for regular sale days.

SCRATCH RECORDS Map pp48–9 Music
☎ 604-687-6355; 726 Richards St; Ⓜ Granville
Initially a tiny specialist record store, Scratch has expanded over the past 15 years to become a record label, concert promoter and international distributor. But the store remains, its bins packed with 99% independent labels, obscure releases and vinyl that the staff know intimately.

SIKORA'S CLASSICAL RECORDS
Map pp48–9 Music
☎ 604-685-0625; 432 W Hastings St; Ⓜ Waterfront
Sikora's blows away the classical inventory of mainstream music stores with its more than 25,000 CD/DVD titles – plus hundreds of LPs for all those traditionalists out there. Opera, organ, choral, chamber and early music are represented, and there's a section devoted to Canadian musicians. The staff are highly knowledgeable and can

SHOPPING AT THE MUSEUM

As if all the regular stores in Vancouver weren't enough to keep your shopping reflexes twitching nervously, the city's museums and galleries also offer some unexpected buying opportunities. You don't have to visit the attraction to visit its shop, and keep in mind that you're helping to fund the institutions you're buying from. Perhaps the best of all the city's museum stores, the UBC Museum of Anthropology (p99) has a fantastic array of authentic First Nations artworks, ranging from elegant silver jewelry to a full headdress for $4000. Back downtown, the Vancouver Art Gallery (p46) gift shop is like a lifestyle store for artsy types, with clever contemporary-coasters, vases and knickknacks to adorn your home, as well as large art books to leave on your coffee table and impress guests. There are also some good educational toys here.

Toys are similarly a large part of the selection at the Vancouver Aquarium (p52), where your sprog will instantly fall in love with the shoal of cuddly sharks, otters and starfish. If you have a tricky young teen to buy for back home, pick up a Shark Pool Predator – an inflatable pool toy that doubles as a squirt gun. Kids are also well served at Science World (p76), where there are lots of pocket money–priced items, including the entertainingly revolting freeze-dried ice cream for astronauts. Finally, if you make it to the Vancouver Police Centennial Museum (p73), you can buy one-pound bags of ground 'cop coffee,' tiny handcuff keychains and T-shirts adorned with 'VPD Police Line: Do Not Cross.' You'll be the envy of everyone back home when you wear that to work.

point you to a hot Mahler or Rachmaninov recording at the drop of a hat.

MOMENTUM Map pp48–9   Personal Care
☎ 604-689-4636; 1237 Burrard St; 🚍 2

In a sign that a well-groomed appearance has become an equality issue, not only can visiting males enjoy a full menu of treatments at locals spas (p186), they can also drop by this men-only grooming shop for the best in quality razors and shaving brushes and enough skin-care products to have you taking over the bathroom cabinets back home. You go guy.

JOHN FLUEVOG Map pp48–9   Shoes
☎ 604-688-2828; www.fluevog.com; 837 Granville St; 🕑 11am-7pm Mon-Wed & Sat, 11am-8pm Thu & Fri, noon-6pm Sun; 🚍 4

While some of the footwear here looks like Doc Martens on acid or as though it could poke your eye out from 20 paces, many of Fluevog's funky shoes also have a reduced 'green footprint.' Check out the synthetic vegetarian shoes and the completely biodegradable 'Earth Angels' range.

CANADIAN MAPLE DELIGHTS
Map pp48–9   Souvenirs
☎ 604-682-6175; 769 Hornby St; 🕑 7:30am-7pm Mon-Fri, 8am-7pm Sat & Sun; 🚍 5

It might seem like a chore but if you have to pick up souvenirs for all those greedy friends back home, this is an ideal one-stop-shop. Specializing in all manner of maple syrup–flavored goodies – think maple sugar, maple tea, maple leaf–shaped

candy, maple tree-growing kits etc – it also has vacuum-packed salmon for those who don't have a sweet tooth.

TRUE VALUE VINTAGE
Map pp48–9   Vintage Clothing
☎ 604-685-5403; 710 Robson St; 🚍 5

'Value' is a bit of a misnomer since the used duds at this subterranean cave of cool-clothing kitsch are sometimes fairly pricey. But if you really need that 1950s bowling shirt or Jimi Hendrix tour hat, you'll pay anything, right? Bargains are to be had on the musty-smelling sale racks.

WEST END

An eclectic and vibrant district of restaurants and coffee shops, the West End also has more than a few stores that are worth nosing around if you have a spare afternoon. The majority of the most distinctive businesses here are located on Davie St and are tailored toward the area's large gay community, but you can also expect bookstores, bakeries, wine shops and just about everything else to be offered along the way. The western end of Robson St delivers some interesting Asian stores; this is the place to pick up Japanese candies and Hello Kitty backpacks (you know you want one).

BOOK WAREHOUSE Map pp66–7   Bookshop
☎ 604-685-5711; 1051 Davie St; 🕑 10am-11pm; 🚍 6

This warm and welcoming outlet of Vancouver's favorite independent bookseller (with several branches around the city) has a good regional and international travel section and also offers large and small discounts on its big stock of new releases, contemporary faves and popular classics. Look out for regular sale days and pre-announced shipments of 'hurt books' – new tomes with minor dings and major discounts.

LITTLE SISTER'S BOOK & ART EMPORIUM Map pp66–7   Bookshop
☎ 604-669-1753; www.littlesistersbookstore.com; 1238 Davie St; ☒ 10am-11pm; 🚌 6

One of the only queer bookshops in western Canada, Little Sister's has a vast bazaar of queer-positive volumes, plus magazines, DVDs and gifts. Proceeds of designated books support the store's long-running legal battle against Canada Customs for its seizures of imported items. A good place to network with the local gay community.

LULULEMON ATHLETICA
Map pp66–7   Clothing
☎ 604-681-5403; 3118 Robson St; 🚌 5

A homegrown local store that's reached far beyond its origins (hence the Tokyo branches), Lululemon kick-started the trend for stretchy yoga togs worn by fashionistas who don't actually do yoga that much. Men and women are catered for here; along with the cute pants and tops, the current hot item is the branded tote bag.

LUSH Map pp66–7   Personal Care
☎ 604-687-5874; www.lush.com; 1020 Robson St; 🚌 4

You'll likely smell this body, bath and beauty store where packaging is generally frowned upon from several meters away. You can stock up here on all its special products – including 'sex bomb' bath ballistics or 'black magic' massage bars – or just peruse the teetering stacks of soap piled up like blocks of cheese. It might look tasty, but try not to eat anything.

GAY-MART Map pp66–7   Specialty
☎ 604-681-3262; www.gaymart.com; 1148 Davie St; 🚌 6

The West End gayborhood's favorite shopping bazaar, Gay-Mart hawks all manner of pride-themed merchandise, including wallets, robes, socks and baseball caps emblazoned with rainbow flags. Jewelry and CDs add to the mix and it does a brisk business in adult movies and 'accessories.'

MINA NO KONBINIYA Map pp66–7   Specialty
☎ 604-682-3634; 1238 Robson St; ☒ 11am-late; 🚌 5

At a point on Robson St where the generic chain stores dry up and the Asian businesses begin, this is the kind of colorful, chaotic, even tacky store frequently seen in Tokyo's clamorous suburbs. It's the best place in town for Pocky chocolate sticks, senbei (rice crackers), take-out bento boxes and Melty Kiss candies – hence the homesick language students shuffling around the aisles. You can even indulge in the Japanese staple of hot, sweet canned coffee here.

RUBBER RAINBOW CONDOM COMPANY Map pp66–7   Specialty
☎ 604-683-3423; 953 Denman St; 🚌 5

A fun funky condom and lube store serving all manner of experiment-inviting accessories, including studded, vibrating and 'full-fitting strawberry flavored' varieties. Ask for a selection pack if you're going to be in town for a while – you never know how lucky you might get.

YALETOWN

Occupying the old brick warehouses, this chichi area is lined with mod furniture outlets and high-end designer boutiques, but it's worth a window-shopping stroll even if your budget isn't up to buying much. It's no surprise that there's a Mini Cooper showroom here – the car is a popular fashion accessory in this part of town. But Yaletown isn't just about designer gear for beautiful young things: there are a couple of art galleries here, too.

COASTAL PEOPLES FINE ARTS GALLERY Map p71 — Arts & Crafts

☎ 604-685-9298; www.coastalpeoples.com; 1024 Mainland St; ⊙ 10am-7pm Mon-Sat, 11am-6pm Sun; ⊜ C23

This sumptuous store houses a fine selection of Northwest Coast and Inuit aboriginal jewelry, carvings and prints. It focuses on the arts end of native crafts, and you'll find some exquisite items that will likely have your credit card sweating within minutes.

ATOMIC MODEL Map p71 — Fashion

☎ 604-688-9989; 1036 Mainland St; ⊜ C23

If having the kind of fashion-forward jeans and tops that are currently being paraded along the catwalks and high-end streets of New York or Tokyo appeals, then it's hard to beat this popular designer haunt where the beautiful young people of Yaletown come to spend their allowances. Watch out for the yappy lapdogs of fellow shoppers.

LOLA HOME & APPAREL

Map p71 — Fashion

☎ 604-633-5017; 1076 Hamilton St; ⊜ C23

A browser's delight, this pink-hued little nook is a smorgasbord of tea sets, Victorian soap leaves and silk dresses. Resembling a boutique from the Victorian era, it showcases modern-day designers who have incorporated antique and vintage aesthetics into their contemporary clothing lines.

BIONIC FOOTWEAR Map p71 — Shoes

☎ 604-685-9696; 1072 Mainland St; ⊜ C23

This little shoe emporium combines form and function with an enticing array of fab footwear for men, women and children who like looks as well as quality. You can slip into pumps, skater shoes or boots from the likes of Camper, Lacoste and Miss Sixty, or check out the small but growing selection of bags.

GASTOWN

While the main Water St thoroughfare is the best place in town to execute all your souvenir shopping in a single leap – especially if you're looking for maple leaf–themed T-shirts and chocolate 'moose dropping' candies – the side streets and alternative walkways of Gastown are increasingly being colonized by hip local designers, making this area a downtown rival to SoMa. Save time to wander a little off the beaten path, and also duck into the art galleries

in the area: they match the clothing stores for edgy local innovation and creativity.

HILL'S NATIVE ART Map p74 — Arts & Crafts

☎ 604-685-4249; 165 Water St; ⊙ 9am-9pm; Ⓜ Waterfront

Launched in 1946 as a small trading post on Vancouver Island, Hill's flagship store has many First Nations carvings, prints, ceremonial masks and cozy Cowichan sweaters, and traditional music and books of historical interest. Artists are often found at work in the 3rd-floor gallery.

BIZ BOOKS Map p74 — Bookshop

☎ 604-669-6431; 302 W Cordova St; Ⓜ Waterfront

This is the city's best source for books on film, theater and the TV industry – collectively known as 'the biz.' Actors, writers and directors studying the craft will find plays, directories, monologue books, scene books, accent tapes and screenwriting software.

CLOTHING SIZES

Women's clothing

Aus/UK	8	10	12	14	16	18
Europe	36	38	40	42	44	46
Japan	5	7	9	11	13	15
USA	6	8	10	12	14	16

Women's shoes

Aus/USA	5	6	7	8	9	10
Europe	35	36	37	38	39	40
France only	35	36	38	39	40	42
Japan	22	23	24	25	26	27
UK	3½	4½	5½	6½	7½	8½

Men's clothing

Aus	92	96	100	104	108	112
Europe	46	48	50	52	54	56
Japan	S		M	M		L
UK/USA	35	36	37	38	39	40

Men's shirts (collar sizes)

Aus/Japan	38	39	40	41	42	43
Europe	38	39	40	41	42	43
UK/USA	15	15½	16	16½	17	17½

Men's shoes

Aus/UK	7	8	9	10	11	12
Europe	41	42	43	44½	46	47
Japan	26	27	27½	28	29	30
USA	7½	8½	9½	10½	11½	12½

Measurements approximate only, try before you buy

SHOPPING GASTOWN

top picks

MUSIC STORES

- Zulu Records (p123)
- Scratch Records (p111)
- Red Cat Records (p117)
- Sikora's Classical Records (p111)
- A&B Sound (p111)

DREAM Map p74   Local Designer Wear
☎ 604-683-7326; 311 W Cordova St; Ⓜ Waterfront
Dream is one of a cluster of small shops in the area near Cambie St spotlighting emerging young local fashionistas. Hip Japanese girls sift through the hats, T-shirts, thongs, purses, jewelry and other urban funk items for that must-have piece. Surprisingly, prices are not sky high.

GOON PACK Map p74   Local Designer Wear
☎ 604-602-8119; 109 W Cordova St; Ⓜ Waterfront
This fantastically eclectic gallery and clothing store offers regular art shows where you can meet the local hipsters. It also showcases some of the city's best, under-the-radar designers on its racks. Look out for duds by Evolt and Paper Bird and check out the unique hoodies and graphic T-shirts that will make everyone back home eternally jealous.

HUNT & GATHER Map p74   Local Designer Wear
☎ 604-633-9559; 225 Carrall St; Ⓜ Waterfront
A crisp white interior showcases the in-house-designed handmade clothing, bags and accessories here as if they are artworks. Some of them are, including a clutch of elegant classics that will likely become mainstays of your wardrobe for years. It's making waves across North America, despite its humble size and location.

NEW WORLD DESIGNS
Map p74   Local Designer Wear
☎ 604-687-3443; 306 W Cordova St; Ⓜ Waterfront
Gothic fetishwear shares rack space with Renaissance ball gowns and brocade corsets here, all of which are a pretty tight squeeze to fit into. Less confining but still a conversation piece are the velvet capes and square-toed witch shoes. Each item of clothing is handmade by the designer-owner.

CANNABIS CULTURE HEADQUARTERS
Map p74   Specialty
☎ 604-682-1172; www.bcmarijuanaparty.ca; 307 W Hastings St; ☯ 10am-7pm Mon-Thu, to 8pm Fri & Sat, noon-6pm Sun; ⊜ 8
For strong arguments in support of legalization, duck into the shop and offices of the BC Marijuana Party, in an area of town that's still known nostalgically as 'Vansterdam.' With books, hemp clothing and associated paraphernalia, this storefront also houses the Vapour Lounge, where you can chill out with some like-minded new buddies.

DELUXE JUNK Map p74   Vintage Clothing
☎ 604-685-4871; 310 W Cordova St; Ⓜ Waterfront
From Victorian-style lace-up boots to a jaunty beret to that rhinestone stick pin you've been coveting – it's all on the racks at this consignment clothing store, as are contemporary skirts, blouses and jeans. Prices slip the longer the items remain on the shelves. A browser's paradise.

CHINATOWN

Chinatown is more a visual experience for most visitors (there are not many other places where you can peer into buckets of live frogs and at teetering pyramids of dried fish), so an hour or two is all you'll need to hit the main drags of Pender and Keefer Sts. The night market is the best time to visit, if you're short on time. Along with these traditional businesses, an intriguing clutch of new shops is emerging between Gastown and Chinatown along both Pender and Columbia Sts. Generally run by younger entrepreneurs, these are among the hippest stores in the city.

CHINATOWN NIGHT MARKET
Map p77   Market
☎ 604-682-8998; 100-200 Keefer St; ☯ 6:30-11pm Fri-Sun mid-May–mid-Sep; ⊜ 3
Smaller but less frenetic than its Richmond brother (p117), this colorful downtown bazaar lures with its sensory combination of cheap trinkets, knock-off designer goods and aromatic hawker food – it's like a walk-through buffet of noodles, fish balls and bubble tea. There's a live music stage on most nights and, once the sun sets and all you can hear are Chinese voices, it's not hard to imagine yourself in Hong Kong. Order a fresh coconut (plus a straw) and you'll fit right in.

NOT YOUR USUAL STREET MARKET

Modeled on London street markets (but sensibly held indoors), the monthly Portobello West (off Map p81; www .portobellowest.com; Rocky Mountaineer Station, 1755 Cottrell St; ☺ noon-7pm last Sun of month; Ⓜ Main St-Science World), near Chinatown, was the city's first arts and fashion market when it launched to a rapturous reception in 2006. Now established and attracting new vendors all the time, the market allows dozens of local artists and artisans to sell their creations direct to the public. The prices are reasonable – no one wants to give away their work here – and you'll find an amazing selection that can include hand-painted boots, striking original paintings, unique ceramics and just about everything else inbetween. Colonizing a high-ceilinged railway station building, the market usually has a party atmosphere, as DJs spin their stuff in the corner and food vendors give you something to munch on while you peruse the goods.

To get here from the Main St–Science World SkyTrain station, walk east along Terminal Ave to Cottrell St. Turn right and the station building is just ahead of you. Alternatively, the market runs a free shuttle bus from the corner of Station St and Terminal Ave (in front of Cloverdale Paints) every 20 minutes for the duration of the market.

FUNHAUSER Map p77 · Specialty
☎ 604-681-8224; 35 E Pender St; 🚍 19
If you need a break from the area's noisy Chinese grocery stores, nip into this kitsch-arama of all things pop culture, where you'll find those must-have tiki mugs, wind-up metal robots and cheetah-print fez hats that no discerning individual should be without. An ideal place to pick up some confusing souvenirs for your friends back home.

TEN LEE HONG ENTERPRISES
Map p77 · Specialty
☎ 604-689-7598; 500 Main St; ☺ 9:45am-6pm; 🚍 3
This authentic Chinese tea and herb shop is a great place to buy supplies of good green, red, white and black teas. The friendly staff – women in cool pink pantsuits – are used to dealing with curious Westerners: they'll instruct you in the art of how to brew and will also serve you samples so you can find your favorite tea.

WANTED – LOST FOUND CANADIAN
Map p77 · Specialty
☎ 604-633-0178; 436 Columbia St; 🚍 19
Nestled in a returning heritage area that was a no-go skid row until recent years, this pioneering shop is like a general store of clever recycling. Old blankets, beach glass and driftwood are among the raw materials that have been cleaned and re-purposed into new patchwork bags, fluffy cushions and cuddly toys, while newspapers found under the floorboards have been transformed into greetings cards. Highly recommended.

SOMA

Lining the stretch along Main St between 20th and 29th Aves, SoMa has a shopping appeal that lies in its unique, independent clothing and jewelry boutiques. Many of these boutiques showcase the exciting creative skills of hot local designers who are fuelling the renaissance of an area once known for little more than its grungy, down-at-heel appearance. This is also a great place to hang out if you want to meet the city's coolest residents – and pick up their fashion sense. If you fancy a break, there are plenty of eclectic coffeehouses and quirky eateries lining the streets.

Just to the west of Main St, the 100-block of W Broadway is 'fleece central' for outdoor-equipment enthusiasts, with more than a dozen pertinent stores.

MODERN TIMES ANTIQUES
Map p81 · Antiques & Collectibles
☎ 604-875-1057; 4260 Main St; 🚍 3
The assortment of furniture, lamps and mirrors is as dichotomous as the name. It's got a bit of everything – old and new, local and global (particularly items from Thailand and Indonesia), Buddhas and Bugs Bunny collectibles. The kind of place you'll find a great stained-glass window that won't fit in your suitcase, it's one of several antique stores lining the 'Antiques Row' section of Main St.

PETRI DISH Map p81 · Arts & Crafts
☎ 604-876-3060; 42 Kingsway; 🚍 3
If you want to pick up a quirky reminder of your time in Vancouver, drop by this eclectic arts and crafts store stuffed with exquisite

WORTH THE TRIP: RICHMOND NIGHT MARKET

Much bigger than Vancouver's Chinatown version (p115), the summertime Richmond Night Market (Map pp44–5; ☎ 604-244-8448; www.richmondnightmarket.com; 12631 Vulcan Way, Richmond; ⌚ 7pm-midnight Fri & Sat, 7-11pm Sun mid-May–mid-Oct) has 350 vendors, who together offer a glimpse of what clamorous Hong Kong–style bazaars are all about. Don't eat anything before arriving and you can taste trip among the 65 food stalls, which offer steaming savory treats such as fish balls, shrimp dumplings, vegetarian *gyoza* (fried Japanese dumplings) and grilled squid. Most dishes cost from $2.50 to $4.

For dessert, drop by one of the Korean stands and watch the staff make Dragon's Beard Candy, then take some with you as you amble around the remainder of the market – rows of neon-lit stalls hawking everything from NYPD dog outfits to glow-in-the-dark singing roosters and reproduction Samurai swords. There's also a fair smattering of fake 'designer' goods – mostly handbags and Bape hoodies – and a few stalls selling Ultra Man collectibles (hence the giant figure of the man himself looming over proceedings).

If you've had your fill of kitsch, there's also a live stage where dance clubs and enthusiastic amateurs strut their stuff: expect to be subjected to some caterwauling karaoke performances if you stick around too long. Even if you don't buy anything, the market is a colorful, sense-pricking place to browse for an hour or two and will likely be a highlight of your BC trip. At the time of research, organizers were considering moving to a new location, so check the website for updates before you set off.

If you're coming by bus from downtown Vancouver, take the 98 B-Line south to Richmond and transfer at Capstan Way to the 407 Bridgeport. If you're driving, head south from Vancouver on Knight St, take the Knight St Bridge and turn right onto Bridgeport Rd once you hit Richmond. Head toward the giant IKEA store and you'll start to see the crowds.

but generally inexpensive creations by local artists. There's an ever-changing selection but items can include treasures such as painted tea bags or collage greeting cards, as well as small but lovable original paintings for less than $50.

EUGENE CHOO Map p81 Local Designer Wear
☎ 604-873-8874; 3683 Main St; 🚍 3
Behind the double-fronted, blue-painted exterior of this Main St favorite beats the heart of a store that reflects the emergence of this area as Vancouver's hip clothing capital. Once a grungy vintage clothing shop, it's now a hotbed of local designer duds for the city's pale and interesting slim-fit set.

MOTHERLAND Map p81 Local Designer Wear
☎ 604-876-3426; 2539 Main St; 🚍 3
Selling cute art-house designer wear for bright young things, Motherland defines Main St's emergence as a fashion center. The clothes – quirky skirts, pants and Ts – are Canadian designed, in-house-made, and well-priced enough that even those on student loans can afford them.

SMOKING LILY Map p81 Local Designer Wear
☎ 604-873-5459; 3634 Main St; 🚍 3
Quirky art-student cool is the approach at this SoMa store, where skirts, belts and halter tops are whimsically accented with

prints of ants, skulls or the periodic table. Men's clothing is slowly creeping into the mix, with some fish, skull and bird-sketch T-shirts available. It's a fun spot to browse and the staff are friendly and chatty.

RED CAT RECORDS off Map p81 Music
☎ 604-708-7422; www.redcat.ca; 4307 Main St; 🚍 3
The best record store in town to dip into the local scene, Red Cat is owned and operated by Buttless Chaps lead singer Dave Gowans (see the boxed text, p28). The store is packed with rare and local CDs and vinyl, and Gowans is often on hand to give you a few pointers on who to see live (and where). At the time of research, he was considering relocating, so check the shop's website for the latest info.

EUROPE BOUND OUTFITTERS
Map p81 Outdoor Equipment
☎ 604-874-7456; 195 W Broadway; 🚍 9
Among the plethora of outdoor stores clustering for economic warmth around the nearby MEC campfire, Europe Bound offers a more branded approach to its selection, including reliable labels such as Columbia, North Face and Canada Goose. Whether you're looking for winter jackets, hydration daypacks, cycling accessories, maps or travel guidebooks, you'll find most of it here.

SHOPPING SOMA

top picks

INDEPENDENT DESIGNER WEAR

- Goon Pack (p115)
- Hunt & Gather (p115)
- Smoking Lily (p117)
- New World Designs (p115)
- Eugene Choo (p117)

MOUNTAIN EQUIPMENT CO-OP

Map p81   Outdoor Equipment

☎ 604-872-7858; www.mec.ca; 130 W Broadway;
☺ 10am-7pm Mon-Wed, 10am-9pm Thu & Fri,
9am-6pm Sat, 11am-5pm Sun; 🚌 9

The granddaddy of outdoor stores, where
grown hikers have been known to weep
at the amazing selection of own-brand
clothing, kayaks, sleeping bags and clever
camping gadgets, MEC has been turning
campers into fully-fledged outdoor enthusiasts for years. You'll have to be a lifetime
member to buy here, but that's easy to
arrange and only costs $5.

REGIONAL ASSEMBLY OF TEXT

Map p81   Specialty

☎ 604-877-2247; www.assembleyoftext.com;
3934 Main St; 🚌 3

This quirky stationery store brims with handmade journals, T-shirts and lexicographical
paraphernalia – the staff might even let you
try one of their vintage typewriters if you
ask nicely. You can join the hipsters for a
monthly letter-writing club (7pm, first Thursday of every month), complete with stationery, tea, cookies and encouragement.

BURCU'S ANGELS Map p81   Vintage Clothing

☎ 604-874-9773; 2535 Main St; 🚌 3

This outrageous place has been known to
rent out its vintage stock to visiting film
crews. It's best known for its collection of
'70s clothing, but there's also a fascinating
selection from the turn of the century to
the 1950s. Consider donating to the '24-
hour free box,' where donated clothes are
left outside for anyone who needs them.

LEGENDS RETRO FASHION

Map p81   Vintage Clothing

☎ 604-875-0621; 4366 Main St; ☺ 11am-5:30pm
Mon-Sat, noon-5pm Sun; 🚌 3

Nestled among antique shops, racks of
elegant clothes from decades past are
sold along with one-of-a-kind hats and
rhinestone jewelry here. Legends has been
around for 20-plus years and has earned its
reputation for having merchandise in
excellent condition.

COMMERCIAL DRIVE

Like a counterculture department store
stretched along both sides of one street, the
Drive is Vancouver's 'anti Robson.' You'll find
17 blocks of eclectic, independent shopping
here, ranging from ethical clothing stores to in-
telligent-minded bookshops. If the area sounds
a little too earnest, keep in mind that Commercial also has plenty of frivolous shopping outlets
where you can pick up handmade chocolates
and pop-culture gifts for your friends back
home. Coffee-shop central (see p154), the Drive
is a great place to shop and sup.

MAGPIE MAGAZINE GALLERY

Map p84   Books & Magazines

☎ 604-253-6666; 1319 Commercial Dr; 🚌 20

Regularly voted among Vancouver's best
magazine stores, Magpie's 2000 titles certainly represent the city's largest and most
varied selection. Prepare for a squeeze
while perusing the narrow aisles, and make
sure you hit the back of the store where a
small selection of discount art, philosophy
and fiction books waits to lure you further.

DUTCH GIRL CHOCOLATES

Map p84   Candy

☎ 604-251-3221; 1002 Commercial Dr; 🚌 20

No one would begrudge you a little
chocolate-flavored R&R after you've been
trawling the sights of the city all day. Nip
into this oasis of chocolatey calm and you'll
be treated to melt-in-your-mouth handmade Belgian confections and more than
70 different types of imported licorice. Only
the brave should mix them.

HT NATURALS Map p84   Clothing

☎ 604-255-5005; 1307 Venables St; 🚌 20

Specializing in sustainable clothing that's
affordable rather than priced for the rich, HT
sells men's and women's T-shirts, hoodies,
pants and tops (expect to pay from $20 to
$60) of the classic, everyday variety. Items
are often made from soy, hemp or organic
cotton blended with bamboo. The hot item

is the Beunostyle ladies' underwear range printed with the phrase 'Eat Organic.'

KALENA'S Map p84 _Shoes_
☎ 604-255-3727; 1526 Commercial Dr; 🚇 20
True to East Van's Italian heritage, Kalena's imports handsome leather shoes and boots from the old country. Men's and women's styles can be had for reasonable prices and there's also a big area devoted to sale items. This is the kind of place where you'll pick up a pair of brogues that'll last you forever.

DREAM DESIGNS Map p84 _Specialty_
☎ 604-254-5012; 956 Commercial Dr; 🚇 20
Visiting greenies will enjoy dipping into this small organic store that sells everything from yoga knickknacks to linen pajamas and hemp bed sheets. Check out the local pottery selection and enjoy a calming chat with the staff about your favorite natural spa treatments.

WOMYNS' WARE Map p84 _Specialty_
☎ 604-254-2543; www.womynsware.com; 896 Commercial Dr; 🚇 20
The female staff at this low-key, couple-friendly shop, which carries one of North America's largest selections of women's sex toys, are happy to explain the workings of the family jewels' harness or nun's habit

flogger. In homage to the 2010 Olympic and Paralympic Winter Games, the store is selling a special edition ring-a-ding in blue, gold, black, green or red. Fair trade committed.

URBAN EMPIRE Map p84 _Toys & Collectibles_
☎ 604-254-4700; 1108 Commercial Dr; 🚇 20
This wacky, all-out, kitsch trinket shop is just the kind of place you can pick up that Crazy Cat Lady action figure you've always wanted. Other must-haves include taste-free nihilist chewing gum and Bill Clinton condoms. Beware: the longer you browse the more you will buy.

VIRGIN MARY'S Map p84 _Vintage Clothing_
☎ 604-844-7848; 1035 Commercial Dr; 🚇 20
Pleasantly jumbled Virgin Mary's carries vintage clothes dating from the 1950s. New and used fashions run the gamut from burlesque-influenced items (such as pasties and bloomers) to 1970s iron-on T-shirts. It's highly browsable; make sure there's room in your suitcase before you go mad with the credit cards.

GRANVILLE ISLAND
Awash with studios where artisans throw clay, blow glass and silversmith jewelry, Granville Island can easily keep you and your wallet

---

FIRST NATIONS ARTS & CRAFTS

Greater Vancouver shops and galleries sell a vast range of First Nations art – everything from tourist kitsch to the very finest in contemporary and traditional designs. For help in determining quality, authenticity and fair costs, read _A Guide to Buying Contemporary Northwest Coast Indian Arts_ by Karen Duffek, available at the Museum of Anthropology (p99). If you're looking for an authentic artwork, buy only from one of the city's established First Nations galleries. But if you're just looking for a unique souvenir, barter with one of the carvers who hang around outside the Vancouver Art Gallery on sunny summer afternoons.

Prominent symbolism used by northwest nations features ravens, killer whales and other powerful mythological animal heroes. These animals appear on masks, ceremonial bowls and tapestries, in wood, stone and bone carvings, and in bright primary-color paintings on paper. You can often buy high-quality prints of the latter, a more affordable option than buying masks or carvings.

Chiefs' 'talking sticks' resemble small totems or are carved with a single family crest, while abstract interpretations of traditional weaving spindles appear in glass works and paintings. Masterful _kerfed_ (or bentwood) boxes are handcrafted by steaming and bending a single wooden plank at three corners, then sealing the box with a watertight joint. Small carvings in argillite (black slate) are produced exclusively by the Haida people of the Queen Charlotte Islands from a special quarry there.

Artists whose works are worth looking out for include Kaka Ashoona, Joe David, Beau Dick, Joy Hallauk, Judas Ooloolah, Kananginak Pootoogook, Bill Reid, Kov Takpaungai, Lucy Tasseor Tutsweetok and Oviloo Tunnillie. Keep your eyes open, too, for Inuit art, especially carvings of dancing polar bears and Inukshuk, human-shaped rock sculptures used as landmarks upon Canada's arctic tundra.

Gastown is a fertile place to begin exploring. Recommended shops in Vancouver include the Coastal Peoples Fine Arts Gallery (p114), Hill's Native Art (p114) and the excellent gift shop of the Museum of Anthropology (p99).

INSIDER'S GUIDE TO THE PUBLIC MARKET

The shopping highlight of any trip to Granville Island is the covered Granville Island Public Market (p86), a colorful cornucopia of delis, produce stalls and ever-changing arts and crafts stands that's worth an afternoon of anyone's time – especially if it's raining. But rather than just wandering aimlessly – not that's there's anything wrong with that – there are some highlights that should not be missed, particularly if you're looking for picnic fixings or searching for a souvenir of the region that isn't salmon or maple syrup.

If you know your Darjeeling from your Hawaiian Rooibos (or you want to learn), head to the Granville Island Tea Company, where 150 varieties are steeped and brewed on site. You can pull up a stool here and sample with the locals and chatty servers. If you're collecting goodies for an alfresco lunch later in the day, drop by Oyama Sausage Company, complete with dozens of smoked sausages and cured meats, and Dussa's Ham and Cheese, with 200 curdy treats and some mouth-melting cold cuts – the Island Ham is recommended. The perfect place to pick up a souvenir for a back-home foodie, Edible BC stocks hundreds of finger-licking products from the Okanagan, Fraser Valley and Vancouver Island. Along with wine and fresh produce, you'll be tempted by Thomas Haas cookies, sharp chili sauces and mason jars filled with wine-soaked cherries. Edible BC also runs fascinating tours (see the boxed text, p131) of the market.

occupied for a day. You'll find a surfeit of artisan studios and shopping nooks colonizing dozens of old industrial buildings – head to the Net Loft building, Railspur Alley or the Granville Island Public Market if you're lacking direction. Make sure you explore as much of the area as possible; duck down the back alleys where you can often see artisans at work in their studios (using the bridge as a landmark should prevent you from getting lost). Buskers hang out here on summer afternoons, making this by far the city's most convivial shopping area.

CIRCLE CRAFT Map p87   Arts & Crafts
☎ 604-669-8021; Net Loft, 1666 Johnston St; 🚍 50
This 30-plus-year-old cooperative hawks 100% BC arts and crafts, including sculptures from found objects, ceramics and sleek jewelry, with hand-sewn puppets and dolls thrown in (not literally) for good measure. Prices vary considerably but there's usually something here to suit most budgets.

CRAFTHOUSE Map p87   Arts & Crafts
☎ 604-687-7270; 1386 Cartwright St; 🚍 50
At this nonprofit gallery run by the Crafts Association of British Columbia (CABC), shelves hold everything from glass goblets and wooden boxes to silver bracelets and decorative paper – all produced by regional artisans, of course. The gallery also keeps schedules of provincial craft shows.

GALLERY OF BC CERAMICS
Map p87   Arts & Crafts
☎ 604-669-5645; 1359 Cartwright St; 🚍 50
The public face of the Potters Guild of BC runs exhibitions for member artists and

sells striking ceramic works, from functional bowls and cups to figurative sculpture, intricate jewelry and ritual objects of art. Artists range from Emily Carr grad newbies to potters with international reputations.

PAPER-YA Map p87   Arts & Crafts
☎ 604-684-2531; Net Loft, 1666 Johnston St; 🚍 50
If you thought stationery was just a pen and paper, think again at this treasure trove of writing-related ephemera. Among the desirable items are cool journals, fountain pens, envelopes and greetings cards, as well as sheaves of breathtakingly beautiful *washi* paper. It's a store that makes you rue the day the internet was invented and long for the return of letter writing.

WOOD CO-OP Map p87   Arts & Crafts
☎ 604-408-2553; 1592 Johnston St; 🚍 50
The silky, highly strokable wood tables and chairs on display here may not be ideal for packing home, but it's hard not to appreciate the artisanship that's gone into their manufacture. Regional woods are often used and there's a striking modern feel to many of the pieces. It's branched out in recent years and now also offers wooden toys and kitchenware – much easier to pack.

SILK WEAVING STUDIO Map p87   Clothing
☎ 604-687-7455; 1551 Johnston St; 🚍 50
Weavers here turn out luxurious, hand-dyed silk dresses, blouses, scarves, shawls, lingerie, belts and hats in a rainbow of colors. Visitors are welcome to wander through the small waterfront studio and watch the weaving process in action. Silk yarns and fabrics are sold, too.

UMBRELLA SHOP Map p87   Specialty
☎ 604-697-0919; adjoining Kids Market, 1496 Cartwright St; 🚌 50
Often the only outdoor gear you need in Vancouver is a good brolly to fend off the torrential rain. This family-run company has just the thing, with hundreds of bright and breezy designs that should put a smile on the face of any drench-weary visitor. Duck inside, choose a great umbrella then launch yourself back into the tempest.

FAIRVIEW & SOUTH GRANVILLE

The main shopping action here is along South Granville. This includes the 'South Granville Rise' area of gallery shops between Granville Bridge and Broadway and the boutiques, homeware emporiums and specialist food stores that dot both sides of the street past Broadway.

BAU-XI GALLERY Map p91   Art
☎ 604-733-7011; 3045 Granville St; 🚌 10
One of the long-established galleries responsible for the city's artistic renaissance in recent years, Bau-xi – pronounced 'bo-she' – showcases the best in local artists and generally has prices to match its exalted position. The main gallery selection changes monthly and the focus is usually on original paintings, although prints, drawings and sculpture are also added to the mix on occasion.

EQUINOX GALLERY Map p91   Art
☎ 604-736-2405; 2321 Granville St; ⏰ 10am-5pm Tue-Sat; 🚌 10
Another veteran of the South Granville scene, the Equinox generally focuses on quality contemporary works from established Canadian and international artists. Some of the leading lights the gallery continues to represent are Jack Shadbolt, Fred Herzog and Liz Magor and, along with the canvasses, there's a commitment to sculpture and provocative installations.

PURDY'S CHOCOLATES Map p91   Candy
☎ 604-732-7003; 2705 Granville St; 🚌 10
Like a beacon to the weary, this purple-painted chocolate purveyor stands at the corner of Granville and W 11th Ave calling

top picks

GALLERIES
- Coastal Peoples Fine Arts Gallery (p114)
- Bau-Xi Gallery (left)
- Gallery of BC Ceramics (opposite)
- Equinox Gallery (left)
- Hill's Native Art (p114)

your name. It's a homegrown family business with outlets dotted like candy sprinkles across the city, and it's hard not to pick up a few treats for the road here. Among the favorites are the chocolate hedgehogs, peanut-butter daisies and sweet Georgia browns – roasted pecans wrapped in caramel and chocolate. Yum.

ZONDA NELLIS Map p91   Clothing
☎ 604-736-5668; 2203 Granville St; 🚌 10
Aretha Franklin and one of those princesses of Monaco are fans of this Vancouver designer's expensive hand-woven and hand-painted evening wear. Nellis is known for her ability to knead luxurious fabrics into simple styles. She also creates a line of accessories, including gold-embossed cushions, beaded necklaces and velvet scarves.

MEINHARDT FINE FOODS
Map p91   Food
☎ 604-732-4405; 3002 Granville St; ⏰ 8am-9pm Mon-Sat, 9am-9pm Sun; 🚌 10
There's a handy take-out service next door to this South Granville cuisine-lovers' paradise – the culinary equivalent of a sex shop for fine-food fans. Check out the narrow aisles of international condiments, then start building your ideal picnic from the impressive bread, cheese and cold cuts selection.

INTERNATIONAL TRAVEL MAPS & BOOKS Map p91   Specialty
☎ 604-879-3621; 530 W Broadway; 🚌 9
For maps, atlases, globes and guides covering nearly every region of the world, drop by this travel-lovers' favorite. It publishes 200 titles of its own and distributes 23,000 titles by other manufacturers. Ask the staff any geographic question and they'll be able to find the map to answer it.

RESTORATION HARDWARE

Map p91   Specialty

☎ 604-731-3918; 2555 Granville St; 🚌 10

Filled with furnishings and interior flourishes that you wish you had in your house and that won't easily fit in your suitcase, this yuppie favorite also carries a kitsch-tastic selection of reproduction toys and old-school gadgets from yesteryear. This is the place to pick up that kazoo you lost when you were six and that clockwork robot you stepped on when you were 10. And then there are the mini Swiss Army knives and hand-cranked radios to keep you busy…

KITSILANO

Though Kits has been well and truly gentrified for years now, a whiff of hippieness still lingers like the scent of patchouli. The neighborhood is rife with Birkenstock stores, hemp shops, crystal-swinging bookstores, yoga-wear retailers and socially conscious merchants, generously layered among the upscale clothing boutiques and homeware shops. W Broadway and W 4th Ave are the main commercial drags. The area makes for a pleasant afternoon stroll and the beach is always nearby if you'd like to discuss your purchases with the driftwood.

HOPE UNLIMITED Map pp94–5   Arts & Crafts

☎ 604-732-4438; 2206 W 4th Ave; 🚌 4

Hope Unlimited selects its giftware stock – beaded jewelry, candles, paper and more – based not only on its appeal, but also on its social and environmental impact. More than 75% of items are Canadian-made. The store donates 10% of its annual profits to charities, such as the YWCA, Children International and AIDS Vancouver.

TEN THOUSAND VILLAGES

Map pp94–5   Arts & Crafts

☎ 604-730-6831; 2909 W Broadway; 🚌 9

You'll find decorative paper from Bangladesh, baskets from Vietnam, hammocks, drums, clothing and other 'fairly traded' handicrafts from around the world. The store is part of a nonprofit program that buys from 120 artisan groups in 30 countries; outlets are located throughout North America.

BARBARA-JO'S BOOKS TO COOKS

Map pp94–5   Bookshop

☎ 604-688-6755; 1740 W 2nd Ave; 🚌 2

Epicureans salivate over more than 2500 food and wine books here, including out-of-print and specialty titles. The best part is the demonstration kitchen, where you can learn from new and notable chefs how to whip up the recipes they've written about. The shop also hosts a full menu of short cooking classes (see p229).

DUTHIE BOOKS Map pp94–5   Bookshop

☎ 604-732-5344; 2239 W 4th Ave; 🚌 4

Once a citywide chain, this independent homegrown bookseller retreated to this single outlet a few years back, but has retained a loyal following. It's a nice place to browse for an hour or two, there's a good selection of Canadiana, and the staff know a thing or two about what to recommend – unlike some ubiquitous chains we could mention.

KIDSBOOKS Map pp94–5   Bookshop

☎ 604-738-5335; 3083 W Broadway; 🚌 9

If you're wondering what your sprogs can read now that the Harry Potter series is over, bring them here. Like a theme park for bookish kids, this fantastic child-friendly store – Canada's biggest kids' bookshop – has thousands of novels, picture books, history titles and anything else you can think of to keep them quiet. There are also regular readings by visiting authors and a selection of quality toys and games.

TRAVEL BUG Map pp94–5   Bookshop

☎ 604-737-1122; 3065 W Broadway; 🚌 9

There's an extensive array of travel guides covering just about every corner of the globe here, plus a good selection of excellent travel literature for those who like to read about other people's epic journeys from the comfort of their armchair. Book launches and travel-related slide shows

top picks

BOOKSHOPS

- Travel Bug (above)
- KidsBooks (above)
- Biz Books (p114)
- Barbara-Jo's Books to Cooks (left)
- Book Warehouse (p112)

WORTH THE TRIP: RAINY-DAY SHOPPING

If the downpours are making you stir crazy and the shops in the hotel lobby are just not cutting it, leave your umbrella behind and head to BC's biggest shopping mall. An ever-expanding homage to materialism, the ginormous Metropolis at Metrotown (Map pp44–5; ☎ 604-438-4715; www.metropolisatmetrotown.com; 🕙 10am-9pm Mon-Fri, 9:30am-9pm Sat, 11am-6pm Sun; Ⓜ Metrotown) is the only shopping center you'll need to visit on this trip. Savvy shoppers arrive early in the morning to beat the crowds then rest their weary credit cards at the sprawling food court – Indian, Japanese and Chinese cuisines are recommended here. All the regular chain-store suspects are on site, as well as bookshops, cinemas, department stores and a large number of intriguing Chinese businesses clustered around the excellent Asian T&T supermarket. The mall is a 20-minute SkyTrain ride from downtown Vancouver – it's big enough to warrant its own station.

are regular events and there are racks of handy gadgets and accessories for serial trekkers.

HIGHEND ORGANICS Map pp94–5   Clothing
☎ 604-792-0022; 1838 W 4th Ave; 🚌 4
Carrying tons of hemp, recycled and organic fiber clothing, this counterculture favorite is also one of the only places in the city where you can buy the sought-after Blackspot sneakers produced by *Adbusters* magazine. Alongside the hoodies, Ts and pants, there's a head-spinning array of bongs, which should please the customs officers when they find one in your suitcase.

ZULU RECORDS Map pp94–5   Music
☎ 604-738-3232; 1972 W 4th Ave; 🕙 10:30am-7pm Mon-Wed, 10:30am-9pm Thu & Fri, 9:30am-6pm Sat, noon-6pm Sun; 🚌 4
Zulu is routinely voted Vancouver's best indie music store – visiting musos can happily spend a rainy afternoon here sifting the racks of new and used vinyl and hard-to-find imports while pretending they're in *High Fidelity*. Check out any of the 30,000 titles at the sweet listening booths with retro chairs. Zulu also sponsors and sells tickets to most of the hip shows that come to town – ask the staff for recommendations.

COAST MOUNTAIN SPORTS
Map pp94–5   Outdoor Equipment
☎ 604-731-6181; 2201 W 4th Ave; 🚌 4
This popular, mainstream outdoor super-store – the kind where SUV drivers shop – occupies the pricey, fashion end of hiking and biking gear and is the kind of place where you'll be tempted to add a matching top or shorts to your trail-boot purchase. End-of-season sales can be good here, if you don't mind wearing sandals

for that snowshoe trek you've arranged for later in the day.

GRAVITY POPE Map pp94–5   Shoes
☎ 604-731-7673; 2205 W 4th Ave; 🚌 4
This temple of great footwear is a dangerous place to come if you have a shoe fetish – best not to bring more than one credit card. Quality and fashion are the keys here and you can expect to slip into runners, boots and shoes by virtually every leading label and designer from Hugo Boss to Etnies to Stella McCartney. The sales are also great here. If you have any money left, head next door to its new branded clothing store.

ART OF LOVING Map pp94–5   Specialty
☎ 604-742-9988; www.theartofloving.ca; 1819 W 5th Ave; 🕙 10am-7pm Mon-Wed & Sat, 10am-10pm Thu & Fri, noon-7pm Sun; 🚌 2
Forget all those grubby sex shops lining the Granville St entertainment strip – this tasteful sex shop is for the nondirty Mac brigade. Among its popular products are the love swing (ask for a demo) and glow-in-the-dark condoms (don't ask for a demo). The store also hosts some entertaining and informative seminars, with titles such as the 'Joy of Flirting' and 'Kissing Class for Couples.'

PD'S HOT SHOP Map pp94–5   Specialty
☎ 604-739-7796; 2868 W 4th Ave; 🕙 noon-6pm Mon-Sat; 🚌 4
PD's sells its own Skull Skates brand of skateboards, snowboards, skimboards, BMX bikes and clothing. The company has been around forever – 'skating since you were swimming in dad's nutsack,' as the official motto goes. It remains *the* place for the boarding scene, and provides resources such as a skate-park directory and tidal-pool charts for skimboarding.

BLUELIST[1] (blu,list) *v.*
to recommend a travel experience.
What's your recommendation? www.lonelyplanet.com/bluelist

EATING

top picks

- **Raincity Grill** (p131)
- **Salt Tasting Room** (p135)
- **C Restaurant** (p127)
- **West** (p139)
- **Go Fish** (p139)
- **Bistrot Bistro** (p142)
- **Vij's** (p140)
- **Templeton** (p128)
- **Tojo's** (p140)
- **Glowbal Grill & Satay Bar** (p133)

EATING

Gourmet dining out in Vancouver – a culinary backwater for decades – used to involve a visit to national fast-food chain Tim Hortons and a sugar-rush box of 12 fresh donuts. Now jostling with Montréal and Toronto for the title of Canadian dine-out capital , the city has undergone a seismic epicurean shift in recent years, due to a couple of major dining movements that have driven adventurous locals to eat just about everything placed in front of them.

The first of these is the city's deep heritage of ethnic cuisines. Vancouver's neighborhoods are heaped with a vast smorgasbord of authentic and highly welcoming international eateries, originally developed to sustain immigrants salivating for a taste of home. Locals now happily taste-trip through France, Mexico, Africa, India and Italy, surrender to Southeast Asia, gorge on Malaysian curries and Chinese dim sum, and frequent the best array of sushi restaurants outside Japan.

Alongside this, West Coast cuisine – also called Pacific Northwest cuisine – has enjoyed a commendable renaissance. The tag was formerly just a fancy way of labeling a menu's salmon dish, but the movement has been fueled by sustainability demands and increasing calls for locally sourced food. Restaurants throughout the city are now foraging for suppliers who can bring them delectable taste-of-the-region ingredients such as Queen Charlotte Islands halibut, Tofino swimming scallops, Fraser Valley chicken and Salt Spring Island lamb – not to mention sweet heirloom tomatoes, juicy local blueberries and piquant regional cheeses.

Most exciting of all, these two dining movements have been rubbing fondly against each other in recent years. Vancouver has one of North America's best fusion dining scenes, meaning that modern French restaurants such as Lumière (p141) embrace Asian approaches to dishes, top-notch Indian eateries such as Vij's (p140) stir contemporary West Coast flavors into their mix, and high-end West Coast favorites such as Raincity Grill (p131) and West (p139) sprinkle their menus with international influences and knowing nods to the foodie approaches of other cultures.

For visitors, the selection can be bewildering – like stopping for lunch at a small café and being presented with a 50-page menu in small print – but the best way to approach what's on offer is to follow your nose around the neighborhoods. Top dining streets, where you can't throw a *kapamaki* without hitting a good eatery, include downtown's Robson St; the West End's Denman and Davie Sts; Yaletown's Hamilton St; Gastown's Carrall and Water Sts intersection; the Commercial Dr drag; and Kitsilano's W 4th Ave.

If the weather's fine, don't hesitate to eat alfresco. Vancouverites love to nosh outdoors amid their stunning environs, so patios and decks are widespread – many are heated and stay open throughout the year. Keep in mind that smoking isn't allowed in restaurants, even on patios. You could also pack your grub and have an impromptu picnic, with Stanley Park, Vanier Park and Kits Beach among the most popular spots.

You can pick up some takeout (or just keep your dining budget down) at some of Vancouver's best homegrown fast-food minichains. Check out branches of Flying Wedge for heaping pizza slices of the gourmet variety, Steamers for bulging burritos that manage to wrap an entire meal into a single roll, and White Spot, BC's own finger-licking burger chain.

Finally, it might be a good idea to do some homework before you start hungrily wandering the streets in search of food. Tap into the latest restaurant openings and reviews in the *Georgia Straight* and *Westender* or pick up a free copy of either *Eat Magazine* or *City Food*. Alternatively, go online and check out the up-to-the-minute Urban Diner blog (see the boxed text, p138).

OPENING HOURS

Restaurants in Vancouver are usually open for lunch from 11:30am to 2:30pm, and most serve dinner daily from 5pm to 9pm or 10pm (often later on weekends). Many also serve weekend brunch, usually from 11am to 3pm. For those that serve breakfast, the time is around 7:30am to 10am. If restaurants take a day off – and not many do – it's usually Monday. Some restaurants may close early or on additional days in winter, and stay open later in summer if there's enough hungry traffic wandering the streets. In the reviews following, only restaurants that deviate from these standard times have their opening hours noted.

BOOKING TABLES

As a general rule, the higher the prices on the menu, the more strongly reservations are advised. Without a reservation, try to show up for an early or late seating, say, before 5:30pm or just after 9pm. Downtown, Yale-town and Kitsilano are probably the most difficult neighborhoods to score an easy table at a high-end joint. Whichever posh spot you end up in, you won't need to dress up, as even the smartest restaurants adopt a fairly casual dress code – this is the fleece capital of the world, after all.

TAXES & TIPPING

Taxes are the only unpleasant taste on the dining scene here. Food gets hit with 5% goods and services tax (GST) and any alcohol on your bill gets whacked with an additional 10%. Then you need to add a tip – 15% of the pre-tax bill is the standard, 20% for exemplary service. So, for example, if you order a burger ($7) and beer ($3), you'll end up paying a total of $12.30 (50¢ GST plus 30¢ alcohol tax plus $1.50 tip). At cafés where you order at the counter, a tip jar will often be displayed prominently: you can drop some change in here if you feel it's warranted.

GROCERIES

The indoor Granville Island Public Market (p120) is as much a sightseeing experience as a destination for take-out meals, snacks and picnic goodies. For vegetarian and health-food eats, local chain Capers (Map pp66–7; ☎ 604-687-5288; 1675 Robson St; ☷ 8am-10pm; ☷ 5) stocks natural and organic foods – the handy wraps are a good take-out option. Small greengrocers also percolate Commercial Dr and the West End. If your recipe calls for more obscure ingredients – say frogs or a giant splayed pig – head to Chinatown. And, hmm, where to go for that $100 loaf of bread flown in fresh from Paris each morning? Yaletown, of course, at uber-upscale Urban Fare (Map p71; ☎ 604-975-7550; 177 Davie St; ☷ 6am-midnight; ☷ C23).

Excellent farmers markets, showcasing crisp seasonal produce and hearty local baking, can be found throughout the city in summer – see p142 for listings. And don't miss the Chinatown Night Market (p115) and much larger Richmond Night Market (p117) with their clamorous, lip-smacking hawker food outlets.

DOWNTOWN

You can't throw a donut in the downtown core without hitting a restaurant. While there are plenty of midrange options and a smattering of celebrity-fave high-end joints lining Robson St, there are also some rewarding ethnic eateries and a few quirky backstreet joints hidden slightly off the beaten path. Try the western end of Robson for Japanese and Korean diners and the grungy strip of Granville between Smithe and Davie for cheap greasy spoons and a clutch of laid-back, food-serving bars.

LE CROCODILE Map pp48–9 French $$$
☎ 604-669-4298; 909 Burrard St, entrance on Smithe St; mains $22-36; ☷ 2
Hidden along a side street in an unassuming building resembling a cast-off from a shopping mall, this surprising Parisian-style dining room is right up there with the city's top-end best. Instead of focusing on experimental shenanigans that only please its chefs, it has perfected a menu of classic French dishes, each prepared with consummate cooking skill. Try the braised veal shank with wild mushrooms, washed down with a smashing bottle from the mother country.

C RESTAURANT Map pp48–9 Seafood $$-$$$
☎ 604-681-1164; 1600 Howe St; mains $18-46; ☷ C21
This pioneering seafood restaurant overlooking False Creek isn't cheap – drop by for lunch if you want to budget a bit – but its revelatory approach to regional fish and shellfish makes it the city's best seafood dine-out. You'll be hard-pressed to find smoked salmon with cucumber jelly served anywhere else, but there's also a reverence for simple preparation that reveals the delicate flavors in dishes such as local side-stripe prawns and Queen Charlotte scallops.

METRO Map pp48–9 West Coast, Fusion $$-$$$
☎ 604-662-3463; 200 Burrard St; mains $18-30; ☷ 11am-10pm Mon-Fri; Ⓜ Waterfront

PRICE GUIDE

The following cost guide is used in this chapter's eating reviews:
$$$	over $25 per main dish
$$	$10 to $25 per main dish
$	under $10 per main dish

top picks

BRUNCH

- Sophie's Cosmic Café (p143)
- Templeton (right)
- Paul's Place Omelettery (p141)
- Fish House in Stanley Park (p130)
- Tomahawk Restaurant (p145)

This chic West Coast eatery – think stone-slab walls and polished wood floors – near the Touristinfo Centre offers a galloping romp through contemporary Canadian fusion cuisine. Its unusual pay-by-the-ounce approach to meat and fish can be pricey if you want to sample a few different flavors. If you're put off by the giant 50-item selection, head to the swanky oyster bar and shuck your way through a few, complemented by a fruity bottle of BC wine.

NU Map pp48–9   Fusion $$
☎ 604-646-4668; 1661 Granville St; mains $16-22; ☾ 11am-1am Mon-Fri, 10:30am-1am Sat, 10:30am-midnight Sun; 🚌 C21
Nestled under the north side of Granville Bridge, this swish eatery has the appearance of a decadent 1970s hotel bar – it's the perfect place to don your gold-colored cravat and velour smoking jacket. The menu is far from old-fashioned, though, combining a host of exciting, French-influenced tasting plates: highlights include tempura-battered olives and duck confit with liquefied foie gras. Don't forget to try a few cocktails, preferably on the lovely wraparound sunset-facing deck.

SANAFIR Map pp48–9   Middle Eastern $$
☎ 604-678-1049; 1026 Granville St; mains $14-20; ☾ 5pm-midnight; 🚌 4
A beacon among Granville St's grubby sex shops, this loungey, Bedouin-themed eatery is dripping with North African style. But it's not all about looks. The menu's small plates are designed for sharing and range from wine-braised short ribs to Indian-spiced scallops. Head to the decadent mezzanine level where you can lay down and feed like royalty. It's packed on weekend evenings, so you might have to sample a few cocktails at the bar as you await your table.

BIN 941 Map pp48–9   Fusion, Tapas $$
☎ 604-683-1246; 941 Davie St; dishes $9-15; ☾ 5pm-2am Mon-Sat, 5pm-midnight Sun; 🚌 6
Funky, bohemian and packed every evening, this late-night, cave-like nook is centered on a candelabra-lit tapas bar and lined with tiny tables. You'll get to know all about your neighbors as they chat noisily nearby. The food is all about hedonistic sampling and taste-tripping small plates – east-west crab cakes or slow-roasted pork tenderloin are recommended – and, like the restaurant itself, there's a small and quirky but perfectly formed wine list.

TEMPLETON Map pp48–9   Diner $-$$
☎ 604-685-4612; 1087 Granville St; mains $6-12; ☾ 9am-11pm Mon-Wed, 9am-1am Thu-Sun; 🚌 6
A funky chrome-and-vinyl '50s diner with a twist, Templeton chefs up plus-sized organic burgers, addictive fries, vegetarian quesadillas and perhaps the best hangover cure in town – try the 'Big Ass Breakfast' and you won't need to eat for days. Sadly, the mini jukeboxes on the tables don't work, but you can console yourself with a waistline-busting chocolate ice-cream float. Beer here is of the local microbrew variety – aka draft Russell Cream Ale.

LA BODEGA Map pp48–9   Tapas $-$$
☎ 604-684-8814; 1277 Howe St; mains $5-12; ☾ 4:30pm-midnight Mon-Fri, 5pm-midnight Sat, 5-11pm Sun; 🚌 4
It's all about the tasting plates at this country-style tapas bar, the most authentic Spanish restaurant in Vancouver. Pull up a chair, order a jug of sangria and decide on a few shareable treats from the extensive menu – if you're feeling spicy, the chorizo sausage hits the spot and the Spanish meatballs are justifiably popular. There's a great atmosphere here, so don't be

top picks

CHEAP EATS

- Go Fish (p139)
- Nuba (opposite)
- Asahi-Ya (p132)
- Belgian Fries (p138)
- Hawkers Delight (p137)

EATING DOWNTOWN

SCHOOL DINNERS

Vancouver is dripping with cooking schools charged with training the hot chefs of tomorrow. For travelers, this means a tasty clutch of training restaurants where you can support the students – don't forget to tip well – and enjoy a bargain gourmet meal. Top tables include the following:

- **Culinaria Restaurant** (Map pp48–9; ☎ 604-639-2055; 609 Granville St, downtown; mains $8-24; 🚌 6) The training restaurant for the Dubrulle Culinary Arts program, this heart-of-downtown dining spot focuses on fine West Coast cuisine. The menu changes weekly and if you don't want to gamble on dinner, the lunch menu is a good deal with gourmet sandwiches, pastas and salads for under $10.
- **JJ's Fine Dining** (Map pp48–9; ☎ 604-443-8479; 250 W Pender St, downtown; mains $7-22; 🚌 6) Lunch or dinner is only an hour long so arrive early at this windowless Vancouver Community College spot and you'll be treated to some excellent West Coast fare served by trainee staff genuinely aiming to please. The ever-changing dinner menu – expect favorites such as salmon and rack of lamb – is a steal at $21.50 for three courses. Lunches are mostly under $10 and Friday night is buffet night ($19.50).
- **Pacific Institute of Culinary Arts** (Map p87; ☎ 604-734-4488; 1505 W 2nd Ave, Granville Island; mains $15-22; 🚌 50) Well-executed West Coast fusion lunches and signature desserts – don't leave without trying a delicate pastry confection – are the menu mainstays at this school near the entrance to Granville Island. But the seafood buffet (lunch/dinner $24/36) is the main reason to come. Expect to un-notch your belt as you tuck into treats such as almond-crusted Arctic char and clams in lemongrass coconut broth.

surprised if you find yourself staying for more than a few hours.

ELBOW ROOM Map pp48–9   Comfort Food $
☎ 604-685-3628; 560 Davie St; mains $4-11; 🕒 8am-4pm; 🚌 C23

Expect some verbal sparring at this local hangout where the jokily abusive servers will greet you with the line 'Move your ass to the table,' then shimmy over to demand 'Are you ready to order, or what?' It's all meant warmly – if they don't insult you, they really don't like you – so make sure you give as good as you get. Breakfasts (including omelets, eggs Benny and 'big-ass pancakes') are legendary here, but the bulging burgers are excellent, too.

NUBA Map pp48–9   Middle Eastern $
☎ 778-371-3266; 1206 Seymour St; mains $4-10; 🕒 11am-10pm; 🚌 20

While the furniture looks like it came from a 1970s IKEA fire sale, the food at this funky Lebanese café, which attracts passing artists and bohemian hipsters in equal measure, more than makes up for it. If you're not sure what to go for, have the great-value falafel plate, heaped with hummus, tabbouleh, salad, pita and brown rice. It'll make you realize what wholesome, made-from-scratch food is supposed to taste like.

GORILLA FOOD Map pp48–9   Vegetarian $
☎ 604-722-2504; 422 Richards St; mains $4-7.50; 🕒 11am-6pm; 🚌 20

More guerrilla than gorilla, this tiny hole-in-the-wall take-out joint is a pilgrimage spot for raw-food devotees. It mimics the diet of its namesake, so nothing is cooked, leading to innovative treats such as crunchy lasagne (strips of zucchini substitute for pasta) and pizza made from a dehydrated seed crust and topped with tomato sauce, tenderized zucchini and mashed avocado. Save room for an icy almond shake dessert.

STANLEY PARK

If you haven't brought a picnic with you – the park has several welcoming beaches and wide grassy expanses made for alfresco noshing – Vancouver's verdant heart has four main dining options covering a range of budgets. There's also a handful of concession stands serving burgers, fries and ice cream. Wherever you dine, try for a window seat so you can enjoy a side dish of dense forest canopy or panoramic sea-to-sky views.

SEQUOIA GRILL Map p54   West Coast $$-$$$
☎ 604-669-3281, 800-280-9893; Ferguson Point; mains $18-40; 🚌 19

Formerly the old Teahouse, the cheery-chic Sequoia combines a bright-painted, artsy interior with a small menu of seasonal classics, often including favorites such as Cornish hen, pan-seared venison and maple-marinated wild BC salmon. Not quite as fashionable as other high-end city

top picks

CHEFS TO DINE FOR

Vancouver's leading chefs seem like a friendly bunch, but beneath those convivial exteriors resides the pure, naked hatred of mortal enemies...or maybe not. Either way, the city's restaurant resurgence in recent years has sparked a healthy competition between its culinary auteurs, creating an ideal climate for visiting gourmands. The top Vancouver chefs worth unleashing your credit cards for:

- The elder statesman of Vancouver's mania for seasonal regional ingredients is John Bishop, an unassuming perfectionist who has been sourcing and serving local scallops, Salt Spring Island lamb and succulent chanterelles for almost two decades. The ambience at Bishop's (p141) perfectly matches the man: warm, modest and sincere.

- A seafood-serving pioneer, Rob Clark has done more than anyone to bring BC's unique aquatic larder to local palates at his popular C Restaurant (p127). Encouraging diners to experiment with unfamiliar flavors and textures, he's a leading light of the Ocean Wise sustainable fishing initiative (see the boxed text, opposite).

- Not content with the success of his stylish, French-inspired Lumière (p141), Rob Feenie, the city's most famous chef, later opened Feenie's (p142), a gourmet faster-food joint, right next door. You have to be confident to name your high-end hot dog 'Feenie's Weenie,' but it's still the delicate innovations at Lumière that draw the serious acclaim. In late 2007 Feenie departed from these popular restaurants but many of the celebrated dishes he created remain. The jury is still out on how his absence from these two kitchens will affect diners.

- A Vancouverite who trained under Marco Pierre White and Raymond Blanc in the UK, David Hawksworth came home to West (p139) in 2000. His strategy of combining the best regional ingredients with surprising, cosmopolitan approaches soon paid off: West is a regular winner in local 'best Vancouver restaurant' polls.

- A colorful character, Hidekazu Tojo has been sharpening his sushi knives in Vancouver for 30 years, polishing his encyclopedic mastery of 2000 traditional Japanese recipes. Moving his landmark Tojo's (p140) restaurant to swanky new premises in 2006 enabled him to draw new plaudits and expand his already impressive sake menu.

restaurants, it nevertheless delivers well-executed contemporary fine dining – and beats the competition with its killer terrace views of English Bay.

FISH HOUSE IN STANLEY PARK

Map p54   Seafood $$-$$$

☎ 604-681-7275, 877-681-7275; 8901 Stanley Park Dr; mains $14-30; 🚍 19

It can be overrun with tourists in summer, but it's hard to blame them for dropping by here for the park's great dine-out views and some of the city's best seafood. The top-end menu changes seasonally, but regular favorites include cedar-planked trout and chili sablefish. There's also a popular fresh oyster bar that attracts in-the-know shuckers. Weekend brunch is a menu highlight: the salmon bagel Benedict is recommended.

PROSPECT POINT CAFÉ

Map p54   Comfort Food $$

☎ 604-669-2737; Stanley Park Dr; mains $13-22; 🚍 19

The highlight of this family restaurant–style eatery perched on a promontory in the center of the park is its views over the forest canopy and the Lions Gate Bridge – snag a patio seat to take full advantage of the vistas. Catering to the tour-bus groups that roll in here relentlessly through the summer, its menu covers the usual suspects from fish-and-chips to chicken linguine. A good fuel-up spot if you're walking around the park.

STANLEY'S PARK BAR & GRILL

Map p54   West Coast, Comfort Food $$

☎ 604-602-3088; 610 Pipeline Rd; mains $11-19; 🚍 19

Overlooking the gardens and close to the Malkin Bowl outdoor theater, this new casual bar and restaurant in the Tudor-style pavilion building has the park's biggest patio. The interior is all about rustic chic – think slate floors and chunky, polished-wood counters – and the menu is a smorgasbord of high-end comfort food such as prime rib burgers and salmon ciabattas. It's equally good for an end of day beer – the bar's regional microbrews include the recommended Red Truck Lager.

WEST END

You could eat out for weeks in the West End and never visit the same place twice. But it's not just the sheer number of restaurants sardined along the streets here that is impressive; the wide variety also makes this one of the city's best midrange dining 'hoods. Stroll along the

FISHING FOR SUSTAINABILITY

Stanley Park's **Vancouver Aquarium** (p52), in partnership with restaurants across the region, spearheads a conservation initiative called Ocean Wise (www.oceanwisecanada.org) that helps eateries and their customers make environmentally friendly menu choices. The aquarium casts its net over a wide range of scientific data then recommends sustainable seafood choices to member restaurants, helping to preserve stocks and ensure the fish and shellfish the restaurants source are caught in ways that minimize environmental impacts, thus ensuring the future health of the oceans. 'Sustainable harvesting, rather than simply depleting our seafood resources, is a major issue for all of us,' says Rob Clark, executive chef at C Restaurant (p127) and an early adopter of the initiative. Diners who want to support the movement can look for the organization's symbol on restaurant menus and check the Ocean Wise website for the latest list of local members.

Stanley Park end of Robson St for great Asian options, or amble up Denman St toward English Bay, where every other business is a restaurant. If you still haven't been tempted, walk along Davie St for some eclectic alternatives.

LE GAVROCHE Map pp66–7 French $$$
☎ 604-685-3924; 1616 Alberni St; mains $29-34; 🚍 5

Hidden along a residential side street, it's easy to overlook this smashing heritage-home restaurant that fuses West Coast ingredients with an array of classic and contemporary French approaches. Emphasizing *les fruits de mer* with unexpected flair – check out the Alaska black cod with burnt orange and anise sauce – it's a good choice for a romantic dinner. Wine lovers should also rejoice: there's a selection here that will have you crying with gratitude.

CINCIN Map pp66–7 Italian $$-$$$
☎ 604-688-7338; 1154 Robson St; mains $22-36; 🕓 5-11pm; 🚍 5

A favored haunt of Hollywood types, casual yet elegant CinCin is the restaurant where you're most likely to find yourself standing next to Robin Williams at the urinal. Don't let that put you off, though. The Tuscan-brushed seasonal menu often includes delectable Salt Spring Island mussels and tender Fraser Valley duck, while gourmet alder-smoked pizzas are another favorite – the wild salmon variety is recommended. There's also a tempting 800-bottle wine menu to keep you merry.

RAINCITY GRILL Map pp66–7 West Coast $$
☎ 604-685-7337; 1193 Denman St; mains $20-30; 🚍 5

Venerable but never blasé, this smashing English Bay restaurant was sourcing and serving unique BC ingredients long before the fashion for Fanny Bay oysters took hold.

It's a great showcase for fine West Coast cuisine; the weekend brunch here is a local legend, and the $30 three-course tasting menu served between 5pm and 6pm is an absolute bargain. If you're on the move, drop by the take-out window and pick up a gourmet $10 sandwich for your jaunt around nearby Stanley Park.

LIFT BAR & GRILL Map pp66–7 West Coast $$
☎ 604-689-5438; 333 Menchions Mews; mains $17-23; 🕓 11:30am-midnight Mon-Fri, 11am-midnight Sat & Sun; 🚍 5

Hanging over the seawall in Coal Harbour near Stanley Park, the swanky Lift serves unrivalled views of the verdant rainforest and mist-cloaked mountains from its wrap-around windows and heated deck. If you can pull yourself away from the vistas, dip into gourmet comfort dishes such as bison strip loin or prosciutto-wrapped salmon then sidle over to the shiny bar for martinis: ask for a Sticky Granny Smith if you dare.

ITALIAN KITCHEN Map pp66–7 Italian $$
☎ 604-687-2858; 1037 Alberni St; mains $15-26; 🕓 11am-10pm Mon-Sat, 4:30-10pm Sun; 🚍 2

Forget terra-cotta tiles and Tuscan color schemes, this is a swish, lounge-style Italian restaurant with a difference. Sit upstairs by

FOOD TRAIL

Epicurious food fans visiting Vancouver for the first time should consider one of the sensory trawls around the city offered by Granville Island's Edible BC (☎ 604-662-3606; www.edible-britishcolumbia .com; Granville Island Public Market; tours from $55). Its three-hour tours include chef-guided ambles around Chinatown, Commercial Dr, Granville Island or the Richmond Night Market, where you'll sample aplenty and learn about unfamiliar ingredients and cooking methods.

the window – open in summer – and tuck into a hearty, well-priced menu of gourmet Mediterranean comfort food. The pastas (crab ravioli is recommended) are perfect, but the antipasto sharing platter – a large dish of delectable finger foods such as tiger prawns, prosciutto-wrapped asparagus and dangerously addictive cheese-filled zucchini flowers – will have you singing an aria or two on your way out the door.

HAPA IZAKAYA Map pp66–7   Japanese $$
☎ 604-698-4272; 1479 Robson St; mains $15-22; ☷ 5:30pm-midnight Sun-Thu, 5:30pm-1am Fri & Sat; 🚍 5
If you think Japanese restaurants are all about sushi, drop by this popular reinvention of a Tokyo tapas bar. Within its cocoon-like windowless interior and black-on-black color scheme, you'll discover comfort-food treats such as steaming hot pots and beef skewers marinated in miso – all best washed down with an ice-cold Sapporo beer. You'll completely forget you're in Vancouver when you stumble out onto the street several hours later looking for the nearest karaoke bar.

SAMBA BRAZILIAN STEAKHOUSE
Map pp66–7   Steakhouse $$
☎ 604-683-2555; 1122 Alberni St; mains $13-25; 🚍 5
In a city with plenty of boring North American steak joints, this unusual subterranean gem is recommended, especially if you're a blood-sucking carnivore. Despite the uninspiring family-restaurant interior and large but oft-ignored salad bar, diners come here to gorge on meat, including beef, lamb and ostrich – all served in a kitschy manner from swords wielded by wandering waiters. It's all-you-can-eat and there's a regular side dish of Brazilian dancers on most evenings.

HAMBURGER MARY'S Map pp66–7 Diner $-$$
☎ 604-687-1293; 1202 Davie St; mains $7-12; ☷ 8am-3am Mon-Thu, 8am-4am Fri & Sat, 8am-2am Sun; 🚍 6
A colorful throwback to the days of chrome trim, jukeboxes and black-and-white checkerboard floors, Mary's is all about fab burgers and mondo milkshakes. The heaping all-day breakfasts and weekend brunches are something to write home about, too. If it's a fine day, you might have to wrestle the locals for a spot

on the people-watching patio. Consider dropping by after a pub night out: this is one of the city's best late-night hangouts.

ASAHI-YA Map pp66–7   Japanese $
☎ 604-688-8777; 1230 Robson St; mains $6-10; 🚍 5
You'll be rubbing shoulders with chatty Asian language students at this friendly and decidedly unpretentious Japanese diner – don't push too hard on the table dividers or they might tumble onto your neighbor's head. Good-value sushi and sashimi classics are fresh and well-presented, but it's the hearty cooked combo meals – especially the sizzling chicken teriyaki – that will bring you back for more. If it's crowded, there are several other good-value Japanese and Korean eateries dotted nearby.

YALETOWN

A favorite hangout for Vancouver's rich and beautiful people – if you really need to see a lap dog carried in a designer handbag, this is where it'll happen – Yaletown is great for a splurge-worthy dinner. Stroll along Hamilton and Mainland Sts and you and your gold credit card will be spoilt for choice. Luckily, style over substance is not the general rule here: even if you spend a little more than usual for your meal, it will be worth it.

BLUE WATER CAFÉ Map p71   Seafood $$$
☎ 604-688-8078; 1095 Hamilton St; mains $22-44; ☷ 5pm-midnight; 🚍 C23
This high-concept seafood restaurant is Vancouver's best posh oyster bar and the pinnacle of Yaletown fine dining. House

top picks

LOCAL EATS

If you're craving some local flavor, try the following restaurants that specialize in serving regional BC ingredients.
- Bishop's (p141)
- Raincity Grill (p131)
- Aurora Bistro (p136)
- Fuel (p141)
- Go Fish (p139)

music gently throbs through the brick-lined, cobalt-blue interior, while seafood towers grace the outdoor patio tables. If you feel like an adventure, head straight to the semicircular raw bar and watch the chef's whirling blades prepare delectable sushi and sashimi, served with the restaurant's signature soya-seaweed dipping sauce.

CIOPPINO'S MEDITERRANEAN GRILL
Map p71   Italian $$$
☎ 604-688-7466; 1133 Hamilton St; mains $20-40; 🚌 C23

Not your standard Italian joint, this fine Mediterranean eatery deploys the *cucina naturale* approach to cooking, which aims to reveal the delicate natural flavors of a range of regionally sourced ingredients. The warm wood and terra-cotta interior is the perfect setting in which to dip into West Coast dishes tweaked with Italian flourishes – try the marinated salmon with potato galette and sour cream – and the international wine list should keep you jolly all evening.

GOLDFISH PACIFIC KITCHEN
Map p71   Seafood $$
☎ 604-689-8318; 1118 Mainland St; mains $14-30; 🕒 4-11pm; 🚌 C23

Don't be blinded by the dazzling blue marble bar and bustling open kitchen at this swanky new joint; it's the menu that should catch your eye. Fusing West Coast seafood with gentle Asian nudges – delivering treats such as roast halibut with pea leaf and coconut pineapple sauce – this place is worth a night out if you're looking for an exciting alternative to the regular Pacific Northwest salmon dinner.

GLOWBAL GRILL & SATAY BAR
Map p71   Fusion $$
☎ 604-602-0835; 1079 Mainland St; mains $14-26; 🚌 C23

Casting a wide net that catches the power-lunch, after-work and late-night crowds, this hip but unpretentious joint has a comfortable, lounge-like feel. Its menu of classy dishes fuses West Coast ingredients with Asian and Mediterranean flourishes – the cheese tortellini with smoked chicken is ace and the finger-licking array of satay sticks is a recommended starter. Good-value lunch specials are offered daily ($10 to $12) and there's a smashing seafood-dominated weekend brunch menu.

top picks

SHARING PLATES

- Six Acres (p134)
- La Bodega (p128)
- Habit Lounge (p136)
- Nu (p128)
- Bin 941 (p128)

RODNEY'S OYSTER HOUSE
Map p71   Seafood $-$$
☎ 604-609-0080; 1228 Hamilton St; mains $9-23; 🕒 11am-midnight Mon-Sat, 3-9:30pm Sun; 🚌 C23

You'll find upwards of a dozen fresh oyster varieties being shucked before your eyes at this decidedly laid-back seafood joint for true bivalve fans. All are best washed down with a simple but effective cold-beer accompaniment and a noisy chat with your neighbors about the much posher places you could be eating at just along the street. On chilly days, the hearty chowders or steamed mussels are like manna from heaven.

GASTOWN

Vancouver's oldest neighborhood is back on the menu for foodie travelers. After years of offering no more than seedy pub dives and a smattering of boring tourist-trap eateries, the heritage buildings are coming back to life with some innovative lounge hangovers and convivial gourmet comfort-food haunts. Things are changing rapidly here, so keep your eyes peeled for regular new openings.

SOCIAL AT LE MAGASIN
Map p74   West Coast $$
☎ 604-669-4488; 332 Water St; mains $22-28; 🕒 11am-midnight Mon-Fri, 10:30am-midnight Sat, 10:30am-10pm Sun; Ⓜ Waterfront

The downstairs oyster bar will entice you through the door but the upstairs dining room, with its ornate tin ceiling, is worth the climb. It's recommended for brunch – try the duck confit eggs Benny – but is also a comfortable dinner spot, with West Coast specials including a mouthwatering lamb shank. If you're on the run, the on-site deli serves bulging gourmet sandwiches ($4 to $9) and heaping bowls of pulled pork chili ($4).

IRISH HEATHER Map p74 — Irish Pub $$

☎ 604-688-9779; 217 Carrall St; mains $14-16;
⏰ noon-midnight; 🚍 7

Vancouver's best traditional pub is also the city's only real exponent of the European gastropub movement, where great draft beers (in this case Guinness and Harp) are offered alongside gourmet comfort food. That explains dishes such as bangers'n'mash, made here with top-table pork sausages, pinot noir gravy and colcannon (a mouthwatering potato-and-cabbage mash). The Belgian-chocolate pâté is a naughtily decadent dessert, but hitting the back courtyard with a beer is also a good way to wind down after dinner. On our visit the Heather was planning a 2008 move immediately across the street.

CHILL WINSTON

Map p74 — West Coast, Fusion $$

☎ 604-288-9575; 3 Alexander St; mains $12-20;
⏰ noon-1am Wed-Sat, 11am-midnight Sun; 🚍 7

Sit on the sprawling patio and squint your eyes and you might almost be in Paris (you'll probably need to be a little merry with drink, too) at this leading exemplar of Gastown's new look. Inside, it's all polished wood floors, exposed brick and a fusion menu of house-smoked salmon and crispy crab cakes. A popular after-work hangout for local business-types, this is a chatty spot in which to line your stomach for a pub crawl.

ALIBI ROOM Map p74 — Comfort Food $$

☎ 604-623-3383; 157 Alexander St; mains $9-18;
⏰ 5pm-midnight Mon-Thu, 4:30pm-2am Fri, 10am-2am Sat & Sun; 🚍 7

Snake up past the Water and Carrall Sts intersection to find this convivial resto-lounge, where the design and film industry crowds congregate at long tables and share comfort food and bitchy stories about work. It's a cozy place on a rainy day – trains rattle forlornly past the windows to remind you of the outside world – and the nosh here includes classics with a twist, such as vegetarian meatloaf with sweet potato mash and macaroni and cheese tossed in crab-and-shrimp cream.

SIX ACRES Map p74 — Comfort Food, Fusion $-$$

☎ 604-488-0110; 203 Carrall St; mains $9-13;
⏰ noon-midnight Tue-Thu, noon-1am Fri & Sat;
🚍 7

This buzzy, brick-lined nook next to the 'Gassy Jack' statue is an ideal spot for hanging out with friends over a plate of excellent grub. The problem is choosing what to have, since the menu – presented to you in an old book cover – includes fusion platters of maple-smoked salmon, baba ghanoush and piquant international cheeses. The Berlin – farmers sausage, havarti, smoked gouda and piping-hot bread – is recommended, washed down with a lip-smacking local beer.

FESTIVAL MENU

Vancouver bulges like an overstuffed sushi roll with events for food and wine nuts. Time your trip right and you can add some enjoyable waist-expanding experiences to your visit.

If you're here in winter, make room for Dine Out Vancouver (p12), when the city's top restaurants offer two- or three-course tasting menus for $15, $20 or $25. There's a similar but more localized event in October called Taste of Yaletown, which promotes that area's excellent dining options.

Lovers of all things foodie should also drop by the annual Eat Vancouver (www.eat-vancouver.com) festival at BC Place Stadium. Western Canada's largest food and cooking event, the three-day extravaganza held in mid-May is dripping with culinary demonstrations, celebrity chef appearances and a tasting area where the city's leading restaurants ply their wares.

If you're more a fan of liquid lunches, stagger into town for the Vancouver Playhouse International Wine Festival (p13), where neophytes and tipple snobs can rub shoulders and pretend they're not getting drunk.

If BC's cornucopia of regional produce intrigues, check into the annual, one-day Feast of Fields (www.feastoffields.com) event held in early September, where great local chefs take over a farm to prepare fresh, finger-licking dishes. The event highlights the importance of regional suppliers and sustainable farming and the $75 entry ticket includes enough food, wine and beer samples to keep you full for days.

If that ticket price seems a bit steep, try the weekend Apple Festival (www.ubcbotanicalgarden.org/events; adult/child $2/free) at UBC in mid-October instead. It's a chance to sample as many seedy treats as you can cram in your mouth, ranging from regional favorites such as Spartan and Macintosh to unusual heritage strains including Ambrosia and Grimes Golden. And, of course, there's the longest peel contest, with prizes for whoever can peel the longest unbroken apple skin.

SALT TASTING ROOM

Map p74   Comfort Food $-$$

☎ 604-633-1912; Blood Alley; mains $5-15;
☽ noon-midnight; 🚌 7

Located along a darkened nook off Carrall
St, this brick-lined wine bar and charcuterie
is a protein-lover's delight with a deceptively simple approach. Pull up a bar stool
at one of the two communal tables and
choose from the ever-changing blackboard
of cured meats and local cheeses, accom
panied by a glass or two of great wine.
The Tasting Plate ($15 for three meats or
cheeses plus tasty condiments) is recommended. Restoring the social aspect to
dining, the room is usually noisy with chat
by the end of the night.

THE MOUSE & THE BEAN CAFÉ

Map p74   Mexican $

☎ 604-633-1781; 207 W Hastings St; mains $4-12;
☽ noon-6pm Mon-Thu, noon-8pm Fri & Sat; 🚌 7

Tucked under the rust-colored heritage
Dominion Building is this great-value family-
run Mexican joint. Everything – including
the salsa and refried beans – is lovingly
made in-house and the prices are eye-
openingly low, which probably explains
why the floor is still unfinished concrete.
There are lots of vegetarian options – ask
the server at the counter for tips on what
to try. The feast-like Plato Mixteco is ideal if
you want to share.

CHINATOWN

Pender and Keefer Sts (between Columbia and
Gore Aves) are your best bet for an authentic
Chinese meal: you'll be rubbing shoulders
with chatty, dim sum–loving locals who have
been noshing here for years. Walk off your
lunch with a stroll around the colorful Chinatown streets, and maybe dip into a bakery for
an almond cookie or creamy chestnut roll
dessert. A few blocks east you'll find dirt-
cheap diners on rough-and-ready E Hastings
St – ideal if you don't mind walking past the
crack addicts.

WILD RICE Map p77   Asian, Fusion $$

☎ 604-642-2882; 117 W Pender St; mains $10-18;
🚌 4

East meets west here in a loungey,
minimalist reinvention of the traditional
Chinese restaurant. Fusing classic dishes
with unexpected culinary influences from

around the world – think tuna *tataki* (lightly
seared tuna) lettuce wraps or wild boar
with jasmine rice and plantain chips –
this is a popular late-night hangout on
weekends. Once you're done stuffing your
face, you can work your way through the
comprehensive martini list as you slide
gracefully off your chair.

HON'S WUN-TUN HOUSE

Map p77   Chinese $-$$

☎ 604-688-0871; 268 E Keefer St; mains $6-18; 🚌 3

Part of the city's favorite Chinese restaurant minichain, Hon's flagship Chinatown
branch is suffused with inviting cooking
smells and clamorously noisy diners. The
giant, 334-item menu ranges from satisfying dim sum brunches to steaming wonton

top picks

ASIAN DINING

- Tojo's (p140)
- Wild Rice (p135)
- Hon's Wun-Tun House (p135)
- Hapa Izakaya (p132)
- Noodle Box (p143)

soups, bobbing with juicy dumplings. For something different, try the congee rice porridge, a fancy-free soul-food dish that takes three hours to prepare and comes in seafood, chicken and beef varieties.

PHNOM PENH
Map p77   Cambodian, Vietnamese $-$$
☎ 604-682-5777; 244 E Georgia St; mains $6-15; 🕒 10am-9pm Mon-Thu, 10am-10pm Fri & Sat; 🚍 19
Arrive early or late because the lines can be long at this locals' favorite eatery. Eschewing the Chinese approach of the area's other restaurants, the dishes here are split between Cambodian and Vietnamese soul-food classics, such as spicy garlic crab, and prawn and sprout filled pancakes. Don't leave without sampling a steamed rice cake, stuffed with pork, shrimp, coconut and scallions, and washed down with an ice-cold bottle of Tsingtao. This is the kind of place that makes Vancouver Canada's most authentic ethnic food city.

NEW TOWN BAKERY & RESTAURANT
Map p77   Chinese $
☎ 604-662-3300; 158 E Pender St; dishes $5-9; 🕒 6:30am-8:30pm; 🚍 3
Arguably the area's best Chinese bakery, this old-school diner specializes in steam buns, Chinese pastries and dim sum, served from giant steamers on the counter. The warm, moist barbecue pork buns are the bakery's signature snack and they make an ideal takeout – there's not much of an ambience here, so there's no real reason to stick around. The buns also come in several vegetarian varieties.

SOMA

Renowned for its alt-shopping options, South Main is also sprouting adventurous new restaurants. Most are clustered at E Broadway and

further south around E King Edward Ave. Well beyond that, along Main St, from E 48th to E 51st Aves, lives the city's Punjabi Market area, where you'll find a plethora of cheap-and-cheerful all-you-can-eat Indian restaurants.

AURORA BISTRO Map p81   West Coast $$
☎ 604-873-9944; 2420 Main St; mains $14-26; 🕒 11am-2:30pm & 5:30-11pm Mon-Fri, 10am-2pm & 5:30-11pm Sat & Sun; 🚍 3
Many foodies come to SoMa for this bistro. Chef Jeff Van Geest takes the region's best seasonal ingredients and transforms them into instant favorites that would cost much more at more fancily located restaurants. Faves include cornmeal-crusted Fanny Bay oysters and a highly recommended wild maitake mushroom risotto. The BC-only wine selection is tip-top and the cheese dessert selection includes the Stilton-like McLennan Blue Capri goat cheese.

NYALA Map p81   African $$
☎ 604-876-9919; 4148 Main St; mains $9-18.50; 🚍 3
While the slow-cooked goat stew and *mafe* (a spicy Creole-style chicken dish with tomato, ochre and hot chili) are menu mainstays at this 20-year-old city favorite, the recently added vegetarian buffet is making waves among veggies and carnivores alike. Available thrice weekly for dinner ($18.50), it's a bargain $9.50 lunch (Tuesday to Sunday only) and includes stews, salads, tabbouleh and Ethiopian flat bread. Check out the colorful African décor and the traditional clay pots made by the owner.

HABIT LOUNGE Map p81   West Coast, Fusion $$
☎ 604-877-8582; 2160 Main St; mains $9-15; 🕒 5pm-1:30am Mon-Sat, 5-11pm Sun; 🚍 3
A smashing cafeteria-style dining room with a welcoming ambience and a knowing

top picks

INTERNATIONAL DINING

- Vij's (p140) Indian
- Nyala (above) African
- Italian Kitchen (p131) Italian
- La Bodega (p128) Spanish
- Le Gavroche (p131) French

TIPS FROM A LOCAL FOODIE

An interview with Stephen Wong, Vancouver food and wine writer.

How would you compare Vancouver's Asian dining scene to other cities in Canada? Favorably. Toronto is the only other city that rivals Vancouver in this regard.

How has the scene changed in recent years? Post-1997, the Chinese restaurant scene has plateaued and, debatably, been in decline. However, other Asian ethnic categories have grown in diversity – Thai, Malaysian/Indonesian, Indian, Nepalese, Filipino, Korean, a rash of Japanese-style *izakaya* (pubs serving food) and Vietnamese *pho* (noodle soup) houses.

If someone's not that familiar with Asian food, what kind of dishes should they sample first? Probably Chinese and Vietnamese. Chinese seafood dishes such as steamed or fried fish, fried crab or shrimp are quite accessible to most inexperienced diners. Vietnamese dishes such as grilled meat brochettes, lemongrass chicken or pork chops will please as well, as will the abundance of aromatic herbs and salads. Japanese restaurants can also be good bets.

In your opinion, what are some of the best Asian dishes to look out for in Vancouver? Steamed Alaskan king crab with minced garlic at any number of Chinese seafood restaurants; batter-fried sea bass (although it's not the most green dish in the world); garlic prawns or squid; chicken wonton soup etc.

Is there anything that very adventurous diners should try while they're here? Order a whole geoduck (large edible clam) and have it sashimi style and/or blanched in a hot pot.

There are lots of Chinese restaurants in the city. How can visitors choose a good one? Look for ones that are crowded with Chinese diners, trust the Chinese grapevine or just ask someone Chinese for recommendations.

What are the various types of Chinese cuisine on offer in the city? Mostly Cantonese, Mandarin/Northern, some Szechuan and some Shanghainese.

The night markets in Vancouver and Richmond are fun for foodies. What particular dishes should travelers try when they visit them? Street foods such as grilled squid, curried fish balls, egg puffs and rustic dim sum.

1980s feel – who knew that orange vinyl benches and minimalist artwork could be so cozy? – this is like a postmodern update of the classic neighborhood bar. Encouraging shared plate experimentation, the well-priced menu includes adventurous treats such as duck ragout, carrot and brie pierogies and pan-roasted halibut, served with broccolini and arugula pesto. Bring an innocent art-school date here and they may just decide to marry you.

ALL INDIA SWEETS & RESTAURANT
Map pp44–5   Indian $

☎ 604-327-0891; 6507 Main St; mains $7; 🚍 3

This is the best of the string of good-value Indian family restaurants lining Main St's Punjabi Market area, with a giant 45-item buffet of vegetarian and nonvegetarian dishes and a continually replenished supply of naan to soak up the sauces. The ambience – chipped 1980s tables and chairs – is nothing to write home about, but the welcome is warm and the food will fill you for a day. Check out the kaleidoscopic array of neon-hued sweets by the door and pick up some for the road.

FOUNDATION Map p81   Vegetarian $-$$

☎ 604-708-0881; 2301 Main St; mains $6-12;
🕐 5pm-1am; 🚍 3

Behind the windows that always seem to be covered in condensation, SoMa's liveliest hangout is a funky vegetarian (mostly vegan) restaurant; it's the kind of place where carefully tousled art students and young intellectuals like to be seen. To fuel all that brainpower, dishes include treats such as mango and coconut pasta and chunky heaps of cheesy nachos, while the beer comes from city fave Storm Brewing.

HAWKERS DELIGHT
Map p81   Malaysian, Singaporean $

☎ 604-709-8188; 4127 Main St; mains $4-6; 🚍 3

This unassuming Asian hole-in-the-wall is easy to miss, but it's worth retracing your steps for a taste of authentic Malaysian and Singaporean soul food, all made from scratch at this family-run favorite. Peruse the photo-menu, with dishes such as aromatic coconut milk curry or yellow noodles with tofu and spicy sweet potato sauce, then head straight to the counter to order. The dishes are super-cheap, making this one of the city's best and most enduring cheap eats.

COMMERCIAL DRIVE

The center of East Vancouver's eclectic dining scene, Commercial Dr – from Venables St to E 8th Ave – is a strollable smorgasbord of adventurous dining. Combining popular ethnic soul-food joints, chatty streetside cafés and the kind of effortlessly convivial pub-style hangouts that give the concept of 'neighborhood bar' a good name, this is the city's most sociable dine-out district. It's also Vancouver's patio capital, so if the weather's good head down here for an alfresco meal.

HAVANA Map p84   Latin, Fusion $$
☎ 604-253-9119; 1212 Commercial Dr; mains $10-20; 🚌 20
The granddaddy of dining on the Drive has still got it, hence its buzzing patio on most summer nights. It combines a rustic Latin American ambience with a roster of satisfying Afro-Cuban-southern soul-food dishes, with highlights ranging from yam fries to slow-roasted lamb curry and a satisfying platter of clams, mussels and oysters. Port, brandy and single malt lead the drink list. Arrive early to beat the crowds.

WAAZUBEE CAFÉ Map p84   Fusion $-$$
☎ 604-253-5299; 1622 Commercial Dr; mains $8-20; 🕑 11:30am-midnight; 🚌 20
One of the Drive's most popular hangouts, bohemian WaaZuBee outfits itself with huge painted murals, velvet curtains and recycled metal sculptures – check out that spoon chandelier. An equally eclectic menu (including plenty of vegetarian options) runs from sesame tuna sashimi to grilled portobello mushroom burgers and maple-soy wild salmon. There's also a good selection of regional beers.

CHARLATAN Map p84   Comfort Food $-$$
☎ 604-253-2777; 1446 Commercial Dr; mains $6-16; 🕑 11:30am-midnight; 🚌 20
Reflecting a recent drink-and-dine resurgence on the Drive, the old Bukowski's bar was transformed into this laid-back pub-style hangout, quickly embraced by the locals. Sports fans can perch at the bar under a flatscreen TV to catch a game; drinkers can hit the patio to watch the buzzing streetscape; and diners can chow down on quality comfort food such as crab cakes with avocado salsa and mussels in exotic broths.

CLOVE Map p84   Indian, Fusion $$
☎ 604-255-5550; 2054 Commercial Dr; mains $3-10; 🕑 5-10pm Mon-Thu, 5-10:30pm Fri & Sat, 5-9:30pm Sun; 🚌 20

This modern fusion reinvention of the Indian restaurant has a menu that mixes traditional approaches with a host of South Asian flourishes, creating an eclectic but fortuitous combination of flavors. You can start with a plate of delectable gyoza (fried Japanese dumplings) before moving on to an aromatic pad thai with prawns, followed by an unusual chai crème brûlée. The room is warm and intimate – you can hang out at the bar or canoodle at a little table – and martinis are a house specialty.

BELGIAN FRIES Map p84   Comfort Food $
☎ 604-253-4220; 1885 Commercial Dr; mains $3-6; 🚌 20
The concept is pure genius: take fresh-cut spuds, fry them, fry them again, toss, salt and serve in a paper funnel. You then dip the beauties into one of a dozen hot or cold mayo-based sauces, including wasabi, hot garlic, Jamaican heat and curry/chutney. What could be better? Beer, which you choose from the Storm brews on tap or the bottled Belgian lambics. Once you've had your fill of spuds and suds, finish yourself off with a deep-fried Mars bar.

GRANVILLE ISLAND
You could easily spend an entire day at this stroller's paradise – ambling around the artisan shops, dipping into the public market and stopping for a coffee overlooking False Creek. But Granville Island is also a sometimes overlooked dine-out haunt. Between catching a show at a theater or grabbing a beer at one of the area's

HOT BLOG

Vancouver's overheated dining scene seems to be ever changing, with new restaurants opening almost weekly. To keep up with the latest developments – and dip into the best gossip – visit Urban Diner (www.urbandiner.ca), Vancouver's best foodie blog. Here, the city's top restaurant reviewer, Andrew Morrison, gives his often irreverent take on area eateries, local chefs and larger-than-life restaurateurs, offering no-holds-barred reviews of new openings for those who want to find out what's hot and what's not before they decide on their dinner destination. The forum pages are often lively, and frequently include entries from chatty local chefs. You can also read Morrison's weekly restaurant column in the Westender newspaper.

bars, you should plan for a convivial meal here, ideally with a sunset view of Burrard Bridge and the shimmering False Creek waterfront.

SANDBAR Map p87
Seafood $$-$$$
☎ 604-669-9030; 1535 Johnston St; mains $18-35; 🚌 50
West Coast seafood heads the menu at this high-ceilinged restaurant-with-a-view under the iron arches of Granville Bridge. The fresh oysters rock and they're best sampled on the fireplace-warmed rooftop deck. The wine list is also something to write home about – there are 1800 bottles nestled in the cellar – but the urban professionals crowding the bar on weekends seem more interested in quaffing cocktails. Reservations recommended.

DOCKSIDE RESTAURANT
Map p87
West Coast $$
☎ 604-685-7070; 1253 Johnston St; mains $14-26; 🕑 7am-10pm; 🚌 50
Wood-grilled steaks, mint-crusted lamb and butter-soft wild salmon are the highlights at this genial dining room adjunct to the Granville Island Hotel (p196). But you can also kick back and enjoy a more casual (and less pricey) meal in the Dockside Brewing Company's (p154) microbrew lounge. Both wood-lined rooms have a warm ambience, and the shared waterfront patio becomes a noisy spot on some summer evenings.

BRIDGES Map p87
West Coast $$
☎ 604-687-4400; 1696 Duranleau St; mains $12-20; 🚌 50
You'll easily spot this bright yellow, shed-like bistro as you pass over the Granville Bridge on your way here. In summer it offers one of the best sunset patios in town from which to enjoy standard but well-executed classics such as chicken quesadillas, fish-and-chips and hearty thin-crust pizzas – the smoked salmon variety is recommended. Diners can also escape the patio clamor at the quieter, more upscale upstairs dining room, which serves a three-course fixed-price menu ($40).

GO FISH Map p91
Seafood $-$$
☎ 604-730-5040; 1505 W 1st Ave; mains $8-13; 🕑 11:30am-6:30pm Wed-Fri, noon-6:30pm Sat & Sun; 🚌 50
Nestled on the seawall between Granville Island and Vanier Park, this seafood shack

top picks

PATIOS

- Havana (opposite)
- Chill Winston (p134)
- Lift Bar & Grill (p131)
- Sequoia Grill (p129)
- Dockside Restaurant (left)

serves the city's best fish-and-chips, offering a choice of halibut, salmon or cod encased in crispy golden batter. The smashing (and lighter) fish tacos are also highly recommended, while the ever-changing daily specials – brought in by the nearby fishing boats – often include praise-worthy scallop burgers or ahi tuna sandwiches. There's not much of a seating area, so pack your grub and head to nearby Vanier Park for a picnic.

FAIRVIEW & SOUTH GRANVILLE

Bordered by SoMa to the east and Kitsilano to the west, the backbone of this area is Broadway, which is suffused with pockets of restaurants for much of its length. While many of these are of the cheap-and-cheerful neighborhood-eatery variety – you'll never have a problem finding budget noodleries and sushi joints here – there are some dining highlights that are worth getting off the bus for. Many of these cluster around the South Granville area that starts from the south side of the Granville Bridge.

WEST Map p91
West Coast $$$
☎ 604-738-8938; 2881 Granville St; mains $22-46; 🚌 10
This multi-award-winning favorite – a regular winner in local 'Restaurant of the Year' contests – combines crisp, friendly service with the kind of exquisite dishes that make you happy to unleash your credit card. While Pacific Northwest treats such as bison and pork cheeks are delicately prepared and architecturally presented, it's the seafood that wins the day: try the blackened lingcod with tiny chanterelles and you'll be in foodie heaven. Ask the waiters if you can try the sliding ladder attached to the wine shelves.

top picks

TAKE-OUTS

- Go Fish (p139)
- Social at Le Magasin (p133)
- Noodle Box (p143)
- Raincity Grill (p131)
- Vij's Rangoli (below)

SEASONS IN THE PARK
Map p91　　　　　　　　West Coast $$-$$$
☎ 604-874-8008, 800-632-9422; Queen Elizabeth Park, W 33rd Ave at Cambie St; mains $21-29; 🚌 15
After a trawl around the gardens of the Bloedel Floral Conservatory (p92), head to this old-school fine-dining joint, making sure your hilltop view overlooks the signature Vancouver vista of glass towers with mountain backdrop. Lucky diners with reservations (to get past the busloads of tourists) can feast on zesty Pacific Northwest cuisine, such as lemon herb-crusted lamb or wild mushroom ravioli. Save room for the delicious sunburned lemon pie.

VIJ'S Map p91　　　　　　　　　　Indian $$
☎ 604-736-6664; 1480 W 11th Ave; mains $20-26; 🕐 5:30-10pm; 🚌 10
Just off S Granville St, sleek modern Vij's is the high-water mark of contemporary East Indian cuisine, fusing regional ingredients, global flourishes and classic ethnic dishes to produce an array of innovative flavors. The unique and, judging by the queues, highly popular results range from wine-marinated 'lamb popsicles' to halibut, mussels and crab in a tomato-ginger curry. Reservations are not accepted, so if you don't want to line up, there's Rangoli, Vij's own take-out café next door.

TOJO'S Map p91　　　　　　　Japanese $$
☎ 604-872-8050; 1133 W Broadway; mains $19-26; 🕐 5-10pm Mon-Sat; 🚌 9
Hidekazu Tojo's legendary skill with the sushi knife has created Vancouver's most revered sushi restaurant. Among his exquisite dishes are favorites such as lightly steamed monkfish, sautéed halibut cheeks and fried red tuna wrapped with seaweed and served with plum sauce. Seats at the sushi bar are more sought-after than a couple of front-row Stanley Cup tickets, so reserve as early

as possible and celebrate with a selection or two from the sake menu.

FIGMINT Map p91　　　　　　European $$
☎ 604-875-3312; Plaza 500 Hotel, 500 W 12th Ave; mains $18-26; 🕐 7am-11pm; 🚌 15
With its Paul Smith–style striped banquettes and mod, lounge-lovers aesthetic, this hotel restaurant seems to have an identity problem: you'll find bemused middle-aged tourists wandering in from their rooms, as well as design fans trying to look hip while families duke it out across the aisle. It's best to drop by in the evening, when the place develops a cooler vibe. The menu is heavy on meat treats; the lamb with goat cheese and spinach is a standout.

OUISI BISTRO Map p91　　　　　　Cajun $$
☎ 604-732-7550; 3014 Granville St; mains $13-22; 🚌 10
The city's best New Orleans–style Creole and Cajun dine-out joint, this atmospheric eatery offers lip-smacking adventurous dishes such as habanero coconut chicken, marinated alligator and vegetarian étouffée. A large selection of single malts and bourbons complements the southern fare and there's regular live jazz to keep things smokin'. Drop by for weekend brunch and partake of a spicy fusion spin on traditional breakfast dishes.

BIN 942 Map p91　　　　　Fusion, Tapas $$
☎ 604-734-9421; 1521 W Broadway; mains $12-15; 🕐 5pm-2am; 🚌 9
This tiny but exceedingly cozy lounge is a convivial late-night hangout if you fancy a few dishes of food and a bottle or two of wine with chatty friends. Among the best 'tapatizers' are sashimi-style ahi tuna and portobello mushroom cutlets, which pair perfectly with a select array of good beers –

top picks

LATE-NIGHT DINING

- Naam (p142)
- Bin 942 (above)
- Hamburger Mary's (p132)
- Foundation (p137)
- Alibi Room (p134)

the Russell Brewing Cream Ale is best – and a compact but well-chosen wine list of Australian, Californian, European and BC tipples. Expect to stay for a few hours if you're in the mood for a relaxing wind-down.

SALADE DE FRUITS CAFÉ BISTRO
Map p91   French $$
☎ 604-714-5987; 1551 W 7th Ave; mains $9-20; ⏲ 10am-2:30pm & 5:30-10pm Tue-Sat; 🚍 10
The simple, well-prepared ethos that prevails here is deceptive: it looks like anyone could chef up that steamy pan of mussels with fries and mayo. Don't be fooled. It takes years of artful practice in French peasant cooking methods to make things look this easy. A real taste of the old country – the staff here chatter away in French to keep things authentic – this is an oasis of fine cooking at a bargain price. Cash only.

PAUL'S PLACE OMELETTERY
Map p91   Comfort Food $-$$
☎ 604-737-2857; 2211 Granville St; mains $7-12; ⏲ 7am-3pm; 🚍 10
You'll be jostling for space with strollers and chatty moms at this unassuming breakfast joint near the south side of Granville Bridge, but it's worth it: this place is far superior to most city bacon-and-egg spots. The menu is short and sweet, but it's grounded on 12 signature omelets, including a chockablock vegetarian option that will make carnivores eye you jealously. It's a great place to warm yourself up on a rainy Vancouver morning; there's also a lunch menu of hearty sandwiches.

KITSILANO
Kitsilano's two main arteries – W 4th Ave and W Broadway – offer a healthy mix of eateries, many of which are the best of their kind in the city: it's well worth the trek here to lounge on a beach or stroll the shopping areas then end your day with a rewarding meal. The neighborhood's hippie past has left a legacy of vegetarian restaurants, but Kits' more recent wealth means that there are also some top-notch high-end eateries well worth a splurge.

BISHOP'S Map pp94–5   West Coast $$$
☎ 604-738-2025; 2183 W 4th Ave; mains $28-38; 🚍 4
A pioneer of fine West Coast cuisine with international flourishes long before the fashion

for delectable local ingredients took hold, chef-owner John Bishop is still at the top of his game. Served in an elegant dining room lined with regional artworks, the weekly-changing menu can range from duck confit salad to steamed smoked sablefish and an addictive maple walnut tart. The service here is pitch-perfect and you can expect Bishop himself to wander over to welcome you.

FUEL Map pp94-5   West Coast $$$
☎ 604-288-7905; 1944 W 4th Ave; mains $27-34; 🚍 4
Despite the bland utilitarian name, this stylish Kits eatery sources exceptional regional ingredients and transforms them with a knowing cosmopolitan flair. Everything is seasonal, so expect regular menu changes – if you're lucky, the crispy rainbow trout with sidestripe shrimp ravioli will be available. If not, console yourself with some Okanagan cherry tart or a satisfying selection of tasty regional cheeses.

GASTROPOD Map pp94-5   European $$$
☎ 604-730-5579; 1938 W 4th Ave; mains $24-32; ⏲ noon-2:30pm & 5:30-10:30pm Wed-Sat, 5:30-10:30pm Sun-Tue; 🚍 4
Part of the new restaurant renaissance sweeping Kits, this striking, wood-lined contemporary dining room is the perfect setting for a modern, French-tweaked menu (expect salivating locals to eye you jealously through the floor-to-ceiling windows). With intriguing dishes such as wasabi-infused salmon and an oyster and horseradish 'snow' creation, the restaurant's three-course prix fixe ($45) dinner is a veritable bargain if you want to go the whole hog.

LUMIÈRE Map pp94-5   French $$-$$$
☎ 604-739-8185; 2551 W Broadway; mains $18-45; ⏲ 5:30-11pm Tue-Sun; 🚍 9
Rob Feenie – the city's most famous chef – created Lumière to serve a growing local demand for fine dining. While other restaurants have followed suit, and Feenie himself has now departed from the kitchen here, this is still one of the best dine-out options in Vancouver. Deceptively unfussy preparations are the order of the day, with French-inspired, Asian-brushed masterpieces such as sake and maple syrup–baked sablefish served amid contemporary-chic splendor. If you really want to push the boat out, loosen your belt, order some good wine and launch

FARMERS MARKETS

A tasty cornucopia of BC farm produce hits the stalls around Vancouver from June to October. Seasonal highlights include crunchy apples, lush peaches and juicy blueberries, while home-baked cakes and treats are frequent accompaniments. Don't be surprised to see zesty local cheese and a few arts and crafts added to the mix. To check out what's on offer, visit www.eatlocal.org.

East Vancouver Farmers Market (Map p84; ☎ 604-879-3276; Trout Lake Community Centre, E 15th Ave at Victoria Dr, Commercial Dr; ☼ 9am-2pm Sat mid-May–mid-Oct; ☐ 20)

Kitsilano Farmers Market (Map pp94–5; ☎ 604-879-3276; Kitsilano Community Centre, 2690 Larch St, Kitsilano; ☼ 10am-2pm Sun mid-Jul–mid-Oct; ☐ 4)

Riley Park Farmers Market (Map p91; ☎ 604-879-3276; Nat Bailey Stadium, Fairview; ☼ 1-6:30pm Wed mid-Jun–mid-Oct; ☐ 15)

UBC Farmers Market (Map p100; ☎ 604-822-5092; 6182 South Campus Rd, UBC; ☼ 9am-1pm Sat mid-Jun–Sep; ☐ 4)

West End Farmers Market (Map pp66–7; ☎ 604-879-3276; Nelson Park, btwn Bute & Thurlow Sts, West End; ☼ 9am-2pm Sat mid-Jun–mid-Oct; ☐ 6)

Winter Farmers Market (Map p84; ☎ 604-879-3276; Wise Hall, 1882 Adanac St, Commercial Dr; ☼ 10am-2pm 2nd & 4th Sat of month Nov-Apr; ☐ 20)

into one of the three multicourse tasting menus (from $110) – it will be the culinary highlight of your trip.

FEENIE'S Map pp94–5　West Coast, Comfort Food $$
☎ 604-739-7115; 2563 W Broadway; mains $16-24; ☐ 9

If you fancy a gourmet nibble but can't afford the prices next door at Lumière, this modern, red-hued diner reinvention – named after the famed chef that launched it – is an excellent alternative. A more laid-back bistro approach reigns here, with high-end comfort dishes such as finger-licking pastas, duck confit shepherd's pie and the now infamous Feenie's Weenie – a cheese smokie with sauerkraut that's only available for weekend brunch.

BISTROT BISTRO Map pp94–5　French $$
☎ 604-732-0004; 1961 W 4th Ave; mains $15-19; ☼ 5-11pm Tue-Thu, 5pm-midnight Fri & Sat, 5-10pm Sun; ☐ 4

Jostling for attention with Kits' other new eateries – which might explain the sunny, colorful interior here that entices you in like a bright flower garden – this snob-free Euro-bistro is at the top end of the French peasant food chain. It fuses robust rustic ingredients with an arsenal of flavor-revealing preparations – you can expect apple-sweetened pork tenderloin still simmering in its skillet, and the kind of hearty

boeuf bourguignon that would make lesser chefs weep. Considering the quality, this place is outstanding value.

ROCKY MOUNTAIN FLATBREAD CO
Map pp94–5　Comfort Food $$
☎ 604-730-0321; 1876 W 1st Ave; mains $14-20; ☐ 2

If you've ever wondered what expensive but decadently gourmet pizza would taste like, now's your chance to find out. This family-friendly West Coast–looking eatery serves pies created with mostly organic ingredients and absolutely no additives, GMOs or trans-fatty acids. They still taste good, though. Varieties such as 'rosemary chicken' and the salmon-and-lobster 'Meet the Ocean' prove popular, and there are pastas and salads available to stop you pigging out entirely on pies.

NAAM Map pp94–5　Vegetarian $$
☎ 604-738-7151; 2724 W 4th Ave; dishes $8-14; ☼ 24hr; ☐ 4

A rare relic of Kitsilano's hippie past, this vegetarian restaurant has the feel of a comfy farmhouse. It's not unusual to have to wait for a table here at peak times, but it's worth it for the hearty stir-fries, Mexican platters and sesame-fried potatoes with miso gravy. This is the kind of veggie spot where carnivores are also happy to dine. There's nightly live music, an array of great organic beers and a popular patio – it's covered, so you can cozy up here with a bowl of broth and still enjoy the rain.

SUSHI AOKI Map pp94–5   Japanese $-$$
☎ 604-731-5577; 1888 W Broadway; mains $8-14; 🚌 9

It's hard to believe that such a tiny restaurant would have the kind of extensive menu usually found in places 10 times bigger, but Sushi Aoki is a fancy-free yet recommended nook that knows exactly how to do the business. Using only the freshest fish (it flies in what it can't source locally), the chefs artfully craft rolls such as the signature shrimp with mayonnaise and apricot sauce and the fab rainbow roll of salmon, clam, tuna and sea bass. Ask for menu recommendations from the friendly owners.

EATERY Map pp94–5   Japanese $-$$
☎ 604-738-5298; 3431 W Broadway; mains $7-18; 🕑 4:30-11pm Mon-Thu, 4:30pm-midnight Fri, 12:30pm-midnight Sat, 12:30-11pm Sun; 🚌 9

Wooden booths, lava lamps and a neon 'miso horny' sign are all part of the ambience at this pop-culture reinvention of the traditional sushi joint. Bring your manga comic and dip into the giant, well-priced menu of soba bowls, curry-rice and several sushi combos, all washed down with a good selection of Japanese and Canadian bottled beers. There are also plenty of vegetarian options, including some shareable platters for all those veggies who travel in packs.

NOODLE BOX Map pp94–5   Asian $-$$
☎ 604-734-1310; 1867 W 4th Ave; mains $7-13; 🚌 4

Although Noodle Box hails from across the water in Victoria, its plans for world

top picks

VEGETARIAN

- Naam (opposite)
- Gorilla Food (p129)
- Planet Veg (right)
- Foundation (p137)
- Nyala (p136)

top picks

GOOD-VALUE GOURMET

- Salade de Fruits Café Bistro (p141)
- Bistrot Bistro (opposite)
- Aurora Bistro (p136)
- Feenie's (opposite)
- Salt Tasting Room (p135)

domination have taken hold in Vancouver, where its winning combination of freshly prepared, good-value Asian nosh has roused Kits locals from their high-end dining ways. The company's kitsch-tastic take-out noodle boxes – almost a fashion accessory – helped spread the word, but diners keep coming back for Malaysian lamb curry, Thai chow mein and the ever-popular spicy Cambodian jungle curry.

SOPHIE'S COSMIC CAFÉ
Map pp94–5   Diner $-$$
☎ 604-732-6810; 2095 W 4th Ave; mains $6-14; 🕑 8am-9:30pm; 🚌 4

With its museum of garage-sale kitsch lining the walls, local legend Sophie's is a cheery diner with burgers, club sandwiches and big-ass milkshakes dominating the menu. There are also a few off-message gems such as BC oyster burgers. A highly popular breakfast and brunch spot – expect to queue on weekends – it's also worth dropping by mid-afternoon for some truck-stop coffee and a slice of pyramid-sized apple pie.

PLANET VEG Map pp94–5   Indian, Vegetarian $
☎ 604-734-1001; 1941 Cornwall Ave; mains $4-7; 🕑 11am-9:30pm May-Sep, 11am-8pm Oct-Apr; 🚌 2

The Indian owners of this small and friendly vegetarian café bake rather than fry their samosas and fill them with wholesome ingredients such as spinach and tofu. Their roti rules – try the Katmandu roll, filled with cabbage and mixed veggies and lined with fried noodles and jalapeno cilantro chutney. The hot pots with rice and the tasty veggie burgers, flavored with yam and apple chutney, are good value. All can be packed up and carried around the corner to Vanier Park for a picnic with the birds.

GREATER VANCOUVER

North Vancouver has plenty of dining options if you've come over the Lions Gate Bridge for the day. Across the rest of the region, West Van has a couple of worthy dine-out spots, Richmond is bristling with Asian food joints (plus some West Coast seafood favorites in its Steveston area) and suburban Burnaby has plenty of neighborhood eateries plus one or two higher-end surprises.

OBSERVATORY Map pp44–5 West Coast $$$

☎ 604-998-4403; Grouse Mountain, North Vancouver; mains $35-40; ⏱ 5-10pm; 🚌 236 from Lonsdale Quay

Perched atop Grouse Mountain, the fine-dining Observatory serves up dishes of seared scallops and roasted beef tenderloin with some of the best views in BC – right down over the crenulated waterfront of Stanley Park and the shiny towers of Vancouver. The views are almost as good and the atmosphere is more laid-back at the adjacent Altitudes Bistro (☎ 604-984-0661; mains $7-17; ⏱ 11:30am-10pm), which offers pub-style food in a casual ski-lodge setting.

SALMON HOUSE ON THE HILL

Map pp44–5 Seafood $$$

☎ 604-926-3212; 2229 Folkestone Way, West Vancouver; mains $24-30; 🚌 251

With Vancouver at your feet, it's tough to beat this place when it comes to views. But it's not just about good looks here; this landmark West Van eatery has been chefing up some of the Lower Mainland's best fish dishes for years. While the salmon is always worthwhile, there's also an ever-changing array of seasonal BC seafood treats – ask for recommendations before you order.

PEAR TREE Map pp44–5 West Coast $$$

☎ 604-299-2772; 4120 E Hastings St, Burnaby; mains $24-29; ⏱ 5-10pm Tue-Sun; 🚌 135

The surprisingly chic contemporary interior here – belying its inauspicious location and discreet storefront – complements a menu of modernized, continental-influenced West Coast classics. Vancouverites are often shocked to find such a place in the 'burbs, but they quickly tell their friends about the amazing lobster cappuccinos and salmon with star anise butter sauce. Make sure you leave a trail of breadcrumbs from your downtown hotel or you might be stuck amid the strip malls forever.

HART HOUSE RESTAURANT

Map pp44–5 West Coast $$-$$$

☎ 604-298-4278; 6664 Deer Lake Ave, Burnaby; mains $20-33; ⏱ 11:30am-2:30pm & 5:30-10pm Tue-Fri, 5:30-10pm Sat, 11am-2pm & 5:30-10pm Sun; 🚌 144

This handsome Tudor-style mansion with a romantic, old-school dining room overlooks the grassy shores of Deer Lake – a natural oasis in the middle of suburban Burnaby. The creative menu has updated northwest cuisine favorites and the weekend brunch – Dungeness crab cake Benedict is recommended – is especially worth the trek. You can walk off your indulgence on the park trails.

GUSTO DI QUATTRO Map pp44–5 Italian $$

☎ 604-924-4444; 1 Lonsdale Ave, North Vancouver; mains $12-24; SeaBus to Lonsdale Quay

A smart-casual but never ostentatious family-run Italian eatery, this welcoming, warm-hued restaurant covers all the pasta classics as well as any other restaurant in town – but the prices make this a better deal than most. More adventurous diners

ALL SCREAM FOR ICE CREAM

If you've been skiing, cycling, kayaking or just on your feet all day exploring the neighborhoods, it may be time to cool down with an ice-cold treat. A visit to La Casa Gelato (Map p84; ☎ 604-251-3211; 1033 Venables St, Commercial Dr; 🚌 20) in the Commercial Dr area is a must, although you'll likely get brain-freeze trying to choose from the bewildering kaleidoscope of flavors – 218 at the last count. All the usual suspects are on offer at this granddaddy of the local ice-cream scene, but if you're feeling adventurous try the garlic or hot chili varieties. If you're closer to Stanley Park on your travels, amble along Denman St and you'll soon come to Mum's Gelato (Map pp66–7; ☎ 604-681-1500; 855 Denman St, West End; 🚌 5), where the popular faves include mocha, pistachio and lemon sorbet. If Yaletown is your rest spot of choice, drop by the Gelato Espresso Bar (Map p71; ☎ 604-689-8531; 1210 Homer St, Yaletown; 🚌 C23) for a sophisticated approach that includes a toasted marshmallow and apple pie variety (the baked pie crust is crumbled in) and a 'drunken gelato,' which comes with a drizzle of booze – limoncello (Italian lemon-flavored liqueur) is recommended.

should make for the duck fusilli or tiger prawn linguini. The wine selection is good and some international tipples have started to infiltrate the mostly Italian selection in recent years.

KELONG SINGAPORE CUISINE
Map pp44–5   Malaysian, Singaporean $$
☎ 604-821-9883; 4800 No 3 Rd, Richmond; mains $9-18; 🚌 403
Spicy Malaysian and Singaporean approaches combine in this bright and breezy restaurant – batik fans will enjoy the interior here. If you're starving, tuck into the hearty beef *redang* or *sambal* chicken, then sit back and eavesdrop on the conversations about who spent too much at the nearby shopping malls. Vegetarians are equally well looked after.

TOMAHAWK RESTAURANT
Map pp44–5   Comfort Food $-$$
☎ 604-988-2612; 1550 Philip Ave, North Vancouver; mains $6-14; 🕑 8am-9pm Sun-Thu, 8am-10pm Fri & Sat; 🚌 240
A blast from Vancouver's pioneering past, the family-owned Tomahawk has been heaping local diners' plates with comfort food since 1926. An excellent weekend breakfast spot – if the giant Yukon bacon and eggs grease-fest doesn't kill your hangover, nothing will – it's also great for lunch or dinner, when chicken potpies and organic meatloaf hit the menu. As you waddle back out the door, check out the First Nations artifacts lining the walls.

DAVE'S FISH & CHIPS
Map pp44–5   Comfort Food $
☎ 604-271-7555; 3460 Moncton St, Steveston; mains $6-8; 🕑 11am-8pm; 🚌 402
Join the throngs of locals strolling the boardwalks in the old fishing village of Steveston on the southern border of Richmond – a great sunset spot – then head a couple of blocks inland to this unassuming old-school fish-and-chippery. With a simple brown-wood and wobbly-table interior that hasn't changed in decades, Dave's puts all its effort into what goes on the plate. All the traditional dishes are here, but for something different try the oysters and chips or the velvet-soft battered salmon and chips. Great value.

BLUELIST[1] (blu list) *v.*
to recommend a travel experience.

What's your recommendation? www.lonelyplanet.com/bluelist

DRINKING

top picks

DRINKING

With swanky new lounges springing up across Vancouver like drunks at an open bar, and neighborhood pubs seemingly as popular as ever to those locals who like a quiet beery chat with friends at the end of the day, it's not hard to find a drink in this city. Visitors are welcome wherever the locals sup – just remember that it's table service at most places, rather than the Brit model of ordering at the bar.

Wherever you end up drinking, avoid the generic national brews by beery behemoths such as Molson and Labatt and head straight for the local selection. BC is one of North America's frothiest microbrewing capitals and Vancouver is home to an impressive array of small producers whose products are well worth sampling (see the boxed text, below). Ask your server for recommendations.

It's not all about beer, of course. Cocktail fans will find plenty of exotic tipples in bars and lounges here. But beyond a couple of staples, wine menus are patchy in many Vancouver drinking holes – see p152 for information on BC wine and where to find it.

If you've had a heavy night mixing it with the locals and your head feels like a melon on a toothpick, recover at one of the city's great coffeehouses. Although Vancouver was the home of the first Starbucks outside the US, there are plenty of quirky independent coffee stops here that could teach Starbucks' baristas a thing or two about great java.

Finally, if you need to pick up a bottle for an impromptu party in your hotel room, head to one of the many government-run liquor stores operated around the city by the Liquor Distribution Branch (☎ 604-252-3000; www.bcliquorstores.com). You'll also find private cold beer and wine stores, but they tend to be a little more expensive.

OPENING HOURS

Pubs and bars that serve lunch usually open before midday, with swankier, lounge-style operations waiting it out until 5pm. Most drinkeries close sometime between midnight and 2am, although they are allowed to stay open until 3am and will do so if they're busy enough, particularly on weekends. Some, especially those on the Granville strip, have licenses to stay open even later. Coffeehouses usually open around 8am and often close before 9pm.

HOW MUCH?

Expect to pay $5 or $6 for a large glass of beer, but always ask if there are any daily specials. A glass of wine will set you back anything over $6, while cocktails often start at $6. Your bill will also include an added 10% liquor tax fee as well as a 5% goods and services tax (GST), extras that are enough to drive anyone to drink.

TIPPING

Table servers get at least $1 per drink, 15% when you're buying a round. Even if you order and pick up your beverage at the bar, consider dropping your change in the prominently placed tip glass.

DOWNTOWN

If you're looking for a bevvie downtown, your best bet is Granville St, between Robson and Davie. This is also nightclub-central on weekends, when a quiet beer is about as likely as a free pint of gold dust.

PUBS

FOUNTAINHEAD PUB Map pp48–9
☎ 604-687-2222; 1025 Davie St; 🚌 6
The West End's loudest and proudest gay neighborhood pub, this friendly joint is all

SIX-PACK OF GREAT LOCAL BREWS

Look out for beers from these Vancouver-area brewers, available at many pubs and bars around the city. Check the brewers' websites for specific info on where to sup 'em.

- R&B Brewing (www.r-and-b.com)
- Russell Brewing (www.russellbeer.com)
- Storm Brewing (www.stormbrewing.com)
- Red Truck Beer (www.redtruckbeer.com)
- Shaftebury Brewing (www.shaftebury.com)
- Granville Island Brewing (www.gib.ca)

about the patio, which spills along Davie St like an overturned wine glass. Expect to take part in the ongoing pastime of ogling the passing locals or retreat to a quieter spot inside for a few lagers (the Red Truck Beer is recommended), some pub-grub classics or a game of darts with the regulars.

LENNOX PUB Map pp48–9
☎ 604-408-0881; 800 Granville St; 🚌 4
This slender Granville St drinkery never seems to have enough tables to go around at the weekend, when the noise levels prevent all but the most rudimentary of conversations. It's a different story during the week, when calm is restored and you can savor a good roster of Belgian drafts – try the Leffe. The décor is reproduction old-school and the upstairs seating area is a popular couples' nook.

RAILWAY CLUB Map pp48–9
☎ 604-681-1625; 579 Dunsmuir St; 🚌 4
A renowned local music venue (see p164), the Rail is also Vancouver's best Brit-style pub. Unlike most Vancouver watering holes, you order at the counter, where an impressive array of regional brews is served in proper dimpled pint glasses. The roster is ever-changing but can include Storm, Russell or Raven – ask for something 'dark' or 'light' and see what you get. Avoid the entertainment cover charge by arriving before 7pm.

BARS
BACCHUS Map pp48–9
☎ 604-608-5319; 845 Hornby St; 🚌 5
A roaring hearth on a chilly day is the main attraction at Bacchus, a decadent bar with a gentleman's club ambience on the lobby level of the Wedgewood Hotel (p191). Sink into a deep leather chair, adjust your monocle and listen to the piano player as you sip on a signature Red Satin Slip martini of vodka, raspberry liqueur and cranberry juice. There's also a good small-plate menu for the incurably esurient.

CHAMBAR Map pp48–9
☎ 604-879-7119; 562 Beatty St; Ⓜ Stadium
This swanky, brick-lined cave – atmospherically lit by table candles at night – is a great place for a lively chat among the

city's urban hipsters. The international wine list is impressive and the cocktail array is exemplary: try a few heady Blue Figs (frozen cooked figs steeped in vodka and served martini-style) and you'll develop a warm glow for your stagger back to the hotel. There's also a frothy Belgian beer selection for added kicks.

GINGER 62 Map pp48–9
☎ 604-688-5494; 1219 Granville St; 🚌 4
Briefly the city's favorite bar until all those fickle fashionistas moved on a couple of years ago, this loungey spot is far more laid-back now – except on busy weekends when the Granville St clubbers stumble in for late-night refreshments. Lured by the calming décor, many of them end up staying for a final round of boogying on the small dance floor or a serious run at the extensive cocktail menu.

COFFEEHOUSES
CAFFÈ ARTIGIANO Map pp48–9
☎ 604-696-9222; 763 Hornby St; 🚌 5
An international award-winner for its barista skills and latte art, Artigiano has the locals frothing at the mouth with its satisfyingly rich java beverages. The drinks appear with leaf designs adorning their foam and there's a good side attraction of gourmet sandwiches and cakes for the hungry. The patio here is almost always packed – grab a table quickly if you see one – and the interior has a Tuscan theme.

MARIO'S Map pp48–9
☎ 604-608-2804; 595 Howe St; Ⓜ Burrard
You'll wake up and smell the coffee long before you make it to the door of this business-district legend. The rich aromatic beverages served up by the man himself are the kind of ambrosia brews that make Starbucks' drinkers weep – you might even forgive the incessant 1980s Italian pop music percolating through the shop as you sip on your tall Americano.

GALLERY CAFÉ Map pp48–9
☎ 604-688-2233; 750 Hornby St; 🚌 5
The mezzanine level of the Vancouver Art Gallery (p46) is home to a chatty indoor dining area complemented by one of downtown's best patios. The food is a little pricey, but it's well worth stopping for a

drink, especially if you take your coffee (or bottled beer) out to the parasol-forested outdoor area where you can top up your tan and watch over Robson St.

WEST END

This clamorous neighborhood has plenty of pubs and bars, including several gay-friendly haunts along Davie St.

PUBS

CARDERO'S MARINE PUB Map pp66–7
☎ 604-669-7666; 1583 Coal Harbour Quay; 🚌 19
Between Coal Harbour's bobbing boats, Cardero's is a stellar waterfront pub with cozy leather sofas, a wood-burning fireplace and great marine views. The small bar has a good menu of comfort food (steamed mussels in a Pernod, garlic and shallot broth is recommended) and the booze selection showcases Granville Island Brewing. On cold days, rib-warming hot toddies include the B52, a coffee made with Grand Marnier and Kahlua.

FOGG 'N SUDS Map pp66–7
☎ 604-683-2337; 1323 Robson St; 🚌 5
The restaurant focuses on standard pasta and burger platters, so decamp to the pub-style counter to dip into the dozens of international beers – try some unfamiliar brews from Africa, South America and the UK. There are also many Canadian drafts to quaff (try the Rickards Red), as well as 'the tower' – a yard-long tube of beer with a tap at the bottom that stands on your table just asking to be knocked over.

MILL MARINE Map pp66–7
☎ 604-687-6455; 1199 W Cordova St; 🚌 19; wi-fi
The food here is nothing to write home about, but the spectacular panoramic patio views of Burrard Inlet and the North Shore mountains more than make up for it. There's a small but impressive beer selection – try the Whistler Export Lager – as well as daily-changing drinks specials throughout the week. Arrive before 5pm in summer or you'll be wrestling the locals for a table.

PUMPJACK PUB Map pp66–7
☎ 604-685-3417; 1167 Davie St; 🚌 6
Expect to get all pumped up at Vancouver's favorite leather bar, where buttoned-up

top picks

PATIOS

- Dockside Brewing Company (p154)
- Backstage Lounge (p154)
- Yaletown Brewing Company (p152)
- Gallery Café (p149)
- Galley Patio & Grill (p155)

(and buttoned-down) uniform nights vie for attention with wandering bears – a beefy group of hairy, often bearded men and their dedicated admirers. Or you could just play pool. It's a popular pick-up joint for the locals, so you can expect queues here on most weekends.

SEVENTY TWO SPORTS BAR Map pp66–7
☎ 604-646-4031; 1025 Robson St; 🚌 5
At this pub, nestled on Robson St, you can pull up a patio chair on the 2nd floor and still hear the chatty shoppers shuffling past below. Head inside to catch a game at a booth with its own built-in TV or stay outside and combine good-quality pub grub (try the chicken quesadillas) with a full complement of local Russell Brewing beers – the cream ale is recommended. You might even get a tan.

BARS

BALTHAZAR Map pp66–7
☎ 604-689-8822; 1215 Bidwell St; 🚌 6
Resembling a Tuscan bordello from the outside and a winery tasting room on the inside, this is a popular hangout for 30-something professionals who like to down a few too many martinis and bitch about their jobs. There's a good array of tapas if you get peckish, but the main menu action is for cocktail fans – try a couple of exotics such as La Petite Mort and the naughty Dirty Sanchez.

BAYSIDE LOUNGE Map pp66–7
☎ 604-682-1831; 1755 Davie St; 🚌 6
A loyal local clientele keeps this 2nd-floor hidden gem alive, but it's worth dropping by just to catch the sunset over nearby English Bay from a seat at the crescent-shaped main window. Rarely crowded, it's a

good spot for a quiet drink with friends or an ideal end-of-day retreat if you just want to wind down with a glass of wine.

THE CALLING Map pp66–7
☎ 604-801-6681; 1780 Davie St; 🚍 6
This is a small but swanky reinvention of the neighborhood bar idea – think silky hardwood floors, mod furnishings and black-clad waiters – where the main draw is the slender covered patio overlooking English Bay, perfect for sunsets and storm-watching. It serves gourmet grub such as smoky bacon and gorgonzola burgers, and the drinks menu includes plenty of European beers, a smattering of wine classics and a roster of serious cocktails.

O'DOUL'S Map pp66–7
☎ 604-661-1400; 1300 Robson St; 🚍 5
Live nightly jazz attracts locals to the on-site watering hole of the Listel Vancouver (p193) hotel, where there's an impressive wine list of Old and New World classics (plus a few quirky cult selections) and some Granville Island brews served in chilled glasses. There's no cover charge for the live shows, which are particularly impressive during the Jazz Festival (p14), when performers drop by to jam.

COFFEEHOUSES

DELANY'S Map pp66–7
☎ 604-662-3344; 1105 Denman St; 🚍 5
A laid-back, wood-lined neighborhood coffee bar that's popular with the West End's gay community, Delany's is a good perch from which to catch the annual Pride Parade (p15) – although you'll have to get here early if you want a front-row seat. The usual array of cookies and muffins will keep you fortified while you wait.

MELRICHE'S Map pp66–7
☎ 604-689-5282; 1244 Davie St; 🚍 5; wi-fi
With its mismatched wooden tables, hearty array of cakes and crowd of journal-writing locals hunkered in every corner, this is an ideal rainy-day nook. Warm your hands on a pail-sized hot chocolate and press your face to the condensation-soaked window to watch the Davie St locals bustle past. This is the kind of place where Morrissey would hang out on a wet Monday afternoon.

YALETOWN
Yaletown is the city's cocktail capital, where the rich and beautiful sup and exchange share-option horror stories.

PUBS & BARS

AFTERGLOW Map p71
☎ 604-602-0835; 1082 Hamilton St; 🚍 C23
Tucked at the back of Glowbal Grill & Satay Bar (p133), the city's tiniest lounge is an intimate, pink-hued room lined with naked women – at least, their silhouettes appear as artwork on the walls. Pull up a stool and experiment with cocktails such as You Glow Girl, or knock yourself out with a few bottles of ultra-strong Québecois beer – complete with images of Satan on the labels.

DIX BBQ & BREWERY Map p71
☎ 604-682-2739; 871 Beatty St; Ⓜ Stadium
The Dix is popular with game-night football fans stumbling in from nearby BC Place, while the regular imbibers are drawn here by the laid-back ambience and well-priced own-brew and regional beers. The southern-style nosh is also a cut above regular pub grease-fests, focusing on velvety brisket sandwiches and a sausage, shrimp and chicken jambalaya that will lure you from your drink.

ELIXIR Map p71
☎ 604-642-0557; 350 Davie St; 🚍 C23
Adjoining the lobby lounge of the Opus Hotel (p195), where nail-perfect gold-diggers pose in hopes of snagging passing pop stars, the Parisian-style Elixir is a complete contrast. Pull up a perch at the bar and try a Bombay Dust, a tasty fusion of scotch and gin. According to a local showbiz legend, Robert de Niro once arrived here, joined later in the evening by Harrison Ford for a quiet drink.

GEORGE ULTRA LOUNGE Map p71
☎ 604-628-5555; 1137 Hamilton St; 🚍 C23
One of hedonistic Yaletown's favorite haunts, the moodily lit George attracts the laser-whitened-teeth crowd with its champagne and wine selection plus a giant list of high-concept cocktails – anyone for a Sazerac, featuring bourbon in an 'absinthe-washed glass'? Work your way down the list, sink further into your comfy chair and figure out what the giant swirly glass thing above the bar is supposed to be.

VANCOUVER UNCORKED

Locals have had a growing love affair with BC wine for decades. But while grapes are grown on Vancouver Island as well as in the Fraser Valley, the majority of the province's 131 wineries and 2000 hectares of wine country are located in the Okanagan Valley, a dry, near-desert region 400km inland from Vancouver. Focusing on popular whites such as chardonnay and pinot gris as well as reds including merlot and pinot noir, the top producers are Quail's Gate, Mission Hill and Sumac Ridge. The region's signature tipple is ice wine, an ultrasweet dessert drink produced from grapes frozen on the vine. Visit www.winebc.com for more information. If you want to sample, drop by a liquor store or head to the following local bars: Bacchus (p149), Dockside Brewing Company (p154), O'Doul's (p151) or SoMa (opposite).

YALETOWN BREWING COMPANY
Map p71

☎ 604-681-2739; 1111 Mainland St; 🚌 C23

As you walk in here, there's a brick-lined pub on the left and a giant dining room on the right; both serve pints of on-site-brewed beer, but the restaurant adds a long menu of comfort foods. In summer the two patios are ideal for ogling the beautiful people of Yaletown as they sashay past toward the chichi restaurants. It's busy on weekends, so arrive early to play pool in the back.

GASTOWN

Gastown's atmospheric old brick buildings have been revitalized with some excellent and distinctive bars, making this an ideal spot for an easy pub crawl.

PUBS & BARS

ALIBI ROOM Map p74

☎ 604-623-3383; 157 Alexander St; 🚌 7

Alibi's low-ceilinged basement lounge creates an ideal setting for Vancouver's film and design crowds to converge over countless martinis, but you're better off sitting at one of the long benches in the convivial and less claustrophobic upstairs area. There's a fair wine and cocktail selection here, and you're more than likely to be tempted by the quality comfort food calling you from the menu (see p134).

CAMBIE Map p74

☎ 604-684-6466; 300 Cambie St; 🚌 4

This is a popular brick-lined watering hole combining cheap booze and hearty, deep-fried pub grub. The clientele is an odd mix of hard-drinking regulars, curious backpackers and Asian language students text messaging each other under the tables, but everyone gets along just fine in this unpretentious spot. Draft specials are a way

of life here and you can expect to pay less than $5 for a cold pint of domestic.

IRISH HEATHER Map p74

☎ 604-688-9779; 217 Carrall St; 🚌 7; wi-fi

A serious Irish pub without all that leprechaun blarney, this wood-floored, exposed-brick hostelry is a breath of fresh air. Head to the rear glass conservatory to sup on Vancouver's best-poured pint of Guinness or settle in at the Shebeen Whiskey House, a tiny, windowless bar out back that stocks dozens of malts: it's the kind of place you end up staying all night without realizing. The Heather's food (see p134) is the best of any pub in town. During the research period for this book, plans were in the works to move the Heather (and Shebeen) directly across the street in the near future.

SIX ACRES Map p74

☎ 604-488-0110; 203 Carrall St; 🚌 7

Ideal for a shared plate of finger food (see p134), but it's just as easy to cover all the necessary food groups with the extensive beer selection here (at least that's what you should tell yourself). There's a small, chatty patio out front but inside – especially the cozy upstairs area – is great for hiding in a corner and working your way through an exotic array of bottled brews, including London Porter and the rather marvelous Draft Dodger from Phillips Brewing.

STEAMWORKS BREWING COMPANY
Map p74

☎ 604-689-2739; 375 Water St; Ⓜ Waterfront; wi-fi

The signature beer at this giant, edge-of-Gastown microbrewery is Lions Gate Lager, a good summer tipple. A favorite of the after-work crowd, the pub downstairs can get noisy, while upstairs is all about serene views across to the North Shore. The menu is packed with pub standards, but the pizzas are a standout.

SOMA

Combining convivial bars and cozy coffee-house hangouts, SoMa is the kind of area you can nurse a drink all afternoon while you pen your latest epic poem.

PUBS & BARS

PUBLIC LOUNGE Map p81
☎ 604 873 5584; 3289 Main St; 🚌 3
The regulars here, in the heart of Main St's hipsterville, spend plenty of time cultivating their tousled, anti-establishment look before they leave home. Once they walk through the door and shuffle to a table, they're already talking about their poetry. Divert their attention by sending over a plate of shrimp wontons or just bury your face in a succession of draft Strongbow ciders. Check out the paintings on the walls, many by local artists.

SOMA Map p81
☎ 604-630-7502; 151 E 8th Ave; 🚌 3
The neighborhood's fave eponymous coffee hangout was kicked out of its popular old location but has re-emerged in a new spot as a wine bar. It's a welcome transformation: while retaining its casual ambience, there's now a tantalizing array of small-plate treats (the baked fondue is fun) as well as a serious BC and international wine menu, some choice local beers and a heartwarming roster of malts.

WHIP Map p81
☎ 604-874-4687; 209 E 6th Ave; 🚌 3
Moodily lit Whip fuses the best in pub and lounge approaches. There's a dare-inviting selection of seven martinis, each named after a deadly sin (lust is always recommended) and a good menu with tempting treats such as yam *frites* and pad thai. But it's the beer that wins regulars, with choice drafts from R&B Brewing, Storm Brewing and Québec's infamous Unibroue.

COFFEEHOUSES

GRIND GALLERY CAFÉ Map p81
☎ 604-874-1588; 4124 Main St; 🚌 3
The artwork-lined Grind is open 24/7, fueling starving students, artists and writers throughout the night. The large, open space hosts an art gallery, concerts and spoken word performances, as well as the philosophical and political musings of its regular patrons who have made this spot a mainstay of the local scene. Alongside the coffee, there are plenty of quality options for those who prefer to quaff tea – try the green tea frappuccino.

LUGZ COFFEE LOUNGE Map p81
☎ 604-874-1588; 2525 Main St; 🚌 3
Bike messengers congregate outside Lugz, while neighborhood artists dream away on the leather couches inside. All enjoy the warming ambience and solid array of fair-trade coffees and exotic teas at this popular Main St haunt. As you sip your cappuccino or elderberry tea, check to see if there are any upcoming events that take your fancy: Lugz often hosts singer-songwriter shows and angsty poetry readings.

COMMERCIAL DRIVE

If you like your drink served with a frothy head of chatty bohemian locals, the Drive's exciting neighborhood bars and expert coffeehouses are hard to beat.

PUBS & BARS

CHARLATAN Map p84
☎ 604-253-2777; 1446 Commercial Dr; 🚌 20
Reinventing the old Bukowski's bar, the charming Charlatan has quickly become a Drive favorite. In summer the windows are flung open and the tiny patio is crowded, while in winter it becomes a cozy joint to watch the game or just chat in a corner. The food (see p138) covers a wide array of comfort dishes, while the sterling beer selection runs the gamut of regional choices, plus selections from Alberta's excellent Big Rock Brewery.

top picks

PLACES TO PICK UP A DATE

- Nevermind (p155)
- Fountainhead Pub (p148)
- Balthazar (p150)
- George Ultra Lounge (p151)

STELLA'S TAP & TAPAS BAR Map p84

☎ 604-254-2437; 1191 Commercial Dr; 🚍 20
Leading the Drive's friendly neighborhood bars, Stella's combines great local beers with a satisfying selection of European brews – it's the best spot in town to taste-test draft Leffe, Kronenbourg and Belle-Vue Kriek. Even better, connoisseurs can dip into an ever-changing array of imported Belgian microbrews, including the legendary Gulden Draak that's strong enough to put hairs on your chest and the chests of everyone sitting nearby.

COFFEEHOUSES

CAFÉ CALABRIA Map p84

☎ 604-253-7017; 1745 Commercial Dr; 🚍 20
When Vancouverites tell you that Commercial is the city's best coffee street, this is one of the places they're thinking about. It tops a healthy handful of great cafés founded here by Italian immigrants, and these guys really know their java. Don't be put off by the chandeliers-and-statues décor (if Liberace had opened a coffee shop, this is what it would have looked like) – just order an espresso and biscotti and pull up a chair outside.

CAFÉ DEUX SOLEILS Map p84

☎ 604-254-1195; 2096 Commercial Dr; 🚍 20
This rambling bohemian coffeehouse is a hip, healthy and child-friendly addition to the Drive. On sunny days, folks relax outside with a beer, while acoustic musicians, performance poets and open-mike wannabes take the stage several nights a week (see p162). There are plenty of good-value vegetarian snacks and meals and this is a great spot if you just want to chill out and meet the counterculture locals.

PRADO CAFÉ Map p84

☎ 604-255-5537; 1938 Commercial Dr; 🚍 20; wi-fi
Eschewing the kitsch-heavy interiors that most coffee shops adopt when they're trying to be cool, the comparatively austere Prado is the kind of place where minimalists sup in peace. But it's not just about aesthetics: the baristas here are serious about their fair-trade coffee, which – don't tell the Italians down the street – may be the best on the Drive. Consider a Nutella chocolate cookie for the road.

top picks

BREWPUBS

- Steamworks Brewing Company (p152)
- Yaletown Brewing Company (p152)
- Dix BBQ & Brewery (p151)
- Dockside Brewing Company (below)
- Granville Island Brewing Taproom (below)

GRANVILLE ISLAND

After a day spent weaving around the public market and artisan stores, wind down at one of Granville Island's decidedly laid-back bars.

PUBS & BARS

BACKSTAGE LOUNGE Map p87

☎ 604-687-1354; 1585 Johnston St; 🚍 50
This recently refurbished but ever-lively Granville Island hangout serves up winning patio views, enticing beer specials (Tuesday night is all about $3 drafts) and some hopping local live bands (see p163). It's popular with an older female crowd. All profits benefit the Arts Club Theatre, so bottoms up.

DOCKSIDE BREWING COMPANY
Map p87

☎ 604-685-7070; Granville Island Hotel, 1253 Johnston St; 🚍 50
Dockside has been self-brewing treats such as Cartwright Pale Ale and fruity, hibiscus-toned Jamaican Lager for more than 30 years. Take your drinks outside to the patio for awe-inspiring views of False Creek's boat traffic and the mountain-backed downtown skyline – this is what supping in Vancouver is all about. If it's raining, stay indoors by the fireplace and sink into a leather couch.

GRANVILLE ISLAND BREWING TAPROOM Map p87

☎ 604-687-2739; 1441 Cartwright St; 🚍 50
Canada's oldest microbrewery started out here in 1984, gradually expanding to become a big player in city bars. Most of its beer is now brewed off-site, but you can still take a tour of the small process (see p86) or just head straight to its pub-style Taproom. Naturally, you're duty bound to sample everything, but the copper-colored Kitsilano Maple Cream Ale stands out.

KITSILANO

You can only hang out at the beach and wander among the shops in Kits for so long. After a while, the bars will start to call your name. Don't be afraid to listen.

PUBS & BARS

BIMINI'S PUBLIC HOUSE Map pp94–5

☎ 604-732-9232; 2010 W 4th Ave; 🚌 4

A KItsilano institution that's been drawing the locals like a booze-soaked magnet for years, Bimini's is a trad-looking bar-restaurant where you'll feel equally comfortable sipping cocktails or knocking back a couple of beers. Drop by on Tuesday, when all draft domestic beer and hi-balls are $3 each, and consider busting your weekend hangover by returning to the scene of the crime for Sunday brunch. A devastating fire had just wrecked the joint during the write-up period for this book, but the owners were planning to rebuild and reopen as soon as possible.

ELWOOD'S Map pp94–5

☎ 604-736-4301; 3145 W Broadway; 🚌 9

A laid-back, low-cost place to quaff a cold beer or three (especially out front on the wooden patio), funky Elwood's is one of those neighborhood pubs that's like your favorite pair of jeans: worn enough to be comfortable whatever the occasion. The owners operate the Metropolitan Bartending School, so they certainly know how to pull a pint and mix a mean martini.

GALLEY PATIO & GRILL Map pp94–5

☎ 604-222-1331; Jericho Sailing Centre, 1300 Discovery St; 🚌 4

This is a terrific, unfussy perch at sunset, with a stunning waterfront view across the beach toward English Bay. Plop down in one of the plastic patio chairs – reservations are not accepted, so arrive early if you want the view – then eyeball all the sailboats steering toward shore. The food is of the fish-and-chips variety, while R&B Brewing highlights the booze side of things.

NEVERMIND Map pp94–5

☎ 604-736-0212; 3293 W 4th Ave; 🚌 4; wi-fi

Casual-chic Nevermind attracts a younger crowd – think UBC students spending their rent money – that's happy to knock back a few cocktails and shimmy around the dance floor when the DJ arrives. Especially packed on weekends, it's a great place to meet 20-somethings. If your chat-up lines aren't working, console yourself with Oral Pleasure – a martini with peach schnapps and cranberry juice.

GREATER VANCOUVER

If you've been skiing your ass off on the North Shore, drop into a neighborhood pub. Not everyone will know your name but they'll likely make you feel welcome.

PUBS

RAVEN PUB Map pp44–5

☎ 604-929-3834; 1052 Deep Cove Rd, Deep Cove; 🚌 212

Raise a glass here to novelist Malcolm Lowry, a one-time local who reportedly enjoyed a glass or two. It's a popular and laid-back neighborhood haunt – especially for the over-30 set – where there are plenty of beers on tap, a pub-classic food menu, and a toasty fireplace to warm you. If you're lucky, there'll also be a live band to keep your toes tapping.

SAILOR HAGAR'S BREWPUB Map pp44–5

☎ 604-984-3087; 86 Semisch Ave, North Vancouver; SeaBus to Lonsdale Quay

A stroll from Lonsdale Quay, this convivial, nautical-themed brewpub has smashing views of the city skyline, plenty of on-tap and bottled beers and a nice greasy menu of pub grub. It's an ideal spot to catch European soccer on TV. The owners also brew some of their own tipples here – the Narwhal Pale Ale is recommended. There are different $4 to $5 beer specials every night and live jazz most Sunday nights.

top picks

LIVE TV SPORTS

- Seventy Two Sports Bar (p150)
- Charlatan (p153)
- Sailor Hagar's Brewpub (right)
- Dix BBQ & Brewery (p151)
- Lennox Pub (p149)

BLUELIST[1] (blu,list) *v.*
to recommend a travel experience.
What's your recommendation? www.lonelyplanet.com/bluelist

NIGHTLIFE

top picks

- **Railway Club** (p164)
- **Commodore** (p164)
- **Media Club** (p164)
- **Shine** (p161)
- **Honey** (p160)
- **Caprice** (p159)
- **Vancouver Theatresports League** (p158)
- **Yale** (p161)
- **Cellar Restaurant & Jazz Club** (p162)
- **Rime** (p163)

Vancouverites have a reputation for healthy living and outdoorsy pursuits, but it's important to remember that not all of them spend their downtime slipping into yoga gear or indulging in a round of naughty rice cakes. Hedonism is never far from the minds of most locals, which might explain the sweet-smelling substances that waft toward you on even the most respectable-looking streets.

But if you've come to the city in search of a rocking good night out, you'll need a few pointers. Although the Granville St entertainment strip between Robson and Davie Sts is Vancouver's traditional night-out area – and it's great if you like big clubs, big noise and big crowds – there are plenty of additional pockets of fun for fans of comedy, clubbing and great live music.

To find out what's on and where, pick up a free copy of the weekly *Georgia Straight,* the city's best listings newspaper. The *Westender* and the *West Coast Life* section of the *Vancouver Sun* also tap into local happenings. All three hit the streets on Thursday.

OPENING HOURS

Nightclubs usually open their doors at 9pm (although they don't really get going until 11pm) and most stay open until 3am or 4am. Few clubs are open every day – many close Monday to Wednesday – and most are at their liveliest on Friday and Saturday. Acts at live-music venues typically hit the stage after 10pm.

HOW MUCH?

Expect to pay $5 to $15 for entry to many clubs, with weekends being top-price time. The cover charge at live-music venues can range from nothing at all to $35, although there are many where $10 is the norm.

COMEDY

Vancouverites apparently have a sense of humor, but the city's live comedy scene is not very large. Along with the dedicated clubs and regular stand-up and improv nights listed following, you can laugh at some hilarious hockey and beaver jokes at one-off events and performances around the city – check the *Georgia Straight* to see what's coming up. If you really need a good laugh, drop by for the annual Global Comedy Fest (p16) or chuckle yourself silly at the International Fringe Festival (p16), where comic plays and stand-up shows hit stages on and around Granville Island.

BALTHAZAR'S HOUSE OF COMEDY
Map pp66–7

☎ 604-689-8822; www.balthazarvancouver.com; Balthazar, 1215 Bidwell St, West End; tickets $5; ☼ 9pm Mon; 🚌 6

The West End's favorite Tuscan-look lounge (see p150) hosts a once-a-week stand-up show where you can expect to see a handful of local comics strutting their stuff while you sip on a round of cocktails that will make you laugh at anything. Students, whip out your ID at the door for half-price entry.

JUPITER CAFÉ Map pp66–7

☎ 604-609-6665; www.jupitercafe.com; 1216 Bute St, West End; tickets $5-8; ☼ 9pm Mon; 🚌 6

Another lounge that likes to add a laughter track to tackle the Monday-night blues, the upstairs Jupiter Café offers a regular comedian-hosted improv night. Reflecting its neighborhood, expect plenty of naughty gay-themed jokes to keep the locals giggling. If you just don't get it, drop by on Thursday instead when it's live jazz night.

URBAN IMPROV Map pp94–5

☎ 604-737-7770; www.chivana.com; Chivana Resto Lounge, 2430 W 4th Ave, Kitsilano; tickets $7; ☼ 9pm Mon; 🚌 4

The best place to tickle your funny bone in Kits, Chivana is a restaurant and lounge most of the week but a live improv comedy venue on Mondays. Expect to see many of the usual improv suspects who appear at Vancouver TheatreSports (below), plus a host of other well-oiled performers who know just how to spin an audience suggestion into a jaw-achingly funny good time.

VANCOUVER THEATRESPORTS LEAGUE Map p87

☎ 604-738-7013; www.vtsl.com; New Revue Stage, 1585 Johnston St, Granville Island; tickets

$10-18; ⊗ 7:30pm Wed, 7:30pm & 9:15pm Thu, 8pm, 10pm & 11:45pm Fri & Sat; 🚌 50

Vancouver's most popular improv group concocts energetic stage romps, loosely connected to themes such as Shakespeare, *Star Trek* or the Olympics. If you're sitting near the front, expect to be picked on or called to the stage, unless you're naked – they tend to leave you alone if you're naked. The recommended 11.45pm Friday and Saturday shows are commendably ribald and if you think it looks easy, try one of their improv classes.

YUK YUK'S Map pp48–9

☎ 604-696-9857; www.yukyuks.com; Century Plaza Hotel, 1015 Burrard St, downtown; tickets $5-15; ⊗ 8:30pm Tue-Thu, 8pm & 10:30pm Fri & Sat; 🚌 2

Stand-up comics from around the city and across North America perform at Yuk Yuk's, part of a Canada-wide chain of dedicated comedy clubs. Tuesday and Wednesday are improv nights, while famous faces usually appear Thursday to Saturday. If you're happy for soup to erupt from your nose at any moment, you can also splash out on a $45 dinner-and-show package.

CLUBBING

While downtown's Granville strip draws the barely clad booties of most mainstream clubbers, there are many other less limelight-hogging joints that cater to just about every musical peccadillo. Cover charges usually run from $5 to $15 ('the ladies' are often free before 11pm) and dress codes are frequently smart-casual – ripped jeans and sportswear will not endear you to the bouncers perusing the queues for people to send home. Make sure you bring ID to get in – most clubs accept over-19s but some want you to be over 25.

You can put yourself on the VIP list (no waiting, no cover) at the websites of individual clubs or via www.clubvibes.com/vancouver and www.clubzone.com/vancouver, where you can also check out events listings for city venues and happenings. Clubs generally open their doors around 9pm or 10pm (some don't really get going until quite a bit later) and most close at around 3am or 4am.

AUBAR Map pp48–9

☎ 604-648-2227; www.aubarnightclub.com; 674 Seymour St, downtown; ⊗ Wed-Sat; Ⓜ Granville

Top 40, hip-hop and house blast from the speakers at this popular, mainstream near-Gastown haunt, complete with three bars and a smallish dance floor. Drop in on Wednesday for $3 beers, highballs and Jägermeisters, or save yourself for Rockstar Saturday, when the locals writhe around each other with abandon.

BAR NONE Map p71

☎ 604 684 3044; www.dhmbars.ca; 1222 Hamilton St, Yaletown; 🚌 C23

Yaletown's favorite haunt for young professionals has a scrubbed beatnik appearance, but within its exposed brick-and-beam shell the main topic of conversation is perfect cocktails and real estate prices. The great and good come to sip and sway at Thursday's Uptown night (hip-hop, soul, disco and funk) and Friday's Open House (house, retro and pop mixes).

CAPRICE Map pp48–9

☎ 604-685-3288; www.capricenightclub.com; 967 Granville St, downtown; ⊗ Wed-Sat; 🚌 4

Originally a movie theater – hence the giant screen evoking its Tinseltown past – Caprice is one of the best mainstream haunts on the Granville strip. The cavernous two-level venue is a thumping magnet for all the local preppies and their miniskirted girlfriends, while the adjoining lounge is great if you need to rest your eardrums and grab a restorative beer. Expect to have to line up here on weekends when the under-25s dominate.

CELEBRITIES Map pp48–9

☎ 604-681-6180; www.celebritiesnightclub.com; 1022 Davie St, downtown; ⊗ Mon-Sat; 🚌 6

The city's other big gay club (see Odyssey, p160), Celebrities hosts a series of sparkling, sometimes sequined event nights

top picks

CLUBS

- Royal Unicorn Cabaret (p160)
- Shine (p161)
- Honey (p160)
- Caprice (above)
- Republic (p160)

throughout the week, including a raucous Wednesday drag night and Saturday's massive dance party, when go-go dancers, live singers and occasional circus performers strut for your viewing pleasure. If you're on a budget, Tuesday is $3 highball night.

HONEY Map p77
☎ 604-685-7777; www.lotussoundlounge.com; 455 Abbott St, Chinatown; Ⓜ Stadium
A refreshing alternative to the Granville St party rabble, this laid-back resto-lounge venue transforms into a hopping club on weekends and is especially renowned for its Friday-night Mod Club, when a welcoming and pretence-free crowd of young hipsters dresses up for a night of pop-soul-and-everything-else fun. Good drinks specials, too.

MODERN Map p74
☎ 604-647-0121; www.dhmbars.ca; 7 Alexander St, Gastown; Ⓨ Fri & Sat; Ⓜ Waterfront
Nestled in a Gastown heritage building, this sleek, classy and ultra-contemporary lounge-nightclub combo attracts an over-20s crowd with money to burn on decadent cocktails. That doesn't mean they don't like to dance: Friday is hip-hop, funk and soul night, while Saturday's This is Not Detroit showcases electro, dance and house.

ODYSSEY Map pp48–9
☎ 604-604-3417; www.theodysseynightclub.com; 1251 Howe St, downtown; 🚌 6
The city's number-one gay club, combining regular drag nights on Wednesday and Sunday with a host of ever-changing special events throughout the week, Odyssey is a thumpingly fun night out. You don't have to be gay to dance here, but it certainly helps if you're planning to meet someone. The vibe is entertainingly risqué – hence Thursday night's Shower Power, when local beefcakes lather up in front of the slavering crowds.

PLAZA CLUB Map pp48–9
☎ 604-646-0064; www.plazaclub.net; 881 Granville St, downtown; Ⓨ Thu-Sat; 🚌 8
Another converted Granville St cinema, the Plaza offers a hopping, mosh pit–style dance floor backed by a circular bar that always seems to be crowded. The music is of the mainstream variety – Saturday's R&B, Top 40 and old-school night is best – and the crowd includes plenty of nonlocals in from the suburbs for their big night out on the town. The club is increasingly showcasing live acts, and low-priced bands are also starting to appear – check the website to see what's coming up.

REPUBLIC Map pp48–9
☎ 604-669-3266; www.dhmbars.ca; 958 Granville St, downtown; 🚌 4
If you make it this far up Granville, you're in for a loungey change of pace from the noisy clubs at the Robson St end; Republic attracts those sophisticated over-25s who have strayed all the way from Yaletown. Start your visit with a cocktail on the 2nd-floor patio while you look over the human wreckage of staggering late-night drunks. Then hit the dance floor, open nightly. Fastlife Thursday is recommended for great 80s, electro and house.

ROXY Map pp48–9
☎ 604-331-7999; www.roxyvan.com; 932 Granville St, downtown; 🚌 4
A raucous old-school nightclub that still has plenty of fans – including lots of partying youngsters who seem to be discovering it for the first time – this brazen old hussy is downtown's least pretentious dance space. Expect to be shaking your booty next to near-teenage funsters, kid-escaping soccer moms and UBC students looking for a bit of rough. On Sunday, don your buttless chaps and drop by for a wild western night out. Open nightly.

ROYAL UNICORN CABARET Map p77
☎ 604-961-5122; www.salbourg.com; 147 E Pender St, Chinatown; 🚌 8
A grungy, uninspiring old-school lounge throughout the week, the Unicorn is trans-

top picks

GAY & LESBIAN NIGHTLIFE

- Odyssey (above)
- Celebrities (p159)
- Fountainhead Pub (p148)
- Pumpjack Pub (p150)
- Fly Girl Productions (www.flygirlproductions.com) – lesbian events across Vancouver

formed on Salbourg Saturdays into perhaps the city's best alternative night out, when it's packed to the rafters with indie lads and lasses celebrating a relentless barrage of ironically cool dance music. They're certainly not here for the beer selection, which runs all the way from Coors to Kokanee. Arrive early to avoid the line-ups.

SHINE Map p74
☎ 604-408-4321; www.shinenightclub.com; 364 Water St, Gastown; Ⓜ Waterfront
With music from electro to funky house and hip-hop, Gastown's sexy subterranean Shine attracts a younger crowd and is divided into a noisy main room and an intimate cozy cave with a 40ft chill-out sofa. The club's Saturday night Big Sexy Funk (hip-hop and rock) is a local legend, while Thursday's 1990s retro night appeals to all those ancient 25-year-old hipsters out there (you know who you are).

SONAR Map p74
☎ 604-683-6695; www.sonar.bc.ca; 66 Water St, Gastown; Ⓨ Wed-Sat; 🚌 7
Many Vancouverites don't know it, but double-roomed Sonar is actually the city's premier club for experimental DJs and live club shows from all over the globe. On any given night you're likely to find progressive house, jazz fusion, soul, hip-hop, reggae or electronica. It's definitely worth braving the atmosphere – which can sometimes be thick with attitude – if you know exactly what you're looking for.

LIVE MUSIC
Vancouver's eclectic live-music scene includes blues, jazz, folk and a double A-side of good rock and alternative venues that should keep most visiting musos happy. Superstar performers typically hit the stages at sports stadiums and downtown theaters, while local stalwarts and rising stars plug in their instruments at the many small, club-style venues dotted around the city. If you're interested in what the locals are listening to, look out for shows by the Buttless Chaps (see the boxed text, p28), New Pornographers, Be Good Tanyas or Bif Naked.

Check p163 for local rock and alternative music promoters or touch base with Global Arts Concerts (www.globalartsconcerts.com), promoters of visiting jazz, roots, world and blues performers. For the usual booking fee, Ticketmaster

top picks
MUSIC FESTIVALS
- Vancouver Folk Music Festival (p14)
- Vancouver International Jazz Festival (p14)
- New Music West (p13)
- Burnaby Blues & Roots Festival (below)
- Festival Vancouver (p15)

(☎ 604-280-4444; www.ticketmaster.ca) sells tickets to concerts throughout the city.

Tickets can also be purchased for many gigs at independent record stores such as Zulu (p123) and Scratch (p111), while it's also worth dropping by Main St's Red Cat Records (p117), where the friendly staff are more than happy to answer questions on the city's music scene and point you in the direction of hot local bands.

Several venues (often those with the word 'club' in their title) offer memberships for $5 to $25 annually, providing discounts to shows, member-night parties and other perks. Some venues may claim you need to be a member to enter, but usually you just need to sign in as a guest and you'll get in without a problem.

BLUES
Downtown (below) is the center of all things blue in Vancouver, but if you fancy a smokin' alfresco day (and night) out, head to the 'burbs and the annual Burnaby Blues & Roots Festival (☎ 604-291-6864; www.burnabybluesfestival.com) in Deer Lake Park.

FAIRVIEW PUB Map p91
☎ 604-872-1262; www.fairviewpub.ca; 898 W Broadway, Fairview; cover $3; 🚌 9
Like a neighborhood pub that time forgot, the Fairview is a great little laid-back joint if all you want to do is grab a few beers, nosh on some chicken wings and catch some great blues licks. The regular house band hits the stage on Thursday with a rumbling back catalogue forged from 12 years on the road. If you miss the big night, there's an eclectic roster of music here most Fridays and Saturdays, including jazz, funk, retro and rock and roll.

YALE Map pp48–9
☎ 604-681-9253; www.theyale.ca; 1300 Granville St, downtown; cover $10-25; 🚌 4

A sassy unpretentious joint with a large stage, a devoted clientele and a beer-sticky dance floor, the Yale is the city's best blues hangout. Photos of Koko Taylor, Junior Wells and other stars who've played here adorn the 19th-century, brick-built interior, while latter-day regulars include Jim Byrnes, who holds court here like a king. Drop by from 3pm to 7pm Saturday and Sunday for free-entry jam sessions.

FOLK & WORLD

Touch base with the Rogue Folk Club (☎ 604-736-3022; www.roguefolk.bc.ca), which presents 50 annual shows and networking events for local and visiting folksters. If you're here in July, indulge in the weekend-long Vancouver Folk Music Festival (p14) at Jericho Beach.

CAFÉ DEUX SOLEILS Map p84

☎ 604-254-1195; www.cafedeuxsoleils.com; 2096 Commercial Dr, Commercial Dr; no cover; 🚌 20

A neighborhood hangout for the Drive's artsy bohemian bunch, this ramshackle gallery-like coffeehouse hosts poetry slams, open-mike nights and live music almost every evening. The eclectic roster of tunesmiths includes singer-songwriters, folk doyens and world-music performers, who sound increasingly good as you down the regional beers on offer.

JERICHO FOLK CLUB Map pp94–5

☎ 604-222-4113; www.discoverysailing.org /folksong; Jericho Sailing Centre, 1300 Discovery St, Kitsilano; cover $8; ⏱ 7:30pm Tue; 🚌 4

Hosted by the Jericho Folk Club in this convivial beachfront sailing center, local folkies stage their regular Tuesday-night event, kicking off at 7:30pm with a fun jam session. The evening then moves on to an open-mike hour – make sure you bring your tambourine – and concludes with a headline act that's guaranteed to have your toes tapping.

MAIN ON MAIN Map p81

☎ 604-709-8555; www.themainonmain.com; 4210 Main St, SoMa; no cover; 🚌 3

Complete with a restaurant serving good Greek comfort food, the warm and welcoming Main is one of Vancouver's liveliest folk and roots music venues. Professional performers – usually heartfelt local soloists or guitar-wielding singer-songwriters – hit

the stage Thursday to Saturday, delivering an ideal accompaniment to your souvlaki or moussaka.

JAZZ

Hep cats should touch base with the Coastal Jazz & Blues Society (☎ 604-872-5200; www.coastaljazz .ca), which orchestrates shows around the city throughout the year. It also runs the hugely successful Vancouver International Jazz Festival (p14), staging Canadian and international megastar shows plus tons of free outdoor concerts every June. Alternatively, drop by St Andrew's Wesley United Church (Map pp48–9; ☎ 604-683-4574; www.standrewswesleychurch.bc.ca; 1012 Nelson St, downtown; 🚌 2) at 4pm on Sundays for an unusual free Jazz Vespers performance.

CAPONES RESTAURANT & LIVE JAZZ CLUB Map p71

☎ 604-684-7900; www.caponesrestaurant.net; 1141 Hamilton St, Yaletown; no cover; 🚌 C23

A convivial restaurant venue – think quality pastas and pizzas – with a surprisingly strong roster of nightly mainstream jazz, this popular Yaletown haunt is an ideal spot if you're hungry for dinner and a show. House pianists and trios make up the early part of the week, while Friday and Saturday are reserved for visiting big acts and Sunday is the regular blues night.

CELLAR RESTAURANT & JAZZ CLUB Map pp94–5

☎ 604-738-1959; www.cellarjazz.com; 3611 W Broadway, Kitsilano; cover from $7; ⏱ Wed-Mon; 🚌 9

A serious muso venue where you're required to keep the noise down and respect the performers on the tiny corner stage, this subterranean 70-seat resto-club is as close as you'll get in Vancouver to a classic

top picks

LIVE JAZZ, BLUES, FOLK & WORLD

- Yale (p161)
- Café deux Soleils (left)
- Rime (opposite)
- Cellar Restaurant & Jazz Club (above)
- O'Doul's (opposite)

jazz venue. Known for showcasing hot local performers, as well as some great touring acts, this atmospheric spot lures aficionados from across the region with its mix of mainstream and edgier fare.

O'DOUL'S Map pp66–7
☎ 604-661-1400; www.odoulsrestaurant.com; 1300 Robson St, West End; no cover; 🚌 5
Free nightly jazz attracts locals and visitors to the Listel Vancouver hotel's laid-back resto-bar (see p151), a romantic, ambient-lit venue showcasing hot soloists, trios and quartets from the city and beyond. The focus is mainstream, but there's always a great buzz here during the Jazz Festival, when performers drop by to jam into the wee hours.

RIME Map p84
☎ 604-215-1130; www.rime.ca; 1130 Commercial Dr, Commercial Dr; cover free-$10; 🚌 20
Presenting a diverse grab-bag of musical genres but focusing on jazz and roots, this warm and welcoming Commercial Dr venue is a truly happening little joint. Enveloped by artworks and a funky décor, the interior is lined with little tables facing performers who know a thing or two about how to engage an audience. Sunday is artist-in-residence night, when a regular celebrated jazz exponent holds court, while the rest of the week ranges from folk to bluegrass and back again. There's a good Mediterranean bistro menu, too.

ROCK & ALTERNATIVE
Some of Vancouver's most beloved old-school rock and alt venues have closed in recent years – goodbye Pic, Lamplighter and Marine Club – as swanky lounges and clubs have taken over the scene. Make sure you support similar stalwarts of the old local scene, such as the Media Club and the Railway Club, on your visit to the city.

To see what's on during your stay, check the *Georgia Straight* or the online rosters of local promoters Live Nation (www.livenation.com) and Sealed With a Kiss (www.sealedwithakisspresents .com). Along with the following venues, these promoters also stage visiting acts at the cavernous GM Place (p47) stadium, the classical Orpheum Theatre (see the boxed text, p169) and the summertime alfresco Malkin Bowl (see Theatre Under the Stars, p175) in Stanley Park. If you're here in May, dip into New

top picks
LIVE ROCK & ALTERNATIVE
- Railway Club (p164)
- Media Club (p164)
- Commodore (p164)
- Cobalt (below)
- Backstage Lounge (below)

Music West (p13), Vancouver's best annual alt-music showcase.

ANZA CLUB Map p81
☎ 604-876-7128; www.anzaclub.org; 3 W 8th Ave, SoMa; no cover; 🚌 9
Local alt-music acts favor this homely, grunge-chic venue that has the ambiance of a worker's club without the edge. Like an eclectic community hall, it has an odd roster of quiz nights and darts events where you can meet and greet the locals, but there's also some fun grassroots music, including local punk and garage bands and the regular Monday-night bluegrass evening.

BACKSTAGE LOUNGE Map p87
☎ 604-687-1354; www.thebackstagelounge.com; 1585 Johnston St, Granville Island; cover free-$10; 🚌 50
This lively, newly smartened Granville Island hangout has been a mainstay of the local night-out scene for years, with daily booze specials (see p154), DJ-led dance nights and a great chill-out patio drawing the regulars. The live music – usually Wednesday to Saturday – is generally of the upbeat local band variety, with West Coast Wednesday showcasing two or three of the best.

COBALT Map p77
☎ 604-764-7865; www.thecobalt.net; 917 Main St, Chinatown; cover free-$10; 🚌 3
Vancouver's punk, hardcore and metal fans have made the grunge pub Cobalt their home in recent years. Don't be put off by its dodgy Downtown Eastside location: there's a welcoming, if mostly black-clad, crowd. The music – thrashed out by bands such as The Fiends, The Pissups and Malhavoc – is of the blistering, ear-bleeding

variety and is scheduled Monday, Wednesday, Friday and Saturday.

COMMODORE Map pp48–9

☎ 604-739-4550; www.livenation.com; 868 Granville St, downtown; cover $15-35; 🚊 4

Up-and-coming local bands know they've finally made it when they play the city's fave mid-sized music venue, a lovingly restored Art Deco ballroom that still has the bounciest dance floor in town – courtesy of stacks of tires placed under its floorboards. If you need a break from your mosh-pit shenanigans, collapse at one of the tables lining the perimeter, catch your breath, grab a beer and then plunge back in.

MEDIA CLUB Map pp48–9

☎ 604-608-2871; www.themediaclub.ca; 695 Cambie St, downtown; cover $5-25; Ⓜ Stadium

This intimate, dimly lit indie space tucked underneath the back of the Queen Elizabeth Theatre books inventive local acts that mix and match the genres, so you may have the chance to see electro-symphonic or acoustic metal groups alongside power pop, hip-hop and country bands – although probably not on the same night. A great place for a loud night out, this rivals the Railway Club for catching up-and-coming Vancouver bands.

PAT'S PUB Map p77

☎ 604-255-4301; www.patspub.ca; 403 E Hastings St, Chinatown; cover $3-15; 🚊 10

Saved from gentrification by its grungy location – the Downtown Eastside is unlikely to see a rash of swanky cocktail bars any-

time soon – the reinvented Pat's Pub used to be one of Vancouver's most happening jazz bars (Jelly Roll Morton was a regular early performer). Now focusing on indie rockers (mostly on Friday and Saturday), you can usually expect two or three bands to blow the roof off while you sup on your brewpub Classic Lager.

RAILWAY CLUB Map pp48–9

☎ 604-681-1625; www.therailwayclub.com; 579 Dunsmuir St, downtown; cover free-$10; Ⓜ Granville

The old-school Rail is great if you just want to grab a beer in a trad-pub setting (see p149), but what really makes it special is its enduring commitment to the indie music scene. Its little stage has seen dozens of rising stars kick-start their careers and it's still the best place in town to catch passionate, consistently high-quality acts, ranging from folk to metal to bluegrass to polka. If you don't like what's on, just slink to the back bar. Arrive before 7pm and there's no cover charge.

WISE CLUB Map p84

☎ 604-254-5858; www.wisehall.ca; 1882 Adanac St, Commercial Dr; cover free-$10; 🚊 20

This comfortably grungy former church hall is a friendly neighborhood gem that's close to the heart of in-the-know locals, who flock here to catch folk and ska bands and dances that remind them of the youth-club discos they used to attend. It's a great place to mix with cool East Vancouverites; the bouncy floor here brings out the mosh-pit desires in the most reluctant of dancers.

BLUELIST[1] (blu.list) *v.*
to recommend a travel experience.
What's your recommendation? www.lonelyplanet.com/bluelist

THE ARTS

top picks

- Vancouver Symphony Orchestra (p167)
- Vancouver Chamber Choir (p172)
- Vancouver New Music Society (p167)
- Pacific Baroque Orchestra (p166)
- Vancity International Film Centre (p171)
- Pacific Cinémathèque (p170)
- Bard on the Beach (p174)
- Scotiabank Dance Centre (p168)
- Philosopher's Café (p173)
- Playhouse Theatre Company (p175)

It's easy to think that Vancouver's Lycra-clad locals are a bunch of philistines when it comes to culture – how can opera and ballet fans also enjoy off-road mountain biking? – but in reality the city is a major regional center for artsy pursuits. On the highbrow side, there's an enormous array of classical music (below) on stage here, while dance (opposite) is one of the city's Canada-leading specialties. There are also dozens of theater troupes (p173) across Vancouver, covering everything from Shakespeare to contemporary and everything in between. And even though the Lower Mainland region is a popular location for Hollywood movie shoots, there's also a healthy domestic movie scene here (p168) and a great love among the locals for art-house productions. Finally, if you're in the mood for something a little more eclectic, the city is home to some regular spoken-word events (p172), including poetry and story slams.

To tap into the local scene, grab a bulging copy of the *Georgia Straight,* and also check the *Westender* and the *West Coast Life* section of the *Vancouver Sun.* All three appear on Thursday every week. Make sure you also check the city's festival calendar (p12) before you arrive; Vancouver is home to some excellent annual arts events that can satisfy the most hungry of traveling arts fans.

CLASSICAL MUSIC

Vancouver has a rich and resonant classical music scene, with particular strengths in baroque and chamber music. Along with recitals at downtown churches, the spectacular Orpheum Theatre and UBC's swanky, state-of-the-art Chan Centre (see the boxed text, p169), the city hosts festivals for fans of many genres. These include the frequently fascinating New Music Festival (p16) and the giant Festival Vancouver (p15). The following societies and orchestras stage shows across the city, usually running from fall to spring.

EARLY MUSIC VANCOUVER

☎ 604-732-1610; www.earlymusic.bc.ca; locations vary; tickets $20-55
Devoted to the performance and study of baroque music from the Middle Ages to the late Romantic era – often played on instruments authentic to the period – this

lively recital society stages a popular summer festival (p15) as well as a rolling roster of concerts throughout the year, usually from late October to May. Talks, workshops and events are also offered, so bring your lute in case there's a jam night.

FRIENDS OF CHAMBER MUSIC

☎ 604-437-5747; www.friendsofchambermusic .ca; Vancouver Playhouse; tickets adult/student $35-40/15
Taking over downtown's Vancouver Playhouse (see the boxed text, p169) for intermittent Tuesday-evening performances between October and April, the Friends stages a tasty menu of shows from international visiting musicians. It's the kind of roster where you'll see chamber musicians from the Lincoln Center one week and the Berlin Philharmonic wind quintet the next.

PACIFIC BAROQUE ORCHESTRA

☎ 604-215-0406; www.pacificbaroqueorchestra .com; locations vary; tickets adult/youth/student/ senior $28/free/12/23
Dedicated to baroque music from the 17th and 18th centuries, this thrilling Vancouver orchestra is highly regarded across North America. Its mandate is to perform the music the way it was originally written, which means using antique or authentic replica instruments and researching the prevalent techniques and styles of the period. Expect to hear plenty of violins and violas, accompanied by visiting harps and

top picks

ARTS FESTIVALS

- Festival Vancouver (p15)
- Vancouver International Fringe Festival (p16)
- Vancouver International Dance Festival (p13)
- Vancouver International Film Festival (p16)
- Vancouver International Writers & Readers Festival (p16)

harpsichords, as you listen in on fresh versions of works by Bach, Handel, Mozart et al.

VANCOUVER CHOPIN SOCIETY
☎ 604-871-4450; www.chopinsociety.org; locations vary; tickets $25-45
One of the city's smaller musical societies, this dedicated group is a must for fans of the French-born Polish piano composer. It usually stages five or six signature piano recitals between October and May from famed national and international soloists (they often add the works of other composers to their performances), and lectures are sometimes offered to sate the hunger of Chopin musos.

VANCOUVER NEW MUSIC SOCIETY
☎ 604-633-0861; www.newmusic.org; locations vary; tickets $15-30
Excitingly innovative and focusing on all manner of contemporary and new composing – from opera to electronica to mixed media – this society's performances can be an adventure in unfamiliar soundscapes. Coordinating a program of regional and visiting acts, its short annual festival (p16) takes place in October. Ask about its popular Soundwalks – free listening journeys around town that uncover the city's complex symphonies of everyday sounds.

VANCOUVER RECITAL SOCIETY
☎ 604-602-0363; www.vanrecital.com; locations vary; tickets $25-75
This group brings in some big international names – think Yo-Yo Ma, Jessye Norman or Kiri Te Kanawa (although not usually on the same bill) – for performances across the city, but it also nurtures up-and-coming hot musicians destined to be the next big classical thing. Straddling opera and orchestral works, you can expect to see great vocal soloists and celebrated ensembles wowing the locals during the society's October to May season.

VANCOUVER SYMPHONY ORCHESTRA
☎ 604-876-3434; www.vancouversymphony.ca; locations vary; tickets $25-60
The city's stirring symphony orchestra offers an accessible season of classics and 'pops.' Shows to look out for include matinees and film nights (when live scores are performed to well-known classics), plus visits from national and international soloists. There's also a series of Kids' Koncerts and a child-centered hands-on Instrument Fair to entice children from their pop-loving ways. Concerts often take place at the Orpheum Theatre (see the boxed text, p169), but the orchestra frequently unpacks its kettledrums at auditoriums throughout the Lower Mainland.

DANCE
Vancouver is a major center for Canadian dance, offering an esoteric array of classical ballet and edgy contemporary fare. The city is home to more than 30 professional companies as well as many internationally recognized choreographers. To touch base with the region's hot-foot crowd, pirouette over to the Scotiabank Dance Centre (p168). If you time your visit right, drop by for one of the region's key dance festivals: March's

LOCAL NOTES
While Vancouver's most popular – OK, its only – series of pre-lunch classical concerts started small in 1988, Music in the Morning (☎ 604-873-4612; www.musicinthemorning.org; locations vary; tickets adult/child/senior from $20/14/18) has grown to become one of the city's favorite daytime cultural fixes. Artists – who run the gamut from solo pianists to classical-guitar exponents to visiting string quartets – give short introductory talks before they blow any vestiges of morning tiredness from their audiences with the kind of stirring, life-enhancing shows that really set you up for the day.

The format has become so successful that themed Composers & Coffee (tickets $15-24) talks have been added, where musicians discuss a musical writer and explore their work via performance, as well as afternoon interactive Family Musik (tickets $14-28) shows aimed at kids. Most exciting of all, a series of bite-sized, one-hour early-evening concerts – under the Rush Hour (tickets $15-20) banner – have been launched, with performers treading the boards in the atmospheric old courtroom of the Vancouver Art Gallery (p46). It's a great way to catch a show in a cool but unfamiliar setting.

Vancouver International Dance Festival (p13) and July's Dancing on the Edge (p14).

BALLET BRITISH COLUMBIA

☎ 604-732-5003; www.balletbc.com; Queen Elizabeth Theatre; adult/child/senior from $27/21/27

A season from Vancouver's favorite dance company often includes the likes of *Giselle* and *Sleeping Beauty* jostling for attention with a world premiere or two and perhaps a night of experimental short pieces. Performing at the Queen Elizabeth Theatre (see the boxed text, opposite), the troupe's season runs from September to April, when it also welcomes visiting shows from acclaimed companies including the Royal Winnipeg Ballet and the National Ballet of Canada.

EXPERIMENTAL DANCE & MUSIC

Map p81

EDAM; ☎ 604-876-9559; www.edamdance.org; 303 E 8th Ave, SoMa; tickets $15-18; 🚊 3

Formed by dancers in 1982, this challenging contemporary troupe adopts a creative multimedia approach that may mix film, music and/or art into its athletic and expressive works, many created through an improvisational process for which EDAM has become famous. If you're lucky, the Echo Case – the company's longest-established improvisational ensemble – will be performing during your visit. With its own on-site studio, EDAM also performs at venues around the city.

HOLY BODY TATTOO

☎ 604-683-6552; www.holybodytattoo.org; locations vary; tickets $10-25

Formed by dancers Noam Gagnon and Dana Gingras, the internationally acclaimed Holy Body Tattoo has been performing riveting, edge-of-your-seat pieces to contemporary dance fans around the world for two decades. Most of their self-choreographed works still start out in Vancouver. They can sometimes be found at the Vancouver East Cultural Centre (see the boxed text, p173), if they're not gallivanting around the globe. Expect a host of multimedia fireworks to accompany the show.

KAREN JAMIESON DANCE

☎ 604-687-6675; www.kjdance.ca; locations vary; tickets $10-25

Bold, striking contemporary choreography and cross-cultural First Nations themes are just two of the hallmarks of this innovative troupe, founded in 1983. The group's work has taken on a more mystical quality in recent years, reinterpreting its older canon and mixing it with some moving new works. Performing at various locations around the city, the troupe often hits the stage at festivals, including Dancing on the Edge and the Vancouver International Dance Festival.

KOKORO DANCE

☎ 604-662-7441; www.kokoro.ca; locations vary; tickets free-$15

The name 'Kokoro' in Japanese means 'heart,' and it sure takes a lot of heart (not to mention guts) to annually perform *Butoh* stark naked on Wreck Beach in front of a crowd of several hundred. Combining modern and traditional Japanese dance approaches, the troupe pops up at venues and festivals (not just dance ones) across the city – check the website to see where it might be next.

SCOTIABANK DANCE CENTRE Map pp48–9

☎ 604-606-6400; www.thedancecentre.ca; 677 Davie St, downtown; tickets $10-25; 🚊 4

The West Coast's de facto dance headquarters, this cleverly reinvented old bank building offers a kaleidoscopic array of activities that actually makes it Canada's foremost dance center. Home to resident companies – Ballet BC is based here – it also houses classes, workshops, performances and events throughout the year. For visiting dance nuts, there's almost always something on that's worth seeing (check the website): if you're really lucky the biennial Dance in Vancouver showcase of BC's best contemporary offerings will be on during your visit.

FILM

Vancouver is a vast, shimmering silver screen of independent, second-run and art-house movie theaters. You'll have no trouble catching the latest mindless blockbuster at a mega-multiplex in the afternoon and following it with a depressing, subtitled dirge about French taxi drivers in the evening. Cheer yourself up the next day with an IMAX movie that will have you soaring over the Grand Canyon or ducking and diving through the Great Barrier Reef. For cinema

PERFORMING-ARTS VENUES

Few of the city's performance groups – from orchestras to dance troupes to theater companies – have their own venues, with most booking space and sharing from the same array of stages across the city. The following venues are the most likely spots for your cultural big night out.

- Centre in Vancouver for Performing Arts (Map pp48–9; ☎ 604-602-0616; www.centreinvancouver.com; 777 Homer St, downtown; Ⓜ Stadium)
- Chan Centre (Map p100; ☎ 604-822-9197; www.chancentre.com; 6265 Crescent Rd, UBC; 🚌 4)
- Orpheum Theatre (Map pp48–9; ☎ 604-665-3050; www.city.vancouver.bc.ca/theatres; 884 Granville St, downtown; 🚌 4)
- Performance Works (Map p87; ☎ 604-687-3020, www.gicculturalsociety.org; 1218 Cartwright St, Granville Island; 🚌 50)
- Queen Elizabeth Theatre (Map pp48–9; ☎ 604-665-3050; www.city.vancouver.bc.ca/theatres; 609 Cambie St, downtown; Ⓜ Stadium)
- Roundhouse Community Arts & Recreation Centre (Map p71; ☎ 604-713-1800; www.roundhouse.ca; 181 Roundhouse Mews, cnr Davie St & Pacific Blvd, Yaletown; 🚌 C21)
- Vancouver East Cultural Centre (Map p84; ☎ 604-251-1363; www.thecultch.com; 1895 Venables St, Commercial Dr; 🚌 20)
- Vancouver Playhouse (Map pp48–9; ☎ 604-873-3311; www.vancouverplayhouse.com; cnr Hamilton & Dunsmuir Sts, downtown; Ⓜ Stadium)
- Waterfront Theatre (Map p87; ☎ 604-685-3005; www.gicculturalsociety.org; 1412 Cartwright St, Granville Island; 🚌 50)

listings and special event schedules, check the weekly *Georgia Straight* or daily *Vancouver Sun*, or visit www.cinemaclock.com to see what's on at all area theaters.

Try not to miss the Vancouver International Film Festival (p16) in late September, where you can rub shoulders with local moviemakers and catch some of the world's most exciting art-house pictures. If it's not on while you're here, drop in to the Vancity International Film Centre (p171), where flicks, lectures and movie events are staged throughout the year.

If you're inspired to direct your own searing indictment of whatever takes your fancy, you might want to look into enrolling at the Vancouver Film School (Map pp48–9; ☎ 604-685-5808, 800-661-4101; www.vfs.com; 198 W Hastings St, downtown), which has programs in animation, game design and visual effects.

Tickets

First-run movie tickets cost $10 to $12 for adults, less for students and seniors, with matinees (shows before 6pm) usually a couple of dollars cheaper. Tuesday is discount day at many cinemas, which means it's often the busiest night of the week. Admission to second-run theaters, repertory cinemas and art-house joints is better value and typically costs $6 to $10.

CN IMAX THEATRE Map pp48–9
☎ 604-682-4629; www.imax.com/vancouver; 999 Canada Place, downtown; adult/child $12/11; Ⓜ Waterfront

Located toward the tip of Canada Place, this giant-format movie theater generally screens worthy documentaries on themes such as the natural world and ancient historic sites – and the directors always find the time to fly the camera over a soaring clifftop vantage point to keep you awake. Occasionally, reformatted *Matrix* or *Star Wars* movies are added to the program. It's a similar story over at Science World, which has its own big-screen Omnimax Theatre (p76).

DENMAN PLACE CINEMA Map pp66–7
☎ 604-683-2201; 1737 Comox St, West End; adult/child $6/4; 🚌 5

The closest cheap-flicks cinema to the downtown core, this subterranean, almost kitsch, 1970s-style joint was a first-run movie house until the multiplexes moved into town. The owners closed it, whacked out half the seats and reopened it as a second-run theater with lots of legroom. It offers an eclectic mix of just-past-their-prime blockbusters and some lesser-known artsy flicks. The cinema is closed Sunday.

FIFTH AVENUE CINEMAS Map pp94–5

☎ 604-734-7469; www.festivalcinemas.ca; 2110 Burrard St, Kitsilano; adult $9-12, child $7-8; 🚍 44
The popular Fifth Ave screens mostly indie and foreign films, although a few handpicked Hollywood releases (the ones requiring more than half a brain) may slip through the net. Moviegoers can belly up to the lobby cappuccino bar for above-par baked goods before the show. A non-mandatory $12 annual membership provides about 15% savings on tickets throughout the year, while on Tuesday seats are $7 for everyone.

GRANVILLE 7 Map pp48–9

☎ 604-684-4000; www.empiretheatres.com; 855 Granville St, downtown; tickets $6.99; 🚍 4
The remaining vestige of a once-thriving cluster of cinemas lining both sides of downtown's old entertainment strip, the Granville 7 might not be around much longer – which probably explains why the escalators are hardly ever switched on – but it still screens a good selection of arty and mainstream flicks. Empire Theatres, its new owners, have recently reduced the ticket price to an enticing $6.99 for all shows.

HOLLYWOOD THEATRE Map pp94–5

☎ 604-738-3211; www.hollywoodtheatre.ca; 3123 W Broadway, Kitsilano; adult/child $7/5; 🚍 9
Two-thirds blockbuster and one-third art house make up the roster here, showing exactly where the funding for this popular local theater comes from. Tickets are a great deal, especially since they include two shows – double bills are every evening

top picks

FOR KIDS

- Carousel Theatre (p174)
- Family Musik, Music in the Morning (p167)
- Spring Break Theatre Festival, Arts Club Theatre Company (p174)
- Kids' Concerts, Vancouver Symphony Orchestra (p167)
- CN IMAX Theatre (p169)

and on weekend afternoons. Bucking the trend, Monday night is cheap night here, when you can catch two movies for just $5.

PACIFIC CINÉMATHÈQUE Map pp48–9

☎ 604-688-3456; www.cinematheque.bc.ca; 1131 Howe St, downtown; adult/student $9.50/8; 🚍 4
This beloved nonprofit repertory cinema operates like an eclectic ongoing film festival with a daily-changing program of movies. A $3 annual membership is required – although if you tell them you're a visitor, they'll usually let you off – before you can skulk in the dark with the chin-stroking movie buffs, who would name their children after Fellini and Bergman if they ever had girlfriends.

RIDGE THEATRE Map pp94–5

☎ 604-738-6311; www.festivalcinemas.ca; 3131 Arbutus St, Kitsilano; adult $9-12, child $7-8; 🚍 16
A community institution mixing foreign films and Hollywood fare, this is a lively and convivial cinema in which to hang out

FILM FESTIVALS

While the leading star of the city's film festival scene is late September's giant Vancouver International Film Festival (p16), several intriguing alternative events hit city screens throughout the year. Butter up your popcorn at one or two of these.

- Vancouver Asian Film Festival (www.vaff.org) Emerging and established North American–Asian filmmakers screen works over four days in November.
- Vancouver International Digital Festival (www.vidfest.com) Digital video, animation and experimental mixed media screenings; held in September.
- Vancouver International Mountain Film Festival (www.vimff.org) A week of movies in February about mountain culture and sports.
- Vancouver Latin American Film Festival (www.vlaff.org) Held in September, it's a week of movies illuminating the region's rich culture and social issues.
- Vancouver Queer Film Festival (www.outonscreen.com) Western Canada's largest film event by and for gays and lesbians; held in August around the same time as Pride Week (p15).

UNEXPECTED SILVER SCREENS

If you're fed up with the multiplex experience or just fancy catching a familiar movie in a quirky new setting, drop by downtown's diner-style Templeton (p128) restaurant on Monday nights. While you tuck into your organic burger and large, old-school milkshake, you can catch a free movie on the projector screen above the counter. Movies start at 8:30pm – call ahead after 4pm and the staff can tell you what's on that night.

Movie buffs will also enjoy a trip to the SoMa area's laid-back Anza Club (p163), where the ongoing Celluloid Social Club (☎ 604-730-8339; www.celluloidsocialclub.com; admission $5; ☼ 7:30pm Wed, mid-month) meets monthly for lively screenings and drinks with local independent film and video artists, who get an audience for their new work and a chance to discuss its themes and techniques. Screenings last a couple of hours and are followed by a short interview and Q&A session.

If that all sounds a little intellectual and all you want to do is catch a mindless classic horror flick, Stanley Park is your best bet, with its irregular summertime Monsters in the Meadow (Map p54; ☎ 604-473-6205; admission free; ☼ 9pm) outdoor movie screenings. Phone ahead to check (movies are cancelled if it's too wet or windy), then bring your blanket and picnic to the Ceperley Meadow area near the Second Beach swimming pool. Expect to hide behind your neighbor as movie baddies such as Dracula and King Kong stalk the screen in front of you.

with the locals. Check out the retro building's glass-enclosed 'crying room,' where parents can take wee noisemakers and still watch the movie without disturbing other patrons. Unlike most cinemas, where the food typically has the nutritional value of a hockey puck, the concession here serves organic fruit.

SCOTIABANK THEATRE Map pp48–9
☎ 604-630-1407; www.cineplex.com; 900 Burrard St, downtown; adult/child $11.95/9.95; 🚌 2
Downtown's shiny new multiplex was big enough to attract its own corporate sponsor when it opened in 2005, but it's actually the city's Odeon chain flagship. It's the most likely theater to be screening that latest must-see *Halloween* sequel or Bruce Willis action flick. The screens here are stacked on top of each other like an apartment building. Like the Grinch, it has no matinee or Tuesday discounts.

TINSELTOWN CINEMAS Map p77
☎ 604-806-0799; www.cinemark.com; 88 W Pender St, Chinatown; adult/child $10.75/8.75; Ⓜ Stadium
A Vancouver favorite, Tinseltown – incongruously located on the 3rd floor of a ghost-town Chinatown shopping mall – combines blockbuster and art-house offerings, screened in a convivial but high-tech multiplex setting. Stadium seating is the norm here and it's the ideal place to shelter on a rainy Vancouver day, especially with its bottomless coffee cup policy. Drop by on bargain Tuesday, when tickets are $8.75 all day.

VANCITY INTERNATIONAL FILM CENTRE Map pp48–9
☎ 604-683-3456; www.viff.org; 1181 Seymour St, downtown; adult/student $9.50/7.50; 🚌 4
The state-of-the-art headquarters of the Vancouver International Film Festival screens a wide array of movies throughout the year in the kind of auditorium that cinephiles usually only dream of: think generous legroom, wide arm rests and great sight lines from each of its 175 seats. It's a place where you can watch a four-hour postmodern epic about a dripping tap and still feel comfortable. Check the ever-changing schedule for shows and special events, and remember that a $12 annual membership is mandatory but the cost of your first movie ticket is deducted from this.

VAN EAST CINEMA Map p84
☎ 604-251-1313; 2290 Commercial Dr, Commercial Dr; adult/child $7.50/5.50; Ⓜ Broadway
This balconied old-school cinema shows an eclectic schedule of critically acclaimed new and classic movies (plus second-run blockbusters to keep the money rolling in), with occasional late-night screenings and special events such as moviemaker lectures. It's a five-minute stroll north of the Broadway SkyTrain station; continue on up the road after the show and discuss the flick at one of Commercial's chatty bars (see p153).

OPERA & CHORAL

Twinned with its classical repertoire, Vancouver has a soaring array of options for visitors who enjoy operatic or choral performances –

most concerts are staged at similar venues throughout the city. Visit the websites of the following performance societies to see what's on the menu during your visit, or check in with **Global Arts Concerts** (www.globalartsconcerts.com), a regional promoter that stages some shows around the city.

VANCOUVER BACH CHOIR
☎ 604-921-8012; www.vancouverbachchoir.com; Orpheum Theatre; tickets $25-50
The city's largest nonprofessional choir, this 150-strong, all-ages group can lift the spirits on the soggiest of Vancouver days. Performing five concerts annually at the Orpheum Theatre (see the boxed text, p169), its Christmastime 'Sing Along Messiah' is guaranteed to raise the hairs on the back of your neck as you join in to try and raise the roof on the auditorium. Rivaling it for fun, May's Last Night of the Proms show is a chance to wave your arms and sing 'Land of Hope and Glory' as if the empire depended on it.

VANCOUVER CANTATA SINGERS
☎ 604-730-8856; www.vancouvercantatasingers .com; locations vary; tickets adult/student from $24/18
Renowned as the city's leading semiprofessional exponent of baroque choral pieces – receiving critical acclaim from across the country – the Vancouver Cantata crew also keeps things current by commissioning and performing works by new composers. Clearing its collective throat at churches and auditoria across the city, its concert series usually runs late October to April.

VANCOUVER CHAMBER CHOIR
☎ 604-738-6822; www.vancouverchamberchoir .com; locations vary; tickets $22-40
Vancouver's top professional choir is an award-winning ensemble of 20 singers recognized around the world for its diverse repertoire, interpretive skills and performing excellence. In addition to busy touring and recording commitments, the choir performs a hotly anticipated season from late September to May at venues around the city. Rarely less than outstanding concerts can range from chant to folksong, traditional to avant-garde, a cappella to orchestra or jazz trio.

VANCOUVER OPERA
☎ 604-683-0222; www.vancouveropera.ca; locations vary; tickets from $25

The city's well-regarded opera company stages four annual productions at the Queen Elizabeth Theatre (p169) during its November to May season. While the shows are typically traditional productions of well-known favorites such as *Pagliacci* and *La Bohème* – complete with lavish sets and costumes – there's usually one show per season that's a little less mainstream or even edgy. Arrive early at the theater for a free 20-minute talk about the show you're about to see.

SPOKEN WORD
There's an array of under-the-radar spoken-word events in Vancouver, which can run from free readings at local libraries to poetry slams at cool cafés and lectures at theaters and halls around the city. If you're a visiting bookworm, check into the dozens of readings and discussions staged during October's annual Vancouver International Writers & Readers Festival (p16), or time your visit for the one-day, late-September Word on the Street (☎ 604-684-8266; www.thewordonthestreet.ca; admission free) event, when authors, poets, booksellers and magazine publishers cluster around the Vancouver Public Library (p47), offering readings, recitals and plenty of lovely books to buy. The library is also home to regular author readings.

COLD READING SERIES Map p91
☎ 604-733-3783, ext 202; www.coldreadingseries .com; Beaumont Studios, 315 W 5th Ave, Fairview; suggested donation $5; 8pm Thu; 15
Visiting actors are cast on the spot – they'll audition you on the night if you feel the urge – to read through an always-changing selection of new plays, movie scripts and TV pilots submitted by nervous local writers. It's like a workshop with an audience and it can be a recipe for a fun night out if you're a creative type who likes to listen. The intimate studio theater space adds to the dynamic, work-in-progress atmosphere.

PANDORA'S COLLECTIVE
www.pandorascollective.com; locations vary; times & dates vary
Promoting self expression through literature, this busy group stages events throughout Vancouver, including open-mike readings, poetry nights and 'word whips,' where you're given 15 minutes to write some engaging prose on a given cue. Locations are

SAVING THE CULTCH

While the city has a good selection of midsized, multipurpose performance venues, where dance, music and theater can comfortably hit the stage, one gable-roofed old Eastside site has gained a special place in the hearts of local arties.

The **Vancouver East Cultural Centre** (Map p84; ☎ 604-251-1363; www.thecultch.com; 1895 Venables St, Commercial Dr; 🚌 20), known by just about everyone as 'The Cultch,' occupies a once-abandoned 1909 church building near Commercial Dr, and has been a gathering place for performers and audiences since being officially designated as a cultural space in 1973.

But after three decades of hard knocks from more than 7500 concerts and shows, the quirky old lady was showing her age and looked like she might have to be retired. Not about to let their old neighbor disappear, the city's arts community – many members of which had performed at the Cultch – kick-started a renovation appeal.

The appeal won an initial $1 million grant from the community fund of a local bank, and plans have been drafted to transform the venerable old hall into a state-of-the-art performance space with a new studio theater and art gallery. With the appeal ongoing, the Cultch is open for business and still offers Vancouver's most diverse and exciting array of live performance arts.

usually coffeehouses around the city. Check the collective's website for upcoming events and consider its annual Summer Dream Literary Arts Festival, a day of readings and bookish shenanigans in Stanley Park.

PHILOSOPHER'S CAFÉ

☎ 604-291-5295; www.philosopherscafe.net; locations vary; admission free-$5; ⏲ times & dates vary

This is a popular series of engaging philosophical discussions staged at restaurants, cafés and galleries in Vancouver and across the Lower Mainland. You can listen to the theories being espoused or wade in with your own choice ideas. Each night has a different theme, which can range from 'marijuana in BC' to 'the meaning of literature' to 'painting is dead,' and the moderated discussions are often brain-fizzingly lively – just try not to hit anyone. Check the online calendar for times, locations and themes.

POETRY SLAM Map p84

☎ 604-254-1195; www.cafedeuxsoleils.com; Café deux Soleils, 2096 Commercial Dr, Commercial Dr; admission $5; ⏲ 9pm 1st & 3rd Mon monthly; 🚌 20

If you think of poetry as a tweedy, pulse-slowing experience, drop by one of the twice-monthly slam events at the Café deux Soleils (p154) for a taste of high-speed, high-stakes slamming. The expert performers will blow your socks off with their verbal dexterity, which often bears more than a passing resemblance to rap. Down a couple of beers and have a go yourself – not that easy, eh?

STORY SLAM Map p81

☎ 604-879-1924; www.boltsoffiction.org; Our Town Café, 245 E Broadway, SoMa; suggested donation $5; ⏲ 8pm 2nd & 4th Wed monthly; 🚌 3

You're guaranteed tons of naughty literary fun at this twice-monthly story-making competition staged at SoMa's popular Our Town Café. Ten storytellers are each given five minutes to write a piece on a given topic; it's then read to the crowd, who are hyped up and ready to kill after several herbal teas and decaf coffees. A great event to meet the local culture vultures.

VANCOUVER PUBLIC LIBRARY

Map pp48–9

☎ 604-331-3602; www.vpl.ca; 350 W Georgia St, downtown; admission free; ⏲ times vary; Ⓜ Stadium

A broad array of Canadian and international novelists, poets and children's storytellers give readings at the VPL, which has a teeming schedule of ever-changing and usually free events, including occasional readings by a Lonely Planet author or two. Check the online schedule for events or just drop in to see what's on when you're passing by.

THEATER

From mainstream to fringe, theater thrives in Vancouver: you can catch an important new work from a major Canadian playwright one night and follow it up the next evening with a quirky off-the-wall production in an intimate studio space. While the season generally runs from October to May, there are a couple of choice theatrical events that ensure the grease-paint is almost a year-round smell here.

These include the summertime Bard on the Beach (below), where locals pack the tents of Vanier Park for atmospheric retellings of *Hamlet, King Lear* et al, and September's Vancouver International Fringe Festival (p16).

If challenging is your theatrical bag and you're in town for a while, consider a See Seven (www.seeseven.bc.ca) pass, which gives you entry to seven out of 12 shows from some of the city's leading independent theater companies for just $87.

Tickets

Ticketmaster (☎ 604-280-4444; www.ticketmaster.ca) is not surprisingly the standard agent for many theatrical productions, although some theaters prefer to bypass it. For advance regular-price tickets and same-day half-price tickets, try the homegrown Tickets Tonight (☎ 604-684-2787; www.ticketstonight.ca). In addition, discounts are normally available for students, seniors and children – ask theater box offices for details.

ARTS CLUB THEATRE COMPANY
☎ 604-687-1644; www.artsclub.com; tickets $30-60; locations vary
Musicals, international classics and works by contemporary Canadian playwrights are part of the mix at this leading theater company. If you're curious about West Coast theatrics, look out for plays by Morris Panych, BC's favorite playwright son. Its two performance spaces are the Granville Island Stage (Map p87; 1585 Johnson St, Granville Island; 📮 50) and the refurbished 1930s Stanley Theatre (Map p91; 2750 Granville St, South Granville; 📮 10). If you've got kids in tow, check the company's Spring Break Theatre Festival (p13), a week of live sprog-friendly shows.

BARD ON THE BEACH
☎ 604-739-0559; www.bardonthebeach.org; Vanier Park, Kitsilano; tickets $17-31; ☒ Jun-Sep; 📮 22
Watching Shakespeare performed while the sun sets behind the North Shore mountains looming through the open back of a tented stage is a singular Vancouver highlight. An enduring favorite summer pastime for city culture hounds, there are usually three or four Bard plays on offer, and a related playwright is sometimes added to the mix. The smaller studio stage showcases slightly less mainstream fare.

Free preshow talks are offered before Tuesday-night performances.

BOCA DEL LUPO
☎ 604-684-2622; www.bocadellupo.com; locations vary; tickets $10-15
Dedicated to the creation of new works of physical theater using collaborative processes and interactions between the performers and audience, this cutting-edge experimental troupe fuses international approaches with its team of local actors. New theater is the name of the game here, and the company often brings in collaborators from across the country (or the world) to keep things fresh.

CAROUSEL THEATRE Map p87
☎ 604-685-6217; www.carouseltheatre.ca; Waterfront Theatre, 1412 Cartwright St, Granville Island; tickets adult/child $20/13; 📮 50
Performing at Granville Island's Waterfront Theatre (see the boxed text, p169), this smashing child-focused theater company stages some great, wide-eyed fantasy productions that adults often enjoy just as much as kids. Adaptations of children's classics such as *The Hobbit, Peter Pan* and *The Wind in the Willows* have featured in the past, with clever versions of Shakespeare and Dickens works added to the mix for older children. The company's free outdoor Shakespeare performances by teen actors is a highlight.

ELECTRIC COMPANY
☎ 604-253-4222; www.electriccompanytheatre.com; locations vary; tickets $20-28
This very exciting company presents original works with lots of visual imagery and nontraditional staging (one recent production took place around a community center's pool). Expect lots of visually stunning

top picks

THEATER COMPANIES

- Playhouse Theatre Company (opposite)
- Bard on the Beach (left)
- Arts Club Theatre Company (left)
- Firehall Arts Centre (opposite)
- Touchstone Theatre Company (opposite)

original imagery, exemplifying the notion that theater really can be magic.

FIREHALL ARTS CENTRE Map p74
☎ 604-689-0926; www.firehallartscentre.ca; 280 E Cordova St, Gastown; tickets $10-30; 🚌 7

The leading player in Vancouver's more challenging avant-garde theater scene, this intimate, studio-sized venue is located inside a historic fire station. It presents culturally diverse, contemporary drama and dance, with an emphasis on showcasing emerging talent. There's an additional outdoor courtyard stage and a convivial licensed lounge where visiting thesps and drama fans discuss the scene over a few beers. The season runs from September to June.

GATEWAY THEATRE Map pp44–5
☎ 604-270-1812; www.gatewaytheatre.com; 6500 Gilbert Rd, Richmond, Greater Vancouver; tickets adult/child $36/19; 🚌 407

The Lower Mainland's third-largest theater company (and Richmond's only professional live theater), the state-of-the-art Gateway has two stages and runs a full roster of shows from October to April. Slick productions of contemporary favorites and older classics – there's usually at least one musical here per season – occupy the main stage, while intriguing and more challenging work fills the studio space, including some premieres of bold new works.

GREEN THUMB COMPANY
☎ 604-254-4055; www.greenthumb.bc.ca; locations vary; tickets $15-30

This long-standing company presenting theater for children addresses social issues in an entertaining and meaningful way. Most of its performances take place at the Vancouver East Cultural Centre (see the boxed text, p173).

MORTAL COIL
☎ 604-874-6153; www.mortalcoil.bc.ca; locations vary; tickets $10-16

You can expect stilts, crazy costumes and fantastic masks to be part of the show with this, one of Vancouver's most determinedly original theatrical troupes. Sensory, visionary and magical, its theatrical extravaganzas usually appeal to adults and children alike.

PLAYHOUSE THEATRE COMPANY
☎ 604-873-3311; www.vancouverplayhouse .com; 600 Hamilton St, downtown; tickets $33-66; 🕒 Oct-Apr; Ⓜ Stadium

Mainstream and generally 'safer' in its selection than the city's edgier companies, Vancouver's pre-eminent city-run theater troupe performs in the purpose-built Vancouver Playhouse (see the boxed text, p169). Its five- or six-play season includes original Canadian and international works featuring top-tier regional actors and directors. There's usually a crowd-pleasing reinvented classic musical thrown into the mix as well. Productions here are slick and impressive.

RADIX THEATRE
☎ 604-254-0707; www.radixtheatre.org; locations & ticket prices vary

This small, highly experimental theater company deploys a variety of multimedia approaches to produce provocative, socially relevant and always entertaining short plays. It often appears at festivals and events around the city and has been known to appear at the FUSE social gathering at the Vancouver Art Gallery (p46).

THEATRE UNDER THE STARS Map p54
☎ 604-687-0174; www.tuts.bc.ca; Malkin Bowl, Stanley Park; tickets adult/child $28/24; 🕒 mid-Jul–mid-Aug; 🚌 19

Stanley Park's old-school Malkin Bowl is an atmospheric open-air venue in which to catch a summertime show. The season never gets too serious, usually featuring two enthusiastically performed Broadway musicals, but it's hard to beat the location, especially as the sun fades over the mountains peeking from behind the stage. Increasingly, the venue is being used for music, with visiting bands such as Wilco and Crowded House performing here recently.

TOUCHSTONE THEATRE COMPANY
☎ 604-709-9973; www.touchstonetheatre.com; locations vary; tickets adult/child $26/15; 🕒 Nov-Apr

One of Vancouver's most vital and refreshing theater companies, Touchstone has been treading the local boards for more than 30 years. It's never lost touch with its commitment to nurture and stage contemporary Canadian theater and it often premieres new work by local writers or stages the first regional productions of important

SCHOOL PLAY

Several of Vancouver's colleges and universities incorporate lively drama departments, offering excellent productions at great prices. If you're a visiting theater buff on a budget, smell the greasepaint at one of these recommended student playhouses.

- **Exit 22** (Map pp44–5; ☎ 604-990-7810; www.capcollege.bc.ca/theatre; Capilano College, 2055 Purcell Way, North Vancouver; tickets $10–20; 🚌 251) North Van's Cap College is home to this well-established theater company, affiliated with its drama department, which performs at the college's smashing 372-seat performance space. Its season – often featuring comedies, classics and contemporary works – runs from November to February, with the theater used by touring musicians the rest of the time.
- **Frederic Wood Theatre** (Map p100; ☎ 604-822-2678; www.theatre.ubc.ca; 6354 Crescent Rd, UBC; tickets $14–20; 🚌 4) UBC's drama students, grads and faculty stage their biggest shows here, but they also have two studio theaters where they try out more challenging fare. The season usually runs September to March, with each production lasting around a week. Expect a roster of classics and contemporary plays.
- **Studio 58** (Map pp44–5; ☎ 604-323-5227; www.langara.bc.ca/studio58; Langara College, 100 W 49th Ave, SoMa; tickets $15.50-20.50; 🚌 3) Named after the room number of the theater space at Langara College campus, which is a two-block walk west of Main St near the Punjabi Market area, Studio 58 has grown to become one of Western Canada's most respected theater companies, hiring professional directors to work on each of its four annual productions. You might catch musicals, Shakespeare or Canadian premieres here.

national works. The company performs around the city – check the website to see what it's up to during your visit.

UP IN THE AIR
☎ 604-715-7580; www.upintheairtheatre.com; locations and ticket prices vary

Challenging, intelligent and often darkly humorous are the keywords with this company, which is renowned across the city for staging works by new playwrights. Audiences are often included in the shows, so expect to be called upon at any moment. It's your big chance for a career on the stage.

BLUELIST[1] (blu,list) *v.*
to recommend a travel experience.
What's your recommendation? www.lonelyplanet.com/bluelist

SPORTS & ACTIVITIES

top picks

- **Vancouver Canucks** (p187)
- **Vancouver Canadians** (p187)
- **BC Lions** (p187)
- **Sun Run** (p182)
- **Kayaking** at Deep Cove (p180)
- **Cycling** the Stanley Park seawall (p178)
- **Hiking** the Grouse Grind (p180)
- **Skiing** at Grouse Mountain (p183)
- **Swimming** at Second Beach (p185)
- Luxury treatments at **Spa Utopia** (p187)

SPORTS & ACTIVITIES

Vancouverites have a passion for the outdoors – it's hard not to when the outdoors is so in your face. But the variety of available activities is what really impresses here: this truly is a city where you can ski in the morning and hit the beach in the afternoon, although it would make for quite a tiring day out. In between, you could hike through a rainforest, swim in a giant saltwater pool, windsurf along the coast or kayak to your heart's content – and it really will be content with the backdrop of a sunset over the city's skyscrapers or the fjords and wilderness of the looming mountains.

If that all sounds a little *too* active, sports fans of the armchair variety will likely enjoy the city's spectator options – from hockey to horse racing to the upcoming 2010 Winter Olympics – while those who just like to be pampered have plenty of opportunities to hit a day spa or two and build a deep and meaningful relationship with a massage table. If you indulge a little too much at the city's bars and restaurants, don't forget there are lots of gyms to lick you back into shape.

ACTIVITIES

It's hard *not* to be active in Vancouver, with its plethora of outdoorsy resources as well as its full menu of indoor facilities for those rainy days when you still want to raise your heart rate. Pick up a Vancouver Board of Parks & Recreation (☎ 604-257-8400; http://vancouver.ca/parks) activity guide from the Touristinfo Centre (p236) or head to the board's website for comprehensive listings covering facilities and courses.

Canada's favorite outdoor-lovers' mega-mart, Mountain Equipment Co-op (p118) rents all sorts of gear and has weekend specials where you collect the goods at 3pm Thursday, bring them back Monday and only pay for Saturday and Sunday. Visit its website (www.mec.ca) for a calendar of local events and activities, ranging from group hikes to guided kayak paddles.

CYCLING

Vancouver is a cycle-friendly city with a good network of designated bike routes. See p223 for info and resources on biking in the city. You can also touch base on local bike issues via Momentum (www.momentumplanet.com) magazine, available free online. Many of the city's routes are urban, but Cypress Mountain also offers a summertime bike park.

The city's favorite (ie most crowded) cycling route is the one-way Stanley Park seawall, where cyclists (plus joggers, walkers and bladers) have to keep their eyes on the road rather than stare open-mouthed at the sea-to-sky vistas. After circling the park to English Bay, you can pedal on along the north side of False Creek toward Science World, where the route

turns up the south side of False Creek toward Granville Island, Kitsilano Beach and, finally, UBC. This extended route is around 25km.

Alternatively, you can cycle through Stanley Park, over the Lions Gate Bridge to West Vancouver, and then along Marine Dr to Horseshoe Bay. If that's not enough, take the ferry over to Bowen Island (p217) and cycle around it before making the trip back. From Vancouver to Horseshoe Bay is about a 40km round-trip. Of course, you could always spend the night on Bowen and return the following morning.

The following businesses rent or service bikes.

BAYSHORE BIKE RENTALS Map pp66–7
☎ 604-688-2453; www.bayshorebikerentals.ca; 745 Denman St, West End; per hr/8hr $5.60/20.80; ⏰ 9am-9pm May-Aug, 9am-dusk Sep-Apr; 🚌 19
This is one of several rival businesses taking advantage of their Stanley Park proximity, and the folks here will rent you just about anything to get you rolling around the seawall. The 21-speed mountain bikes are its bread and butter, but it also hires in-line skates, tandems (you know you want one) and rugged baby strollers for parents who like to jog.

DENMAN BIKE SHOP Map pp66–7
☎ 604-685-9755; www.denmanbikeshop.com; 710 Denman St, West End; ⏰ 10am-5pm Sun & Tue, 10am-6pm Fri & Sat, 9am-6pm Mon, 9am-7pm Wed & Thu; 🚌 19
If you've brought your own wheels with you and need a tune-up or repair, this is perhaps the best spot in the city to get

some help. The owners are real bike aficionados – hence the tempting array of '50s-style cruisers for sale – and they can tell you all you need to know about tapping into the local bike scene.

RECKLESS BIKE STORES Map p91
☎ 604-731-2420; www.rektek.com; 1810 Fir St, Granville Island; per half/full day $25/32.50; ⏲ 9am-7pm Mon-Sat, 10am-5pm Sun May-Aug, 10am-dusk Sep-Apr; 🚌 50
The friendly folk at Reckless have been big players in the city's bike community for years, sponsoring events and supporting initiatives across the region. There's a good selection of rental cruisers and mountain bikes and it can provide maps of regional road routes. It's located in a no-man's-land of mismatched businesses near the entrance to Granville Island (it also has a Yaletown location at 110 Davie St).

SPOKES BICYCLE RENTALS Map pp66–7
☎ 604-688-5141; www.vancouverbikerental.com; 1798 W Georgia St, West End; adult per hr/6hr from $7/20; ⏲ 9am-7pm May-Aug, 10am-dusk Sep-Apr; 🚌 19
On the corner of Georgia and Denman Sts, Spokes is the biggest of the bike shops crowding this stretch – these are the guys mostly responsible for all those tourists wobbling across the nearby road as if they've never ridden a bike in their lives. It can kit you and your family out with all manner of bikes, including choppers, tandems and kiddie one-speeds.

GOLF
Vancouverites love to swing their sticks, and the city's mild climate allows for year-round putting. Green fees average $40 to $50 (early-bird specials are often available) and many courses have highly convivial clubhouses where you can hang with the locals and their dimpled balls.

FRASERVIEW GOLF COURSE Map pp44–5
☎ automated tee times 604-280-1818; www.fraserviewgolf.ca; 7800 Vivian Dr, South Vancouver; green fees adult/youth/senior 58/29/41; ⏲ dawn-dusk; par 72, 6700yd; Ⓜ 29th Ave Station, then 🚌 29
Surrounded by mature trees, this city-run facility near E 54th St overlooks the Fraser River and consistently wins awards for

top picks
SPORTY THINGS TO DO
- Kayak the waters of False Creek or Indian Arm (p180)
- Skimboard at Spanish Banks (p183)
- Cycle the Stanley Park seawall (opposite)
- Take a saltwater swim at Kitsilano Pool (p185)
- Ski or snowboard at Cypress, Grouse or Seymour mountains (p183)

being one of Canada's best public courses. Its clubhouse serves a full menu and you can also grab a consolatory beer if you've been hacking unsuccessfully all day.

GLENEAGLES GOLF COURSE Map pp44–5
☎ 604-921-7353; www.westvancouver.ca/golf; 6190 Marine Dr, West Vancouver; green fees adult/youth/senior $20/14/14; ⏲ dawn-dusk; par 35, 2800yd; 🚌 250
This excellent but challenging nine-hole public course has a long history and must have been named by a fan of the Great Game. Nestled between the mountains and sea near Horseshoe Bay, its lovely views entice many to keep coming back. Beware of the third hole, known as Cardiac Hill.

LANGARA GOLF COURSE Map pp44–5
☎ automated tee times 604-280-1818, pro shop 604-713-1816; http://vancouver.ca/parks/golf; 6706 Alberta St, South Cambie; green fees adult/youth/senior $52/27/37; ⏲ dawn-dusk; par 71, 6100yd; 🚌 15
Another city-owned facility (near W 49th St), with large rolling greens and narrow fairways, Langara is regarded as a challenging course. You can practice a few strokes on the putting green before you hit the main attraction.

UNIVERSITY GOLF CLUB Map p100
☎ 604-224-1818; www.universitygolf.com; 5185 University Blvd, UBC; green fees adult/youth/senior $45/35/35; ⏲ dawn-dusk; par 72, 6157yd; 🚌 4
Tucked inside the tree-lined Pacific Spirit Park on UBC Endowment Lands, this popular course and driving range has been luring locals of all skill levels to knock off early from work for 80 years. Lessons are available and there's also a driving range.

HIKING

Hiking opportunities abound in the regional and provincial parks here. A rite of passage for many Vancouverites, the Grouse Grind (p103) is the most infamous huffer-and-puffer: it takes locals about 90 minutes. Lighthouse Park (p105) and Whytecliff Park (p105) are scenic gems with gentle trails to tramp around. Many locals agree that Mt Seymour Provincial Park (p104) has the area's best hiking, though Cypress Provincial Park (p105) and Pacific Spirit Regional Park (p100) rank up there, too.

In you're heading for any of the North Shore parks, be prepared for continually changing mountain conditions – the weather can change suddenly and a warm sunny day in the city might not mean it's going to be the same, or stay the same, in the mountains. Take along a warm waterproof jacket, wear sturdy shoes and a hat, and carry a water bottle. Call for a mountain weather forecast (☎ 604-664-9021) before heading out for the day.

For maps and information about regional parks, contact the Greater Vancouver Regional District (☎ 604-432-6350; http://vancouver.ca/parks). For maps and information on provincial parks in the Vancouver area, go to BC Parks (www.bcparks.ca) online.

ICE SKATING

If you're itching to practice your sequined ice-dance routine in time for the 2010 Winter Olympics, Vancouver has several facilities where no one would mind at all. If you're up at Grouse Mountain (p103) in winter, there's a small outdoor rink where you'll be fighting the five-year-olds for ice time. The city also has eight good-value public indoor rinks.

BRITANNIA COMMUNITY CENTRE
Map p84

☎ 604-718-5800; www.britanniacentre.org; 1661 Napier St, Commercial Dr; ☒ 8am-9pm Mon-Thu, 8:30am-7pm Fri, 9am-5pm Sat, 10am-4pm Sun; adult/child/senior $4.85/2.45/3.40, skate rental $2.45; ▣ 5

Handily open for ice all year round, this popular community-center rink offers skate lessons and a weekly roster of regulars, including Friday's women's drop-in hockey, Wednesday evening's adults-only skate (the perfect place to meet your new ice-dance partner) and Thursday's midnight adult hockey session.

WEST END COMMUNITY CENTRE
Map pp66–7

☎ 604-257-8333; www.westendcc.ca; 870 Denman St, West End; ☒ 6am-10pm Mon-Thu, 6am-9pm Fri, 8am-5pm Sat & Sun Nov-Mar; adult/child/senior $4.85/2.45/3.40, skate rental $2.45; ▣ 5

This busy and bustling community center, with a full range of events, activities and classes to keep the locals on their toes, has its main hall transformed into an ice rink for the winter and early spring. You don't have to pack your skates because rentals are available. Like all the city-owned rinks, public skating times vary, so call ahead for the latest schedule.

KAYAKING

It's hard to beat the joy engendered by a sunset paddle around the coastline here, with the sun sliding languidly down the mirrored glass towers that forest the skyline. With its calm waters, Vancouver is a popular spot for both veteran and novice kayakers. For an alternative, try a tranquil, sigh-inducing summer excursion around the glassy waters of Deep Cove (p106).

DEEP COVE CANOE & KAYAK CENTRE
Map pp44–5

☎ 604-929-2268; www.deepcovekayak.com; 2156 Banbury Rd, North Vancouver; 2hr/5hr rental $28/56; ☒ 9am-6pm; ▣ 212

Enjoying Deep Cove's sheltered waters, this is an ideal spot for first-timers to try their hand at paddling. The staff here will gently show you all you need to know on a three-hour introductory course ($70), where you'll learn that getting in and out of the boat are the hardest parts. For those with a little more experience, it also offers rentals

top picks

FOR KIDS

- Cycling the seawall at Stanley Park (p178)
- Swimming with the local kids at Second Beach (p185)
- Learning to sail at Jericho Beach (p182)
- Snowboarding like a star at Grouse Mountain (p183)
- Enhancing your rock-climbing skills at Cliffhanger Vancouver (opposite)

top picks

SPORTING EVENTS

- Sun Run (p182)
- Polar Bear Swim (p12)
- Alcan Dragon Boat Festival (p14)
- Tour de Gastown (p14)
- BC Cup Day (p188)

and some smashing tours (adult/child from $80/50) of the Indian Arm region.

ECOMARINE OCEAN KAYAK CENTRE
Map p87

☎ 604-689-7575, 888-425-2925; www.ecomarine .com; 1668 Duranleau St, Granville Island; 2hr/day rental $34/59; ⏰ 10am-6pm daily Sep-May, 9am-6pm Sun-Thu, 9am-9pm Fri & Sat Jun-Aug; 🚌 50
Headquartered on Granville Island, the friendly folk at Ecomarine offer guided tours (from $54) and equipment rentals – Tuesday is two-for-one rental day. At the center's Jericho Beach branch (Map pp94–5; ☎ 604-222-3565; Jericho Sailing Centre, 1300 Discovery St; ⏰ 10am-dusk Mon-Fri, 9am-9pm Sat & Sun May-Aug, 10am-dusk Sep; 🚌 4), they also organize events and seminars where you can rub shoulders with local paddle nuts.

ROCK CLIMBING

There's rock climbing close to Vancouver at places such as Juniper Point in West Vancouver's Lighthouse Park (p105) and the bluffs overlooking Indian Arm in Deep Cove (see the boxed text, p106). Serious climbers, however, head up Hwy 99 to Squamish (p215) to scale the Stawamus Chief. The BC Mountaineering Club (☎ 604-268-9502; www.bcmc.ca) offers programs and courses and is a good way to network with the local upwardly mobile community.

In the city, Vancouverites are restricted to indoor climbing centers, which generally charge around $15 to $20 for entry; courses are extra. Recommended centers – both with additional kid-friendly programs – include the following.

CLIFFHANGER VANCOUVER Map p81

☎ 604-874-2400; www.cliffhangerclimbing.com; 106 W 1st Ave, SoMa; ⏰ noon-10:30pm Mon-Thu, noon 9:30pm Fri-Sun; Ⓜ Main St-Science World

The city's best and biggest indoor-climbing facility has a chatty, welcoming vibe and offers tons of courses for beginners and more advanced climbers alike. The two-hour intro course runs four nights a week and is ideal if you're a climbing virgin. Kids are also welcome here.

EDGE CLIMBING CENTRE Map pp44–5

☎ 604-984-9080; www.edgeclimbing.com; Suite 2, 1485 Welch St, North Vancouver; ⏰ 1-11pm Mon-Fri, noon-9pm Sat & Sun; 🚌 240
This high-tech North Van facility has a large climbing gym with more than 15,000 sq ft of climbing surfaces for those who like hanging around for fun. There are plenty of courses, from introductory level to advanced classes, where you can learn all about diagonalling and heel-and-toe hooking. If you enjoy this, you can drive straight from here to the Stawamus Chief in Squamish.

RUNNING

For heart-pounding runs (or even just an arm-swinging speed walk), the Stanley Park seawall remains the city's number-one circuit. It's mostly flat, apart from a couple of uphill sections where you might want to hang onto a passing bike. While a devastating late-2006 storm affected the park's interior trails (see the boxed text, p56), most are expected to be restored, including the popular 4km trek around Lost Lagoon. UBC is another popular running destination, with trails marked throughout the University Endowment Lands.

NIKE RUNNER'S LOUNGE Map pp66–7

☎ 778-786-7463; www.nikerunning.ca; 510 Nicola St, West End; ⏰ 4-8pm Mon-Thu, 8am-1pm Sat & Sun; 🚌 19
If you want to hook up with some Vancouver joggers, drop in to this swanky operation on the Coal Harbour side of Stanley Park. You can check your bags, collect an area running map and borrow an iPod for your trek.

RUNNING ROOM Map pp66–7

☎ 604-684-9771; www.runningroom.com; 679 Denman St, West End; ⏰ 9:30am-9pm Mon-Fri, 9:30am-6pm Sat, 8:30am-5pm Sun; 🚌 19
Where local runners and those hitting the streets for the first time come to hang out, discuss training regimes and choose their

RUNNING THE CITY

Elite runners, regular joggers and the kind of people who would normally rather have a beer than pull on jogging shoes join together once a year for the city's 10km Sun Run (www.sunrun.com). North America's second-biggest street race – numbers creep up every year and currently hover around 55,000 – the April event is like a gargantuan rolling street parade, complete with laughing locals, bands that buoy your spirits along the route and a party-like group hug that awaits the triumphant at BC Place stadium, where everyone tucks into bagels and yogurt while rubbing their aching muscles. It's a great way to see the city, too – you'll wind through Stanley Park, over the Burrard Bridge and through residential streets where the cheering locals will be out in force. And the satisfaction as you limp toward the finish line – usually with some stirring music to trigger a final sprint – will live with you long after you return home.

next pair of well-supported athletic shoes, this shop is at the center of Vancouver's jogging community. It also offers regular clinics and group runs.

SAILING & WINDSURFING

English Bay gets some good winds whipping through, attracting summertime sailors and windsurfers to duke it out over the water. For lessons and equipment rentals, Jericho Sailing Centre (Map pp94–5; 1300 Discovery St, Kitsilano; ☎ 4) is the best place in town. Many companies are based here, along with the Galley Patio & Grill (p155), where the patio views are breathtaking. Hard-core windsurfers should also try Squamish (p215), where the winds are fiercer. The following companies occupy the Jericho Sailing Centre.

MAC SAILING Map pp94–5
☎ 604-224-7245; www.macsailing.com; rental per hr $35-50, courses per hr from $70; ☼ 9am-7pm Mon-Fri, noon-6pm Sat & Sun May-Sep
This excellent operation, catering to sailing veterans and newbies who want to learn the ropes, has six boats available for rent – the super-fast and easy-to-sail *Hobie Getaway* is recommended. Lessons usually run for four days and some are tailored specifically for kids.

WINDSURE ADVENTURE WATERSPORTS Map pp94–5
☎ 604-224-0615; www.windsure.com; board/skim board rental per hr $17.55/4.40; ☼ 9am-8pm Apr-Sep
For those who want to be at one with the sea breeze, Windsure specializes in kiteboarding, windsurfing and skimboarding and offers lessons and equipment rentals. Novices are more than welcome here: the two-hour windsurfing introductory group lesson ($49) is recommended.

SCUBA DIVING

Despite extremely cold temperatures, the North Shore waters have a lot to offer divers, though the general consensus is that you can find more comfortable diving elsewhere in the province. Among the most popular dive areas near the city is Whytecliff Park (p105), which contains an underwater reserve that's best explored between October and April. Divers in this area will need a 6mm neoprene wetsuit as temperatures below the thermocline stay at about 10°C (50°F).

A number of outfitters offer equipment, training and trips, including the following.

DIVING LOCKER Map pp94–5
☎ 604-736-2681, 800-348-3398; www.vancouver divinglocker.com; 2745 W 4th Ave, Kitsilano; rentals from $70, courses from $50; ☼ 10am-6pm Mon-Fri, 9:30am-5:30pm Sat, 9:30am-4pm Sun; ☎ 4
A long-established favorite with local snorkelers and scuba divers, the Diving Locker is not just for experienced practitioners. Along with its regular series of PADI training courses, there's a great introductory course ($50, including equipment) for first-timers. Basic, full-gear equipment rental is $70 daily.

INTERNATIONAL DIVING CENTRE Map pp94–5
☎ 604-736-2541, 866-432-3483; www.diveidc .com; 2572 Arbutus St, Kitsilano; rentals from $49.95, courses from $40; ☼ 10am-7pm Mon-Thu, 10am-8pm Fri, 9:30am-6pm Sat, 10am-5pm Sun; ☎ 16
Equipment rentals and courses are part of the mix here, but the center also organizes regular trips around the region that can take you to revered dive sites on the Sunshine Coast and off Vancouver Island – treks to the sunken HMCS *Cape Breton* near Nanaimo are especially recommended. There's also a Dive Buddies program where

you can team up with locals looking for dive partners.

SKATEBOARDING

Vancouver is one of the world's premier skateboarding destinations; rumor has it some tourists come here exclusively to check out the more than 30 skateparks splashed across the Lower Mainland. Held in August, the annual three day Slam City Jam (www.slamcityjam .com), the largest and most rippin' skateboard competition around, originated in Vancouver. Connect with the Vancouver Skateboard Coalition (www.vsbc.ca) to see what's new.

Tap into the local scene at PD's Hot Shop (p123), where you can pick up a directory of regional skateparks that includes detailed directions and facility descriptions. Directory in hand, check out the following favored haunts.

DOWNTOWN SKATE PLAZA Map p77
near cnr of Quebec & Union Sts & southeast cnr of Andy Livingstone Park, Chinatown; ⏱ 24hr; Ⓜ Main St-Science World
The city's excellent street-style skatepark was opened in 2004 and offers plenty of ramps, curbs, walls, steps and replica rails, plus surfaces such as granite, steel and brick. It's also covered, so you can happily skate in the rain.

HASTINGS SKATEPARK Map pp44–5
☎ 604-718-6222; 2901 E Hastings St, East Vancouver; ⏱ dawn-dusk; 🚌 10
This has a traditional-style skatepark layout with three large, extremely popular concrete bowls plus an added street course. Designed by boarders, the bowl area offers hips, curves and metal coping while the street section has ledges, rails and quarter pipes.

SKIMBOARDING

A cross between skateboarding and surfing, skimboarding – where participants ride a small, surf-like board on the incoming tide, and move down the beach via shallow shoreline washes and tidal pools – is a popular pastime on some Vancouver beaches. Spanish Banks (p101) and Wreck Beach (p101) are generally considered the best places to skim, and you can watch riders throw down ollies, railslides and other cool moves. PD's Hot Shop (p123) sells skimboards and provides free tidal charts.

SKIING & SNOWBOARDING

While Whistler (p211) is the regional king of the snowy hill, there are excellent alpine skiing and snowboarding areas as well as cross-country skiing trails on the edge of the city, less than 30 minutes from downtown. The season typically runs from late November to early April. Following are the three main powder kegs.

CYPRESS MOUNTAIN Map pp44–5
☎ 604-926-5612; www.cypressmountain.com; West Vancouver; adult/child/youth $50/27/46; ⏱ 9am-4pm Dec, 9am-10pm Jan-Mar; 🚌 free winter shuttle
Around 8km north of West Van via Hwy 99, Cypress Provincial Park (p105) transforms into Cypress Mountain ski resort in winter, attracting well-insulated sporty types with its 38 ski runs, increasingly popular snowshoe trails and a snowtubing course. As the snowboarding and freestyle skiing venue (plus the new ski cross event) for the 2010 Olympics, new facilities and upgrades are being added all the time, including a new day lodge, high-speed chair lift and nine ski and snowboard runs. A shuttle bus from Lonsdale Quay runs in winter.

GROUSE MOUNTAIN Map pp44–5
☎ 604-980-9311; www.grousemountain.com; 6400 Nancy Greene Way, North Vancouver; Skyride adult/child/youth/senior $47/21/37/37; ⏱ 9am-10pm mid-Nov–mid-Apr; 🚌 236 from Lonsdale Quay
Vancouver's favorite wintertime hangout (see p103 for summertime info), family-friendly Grouse offers 26 ski and snowboard runs, an outdoor ice-skating rink and a large helping of Christmastime shenanigans – if you're looking for Santa in Vancouver, this is where you'll find him. Night skiing is popular here, there are plenty of lessons available for beginners and the snowshoe park is excellent. There are also some good dining options if you just want to hang out.

MT SEYMOUR Map pp44–5
☎ 604-986-2261; www.mountseymour.com; 1700 Mt Seymour Rd, North Vancouver; adult/child/youth $39.50/20/33; ⏱ 9:30am-4pm Mon-Fri, 8:30am-4pm Sat & Sun late Nov–mid-Dec, 9:30am-10pm Mon-Fri, 8:30am-10pm Sat & Sun mid-Dec–Mar; 🚌 free winter shuttle
A year-round outdoor hangout for Vancouverites (see p104), the third branch of the

SNOWSHOE SHENANIGANS

If you lack the pose-worthy skills for the ski and snowboard slopes around Vancouver but you'd still like to gambol through the powder, snowshoeing is an ideal alternative – especially since the only requirement is the ability to walk. If you can manage that, head to Grouse Mountain (p183; there are also trails at the other two resort mountains) where you can rent shoes (adult/child $15/10) and hit the 10km of winding trails in Munday Alpine Snowshoe Park.

Within minutes, you'll feel like you're the only person on the mountain, as the fading voices are replaced by the crunch-crunch of ice-caked snow, along with the ever-present cawing of scavenging ravens – you might also glimpse an eagle or two. Passing through the forest of mountain hemlocks and Pacific silver fir trees – many with straggles of moss hanging from them like Marxian beards – you'll sometimes break into open ground where you'll catch some stunning panoramic views. Burnaby Mountain, topped by Simon Fraser University, is usually visible, while the ghostly face of Mt Baker can often be glimpsed shimmering 130km away.

Continuing upwards, you'll eventually hit the park's broad Evian Express Trail. The route overlooks the silver surface of Capilano Reservoir far below and the distant crags of Vancouver Island on the watery horizon. Once you've had enough, head downhill (at a rate of knots) to the lodge for a well-deserved Granville Island brew or two.

region's winter playground network has a 21-run downhill ski area, plus snowboard and tobogganing courses. The nighttime snowshoe tours are also popular. It's usually far less crowded than Grouse and you're much more likely to meet the locals. There's no transit service to the park, but a free shuttle operates from Lonsdale Quay throughout the season.

HEALTH & FITNESS

You might think Vancouver is the perfect place to mumble the 'I can't go for a run today because it's raining' excuse. Wrong. The city hosts a sweaty kit bag full of gyms, yoga and Pilates studios, and offers other indoor ways to stay fit. Or maybe you could start a new trend for jogging with an umbrella.

GYMS & HEALTH CLUBS

Private gyms charge up to $20 per day: ask about weekly or monthly membership if you're sticking around. Vancouver's community centers charge about $5 to use their workout rooms, and the same for aerobics or other fitness classes. The West End Community Centre (p180) is a convenient option, with both a fitness facility and classes. Contact the Vancouver Board of Parks and Recreation (☎ 604-257-8400; http://vancouver.ca/parks) for other community centers offering fitness programs.

FITNESS WORLD Map pp66–7
☎ 604-662-7774; www.fitnessworld.ca; 1185 W Georgia St, downtown; ⏰ 24hr Mon-Fri, 8am-7pm Sat & Sun; Ⓜ Burrard
Known as 'Fatness World' by locals, this downtown 2nd-floor gym – you'll see the

bedraggled staggering back to their apartments after overdoing it – has long opening hours, so you can usually find some quiet time. Hop on a running machine by the window and work out while you look down over the unfit masses below. The company has several other city branches.

KITSILANO WORKOUT Map pp94–5
☎ 604-734-3481; www.kitsilanoworkout.com; 1923 W 4th Ave, Kitsilano; ⏰ 24hr Sun-Fri, 7am-10pm Sat; 🚌 4
You can exercise among the stringy fitness nuts and 'yummy mummies' of Kitsilano at this highly popular gym. If you want to mix up your routine, regular classes include step, yoga, Pilates and Latin Funk – dance aerobics is a specialty here. After you've reached your sweat quotient, you can nip along the street to Sophie's Cosmic Café (p143) and blow all your hard work.

YWCA HEALTH & WELLNESS CENTRE Map pp48–9
☎ 604-895-5777; www.ywcavan.org/health; 535 Hornby St, downtown; ⏰ 6am-10pm Mon-Fri, 8am-5:30pm Sat & Sun; Ⓜ Burrard
Despite its name, this excellent downtown gym is open to men and women. It has three studios with wood-sprung floors, and combined and women-only weight rooms, a cardio room, steam room, meditation room and a 25m pool. There are also kickboxing, cycling, Pilates and other classes. A day membership ($16) gets you access to all.

SWIMMING
Ten beaches around the city are fine for swimming and have lifeguards on duty from May to

early September (11:30am to 8:45pm). Among the best are Second Beach (p54), Third Beach (p54), English Bay Beach (p65) and Kitsilano Beach (p96).

Kits is the busiest of the lot – as many as 10,000 people may hit the sand here on a hot summer day. It gets less crowded the further you move toward UBC. Vancouver's waters are never exactly warm; they reach a high in summer of around 21°C (70°F).

If you prefer to swim in fish-free waters, Vancouver's best public pools include the following.

KITSILANO POOL Map pp94–5
☎ 604-731-0011; http://vancouver.ca/parks; 2305 Cornwall Ave, Kitsilano; adult/child/youth/senior $4.85/2.45/3.40/3.65; ☼ 7am-8:45pm mid-May–mid-Sep; 🚌 2

This giant, heated 137m saltwater outdoor pool provides the best dip in town. It has a designated kids' area, where young families often teach their kids to swim, and some unfettered lanes so you can practice your laps.

SECOND BEACH POOL Map p54
☎ 604-257-8371; http://vancouver.ca/parks; cnr N Lagoon Dr & Stanley Park Dr, Stanley Park; adult/child/youth/senior $4.85/2.45/3.40/3.65; ☼ late May–mid-Sep; 🚌 19

This outdoor pool shimmers like an aquamarine right beside the beach. It has lanes for laps but you'll be weaving past kids on most summer days; the kids take over here during school vacations, making it very hard to get anywhere near the waterslide.

UBC AQUATIC CENTRE Map p100
☎ 604-822-4522; www.aquatics.ubc.ca; 6121 University Blvd, UBC; adult/child & senior/youth $4.75/2.75/3.75; ☼ hours vary; 🚌 4

The city's best indoor pool is on the UBC campus, so it's a bit of a hike from downtown. Also the students take precedence in the water so you'll have to plan your visit around them – check the website for the latest schedules. If you negotiate those obstacles, you'll find a 50m pool, saunas and exercise areas for public use.

VANCOUVER AQUATIC CENTRE
Map pp66–7
☎ 604-665-3424; http://vancouver.ca/parks; 1050 Beach Ave, West End; adult/child/youth/senior $4.85/2.45/3.40/3.65; ☼ 6:30am-9:30pm Mon-Fri, 8am-9pm Sat & Sun; 🚌 6

At Sunset Beach beside the Burrard Bridge (the concrete monstrosity that looks like a nuclear bunker), this busy aquatic center has a 50m pool, whirlpool, diving tank and sauna. There's also a gym if you want to continue your exercise purge.

YOGA

Yoga is huge in Vancouver, as you'd expect in the city that birthed Lululemon Athletica (p113) and made yoga wear into a fashion statement. Most of the city's community centers (see p229), including those in the West End, Coal Harbour and Yaletown, offer drop-in classes.

BIKRAM'S YOGA COLLEGE OF INDIA
Map pp66–7
☎ 604-662-7722; www.bikramyogavancouver .com; Suite 101, 1650 Alberni St, West End; drop-in session $20; ☼ 10am-8pm Mon-Thu, 10am-6pm Fri-Sun; 🚌 5

Dynamic yoga performed in a heated room, Bikram is a 26-asana series designed to warm and stretch muscles, ligaments and tendons. It is reputedly good at providing relief for arthritis, back problems and other chronic conditions. Also has branches on Cambie St and W Broadway.

WANDERING YOGI Map p84
☎ 604-251-1915; www.wanderingyogi.com; 1707 Grant St, Commercial Dr; courses from $80; ☼ hours vary; 🚌 20

This studio offers classes on a lightly heated floor to encourage the release of toxins and muscular tension. There are also kirtan courses that revolve around chanting, and a 60-minute mantra/chant class in which participants recite the Mahaa Mrityunjaya mantra 108 times for healing and peace.

top picks

WORKOUTS
- Cycling from Stanley Park to UBC (p178)
- Running – not hiking – the Grouse Grind (p180)
- Hitting the cardio room at the YWCA Health & Wellness Centre (opposite)
- Hiking the forested trails at UBC's Pacific Spirit Regional Park (p180)
- Hanging from the climbing wall at the Edge Climbing Centre (p181)

YALETOWN YOGA Map p71
☎ 604-684-3334; www.yaletownyoga.com; Suite 280, 1050 Homer St, Yaletown; drop-in session $15-20; ⏱ 7am-9:15pm Mon-Fri, 8am-9:15pm Sat & Sun; 🚌 C23

This studio specializes in Moksha, another 'hot' yoga like Bikram yoga. The room is heated, and participants go through 40 postures in 90 minutes designed to strengthen the upper body, open the hips and release tension. There's also a kids' program for enlightened sprogs.

SPAS & PERSONAL CARE

If you've had enough of fighting the crowds and all you want is a little 'me' time, Vancouver has plenty of hair salons and a healthy clutch of spas to cheer you up. Expect to tip around 15% to 20% at these places.

HAIR SALONS
Expect to pay at least $50 for a haircut and style. Try to make appointments at least a day in advance.

KNOTTY BOY Map p84
☎ 604-473-9651; www.knottyboy.com; 1721 Grant St, Commercial Dr; ⏱ 10am-6pm Mon-Fri; 🚌 20

This is a 'one-stop lock shop' where you can get natural or synthetic dreadlocks done, undone, colored, extended, deep cleaned, tidied up, beaded and more. If you prefer to do it yourself, you can buy a kit that provides instructions on how to start dreads from scratch. Dread combs, all-natural dreadlock wax, itch-fighting dreadlock shampoo bars, and myriad other dread specialty products are available.

top picks

PAMPERING TREATS

- Steam room at the Vancouver Aquatic Centre (p185)
- 'Seaweed Journey' treatment at Spa Utopia (opposite)
- Dinner at Grouse Mountain after a snowshoe trek (p184)
- Yoga stretch at Bikram's Yoga College (p185)
- Great new hairstyle at Suki's International (right)

PROPAGANDA HAIR SALON Map pp94-5
☎ 604-732-7756; www.propagandasalon.com; 2090 W 4th Ave, Kitsilano; ⏱ 10am-6pm Mon-Wed & Sat, 10am-8pm Thu & Fri, 10am-5pm Sun; 🚌 4

Propaganda features excellent hair washing complete with relaxing scalp massages. The staff is a mix of trendy and cool but stylistically sensible hair professionals, and hey, dogs are welcome inside to help their owners make those all-important new-look decisions.

SUKI'S INTERNATIONAL Map p91
☎ 604-738-7713; www.sukis.com; 3157 S Granville St, South Granville; ⏱ 9am-6pm Mon-Wed, Sat & Sun, 9am-9pm Thu & Fri; 🚌 10

If you're jealous of all those stunningly coiffed people you keep seeing in the clubs here, don't get mad, get even. They generally get their 'dos and colors at Suki's, the city's fave salon minichain. There are four other Suki's around town.

MASSAGE & DAY SPAS
Given Vancouver's healthy lifestyle, it's no wonder that spas flourish here. Expect to pay upwards of $85 for an hour-long massage and at least $30 for a 'quickie' facial.

ABSOLUTE SPA AT THE CENTURY Map pp48-9
☎ 604-648-2772, 877-684-2772; www.absolute spa.com; Century Plaza Hotel & Spa, 1015 Burrard St, downtown; ⏱ 8am-9pm; 🚌 2

This popular, hotel-based day spa has a calming earth-toned interior and offers a full menu of treats from facials to hydrotherapy to make-up sessions. If you're a chocoholic, splurge for the hot-choc and whipped-cream body scrub ($260) – you'll be craving Cadbury's for the rest of the day. Men-only treatments also available.

MIRAJ HAMMAM SPA Map p91
☎ 604-733-5151; www.mirajhammam.com; 1495 W 6th Ave, South Granville; ⏱ 11am-7pm Tue & Wed, noon-8pm Thu & Fri, 10am-6pm Sat, 2-6pm Sun; 🚌 10

Canada's only hammam is based on the real Middle Eastern deal. Step into the arched and tiled interior for a steam followed by *gommage* (a full-body scrub with authentic black Moroccan soap, starting at $99). Men are only admitted from 4pm to 8pm Saturday and 2pm to 6pm Sunday; it's women only the rest of the time.

SKOAH Map p71

☎ 604-642-0200; www.skoah.com; 1011 Hamilton St, Yaletown; ⏱ 10:30am-7:30pm Mon-Fri, 10am-7pm Sat & Sun; 🚌 C23

'No whale music and no bubbling cherubs,' as they say at this tongue-in-cheek, trying-hard-not-to-be-pretentious spa. There are deep-cleansing masks, facial massages, scalp massages, foot 'facials' and muscle stimulation treatments, all done by your 'personal skin care trainer.' Skoah also sells its own line of all-natural products.

SPA UTOPIA Map pp48–9

☎ 604-641-1351, 866-700-9008; www.spautopia.ca; Pan Pacific Hotel, 999 Canada Pl, downtown; ⏱ 9am-8pm Tue-Fri, 9am-5pm Sat-Mon; Ⓜ Waterfront

Welcome to the height of luxury. Spa Utopia is just that: a perfect world of relaxation and pampering specializing in 'spa suites,' where you hold court in a private, hotel-style room while various treatments and their practitioners come to you. Along with its massive range of treatments – the West Coast Seaweed Journey is recommended – there are lots of deep massage options (from $115).

SPECTATOR SPORTS

Vancouver's sports scene is tightly intertwined with the city's culture, and if residents aren't engaging in some sort of sporting activity themselves, they're likely to be watching one. Hockey generates the most madness. Despite the fact the Vancouver Canucks have never won a Stanley Cup, hope springs eternal. And just remember: those pesky Toronto Maple Leafs haven't won a Cup since 1967, so Vancouver fans needn't feel too bad.

Canadian football is also popular; it's vaguely like American football, but with key differences best summed up as 'longer, wider and faster.' The BC Lions is the local team, and they've done a pretty good job in recent years. Vancouver does have a baseball team, the minor-league Vancouver Canadians, which serves as the training ground for Major League Baseball's (MLB) Oakland As. However, games are more about the nostalgic summertime ambience than serious sports watching.

Tickets & Reservations

Ticketmaster (☎ 604-280-4400; www.ticketmaster.ca) sells advance tickets, but be aware of the booking fee. You can also pick up tickets at Tickets Tonight (☎ 604-684-2787; www.ticketstonight.ca). Box offices

top picks

SPORTY THINGS TO SEE

- Vancouver Canucks NHL hockey game (below)
- Vancouver Canadians baseball game (below)
- Horse racing at Hastings Racecourse (p188)
- Skateboarders at the Downtown Skate Plaza (p183)
- Windsurfers at Jericho Beach (p182)

at GM Place and BC Place also sell tickets. Scalpers congregate on the corner of Georgia and Beatty Sts for GM Place events, and at the Expo Blvd entrances for BC Place events.

BASEBALL

VANCOUVER CANADIANS Map p91

☎ 604-872-5232; www.canadiansbaseball.com; Nat Bailey Stadium, 4601 Ontario St, Fairview; tickets $8-12.50; ⏱ regular season mid-Jun–mid-Sep; 🚌 15

The minor-league farm team to the MLB's Oakland As, the Canadians play at old-school Nat Bailey Stadium by Queen Elizabeth Park. Recently refurbished, it's known as 'the prettiest ballpark in the world' thanks to its mountain backdrop. Afternoon games – called 'nooners' – are perfect for a nostalgic bask in the sun. Hotdogs and beer rule the menu, but there's also sushi and fruit – this is Vancouver, after all.

FOOTBALL

BC LIONS Map p71

☎ 604-589-7627; www.bclions.com; BC Place Stadium, 777 Pacific Blvd, Yaletown; tickets $27-70; ⏱ regular season Jun-Oct; Ⓜ Stadium

The Lions is Vancouver's team in the Canadian Football League (CFL), arguably a more exciting game than its US counterpart. The Lions have had some decent showings in the last few years, winning the Grey Cup championship most recently in 2006. The team relies on its jump-out-of-your-seat offense. Tickets are easy to come by – unless the boys are laying into their Calgary rivals.

HOCKEY

VANCOUVER CANUCKS Map pp48–9

☎ 604-899-4600; www.canucks.com; GM Place, 800 Griffiths Way, downtown; tickets $33-94; ⏱ regular season Oct-Apr; Ⓜ Stadium

LOSING YOUR SHIRT FOR FUN

What it lacks in stature – this isn't exactly the Kentucky Derby – Vancouver's mountain-view Hastings Racecourse (Map pp44–5; ☎ 604-254-1631, 800-677-7702; www.hastingspark.com; Pacific National Exhibition grounds, East Vancouver; admission free, minimum bet $2; ☷ Fri-Sun Jun-Sep, Sat & Sun Apr, May, Oct & Nov; ⊟ 10) more than makes up for in good old-fashioned fun. It's an alternative day out if you've covered all the usual sporting activities; they're used to seeing first-timers who don't know how to place a bet here and will be more than happy to show you how to lose your money. Even if you bet small (or not at all), there's an undeniable thrill when the bell sounds, the gates open and the thoroughbreds speed off around the dirt track. If you're here in August, drop by for BC Cup Day, the biggest race card of the year, complete with live music, family-friendly activities and a three-day weekend of racing.

The city's beloved National Hockey League (NHL) team toyed with fans in 1994's thrilling Stanley Cup finals before losing Game 7 to the New York Rangers, triggering local riots. But love runs deep and 'go Canucks go!' is still boomed out from packed-to-capacity GM Place at every game. Book your seat way before you arrive in town or just head to a local bar for some game-night atmosphere.

VANCOUVER GIANTS Map pp44–5

☎ 604-444-2687; www.vancouvergiants.com; Pacific Coliseum, 100 N Renfrew St, East Vancouver; tickets $21.50-23.50; ☷ regular season Oct–mid-Mar; ⊟ 16

If you can't score Canucks tickets, the Western Hockey League's (WHL) Vancouver Giants is a good-value alternative. Games are held at the Pacific Coliseum and often have a buzzy locals feel with lots of families and die-hard fans, all united in awaiting the next big punch-up on the ice. Tickets cost a lot less than Canucks ones, unless you factor in the beer you'll be sipping throughout the game.

SOCCER

VANCOUVER WHITECAPS Map pp44–5

☎ 604-669-9283; www.whitecapsfc.com; Swangard Stadium, cnr Boundary & Kingsway Rds, Burnaby; tickets $16-35; ☷ regular season May-Sep; Ⓜ Patterson

They've been angling for a new downtown stadium for years, but until that happens you'll have to hit the SkyTrain to Burnaby to catch the region's top men's and women's soccer teams – men play in the A-League and women play in the W-League. Only covered on one side, the 5000-seat stadium is great on hot summer days but bloody freezing when the wind whips up, so dress warmly or insulate yourself in the beer tent.

lonely planet Hotels & Hostels

Want more Sleeping recommendations than we could ever pack into this little ol' book? Craving more detail – including extended reviews and photographs? Want to read reviews by other travellers and be able to post your own? Just make your way over to **lonelyplanet.com/hotels** and check out our thorough list of independent reviews, then reserve your room simply and securely.

SLEEPING

top picks

- Wedgewood Hotel (p191)
- Opus Hotel (p195)
- Fairmont Hotel Vancouver (p191)
- Granville Island Hotel (p196)
- Sylvia Hotel (p195)
- O Canada House (p193)
- West End Guest House (p194)
- Pacific Palisades Hotel (p193)
- Victorian Hotel (p192)
- Shaughnessy Village (p197)

SLEEPING

Although there are 25,000 hotel, B&B and hostel rooms in Vancouver, the city is completely colonized by tourists in summer months, so booking ahead is a smart move, unless you want to be sleeping with your head on a damp log in Stanley Park. While rates are at their highest in July and August, there are some genuinely good deals in spring and fall, when you can avoid the school-holiday crush and join the locals in enjoying a day or two of wild 'Wet Coast' rainfall.

With the Olympics on the horizon, the city is launching a rash of new, mostly high-end hotel developments. The Loden and L'Hermitage will be joining downtown's designer boutique offerings, while the Shangri-La, the Ritz-Carlton, Coast Coal Harbour, Fairmont Pacific Rim and the revamped Crowne Plaza will be luring the gold-card crowd with their top-of-the-range amenities and central locations.

But Vancouver is not just about high-end sleepovers. There are many good midrange hotels – especially in the downtown core – as well as pockets of homely heritage B&Bs in the West End and Kits. If you want to be closer to the forests and mountains yet not too far from downtown, the North Shore is ideal. And for those on a limited budget, there are hostels scattered across the city, as well as some good student-style digs out at UBC.

From high end to budget, lodgings are increasingly adding free wireless internet access to their offerings, while spas, pools, air-conditioning and laundry facilities are more sporadically applied: see the symbols in each listing to see what's available and call ahead to see what's new.

Accommodation reviews here are arranged by neighborhood and then by budget – most expensive first. Quoted prices are for the height of the summer season, but rates can drop by as much as 50% in the off-season and many hotels also offer good-value packages that might include restaurant deals, spa treatments or entry to local attractions. Check hotel websites and call ahead for the best deals and a selection of available packages. Also check online or call for the dedicated accommodation services offered by Tourism Vancouver (☎ 604-966-3260, 877-826-1717; www.tourismvancouver.com) and Hello BC (☎ 604-663-6000, 800-663-6000; www.hellobc.com) for up-to-the-minute deals and packages.

Be aware that there are some significant additions to most quoted room rates. These include taxes of up to 16% – an 8% to 10% hotel tax (PST) and 5% federal goods and services tax (GST). Overseas visitors may be able to claim back the GST (see p235). Many hotels, particularly in the downtown core, also charge parking fees that often range between $10 and $20 per night. You can avoid this by staying at B&Bs, which generally don't charge for parking.

BOOKING B&BS

B&Bs across the city run from homely rooms in residential neighborhoods that start at under $100 per night to sumptuous, antique-lined heritage mansions at prices over $250, where every pampering treat is offered. The average is around $150 and you can expect a warm welcome and plenty of friendly personal attention. It's not all smiles, though:

some B&Bs require a two-night minimum stay – especially on summer weekends – and cancellation policies can cost you an arm and a leg if you decide not to turn up.

There are several handy regional agencies that allow you to search and book Vancouver-area properties online. These generally show photos and available amenities at local properties and can save you a lot of time when you're on the road. You can do your pre-trip homework via the recommended agencies BBCanada (www.bbcanada.com) or Western Canada B&B Innkeepers Association (www.wcbbia.com). Alternatively, you can contact Tourism Vancouver or Hello BC (above) for area listings and late-availability deals.

TIPPING

Bellhops typically get $2 for hailing you a cab at the front of the hotel and $2 per item for carrying your bags to your room. Housekeepers can be tipped $2 to $5 per night of your stay, although this is entirely optional.

DOWNTOWN

With few B&B options – head to the West End if you want an antique-lined, home-style sleepover – the downtown area is bristling with swanky hotel towers, and also has a handful of refurbished heritage properties and a couple of party-central hostels. You'll be within staggering distance of many of the city's best nightlife options plus a smorgasbord of good restaurants. Be aware that some front-facing rooms can be noisy; request a quieter back room if you're a light sleeper.

PAN PACIFIC VANCOUVER
Map pp48–9 Luxury Hotel $$$
☎ 604-662-8111, 800-663-1515; www.vancouver.panpacific.com; 999 Canada Place; r from $450; Ⓜ Waterfront; ⊠ ⌲
This deluxe convention hotel inside Canada Place starts with a cavernous lobby, complete with its own clutch of totem poles. The large rooms, many with panoramic views across Burrard Inlet, are no less impressive and come complete with rich maple-wood furnishings and the kind of beds where the linen thread-count is off the scale. The three on-site restaurants include the recommended Five Sails.

FAIRMONT HOTEL VANCOUVER
Map pp48–9 Historic Hotel $$$
☎ 604-684-3131, 800-441-1414; www.fairmont.com/hotelvancouver; 900 W Georgia St; r from $450; Ⓜ Burrard; ⊠ ⌲
Built in the 1930s by the Canadian Pacific railroad company, this sparkling grand dame of city hotels is a Vancouver landmark. Despite the snooty provenance, the hotel carefully balances comfort with elegance: the lobby is decked with crystal chandeliers but the rooms have an understated business hotel feel. If you have the budget, check in to the Gold Floor for a raft of pampering services.

WEDGEWOOD HOTEL
Map pp48–9 Boutique Hotel $$$
☎ 604-689-7777, 800-663-0666; www.wedgewoodhotel.com; 845 Hornby St; r from $350; ▤ 5; ⊠
The last word in personalized boutique luxury, the elegant Wedgewood is dripping

PRICE GUIDE
The following price guide (based on a double room) is used in the accommodation reviews in this chapter:
$$$	over $200 per night
$$	$100 to $200 per night
$	under $100 per night

with top-hatted charm. The friendly staff is second to none, the rooms are stuffed with reproduction antiques and the balconies enable you to smirk at the grubby plebs shuffling past below. Steam up your monocle with a trip to the spa, where a shiatsu massage should work off those sore shopping muscles.

METROPOLITAN HOTEL
Map pp48–9 Boutique Hotel $$$
☎ 604-687-1122, 800-667-2300; www.metropolitan.com/vanc; 645 Howe St; r from $300; Ⓜ Granville; ⊠ ⌲
This swish boutique property has a swank, modern take on style that will appeal to urban sophisticates. It's also right in the heart of downtown for those who like to be close to all the action. Bold contemporary artworks add a splash of color to the atmospheric, subtly decorated rooms, and there's a good on-site restaurant, an indoor pool and a squash court to keep you busy.

CENTURY PLAZA HOTEL & SPA
Map pp48–9 Hotel $$
☎ 604-687-0575, 800-663-1818; www.century-plaza.com; 1015 Burrard St; r/ste from $189/249; ▤ 2; ⌲
Renovated in recent years, this central tower-block sleepover combines standard business hotel–style rooms (many with handy kitchenettes) with a raft of on-site amenities: there can't be many North American hotels that have both their own spa and comedy club. There's also an indoor pool and steam room, plus the good lounge-style Figmint (p140) restaurant.

SANDMAN HOTEL DOWNTOWN
Map pp48–9 Chain Hotel $$
☎ 604-681-2211, 800-726-3626; www.sandman.ca; 180 W Georgia St; r from $159; Ⓜ Stadium; ⊠ ⌲
If you're looking for a reliable, well-located downtown hotel, it's hard to beat the solid standards and friendly approach of this Canadian chain property. The rooms have a dependable, business-hotel feel but there

are plenty of handy amenities – including a pool and fitness center – that make a stay worthwhile. The on-site bar-restaurant is popular on hockey game nights, so head down and join the noisy throng.

ST REGIS HOTEL Map pp48–9   Hotel $$
☎ 604-681-1135, 800-770-7929; www.stregis hotel.com; 602 Dunsmuir St; r & ste from $149; Ⓜ Granville; wi-fi 🖳
Recently upgraded from its previous down-at-heel incarnation, this near-Gastown heritage sleepover combines pokey standard rooms with swankier quarters on its higher floors. Rates include continental breakfast, access to a small on-site business center and entry to a nearby gym. The excellent Railway Club (p164) is just across the street, indicating that this is a busy part of town: ask for a back room if noise is an issue.

COMFORT INN DOWNTOWN
Map pp48–9   Hotel $$
☎ 604-605-4333, 888-605-5333; www.comfortinn downtown.com; 654 Nelson St; d/tw $129/149; 🚍 4
Combining a winning location with jazzy, brightly painted rooms – not ideal if you wake up with a hangover – this renovated heritage building is within crawling distance of the Granville entertainment strip. The corner suites, with fireplaces and Jacuzzis, are the best rooms. Continental breakfast and access to a nearby health club are included, and there's a popular Irish bar downstairs if you need to wave your shillelagh around.

VICTORIAN HOTEL Map pp48–9   Hotel $$
☎ 604-681-6369, 877-681-6369; www.victorian hotel.ca; 514 Homer St; r from $129, with shared bathroom from $99; Ⓜ Granville; wi-fi
Housed in a couple of expertly renovated older properties, the lovely, high-ceilinged rooms at this Euro-style pension combine

glossy hardwood floors, a sprinkling of antiques, an occasional bay window and bags of heritage charm. Most rooms have en suite bathrooms, with summer fans, TVs and robes provided, but the best rooms are in the newer extension, complete with its marble-floored bathrooms. Muffins, tea and coffee are served each morning.

MODA HOTEL Map pp48–9   Hotel $$
☎ 604-683-4251, 877-683-5522; www.modahotel .com; 900 Seymour St; d from $119; 🚍 4; wi-fi
The dodgy old Dufferin Hotel has been reinvented as this white-fronted, designer-flecked boutique property one block from the Granville St party area. The new rooms have loungey flourishes such as mod furnishings and bold paintwork and the bathrooms have been given a swanky makeover. The flat-screen TVs are a nice touch – great if you decide to have a night in.

KINGSTON HOTEL Map pp48–9   Hotel $$
☎ 604-684-9024, 888-713-3304; www.kingston hotelvancouver.com; 757 Richards St; s/d/tw $115/145/160; Ⓜ Granville
While some recent revamping has taken place, most rooms at this Euro-style pension are still basic and a bit worn, except for the recommended en suite rooms, which have new furniture, flatscreen TVs and fresh floral bedspreads. Rates include continental breakfast and there's a popular on-site patio bar. You're also within walking distance of most of the city's main action.

BOSMAN'S VANCOUVER HOTEL
Map pp48–9   Motel $$
☎ 604-682-3171, 888-267-6267; www.bosmans hotel.com; 1060 Howe St; r from $109; 🚍 4; wi-fi 🚸 🖳
It calls itself a hotel but heart-of-the-action Bosman's is an old-school motel with large, slightly faded rooms heavy on the pink décor. Friendly front-desk staffers can help with your day-out plans, and there's a popular on-site restaurant and a small pool to cool off after your long drive. Avoid front-facing ground floor rooms: they're usually noisy.

HI VANCOUVER CENTRAL
Map pp48–9   Hostel $
☎ 604-685-5335, 888-203-8333; www.hihostels .ca/vancouvercentral; 1025 Granville St; dm/r $27.50/66; 🚍 4; wi-fi 🖳

top picks

SPA HOTELS

- Wedgewood Hotel (p191)
- Pan Pacific Vancouver (p191)
- Fairmont Hotel Vancouver (p191)
- Pacific Palisades Hotel (opposite)
- Century Plaza Hotel & Spa (p191)

Opposite the rival Samesun, this labyrinthine former hotel building has a calmer ambience, four-bed dorms with sinks, and lots of recommended private rooms – some with en suite bathrooms. If you're new to the city, ask about taking a tour with the legendary Erik, HI volunteer extraordinaire who leads groups on a 101 trek around Vancouver. Rates include a continental buffet breakfast.

SAMESUN BACKPACKERS LODGE
Map pp48–9   Hostel $
☎ 604-682-8226, 888-203-8333; www.samesun.com; 1018 Granville St; dm/r $25/65; ◻ 4; wi-fi
Expect a party atmosphere at this lively hostel in the heart of the Granville nightclub area. There's also the Beaver, a hopping on-site bar if you don't quite make it out the front door. The dorms, complete with funky paint jobs, are comfortably small and there's a large kitchen for your mystery-meat pasta dishes. There's a strong lineup of social events here, so make sure you check the roster daily.

WEST END
Vancouver's B&B central, the West End is dripping with clapboard heritage houses that tend toward the high-end range of comfortable – expect lots of pampering extras. The main draw is that you're within walking distance of the downtown bustle without the attendant noise; the West End is crisscrossed with quiet residential streets but is also ringed with shops and restaurants. Also, Stanley Park is on your doorstep, enticing you for a sigh-inducing seawall stroll.

PACIFIC PALISADES HOTEL
Map pp66–7   Boutique Hotel $$$
☎ 604-688-0461, 800-663-1815; www.pacificpalisadeshotel.com; 1277 Robson St; r from $230; ◻ 5; wi-fi 🏊
Like the nearby Listel, this urban hipster has a love of artistic flourishes but is much bolder in its palette, from the swirly glassware behind its front desk to the striking primary colors in every room. The Palisades offers comfortable accommodations and a raft of quality services, including a large pool, a health club and an evening wine-tasting hour. Rooms are mostly large and sunny and all have kitchenettes. It's also one of the city's greenest sleepover options (see p62).

top picks
HERITAGE SLEEPOVERS
- O Canada House (below)
- Fairmont Hotel Vancouver (p191)
- Victorian Hotel (opposite)
- English Bay Inn (p194)
- West End Guest House (p194)

LISTEL VANCOUVER
Map pp66–7   Boutique Hotel $$$
☎ 604-684-8461, 800-663-5491; www.listel-vancouver.com; 1300 Robson St; d from $220; ◻ 5; wi-fi 🔀 ◻
A sophisticated, self-described 'art hotel,' the Listel attracts grown-ups with its on-site installations and package deals with local art galleries. There's original artwork, including some First Nations creations, in the rooms, which all have a relaxing, mood-lit West Coat ambiance. Adding to the artsy appeal, the hotel's on-site bar, O'Doul's (p151), hosts nightly jazz shows and is a performers' hangout during the annual Jazz Festival (p14).

O CANADA HOUSE
Map pp66–7   B&B $$$
☎ 604-688-0555, 877-688-1114; www.ocanadahouse.com; 1114 Barclay St; r from $210; ◻ 5; wi-fi ◻
The home where Canada's national anthem was penned is now an immaculate, adult-oriented B&B, packed with antiques and Queen Anne flourishes. Its seven rooms are a respite from the city bustle and the wraparound veranda is a popular spot from which to watch the world go by. There's also a guest pantry with sherry and baked goodies if you can't wait for your next meal.

BARCLAY HOUSE B&B
Map pp66–7   B&B $$$
☎ 604-605-1351, 800-971-1351; www.barclayhouse.com; 1351 Barclay St; d from $195; ◻ 5; wi-fi ◻
This bright-yellow Victorian heritage property has a sophisticated boutique twist on the usual B&B approach. Rather than a mothballed museum look – think delicate chintzy antiques – the rooms have a loungey, designer élan and are lined with local modern artworks. Home comforts haven't been lost to aesthetics, though, and four of the five rooms have deep soaker tubs.

ENGLISH BAY INN Map pp66–7   B&B $$$

☎ 604-683-8002, 866-683-8002; www.english bayinn.com; 1968 Comox St; r $190-295; 🚌 5; wi-fi 💻

Each of the six rooms in this Tudoresque B&B near Stanley Park has a private bathroom and two have sumptuous four-poster beds: you'll think you've arrived in Victoria, BC's determinedly Olde English capital, by mistake. There's complimentary port in the parlor, a secluded garden for hanging out with your copy of the London *Times* and a three-course breakfast – arrive early to snag the alcove in the upstairs breakfast room.

EMPIRE LANDMARK HOTEL
Map pp66–7   Hotel $$

☎ 604-687-0511, 800-830-6144; www.empireland markhotel.com; 1400 Robson St; r from $190; 🚌 5

Housed in a generic tower block, the Landmark has rooms with a slightly dated business-hotel look, despite being recently renovated. All rooms have balconies – ask for one with a view of English Bay or Stanley Park – and there's a raft of amenities, including a gym and business center. Save time for a cocktail (meals are better value elsewhere) at the lofty revolving restaurant on the 42nd floor, which has some of the city's best panoramic views.

ROBSON SUITES
Map pp66–7   Serviced Apartments $$

☎ 604-685-9777, 800-404-1398; www.robson suitesvancouver.com; 777 Bidwell St; r/ste $185/195; 🚌 5; wi-fi

A comfortable home away from home – especially if your home looks like a well-maintained 1980s bachelor suite – this quiet apartment hotel on a residential side street is a relaxing alternative sleepover. The rates are a good deal when you factor in the full kitchens, in-suite laundry facilities, free

parking and the shuttle bus that ferries guests around the town on request. Off-season and weekly deals are a steal here.

BLUE HORIZON HOTEL Map pp66–7 Hotel $$

☎ 604-688-1411, 800-663-1333; www.bluehori zonhotel.com; 1225 Robson St; r from $165; 🚌 5; wi-fi ❌ 💻 🅿

This slender tower-block property offers good rooms with the kind of quality, business hotel furnishings common in pricier joints. All rooms are corner suites and each has a balcony – the top floors look across to English Bay or the North Shore. The on-site restaurant has a summertime patio – look out for the blueberry pancakes – while the 9th floor is the 'Green Floor,' with energy-efficient lighting, low-flow showerheads and recycling bins.

ROBSONSTRASSE HOTEL & SUITES
Map pp66–7   Hotel $$

☎ 604-687-1674, 888-667-8877; www.robson strassehotel.com; 1394 Robson St; r & ste from $145; 🚌 5; ❌

Many travelers have recommended this place, with its large rooms, helpful staff and accessible Robson St location. The corridors may smell like your grandma's house but all the suites and rooms, decorated in a standard chain hotel manner, have been recently renovated and now include microwaves and mini-fridges. There's a handy on-site laundry and a tortoise-paced elevator that may well qualify as the slowest in the world.

WEST END GUEST HOUSE
Map pp66–7   B&B $$

☎ 604-681-2889, 888-546-3327; www.westend guesthouse.com; 1362 Haro St; s/d from $140/205; 🚌 5; 💻

A superior, century-old heritage B&B dripping with antique charm, this inviting nook has the kind of extras that induce a highly civilized sleepover. Among the eight elegant rooms, the downstairs suite – with private sauna-style steam shower – is recommended for hedonists. There are free loaner bikes available, a guest pantry of freshly baked cookies and a summer-afternoon iced-tea gathering on the home's sunny deck.

TROPICANA SUITE HOTEL
Map pp66–7   Hotel $$

☎ 604-687-6631; www.tropicanasuites.com; 1361 Robson St; s/d $129/139; 🚌 5; 🅿

top picks

CHEAP SLEEPS

- Shaughnessy Village (p197)
- Samesun Backpackers Lodge (p193)
- HI Vancouver Central (p192)
- Buchan Hotel (opposite)
- YWCA Hotel (p196)

The Tropicana is the best of the three age-old self-catering hotels crowding this corner of Robson and Broughton Sts. Rooms here combine faded pink-trimmed walls and clashing green comforters. While it will never be cool, it's good value and has a great location near both Stanley Park and the Robson St shopping core. Most suites have full kitchens with stoves and large refrigerators and there's a heated indoor pool and sauna.

SYLVIA HOTEL Map pp66–7   Hotel $$
☎ 604-681-9321; www.sylviahotel.com; 1154 Gilford St; s/d/ste from $110/165/195; ☐ 5
Built in 1912 and named after the original owner's daughter, the beloved, ivy-covered Sylvia enjoys a prime location on English Bay near Stanley Park. With the lobby of a Bavarian pension – think stained-glass windows and dark wood paneling – the hotel has a wide array of comfortable, home-style room configurations. The best are the 12 apartment suites, each with full kitchens and panoramic waterfront views. Book ahead and you'll have a front row seat for the Celebration of Light (p15) fireworks festival in July.

NELSON HOUSE B&B Map pp66–7   B&B $$
☎ 604-684-9793, 866-684-9793; www.downtown bedandbreakfast.com; 977 Broughton St; s/d from $108/118; ☐ 5
Each of the five rooms in this gay-friendly heritage B&B has a kitschy travel theme – check out the wood-lined Cabin room, where you can sleep like a pioneer-era lumberjack. All rooms have sinks and four have private bathrooms. Breakfast takes a gourmet approach with finger-licking mains such as Swiss cheese and asparagus omelets. Close to Robson St, Stanley Park and Barclay Heritage Sq.

BUCHAN HOTEL Map pp66–7   Hotel $
☎ 604-685-5354, 800-668-6654; www.buchan hotel.com; 1906 Haro St; r from $72; ☐ 5
This cheerful, charming and good-value heritage hotel near Stanley Park combines cheaper rooms – many with shared bathrooms, dinged furnishings and older blankets – with higher quality and pricier en suite rooms. The smiley front-desk staff is ever helpful, and there's a useful on-site laundry as well as storage facilities for bikes and skis.

top picks

CELEB-SPOTTING HOTELS

- Opus Hotel (below)
- Pan Pacific Vancouver (p191)
- Fairmont Hotel Vancouver (p191)
- Wedgewood Hotel (p191)
- Metropolitan Hotel (p191)

HI VANCOUVER DOWNTOWN
Map pp66–7   Hostel $
☎ 604-684-4565, 888-203-4302; www.hihostels .ca/vancouverdowntown; 1114 Burnaby St; dm/r $27.50/66; ☐ 6; wi-fi ☐
This hospitable hostel enjoys the best of both worlds: located on a quiet residential West End street, it's also walking distance to all the downtown action. Quieter and more institutional than other Vancouver HI hostels, it's popular with families. The dorms are all small, and added extras range from bike rentals to internet-access computers. Rates include a free continental breakfast.

YALETOWN

Lined with fancy restaurants and loungey bars, Yaletown claims to be Vancouver's little Soho. That may be a bit of a stretch – it's not quite cutting edge or bohemian enough to be quite so cool – but this is still an excellent location for a sleepover. You'll be just a couple of blocks from the Granville St entertainment area and you'll also find plenty of great places to eat, drink and shop like there's no tomorrow just steps from your hotel door.

OPUS HOTEL Map p71   Boutique Hotel $$$
☎ 604-642-6787; 866-642-6787; www.opushotel .com; 322 Davie St; r from $340; ☐ 4; wi-fi ☒ ☐
Visiting Hollywood celebs flicking through these pages looking for a place to be seen should flick no further. The city's best designer hotel has been welcoming the likes of Justin Timberlake and that bloke from REM for years. They come for the chic suites – think mod furnishings and feng shui bed placements – and the paparazzi-friendly bathrooms with their clear windows overlooking the streets. It's a model of excellent service and there's a stylish on-site bar and restaurant, as well as a small gym.

top picks

HOTEL BARS

- Opus Hotel (p195)
- Sylvia Hotel (p195)
- Listel Vancouver (p193)
- Kingston Hotel (p192)
- Samesun Backpackers Lodge (p193)

GEORGIAN COURT HOTEL

Map p71   Hotel $$

☎ 604-682-5555, 800-663-1155; www.georgian court.com; 773 Beatty St; r from $190; Ⓜ Stadium; wi-fi ✕

A recent makeover for this discreet, European-style property hasn't changed its classic, old-school approach to high service levels and solid, dependable amenities. The spruced-up standard rooms have new carpets and curtains but the apartment-style corner suites, with their quiet recessed bedrooms, are recommended. There's a small on-site fitness room and the Swiss-flavored William Tell restaurant draws plenty of outside diners.

YWCA HOTEL Map p71   Hostel $

☎ 604-895-5830, 800-663-1424; www.ywcahotel .com; 733 Beatty St; s/d/tr $64/77/102; Ⓜ Stadium; ✕ ▣

One of Canada's best Ys, this well-located tower is a popular option for those on a budget. Accommodating men, women, couples and families, it's a bustling place with a communal kitchen on every other floor and a wide array of rooms ranging from compact singles to group-friendly larger quarters. All rooms are a little institutionalized – think austere student study/bedroom – but each has a sink and refrigerator. Handy weekly rates are available and guests can access the nearby YWCA Health & Wellness Centre (p184) for free.

SOMA

You won't find too many sleepover options in the SoMa area of the city, which means you'll likely have a long walk back to your room with your shopping bags from all those tempting local designer stores. Luckily, transit links to downtown are pretty good and there are many pit-stop coffee joints if you need to rest your weary credit cards en route.

PILLOW SUITES

Map p81   Serviced Apartments $$

☎ 604-879-8977; www.pillow.net; 2859 Manitoba St; ste from $145, house $265; ▣ 9; wi-fi

Not far from the Gothamesque City Hall, between W 12th and W 13th Aves, this clutch of three brightly painted heritage homes is ideal if you're looking for a longer stay where you can spread out and feel like you're home. The six art-lined, self-catering chintzy apartments each have full-sized kitchens, but the best deal is for those traveling in groups: rent the 'West Coast' and you'll have a complete house to yourself that's suitable for up to six people. Officially, there's a minimum two-week stay, but shorter stopovers are often available – call ahead.

GRANVILLE ISLAND, FAIRVIEW & SOUTH GRANVILLE

While shopping-friendly Granville Island has just one lodging option – it's ideal if you want to enjoy a retreat-like location with waterfront views that's also close to all the city action – Fairview has some good B&Bs and a couple of recommended hotels. Transit from these areas to the downtown core is generally good.

GRANVILLE ISLAND HOTEL

Map p87   Boutique Hotel $$$

☎ 604-683-7373, 800-663-1840; www.granville islandhotel.com; 1253 Johnston St, Granville Island; d from $215, ste $250; ▣ 50; wi-fi ✕

This gracious, 85-room boutique hotel hugs the quieter eastern tip of Granville Island and has great views of False Creek and the glassy downtown towers. You'll be close to the island's public market, restaurants and theaters, and five minutes away from downtown via the miniferries that ply the surrounding waters. Rooms have exposed beams and earth-toned walls – the suites with their floor-to-ceiling views are recommended – and there's a good on-site brewpub and restaurant.

PLAZA 500 HOTEL Map p91   Hotel $$

☎ 604-873-1811, 800-473-1811; www.plaza500 .com; 500 W 12th Ave, Fairview; r from $180; ▣ 15; wi-fi ✕

With great views looking over the downtown towers dwarfed by the region's

SLEEPING SOMA

looming mountains, rooms at the Plaza 500 have received a recent makeover, delivering a more contemporary aesthetic – think loungey business hotel. This look is taken to the max in the property's Euro-chic on-site restaurant. Rates include passes to a nearby gym and there's also a free shuttle bus to downtown if you don't want to negotiate the nearby transit buses.

WINDSOR GUEST HOUSE

Map p91   B&B $$

☎ 604-872-3060, 888-872-3060; www.dougwin .com; 325 W 11th Ave, Fairview; r from $105, with shared bathroom from $95; 🚌 15
Sister property of the Douglas Guest House (p198), this 1895 heritage home is covered from top

to toe with blue-painted shingles and has a similar homey feel, with a charming veranda and stained-glass windows. The rooms vary greatly in size and some have shared bathrooms. The recommended top floor 'Charles Room' is quaint and quiet with a patio – shared with the next room – overlooking downtown. A filling cooked breakfast is included, along with free off-road parking.

SHAUGHNESSY VILLAGE

Map p91   Serviced Apartments $

☎ 604-736-5511; www.shaughnessyvillage.com; 1125 W 12th Ave, Fairview; s/d $79/89; 🚌 9; 🚇
This immaculate but kitsch place, with pink carpets, flowery sofas and maritime

---

HOTEL STORIES

An interview with Daniel Craig, general manager of Opus Hotel (p195), infamous hotel-industry blogger and first-time mystery-novel author.

You must get blasé about meeting famous people at Opus. Blasé about famous people? Never! But it does get easier over time.

Are there any that have really impressed you when they've walked through the door? I love hosting musicians, particularly those that have been around so long they've become legends, such as REM, Annie Lennox, Janet Jackson, Cher and Sting. Having the band members of U2 on the property was quite a thrill. I've also been particularly impressed with Bill Clinton, who, since I first encountered him during his summit in Vancouver with Boris Yeltsin, has evolved into such an admirable former statesman.

Are celebrities very demanding guests? Earlier in my career challenges were more common – I've been verbally abused by my share of famous names! But I'm happy to report that the days of outrageous celebrity demands and bad behavior seem to have passed. A perfect example of this is the riders that music groups send to hotels detailing special arrangements: they used to specify the brand of hard liquor that must be waiting in suites for the band's arrival, but these days it's the brand of mineral water.

Your blog (www.opushotel.com/blog) has become infamous. What is it about and why do you write it? The General Manager's Blog gives a frank, behind-the-scenes look at the challenges and rewards of managing an upscale boutique hotel. It's become popular worldwide because it addresses some of the taboo subjects that a hotel manager would normally not discuss – without ever compromising the privacy of our guests, of course.

What are some of the stories you've related on your blog? Popular blog posts have included a challenging weekend of guests behaving badly – including a drag queen who painted the walls of her room with makeup – and a story called 'Demystifying Minibars' where I explain why minibar items are so expensive and fret over whether Opus should offer sex toys in the minibar.

You've also written a novel. What is it about and how does it relate to your hotel industry experience? My novel, *Murder at the Universe* (2007), is a mystery about a manager of a luxury New York hotel who becomes a reluctant sleuth when the hotel's owner is murdered on site. The story involves harried employees, demanding guests and three hotel executives who become prime suspects in the murder. While the novel is pure fiction, it draws from many of the colorful characters and bizarre situations I've encountered in the hotel business.

The high-end hotel scene is hotting up in Vancouver. What do you think about the competition that's about to come your way? Opus was opened in 2002 and has enjoyed being the newest upscale hotel in the city for over five years. That's all changing. A number of hotels are under construction as Vancouver approaches the 2010 Winter Olympics. Fortunately for Opus, they are mostly branded hotels such as Fairmont, Shangri-La and the Ritz-Carlton. Opus will continue to be one of the only boutique hotels in the city and the only boutique hotel in Yaletown.

What do you like to do in the city when you have time off? I live in Yaletown, two blocks from the hotel, and I love to grab a coffee at one of the many cafés in the area and read, daydream and people-watch. I also love to hike the Grouse Grind (p103) and experience the city's great restaurants, such as West (p139) and Glowbal (p133). You'll often see me on the seawall walking, running, biking, rollerblading – or plotting my next murder mystery.

top picks

UNEXPECTED HOTEL PERKS

- On-site comedy club – Century Plaza Hotel & Spa (p191)
- Free in-room yoga kits – Pacific Palisades Hotel (p193)
- Landscaped garden with crazy golf – Shaughnessy Village (p197)
- Dog available for walking – Fairmont Hotel Vancouver (p191)

memorabilia, describes itself as a tower block 'B&B resort.' Despite the old-school approach, the hotel is perfectly shipshape, right down to its clean, well-maintained rooms, which, like boat cabins, are lined with wooden cupboards and include microwaves, refrigerators and tiny en suite bathrooms. Extras include cooked breakfasts, an outdoor pool, a large laundry and, of course, a large display of petrified wood.

DOUGLAS GUEST HOUSE Map p91 B&B $$
☎ 604-872-3060, 888-872-3060; www.dougwin.com; 456 W 13th Ave, Fairview; r/ste from $75/145; 🚍 15

A tangerine-hued Edwardian B&B in a quiet characterful neighborhood near City Hall, the Douglas offers good rates (especially in winter) and the kind of laid-back feel where you don't have to worry about creaky floors and knickknacks being knocked over. Its six rooms – comfortable and old-school rather than antique-lined – include flowery singles with shared bathrooms, larger doubles with en suite bathrooms and two family-friendly suites. Free off-street parking is included.

KITSILANO & UBC

Vancouver's original hippie haven has come a long way since all the flower children used to hang out here in their parent's basements smoking naughty cigarettes. The counterculture rebels who stayed behind now own some of the city's most expensive heritage-home properties. Some of these are now B&Bs, combining the best of both Vancouver worlds: they're walking distance to great beaches and close to a large serving of browseworthy shops and good restaurants. Head further west for some budget options at UBC.

MAPLE HOUSE B&B Map pp94–5 B&B $$
☎ 604-739-5833; www.maplehouse.com; 1533 Maple St, Kitsilano; d $130; 🚍 2; wi-fi

Located in an old heritage property close to Kits Beach, this cozy, bright-blue little B&B is less about antiques and more about home comforts. Fusing elegant old flourishes with modern chintz touches, the three rooms – the hardwood-floored blue room is our favorite – all have private bathrooms. Your cooked breakfast is served in the high-ceilinged dining room downstairs and there's free off-street parking if you've brought a car.

MICKEY'S KITS BEACH CHALET
Map pp94–5 B&B $$
☎ 604-739-3342, 888-739-3342; www.mickeysbandb.com; 2142 W 1st Ave, Kitsilano; r $120-160; 🚍 2; wi-fi

Eschewing the heritage-home approach of most B&Bs in the area, this modern, Whistler-style chalet has three rooms and a tranquil, hedged-in garden terrace. Behind its slender, chimney-dominated exterior, its quarters – including the gabled, top-floor York Room – are decorated in a comfortable contemporary style, but only the York Room has an en suite bathroom. It's a family-friendly place: the hosts can supply toys, cribs and even babysitters. Rates include continental breakfast.

UNIVERSITY OF BRITISH COLUMBIA
Map p100 Hostel/University Housing $-$$
☎ 604-822-1000, 888-822-1030; www.ubcconferences.com; 5961 Student Union Blvd, UBC; dm & r from $29, ste from $69; 🚍 99 B-Line; wi-fi

You can pretend you're still a student by staying at UBC, but you'll need to hop on the bus for the 40-minute ride to

top picks

GAY STAYS

The following are gay-friendly but nonexclusive Vancouver sleepover options:

- Nelson House B&B (p195)
- West End Guest House (p194)
- Barclay House B&B (p193)
- Blue Horizon Hotel (p194)
- Granville Island Hotel (p196)

AIRPORT ALTERNATIVES

Staying near the airport in Richmond is not required since downtown Vancouver is only a 30-minute cab ride away. But if you're a dogged plane spotter or have an early-morning flight to catch (or a late-night one to recover from), you might want to consider these two recommended options:

- **Delta Vancouver Airport Hotel** (Map pp44–5; ☎ 604-278-1241, 800-268-1133; www.deltavancouverairport .ca; 3500 Cessna Dr, Richmond; r from $150; 🚌 98 B-Line; wi-fi) Situated on nine acres fronting the Fraser River and a five-minute drive from the airport, the Delta has standard, comfortable, business-class rooms, some with high-speed internet access (ask when you book). It provides a 24-hour airport shuttle (or free taxi during the wee hours), a 24-hour health club and an outdoor pool. Check online for price-lowering package deals.
- **Fairmont Vancouver Airport** (Map pp44–5; ☎ 604-207-5200, 800-441-1414; www.fairmont.com/vancouver airport; Vancouver International Airport, Richmond; r from $250; 🚌 424;) You can wave from the overhead walkway to the harried economy-class plebs below as you stroll toward the lobby of this luxe airport hotel in the US departure hall. This is a great option for boarding long-haul flights in a Zen-like state of calm – if you've booked an economy-class seat yourself, you're in for a rude awakening after staying here. The rooms are elegantly furnished with high-end flourishes including remote-controlled curtains and marble-lined bathrooms.

downtown to hang out with the regular people. Room types include basic hostel-style layouts with one or two single beds in each; study rooms with en suite bathrooms and kitchenettes (these are recommended); and swanky hotel-style suites with flat-screen TVs and wood and stone interior flourishes. Most are available from May to August only, but the pricey West Coast suites are offered year-round.

HI VANCOUVER JERICHO BEACH
Map pp94–5   Hostel $

☎ 604-224-3208, 888-203-4303; www.hihostels .ca; 1515 Discovery St, Kitsilano; dm/r $27/71; May-Sep; 4;

For the activity-minded budget traveler, this is the best place to stay in Vancouver. Canada's largest hostel, it's superbly located seconds from Jericho Beach, close to the restaurants on W 4th Ave and 20 minutes from downtown by bus. The large, basic dorm rooms are fine if you like a crowd, but book ahead if you'd prefer one of the handful of private rooms. Outdoorsy types can rent bikes and sports equipment here or just stroll to the nearby kayaking and surfing operators.

GREATER VANCOUVER

Across the Burrard Inlet, North Vancouver and West Vancouver (particularly the former) have a smattering of lodging options for those who like to be closer to the mountains yet also only a short drive (or SeaBus trip) from

downtown. In addition, you're in a good spot if you plan to explore further afield to Whistler. South of the city, Richmond is close to the airport if you want to be sure you make that bleary-eyed early-morning flight.

THISTLEDOWN HOUSE B&B
Map pp44–5   B&B $$

☎ 604-986-7173, 888-633-7173; www.thistle -down.com; 3910 Capilano Rd, North Vancouver; r $150-275; 236 from Lonsdale Quay

Located on the road to Grouse Mountain, this romantic adult-oriented place is a notch above standard B&Bs: just check its gourmet breakfast menu. Among its five elegantly decorated rooms, the most palatial suite – called Under the Apple Tree – is surprisingly secluded and includes a beautiful fireplace, sunken sitting room, Jacuzzi and large windows opening onto a private patio. The owners are friendly and helpful and intent on making your stay as comfortable as possible.

LONSDALE QUAY HOTEL
Map pp44–5   Hotel $$

☎ 604-986-6111; www.lonsdalequayhotel.com; 123 Carrie Cates Crt, North Vancouver; d/ste $149/189; SeaBus to Lonsdale Quay; wi-fi

Ask for a waterfront room at this hotel, a short walk from the SeaBus terminal and steps from Lonsdale Quay Market, and you'll be treated to grand views of the shimmering Vancouver skyline across Burrard Inlet. Most of the room interiors will be familiar to the business traveler, but there are also two colorful family rooms with bunk beds and bath toys. There are plenty of shops and restaurants nearby to keep you occupied and a bus terminal if you want to head up to Grouse Mountain or Capilano Suspension Bridge.

OCEAN BREEZE B&B Map pp44–5   B&B $$
☎ 604-988-0546, 800-567-5171; www.oceanbreeze vancouver.com; 462 E 1st St, North Vancouver; r from $145; 🚌 228 from Lonsdale Quay; wi-fi
This place may look like it was designed for Hansel and Gretel, but beneath the filigree woodwork and brightly painted exterior beats the heart of a warm, welcoming B&B. The flowery flourishes are continued inside where pastel shades compete with reproduction antiques, while most of the rooms have fireplaces and overlook the waterfront

where you can watch the cruise ships sliding by. Breakfast is served in a sunny dining area – check out the salmon omelet.

GROUSE INN Map pp44–5   Motel $$
☎ 604-988-1701, 800-779-7888; www.grouseinn .com; 1633 Capilano Rd, North Vancouver; s/d/ste from $99/109/145; 🚌 236 from Lonsdale Quay; 🚗
While it looks like a stuccoed shopping mall from the outside, this family-friendly motel is a favorite among winter skiers and summer hikers. Its great amenities include a playground, restaurant, outdoor pool and free continental breakfast. Rooms have bright and breezy interiors – especially if you like busy, 1980s-style bedspreads – and come in a wide array of configurations, including Jacuzzi suites and larger rooms for groups. Free parking.

DAY TRIPS & EXCURSIONS

Wherever you wander in Vancouver, the rest of the province seems to be calling you from almost every corner. It could be the snow-capped crags peeking at you between the glass towers of downtown; the region's dense and ancient forests waving at you from the other side of an inlet; or the nearby islands whispering your name as you stroll along the waterfront. Your best response to all these enticements is to go with the flow. Vancouver may be an enjoyable place to visit but it's the surrounding treasures that truly make it a great vacation destination – if you don't get away to one or two of these while you're here, you haven't really seen BC.

Victoria, the provincial capital, and Whistler, BC's favorite outdoor playground, are the region's big-ticket locales and both are possible day trips if you're on a tight timeline, although an overnight trip is preferable, if you can manage it.

The former has a reputation as a tweed-curtained 1950s evocation of old-empire England, but this image has slowly receded in recent years. The city's iconic landmark buildings are still there, but the tourist-trap olde-world restaurants and Tudor-framed shops have been reinvigorated with a new generation of funky eateries and businesses, without abandoning the charming aesthetic that draws two million visitors yearly.

Whistler is North America's top ski resort and is fast becoming a year-round destination with its menu of summertime adrenaline-rush activities. Despite getting all gussied up for the 2010 Olympic and Paralympic Winter Games (see p25), the town retains a bit of a nonconformist image and draws people from all walks of life. You can see baggy pants–wearing snowboarders, muddied-up mountain bikers and women in business suits all downing coffee within 15m of each other.

En route to Whistler along winding Hwy 99, Squamish is the place to go for rock climbing and eagle watching. The colorful Southern Gulf Islands lure art fans and retreat seekers with their bewitching bluffs, bays and teensy, often quirky communities. And for those who think they have no time for excursions when visiting the region, consider Bowen Island, little more than a stone's throw from West Vancouver, or Buntzen Lake, just an hour from the city and a breathtaking natural spot that's far from the madding tourists crowds.

The accommodation prices listed in this chapter are for peak season, which runs from late May to early September. Whistler is the exception, when winter is the prime time, with prices to match.

OUTDOOR ACTIVITIES

Tottering around Vancouver's Stanley Park seawall on a rented bike does not count: you really have to dive head first (not always literally) into the activity side of BC's outdoor wonderland if you want some stories to tell when you get back home. Highlights include scuba diving or kayaking (try a sunset kayak tour) in Victoria (p204), where you should also hop on a bike: the city constantly brags about having more cycling routes than any other in Canada. For breadth of activities, you can't beat Whistler (p211) – especially if your idea of thrills includes screaming like a banshee or wetting yourself (or both). In summer, the popular alpine resort attracts zipliners, hikers, rock climbers and white-water rafters, while winter delivers action from skiing to snowboarding to nighttime snowshoeing. If you prefer rock climbing in the morning and

a choice of kiteboarding or mountain biking in the afternoon, Squamish (p215) is ideal, while surfers and storm watchers won't want to leave Tofino (p210) on the wild west coast of Vancouver Island. Alternatively, if you're just craving a quick nature break from the city, Buntzen Lake (p216) is a spectacular tree-hugger's fave.

PLANES, TRAINS & BOATS

While getting around is usually the least exciting part of any vacation, in BC the reverse is true. The region is blessed with some great transportation options that also turn out to be among the best ways to encounter the forests, islands and coastlines for which the province is justly famous. You'll understand exactly what we mean if you take a 30-minute floatplane trip (p205) between Vancouver and Victoria: you'll be glued to the window watching the forested

islands and expansive ocean slide past below. You'll likely fall in love with Mother Nature again if you make the return trip via BC Ferries (opposite), where you can stand on deck and sigh as deeply as you want. The operator also runs services between the Southern Gulf Islands (p218), which tend to be even more peaceful and laid-back. Slow-travel fans can also hit the rails in Victoria on board the charming Malahat train (p208), which trundles up-island over trestle bridges and through forests to Courtenay. Trainspotters will also enjoy the scenic Whistler Mountaineer (p211) service that winds between the resort and North Vancouver. (If you're a true train nut, drop by the giant West Coast Railway Heritage Park – see p216 – home to BC's favorite steam engine and a rolling cavalcade of historic locomotives.) Finally, consider soaring in solitude with a breathtaking glider excursion (p214) in Pemberton.

ISLAND HOPPING

You won't go wrong visiting any of the region's main islands, so let time be the deciding factor. If you only have half a day, sample the 'Happy Isle,' Bowen (p217), a 20-minute ferry ride from West Vancouver and a fine place for a quick hike or nautical-style pint. Vancouver Island's Victoria (right) can be visited in a day, but it'll be a long-ass one, so consider spending at least a night. You can also use Victoria as a base for traveling further afield: Vancouver Island is ripe for exploring and is relatively drivable, or you can take the train as far as Courtenay, stopping at the colorful communities en route.

The Southern Gulf Islands (p218) recharge the soul with their aqua skies seemingly close enough to touch. The islands aren't that far away, but the infrequent ferries mean you should give yourself plenty of time to get around – it's never too late to adopt the slower-paced island approach to life. The BC Ferries (p224) network services all these places, and the ride itself – as the boat slithers through a labyrinth of lighthouse-punctuated islands – can be just as rewarding as the destination. The operator sells a special SailPass aimed at island-hoppers: check its website for the latest prices and information.

WILDLIFE WATCHING

The most popular BC excursions for those who want to commune with nature are whale watching (p208) in Victoria, usually a three-hour boat tour where mostly orcas are viewed; and eagle watching (see Brackendale Art Gallery, p216) in Brackendale, near Squamish, where birds feast on the local rivers' spawning salmon. But keeping your eyes peeled when you're in BC can also reveal a few wildlife surprises: BC Ferries services often slip past seals and the occasional whale pod (the captain will announce anything worth getting your camera out for); Victoria's Beacon Hill Park (p208) is home to a few bold raccoons; and it's not too difficult to spot a marmot or two diving between the rocks around Whistler (p211). In the wilderness, of course, anything goes: near Tofino, the Pacific Rim National Park Reserve (see the boxed text, p210) has rainforests of huge cedar and fir trees and is home to a teeming mass of critters large and small. Take a guided wildlife trek here and you'll find out all about them.

VICTORIA

BC's ivy-covered, picture-postcard capital was long touted as North America's most English city. This was a surprise to anyone who actually came from Britain, since Victoria promulgated a dreamy version of England that never really was: every garden (complete with the occasional palm tree) was manicured; every flagpole flew the Union Jack; and every afternoon was spent sipping imported Marks & Spencer tea from bone-china cups.

Thankfully this sleepy theme-park version of Ye Olde England has gradually faded in recent years. Fuelled by an increasingly younger demographic, a quiet revolution has seen lame tourist pubs, eateries and stores transformed into the kind of brightly painted bohemian shops, wood-floored coffee bars and surprisingly innovative restaurants that would make any city proud. It's worth seeking out these enclaves on foot, but activity fans should also hop on their bikes: Victoria has more cycle routes than any other Canadian city.

Centered on the twin Inner Harbour landmarks of the Parliament Buildings and the Fairmont Empress Hotel, downtown Victoria is compact and strollable. Stretching north from here, Government St is the main shopping promenade (especially for souvenirs) and it leads to Bastion Square, lined with historic buildings now colonized by cafés and restaurants. At the northern edge of downtown, Victoria's small Chinatown is the oldest in Canada. Just south is Market Square, adjoined by the funky LoJo shopping area. Once you've got your bearings, you're ready to go.

The excellent **Royal British Columbia Museum** (☎ 250-356-7226, 888-447-7977; www.royalbcmuseum .bc.ca; 675 Belleville St; adult/child $18/12; ⏰ 9am-6pm Jul–mid-Oct, 9am-5pm mid-Oct–Jun) is the best in the province and should be a highlight of any visit here. It's an evocative introduction to the prehistoric and human history of the region – the old woolly mammoth diorama still packs a punch. Don't miss the museum's stirring First Nations gallery and detailed pioneer town re-creation.

Across the street, the handsome, multi-turreted **Parliament Buildings** (☎ 250-387-1400; www .leg.bc.ca; 501 Belleville St; admission free; ⏰ 8:30am-5pm daily May-Sep, Mon-Fri Oct-Apr) offers more history and an entertaining 30-minute **tour** (☎ 250-387-3046, 800-663-7867; admission free; ⏰ 9am-4pm daily May-Sep, Mon-Fri Oct-Apr), where costumed Victorians will regale you with plenty of quirky stories about the old dame. Consider returning for lunch – one of the city's best dining secrets, the **Legislative Dining Room** (p209), is hidden downstairs – and come back to the area at night, when the building's exterior is lit up like a Christmas tree.

Even if you're not staying there, it's well worth strolling through the nearby **Fairmont Empress Hotel** (p210) as if you own the place. You can stop for afternoon tea ($55), a pricey but popular experience that attracts many tourists, or just walk haughtily through then continue your stroll up **Government St**.

The buskers here will keep you entertained as you duck into the **Artisan Wine Shop** (☎ 250-384-9994; 1007 Government St; ⏰ 10am-9pm) for a tasting of the Okanagan Valley's finest, or **Rogers' Chocolates** (☎ 250-727-6851; 913 Government St; ⏰ 9am-7pm Sun-Wed, 9am-9pm Thu-Sat) for some dessert-sized Victoria Creams or ice cream. If it's a Sunday in summer, the **Government St Public Market** (☎ 250-598-2593; 1600 Government St; ⏰ 11am-4.30pm Sun May-Sep) will be open, offering an eclectic mix of street performers and craft stalls.

This end of town (Fisgard St) is the doorstep of **Chinatown**, complete with chatty grocery-store and trinket-shop owners, as well as **Fan Tan Alley** – a narrow passageway between Fisgard St and Pandora Ave that's a mini-warren of traditional and trendy stores hawking cheap-and-cheerful trinkets, cool used records and funky artworks. Consider signing up with **Hidden Dragon Tours** (☎ 250-920-0881, 866-920-0881; www.oldchinatown.com; 541 Fisgard St; adult/child $29/14.50) for a three-hour evening lantern tour of the area, where you'll learn all about opium dens and the hardships of 19th-century immigration.

Close by, the old colonial buildings on **Lower Johnson St** have been repainted and occupied by Victoria's best independent shops; this area is now called **LoJo** and is worth an hour or so

TRANSPORTATION: VICTORIA

Distance from Vancouver 100km
Direction Southwest
Travel time Three to 3½ hours (including ferry) by vehicle; 35 minutes by floatplane or helicopter; 25 minutes by plane
Air Services by Air Canada Jazz (☎ 514-393-3333, 888-247-2262; www.aircanada.ca) arrive from Vancouver International Airport (from $91, 25 minutes, up to 21 daily) at Victoria International Airport (☎ 250-953-7500; www .victoriaairport.com), 26km north of the city. Much more convenient, Harbour Air Seaplanes (☎ 604-274-1277, 800-665-0212; www.harbour-air.com) services arrive in the Inner Harbour from downtown Vancouver ($120, 35 minutes) throughout the day. There are similar services by West Coast Air (☎ 604-606-6888, 800-347-2222; www.westcoastair .com) and Helijet (☎ 604-273-4688, 800-665-4354; www.helijet.com).
Bus From Vancouver, Pacific Coach Lines (☎ 250-385-4411, 800-661-1725; www.pacificcoach.com) services arrive, via ferry, several times daily. The Victoria Regional Transit (☎ 250-382-6161; www.busonline.ca) bus 70 runs from Swartz Bay ferry terminal to downtown (adult/child $3/2.25), while bus 11 trundles from downtown to the Art Gallery of Greater Victoria and Craigdarroch Castle (adult/child $2.25/1.40). Day passes cost $7/5 per adult/child.
Car Drive from downtown Vancouver to the BC Ferries Tsawwassen terminal – via S Oak St, Hwy 99 and Hwy 17 – then board the Victoria ferry. From Swartz Bay on Vancouver Island, take Hwy 17 into Victoria (32km).
Ferry Services from BC Ferries (☎ 250-386-3431, 888-223-3779; www.bcferries.com) Tsawwassen terminal on the mainland (adult/child/vehicle $10.30/5.15/34.20, 90 minutes) arrive at Swartz Bay every hour between 10am and 7pm in summer (reduced hours in winter). The little boats of the Victoria Harbour Ferry (☎ 250-708-0201; www.victo riaharbourferry.com; adult/child $4/2) wobble between the Inner Harbour, Songhees Park (for Spinnakers Brewpub), Reeson's Landing (for the LoJo shopping area) and other stops along Gorge Waterway.

VICTORIA

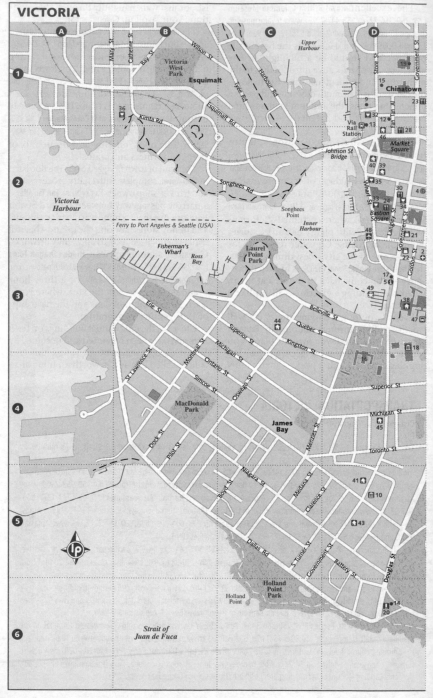

A B C D

1 Victoria West Park
Esquimalt
Upper Harbour
Store St
19
15 **Chinatown**
Government St
Mary St
Catherine St
Bay St
Wilson St
9
32
Fisgard St
12
28
13
23
46 Market Square
35
40 39
33 24 30
Bastion Square
4
Langley St
Government St
21
22
Caddon St
2
48
17
5
49
38
47
36
Kimta Rd
Esquimalt Rd
Tyee Rd
Harbour Rd
Johnson St Bridge
Songhees Rd
Songhees Point
Inner Harbour
Wharf St

2 Victoria Harbour

Ferry to Port Angeles & Seattle (USA)

3 Fisherman's Wharf
Ross Bay
Laurel Point Park
Belleville St
Erie St
Superior St
44 Quebec St
Kingston St
18

4 Michigan St
Montreal St
Ontario St
St Lawrence St
Simcoe St
Oswego St
Superior St
MacDonald Park
James Bay
Menzies St
Michigan St
45
Toronto St
Dock St
Pilot St

5 Niagara St
Boyd St
41
10
Medana St
Clarence St
43

6 Strait of Juan de Fuca
Dallas Rd
S Turner St
Government St
Battery St
Douglas St
Holland Point
Holland Point Park
14
20

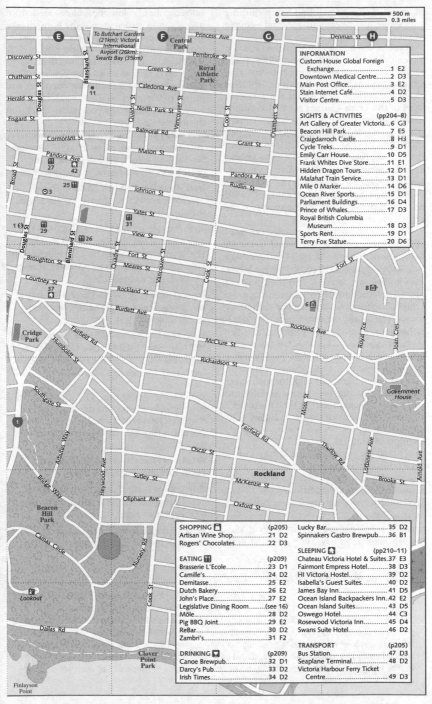

0 ――――――― 500 m
0 ――――――― 0.3 miles

INFORMATION
Custom House Global Foreign
  Exchange..........................1 E2
Downtown Medical Centre.....2 D3
Main Post Office..................3 E2
Stain Internet Café...............4 D2
Visitor Centre......................5 D3

SIGHTS & ACTIVITIES (pp204–8)
Art Gallery of Greater Victoria..6 G3
Beacon Hill Park....................7 E5
Craigdarroch Castle................8 H3
Cycle Treks...........................9 D1
Emily Carr House..................10 D5
Frank Whites Dive Store.........11 E1
Hidden Dragon Tours............12 D1
Malahat Train Service..........13 D1
Mile 0 Marker......................14 D6
Ocean River Sports...............15 D1
Parliament Buildings.............16 D4
Prince of Whales..................17 D3
Royal British Columbia
  Museum...........................18 D3
Sports Rent..........................19 D1
Terry Fox Statue...................20 D6

SHOPPING (p205)
Artisan Wine Shop................21 D2
Rogers' Chocolates...............22 D3

EATING (p209)
Brasserie L'Ecole..................23 D1
Camille's.............................24 D2
Demitasse............................25 E2
Dutch Bakery.......................26 E2
John's Place.........................27 E2
Legislative Dining Room.......(see 16)
Môle...................................28 D2
Pig BBQ Joint......................29 E2
ReBar..................................30 D2
Zambri's..............................31 F2

DRINKING (p209)
Canoe Brewpub....................32 D1
Darcy's Pub.........................33 D2
Irish Times..........................34 D2

Lucky Bar............................35 D2
Spinnakers Gastro Brewpub...36 B1

SLEEPING (pp210–11)
Chateau Victoria Hotel & Suites.37 E3
Fairmont Empress Hotel.........38 D3
HI Victoria Hostel.................39 D2
Isabella's Guest Suites...........40 D2
James Bay Inn......................41 D5
Ocean Island Backpackers Inn..42 E2
Ocean Island Suites..............43 D5
Oswego Hotel......................44 C3
Rosewood Victoria Inn..........45 D4
Swans Suite Hotel................46 D2

TRANSPORT (p205)
Bus Station..........................47 D3
Seaplane Terminal................48 D2
Victoria Harbour Ferry Ticket
  Centre.............................49 D3

207

of anyone's time. You'll find hemp clothing stores, one-off design boutiques and a couple of good coffee shops.

If you're still hungry for activities (and you haven't run out of time), Beacon Hill Park is the locals' favorite outdoorsy hangout – enter on Douglas St and check out the windswept trees along the clifftop. You'll find a marker for Mile 0 of the Trans-Canada Hwy, alongside a statue of Terry Fox, the heroic, one-legged runner whose attempted cross-Canada trek gripped the nation in 1981. It's not far from here to the Emily Carr House (☎ 250-383-5843; www.emilycarr .com; 207 Government St; admission by donation; ☺ 11am-4pm daily Jun-Aug, Tue-Sat Sep-May), the birthplace of BC's best-known painter, complete with re-created period rooms and displays on the artist's life and work.

If her swirling nature-dominated canvases appeal, drive or take transit bus 11 to the Art Gallery of Greater Victoria (☎ 250-384-4101; www.aggv .bc.ca; 1040 Moss St; adult/child $12/2; ☺ 10am-5pm Fri-Wed, 10am-9pm Thu), where you'll find the country's best Carr collection. There's also an extensive array of Japanese art and regular temporary shows. The nearby Craigdarroch Castle (☎ 250-592-5323; www.thecastle.ca; 1050 Joan Cres; adult/child $11.75/3.75; ☺ 9am-7:30pm mid-Jun–Aug, 10am-5pm Sep–mid-Jun) is also worth a stop. A handsome, 39-room landmark built by a 19th-century coal baron with money to burn, this multiturreted stone mansion is dripping with period architecture and antique-packed rooms. Climb the tower's 87 steps (checking out the stained-glass windows en route) for views of the snow-capped Olympic Mountains.

With all the rugged natural beauty in BC, it's a bit ironic that one of the province's top tourism draws is the 20 hectares of elaborate manicured foliage at Butchart Gardens (☎ 250-652-5256, 866-652-4422; www.butchartgardens.com; 800 Benvenuto Ave; adult/child/youth $25/3/12.50; ☺ 9am-10:30pm mid-Jun–Aug, earlier closing at other times), 21km north of Victoria in Brentwood Bay. With its year-round

kaleidoscope of colors, the grounds are divided into separate garden areas – the tranquil Japanese Garden is a favorite. Summer can be crowded but the Saturday-night fireworks display (July and August only) makes it all worthwhile.

Victoria is a whale-watching center and is also home to kayaking and diving operators and plenty of bike routes, so if you're looking for a bit more action from your visit, check out the following:

Cycle Treks (☎ 250-386-2277, 877-733-6722; www .cycletreks.com; 450 Swift St; from $50; ☺ 9:30am-6pm Mon-Sat) Leads three- to four-hour seafront-themed cycling tours – one of the best ways to encounter Victoria.

Frank Whites Dive Store (☎ 250-385-4713; www .frankwhites.com; 1620 Blanshard St; ☺ 9am-5:30pm) Scuba equipment rentals.

Ocean River Sports (☎ 250-381-4233, 800-909-4233; www.oceanriver.com; 1824 Store St; rental 2hr/24hr $25/50; ☺ 9:30am-6pm Mon-Thu & Sat, 9:30am-8pm Fri, 11am-5pm Sun) Rents kayaks and leads tours, including popular 2½-hour sunset tours ($59).

Prince of Whales (☎ 250-383-4884, 888-383-4884; www.princeofwhales.com; 812 Wharf St; adult/child $85/69) Whale-watching tours.

Sports Rent (☎ 250-385-7368; www.sportsrentbc.com; 1950 Government St; rental 5hr/24hr $29/45; ☺ 9am-5:30pm Mon-Thu & Sat, 9am-6pm Fri, 10am-5pm Sun) Rents kayaks, bikes and other equipment.

If you want to time your Victoria visit to take in a festival or two, consider these events:

Moss Street Paint-In One hundred artists demonstrate their skills at this popular one-day community event held in mid-July.

Victoria Day Parade Street fiesta shenanigans with dancers and marching bands; mid-May.

Victoria Fringe Theatre Festival (www.victoriafringe .com) Two weeks of quirky short plays staged throughout the city during late August.

Victoria Jazzfest International (www.vicjazz.bc.ca) Ten days of jazz performance; late June.

DETOUR: MALAHAT TRAIN

The under-the-radar but undeniably charming Via Rail (☎ 888-842-7245; www.viarail.com) *Malahat* train service departs from Victoria every morning and is a great-value way to see more of Vancouver Island without having to rent a vehicle. The two-car train leaves from the little station near downtown's sky-blue Johnson St Bridge and trundles through the forest, passing alongside small communities and inching over trestle bridges that span deep, tree-lined valleys. You can break your trip up with an overnight or two along the way – artsy Chemainus, seaside Parksville or portside Nanaimo are recommended – or you can get off for a day trip and be back at the station in time to catch the train back to Victoria later in the day. One-way tickets cost no more than $49, depending on where you're planning to get off.

Victoria SkaFest (www.victoriaskafest.ca) Held in mid-July, this is Canada's largest ska music event.

INFORMATION

Custom House Global Foreign Exchange (☎ 250-412-0336; 1150 Douglas St; ☺ 9:30am-6pm Mon-Sat, 11am-6pm Sun) Well-located exchange.

Downtown Medical Centre (☎ 250-380-2210; 622 Courtney St; ☺ 9am-6pm) Handy walk-in clinic.

Main Post Office (☎ 250-953-1352; 706 Yates St; ☺ 8am-5pm Mon-Fri) Central post office at the corner of Yates and Douglas Sts.

Stain Internet Café (☎ 250-382-3352; 609 Yates St; per hr $3.50; ☺ 10am-2am) Late-opening internet spot.

Visitor Centre (☎ 250-953-2033; www.tourismvictoria .com; 812 Wharf St; ☺ 9am-5pm) Flyer-lined tourist information center overlooking the Inner Harbour.

EATING

Camille's (☎ 250-381-3433; 45 Bastion Sq; mains $18-26; ☺ 5:30-10pm Tue-Sat) A charming subterranean dining room with a lively, ever-changing menu reflecting great local ingredients. With its good wine list, this spot invites adventurous foodies.

Brasserie L'Ecole (☎ 250-475-6260; 1715 Government St; mains $19-28; ☺ 5:30-11pm Tue-Sun) This country-style French bistro has a warm casual atmosphere and delectable menu favorites, such as lamb shank served with mustard-creamed root vegetables and braised chard.

Zambri's (☎ 250-360-1171; 911 Yates St; mains $20-25; ☺ 11:30am-2:45pm & 5-9pm Tue-Sat) An unassuming restaurant with a gourmet, Italian-influenced menu. Savvy diners drop by on Saturdays, when a creative five-course tasting menu hits the blackboard.

John's Place (☎ 250-389-0711; 723 Pandora Ave; mains $7-16; ☺ 7am-9pm Mon-Thu, 7am-10pm Fri, 8am-10pm Sat, 8am-9pm Sun) An idyllic weekend brunch spot, with wood floors, high ceilings and funky memorabilia lining the walls. Dinner is also good here, including international comfort foods from calamari to pierogies.

Möle (☎ 250-385-6653; 554 Pandora Ave; mains $10-18; ☺ 8am-3pm & 5:30-11pm Wed-Mon, 8am-3pm Tue) This wood-floored joint attracts the hip crowd with its comfort classics and adventurous fusion dishes (think organic hamburgers and yam wraps). Beer includes the recommended Phillips brews.

Legislative Dining Room (☎ 250-387-3959; Room 606, Parliament Buildings, 501 Belleville St; mains $6-16; ☺ 9am-3pm Mon-Thu, 9am-2pm Fri) This is the Parliament Buildings' subsidized restaurant, where anyone can drop by for dishes such as shrimp quesadillas and smoked tofu salad. Enter via the security desk at the building's entrance.

Pig BBQ Joint (☎ 250-381-4677; 749 View St; mains $5; ☺ 9am-7pm Mon-Fri) Hulking sandwiches of the melt-in-your-mouth pulled-pork variety (beef brisket and smoked-chicken variations are also offered) dominate the simple menu here, washed down with homemade iced tea.

ReBar (☎ 250-360-2401; 50 Bastion Sq; mains $9-14; ☺ 8:30am-9pm Mon-Wed, 8:30am-10pm Thu-Sat, 8:30am-3:30pm Sun) This place fuses colorful interiors with a clever, mostly vegetarian menu, but carnivores will be just as happy noshing here. It's a good weekend brunch spot.

Dutch Bakery (☎ 250-385-1012; 718 Fort St; mains $4-7; ☺ 7:30am-5:30pm Mon-Sat) Rub shoulders with the regulars at this old-school nook and they'll recommend a beef pie with potato salad. Pick dessert from the handmade candies on display near the entrance.

Demitasse (☎ 250-386-4442; 1320 Blanshard St; mains $7-11; ☺ 7am-4pm Mon-Fri, 9am-2pm Sat & Sun) Soups, wraps and sandwiches dominate the menu and there are plenty of veggie-friendly options at this laid-back, student-friendly spot.

DRINKING & NIGHTLIFE

Spinnakers Gastro Brewpub (☎ 250-386-2739; 308 Catherine St) Lip-smacking craft brews here include light Honey Blonde Ale and dark Nut Brown. The superior food menu includes excellent seafood.

Canoe Brewpub (☎ 250-361-1940; 450 Swift St) Its own-brewed beers include the hoppy Red Canoe Lager and the summer-friendly Siren's Song Pale Ale. It's also good for a meal and there's a great waterfront patio.

Darcy's Pub (☎ 250-380-1322; www.darcyspub.ca; 1127 Wharf St) This laid-back downtown bar offers free live acts every night, ranging from weekend cover bands to a Monday-night open-mike session. There's beer from Vancouver Island Brewing.

Lucky Bar (☎ 250-382-5825; www.luckybar.ca; 517 Yates St; cover free-$10) This club, a Victoria institution, offers live music from ska and indie to electroclash, plus dance-floor tunes when there's no band on.

Irish Times (☎ 250-383-7775; 1200 Government St) A lively Celtic bar serving drafts from Ireland, France and Belgium. Daily food specials are offered (pizza and beer is $9.99 on Wednesday), plus there's nightly live Irish music.

DETOUR: TOFINO

Like a waterfront Whistler-in-the-making, lovely Tofino – hugging itself against the crashing surf on the west coast of Vancouver Island – has boomed in recent years, becoming the de facto capital of the stunningly rainforested Pacific Rim National Park Reserve. You'll find plenty of seaside hotels and resorts and a smattering of good seafood restaurants in and around the town – the Visitor Centre (☎ 250-725-3414; www.tourismtofino.com; 1426 Pacific Rim Hwy; ☺ 10am-6pm May-Sep) can help with info on where to stay and what to do.

It's really all about the outdoors here: Clayoquot Sound is famed for kayaking; the area's tumultuous waves attract surfers and storm watchers in equal measure; and there are plenty of hiking trails and wilderness treks to attract the active. You don't need calves of steel to enjoy yourself, though: there are plenty of nature tours and laid-back activities for those who prefer the soft-eco approach.

You can drive here via Hwy 1 and Hwy 4 from Victoria (314km). You can also fly: Orca Airways (☎ 604-270-6722, 888-359-6722; www.flyorcaair.com) services arrive at Tofino Airport (☎ 250-725-2006) from Vancouver International Airport's South Terminal ($159, 55 minutes, one to three daily). Alternatively, Tofino Bus (☎ 250-725-2871, 866-986-3466; www.tofinobus.com) runs an 'Express Service' from Vancouver ($61, ferry fare extra, seven hours) and Victoria ($65, 5½ hours). The bus route runs daily year-round and twice daily from mid-March to mid-November.

SLEEPING

Prices indicated are for the May to September peak season (sans taxes), when it is difficult to find something for less than $100 a night; rooms are reduced by up to 50% off peak, when the weather is usually pleasantly mild. Tourism Victoria's room reservation service (☎ 250-953-2033, 800-663-3883; www.tourismvictoria.com) books B&Bs, hotels and everything else.

Swans Suite Hotel (☎ 250-361-3310, 800-668-7926; www.swanshotel.com; 506 Pandora Ave; d/ste $199/289) An old brick warehouse transformed into an art-lined boutique hotel, it has rooms decorated with a comfy combination of wood beams, rustic chic furniture and deep leather sofas. The full kitchens are also handy.

Ocean Island Suites (☎ 250-385-1788, 888-888-4180; www.oisuites.com; 143 Government St; ste $120; wi-fi) This renovated heritage home has four individually styled suites (the Burma room is recommended), all with kitchens and hardwood floors. There's a shared laundry ($1.50 per washing load) plus a large, summer-friendly deck.

Fairmont Empress Hotel (☎ 250-348-8111, 866-540-4429; www.fairmont.com/empress; 721 Government St; r from $249; 🌐 💻 🐾) Rooms at this ivy-covered, century-old landmark are elegant but conservative and some are quite small, but the overall effect is regal and old-school class.

Isabella's Guest Suites (☎ 250-812-9216; www.isabellasbb.com; 537 Johnson St; ste from $150; wi-fi) A pair of self-contained adult-oriented suites with hardwood floors, elegant interiors and full kitchens. If you don't fancy cooking, your included dining voucher covers breakfast at the downstairs bakery.

Rosewood Victoria Inn (☎ 250-384-6644, 866-986-2222; www.rosewoodvictoria.com; 595 Michigan St; d from $150; wi-fi) The rooms at this superior heritage B&B are immaculate and the gourmet breakfast runs from spinach crêpes to coconut and almond scones. Bring your laptop to the lounge for wireless access.

Oswego Hotel (☎ 250-294-7500, 877-767-9346; www.oswegovictoria.com; 500 Oswego St; d/ste from $220/300) Victoria's swankiest new hotel, this designer lounge place in a quiet residential location comes complete with granite floors, cedar beams, deep baths and (in most rooms) small balconies.

Chateau Victoria Hotel & Suites (☎ 250-382-4221, 800-663-5891; www.chateauvictoria.com; 740 Burdett Ave; d/ste/penthouse from $152/202/400; wi-fi 🌐 💻 🐾) There's an '80s feel at this tower-block hotel but the rooms are clean and well-maintained, and many have kitchens. The hotel's top-floor restaurant has the city's best views.

James Bay Inn (☎ 250-384-7151, 800-836-2649; www.jamesbayinn.bc.ca; 270 Government St; r from $129) This well-maintained old charmer has an array of room types, most with busy patterned carpets and furniture that's not quite antique. Some rooms have kitchenettes and there's a downstairs bar serving pub grub.

Ocean Island Backpackers Inn (☎ 250-385-1788, 888-888-4180; www.oceanisland.com; 791 Pandora Ave; dm/s/d from $24/39/44; wi-fi 💻) A funky, multicolored sleepover option with a labyrinth of dorms and private rooms. There's also a communal kitchen and a licensed lounge for bands and DJs. Regular tours offered to guests.

HI Victoria Hostel (☎ 250-385-4511, 888-883-0099; victoria@hihostels.ca; 516 Yates St; dm/d $25/60; wi-fi 💻) This quiet, somewhat institutionalized but well-located hostel has two large single-sex dorms, three small co-eds and a couple of private rooms. It offers free weekly city tours to guests.

WHISTLER

Named for the furry marmots that populate the area and whistle like deflating balloons, this gabled alpine village is one of the world's most popular ski resorts. Home to many of the outdoor events at the 2010 Olympic and Para-lympic Winter Games (see p25) – it's never too late to slip on your luge outfit and try out for your country's national team – the town nes-tles in the shade of its formidable twin peaks, Whistler and Blackcomb mountains.

Despite the frosted, Christmas-card aes-thetics, it's not just about the winter season here. The area's summer visitor numbers have leaped in recent years, with Vancouver-ites and international travelers lured to the lakes and crags by a wide array of activities, from mountain biking to ziplining to alpine meadow hiking.

Comprised of four neighborhoods – ap-proaching via Hwy 99 from the south, you'll hit Creekside first – the central Whistler Vil-lage is the area's hub for hotels, restaurants and businesses. You'll find plenty of B&B-type accommodations in the quieter Village North area, while the Upper Village is home to some swanky hotels, clustered around the base of Blackcomb. Don't be surprised if you get lost when you're wandering around on foot – luck-ily, there are plenty of street signs and lots of people around to help with directions.

One of North America's largest ski and snowboard areas, twin-mountain Whistler-Blackcomb (☎ 604-904-7060, 888-403-4727; www.whistler blackcomb.com; 2-day lift ticket adult/child/youth $81/42/69) has 200 runs and Canada's longest season – November through June on Blackcomb and November through April on Whistler. There are dozens of lifts to transport the powder fans, including a hotly anticipated 4.4km peak-to-peak gondola – linking both mountains for the first time – opening in late 2008.

Not surprisingly, it can get very busy here at peak times, but ski nuts and board freaks can beat the crowds with an early-morning Fresh Tracks ticket (adult/child $17/12). Book in advance at the Whistler Village Gondola and be there for a 7am start the next day – rates include breakfast at the up-top Roundhouse Lodge. Evening skiers might prefer the Night Moves (adult/child/youth $16/11/13; ☾ 5-9pm Thu-Sat) program operated via Blackcomb's Magic Chair lift.

If you didn't bring your own gear, Whistler Adventure Centres (☎ 604-904-7060, 888-403-4727; www .whistlerblackcomb.com/rentals; 1-day ski or snowboard rental adult/child from $38/20) runs several equipment rental outlets around town. It also offers on-line reservations, so you can choose your look before you arrive, and provides lessons for ski and snowboard first-timers.

A free shuttle bus away from the village, Lost Lake (☎ 604-905-0071; www.crosscountryconnection .bc.ca; day pass adult/child/youth $15/7.50/9; ☾ 8am-9pm Nov-Mar) is home to 32km of wooded cross-country ski trails, suitable for novices and experts alike. The routes are lit at night and its 'warming hut' provides rentals, lessons and maps. Snowshoers are also well served

TRANSPORTATION: WHISTLER

Distance from Vancouver 125km
Direction North
Travel time Two to 2½ hours by vehicle; three hours by train
Bus Services from Greyhound (☎ 800-661-8747; www.greyhound.ca) arrive at Creekside and Whistler Village from Vancouver ($18.80, 2½ hours, eight daily). Buses from Perimeter Tours (☎ 604-266-5386, 877-317-7788; www.pe rimeterbus.com) also arrive from Vancouver ($67, 2½ hours, seven to 11 daily) and Vancouver Airport ($67, three hours, nine daily). Snowbus (☎ 604-685-7669, 866-766-9287; www.snowbus.ca) operates a November to April service from Vancouver ($21, 2½ hours, two daily). Whistler and Valley Express (WAVE; ☎ 604-932-4020; www.busonline.ca; adult/child/one-day pass $1.50/1.25/4.50) transit buses are equipped with ski and bike racks. In winter, buses are free between Marketplace and the Upper Village loop and in summer between the village and Lost Lake.
Car Take Georgia St through Stanley Park and over the Lions Gate Bridge. Exit the bridge on the Marine Dr W turnoff. Take the first right on to Taylor Way. Travel up the hill and turn left on to Hwy 1. Follow the signs and take Exit 2 to Hwy 99, which takes you all the way to Whistler Village.
Train The popular Whistler Mountaineer (☎ 604-606-8460, 888-687-7245; www.whistlermountaineer.com) trun-dles in from North Vancouver (from $105, three hours, May to mid-October).

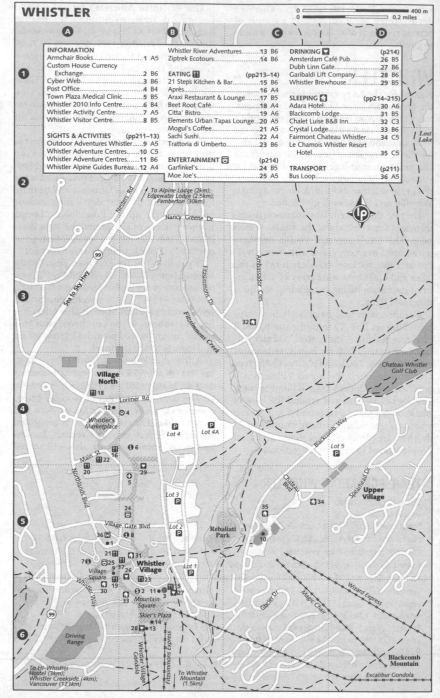

WHISTLER

0 — 400 m
0 — 0.2 miles

INFORMATION	
Armchair Books	1 A5
Custom House Currency Exchange	2 B6
Cyber Web	3 B6
Post Office	4 B4
Town Plaza Medical Clinic	5 B5
Whistler 2010 Info Centre	6 B4
Whistler Activity Centre	7 A5
Whistler Visitor Centre	8 B5

SIGHTS & ACTIVITIES	(pp211–13)
Outdoor Adventures Whistler	9 A5
Whistler Adventure Centres	10 C5
Whistler Adventure Centres	11 B6
Whistler Alpine Guides Bureau	12 A4

Whistler River Adventures	13 B6
Ziptrek Ecotours	14 B6

EATING	(pp213–14)
21 Steps Kitchen & Bar	15 B6
Après	16 A4
Araxi Restaurant & Lounge	17 B6
Beet Root Café	18 A4
Citta' Bistro	19 A6
Elements Urban Tapas Lounge	20 A5
Mogul's Coffee	21 A5
Sachi Sushi	22 A4
Trattoria di Umberto	23 B6

ENTERTAINMENT	(p214)
Garfinkel's	24 B5
Moe Joe's	25 A5

DRINKING	(p214)
Amsterdam Café Pub	26 B5
Dubh Linn Gate	27 B6
Garibaldi Lift Company	28 B6
Whistler Brewhouse	29 B5

SLEEPING	(pp214–215)
Adara Hotel	30 A6
Blackcomb Lodge	31 B5
Chalet Luise B&B Inn	32 C3
Crystal Lodge	33 B6
Fairmont Chateau Whistler	34 C5
Le Chamois Whistler Resort Hotel	35 C5

TRANSPORT	(p211)
Bus Loop	36 A5

To Alpine Lodge (2km);
Edgewater Lodge (2.5km);
Pemberton (30km)

Nancy Greene Dr

Nexen Rd

Sea to Sky Hwy

99

Fitzsimmons Dr

Ambassador Cres

Fitzsimmons Creek

Lost Lake

Chateau Whistler Golf Club

Village North

Lorimer Rd

Whistler's Marketplace

Lot 4

Lot 4A

Blackcomb Way

Lot 5

Main St

Northlands Blvd

Lot 3

Chateau Blvd

Upper Village

Spearhead Dr

Village Gate Blvd

Lot 2

Rebaliati Park

Whistler Village

Lot 1

Village Square

Whistler Way

Mountain Square

Glacier Dr

Magic Chair

Wizard Express

Driving Range

99

Skier's Plaza

Whistler Village Gondola

Fitzsimmons Express

To Whistler Mountain (1.5km)

Blackcomb Mountain

Excalibur Gondola

To HI-Whistler Hostel (3km);
Whistler Creekside (4km);
Vancouver (123km)

here: you can stomp off on your own or rent equipment and hire guides.

If you prefer your outdoor treks to be a little more pampered, **Outdoor Adventures Whistler** (☎ 604-932-0647; www.adventureswhistler.com; 4205 Village Sq; tours adult/child from $69/39) offers snowshoeing tours, including a three-hour fondue excursion (adult/child $109/49) that culminates in a rewarding feast for all your hard work. This company offers plenty of other activities if you want to try something different – check its website for options.

Whistler is also an increasingly popular summer destination for weary Lower Mainlanders looking for a break from the city. Exploring the wilderness on two wheels has begun to rival skiing as a favored Whistler activity. The giant **Whistler Mountain Bike Park** (☎ 604-904-8134, 866-218-9690; www.whistlerbike.com; 1-day lift access adult/child/youth $40/21/35; ☺ mid-May–mid-Oct) is served by three lifts and offers more than 1200m of vertical drops, plus plenty of ramps, high-octane jumps and 45 forested trails – pick up a free route map from the **Whistler Visitor Centre** (right). To tap into the 100km of additional bike trails in the region, visit the website of the **Whistler Off-Road Cycling Association** (www.worca.com).

Two legs are almost as handy as two wheels here. With more than 40km of flower-and-forest alpine trails, most accessed via the Whistler Village Gondola, this region is ideal for those who like nature of the strollable variety. Favorite routes include the **High Note Trail** (8km), which traverses pristine meadows and has stunning views of the blue-green waters of **Cheakamus Lake**. Route maps are available at the Visitor Centre. Guided treks are also offered by the friendly folk at the **Whistler Alpine Guides Bureau** (☎ 604-938-9242; www.whistlerguides.com; Unit 113, 4350 Lorimer St; guided hikes adult/child from $89/69), who can also help with rock climbing and rap jumping excursions.

If adrenaline-rush thrills are more your bag, consider a fully-harnessed ziplining swoop through the trees with **Ziptrek Ecotours** (☎ 604-935-0001, 866-935-0001; www.ziptrek.com; adult/child $98/78), or have a splashing good time on a white-knuckle rafting trip with **Whistler River Adventures** (☎ 604-932-3532, 888-932-3532; www.whistlerriver.com; Whistler Village Gondola; adult/child/youth from $89/44/59; ☺ mid-May–Aug). Wetting your pants has never been so much fun.

If you time your visit right and you still have energy to spare, Whistler hosts a few party-worthy events throughout the year, including the following:

Cornucopia (www.whistlercornucopia.com) Bacchanalian food and wine fest held in mid-November.

Kokanee Crankworx (www.crankworx.com) Bike stunts, speed demons and general two-wheeled shenanigans; mid-July.

Telus World Ski & Snowboard Festival Mid-April showcase of pro ski and snowboard competitions.

Whistler Film Festival (www.whistlerfilmfestival.com) Four days in late November of movie screenings and industry glad-handing.

Winter Pride (www.gaywhistler.com) Gay-friendly snow action and late-night partying in early February.

INFORMATION

Armchair Books (☎ 604-932-5557; 4205 Village Sq; ☺ 9am-9pm) Well-located bookstore with good travel section.

Custom House Currency Exchange (☎ 604-938-6658; 4154 Village Stroll; ☺ 9am-5pm May-Sep, 9am-6pm Oct-Apr) Central exchange.

Cyber Web (☎ 604-905-1280; 4340 Sundial Cres; per 10min $2.50; ☺ 9am 10:30pm May-Sep, 8am-10pm Oct-Apr; wi-fi) Large internet café.

Post Office (☎ 604-932-5012; Unit 106, 4360 Lorimer Rd; ☺ 8am-5pm Mon-Fri, 8am-noon Sat)

Town Plaza Medical Clinic (☎ 604-905-7089; 4314 Main St; ☺ 8:30am-7:30pm Oct-Apr, 9am-5:30pm Mon-Sat, 10am-4pm Sun May-Sep) Walk-in medical center.

Whistler 2010 Info Centre (☎ 877-408-2010; www .winter2010.com; 4365 Blackcomb Way; ☺ 11am-5pm Thu-Mon) Olympics info and resources.

Whistler Activity Centre (☎ 604-938-2769, 877-991-9988; 4010 Whistler Way; ☺ 9am-5pm) Bookings for local activities.

Whistler Visitor Centre (☎ 604-935-3357, 877-991-9988; www.tourismwhistler.com; 4230 Gateway Dr; ☺ 8am-8pm) Flyer-lined visitor center.

EATING

Araxi Restaurant & Lounge (☎ 604-932-4540; 4222 Village Sq; mains $30-45; ☺ 5-11pm) This restaurant has an exquisite Pacific Northwest menu plus courteous service. Try the Queen Charlotte Islands cod and drain the 15,000-bottle wine selection.

Après (☎ 604-935-0200; Unit 103, 4338 Main St; mains $18-35; ☺ 6pm-midnight) This contemporary French-influenced West Coast bistro is dripping with quality.

21 Steps Kitchen & Bar (☎ 604-966-2121; 4320 Sundial Cres; mains $14-22; ☺ 5:30pm-1am Mon-Sat,

DETOUR: PEMBERTON

A 30km drive north of Whistler on Hwy 99 delivers you to the cowboy country town of Pemberton (www.pemberton .net). Get some background on the region at the charming museum (☎ 604-894-5504; Prospect St; admission by donation; 10am-5pm Jun-Sep), a village of rescued pioneer shacks and elderly volunteers who look like they might have been here from the start. If you're inspired to find your inner cowboy, saddle up with Adventures on Horseback (☎ 604-894-6269; www.adventuresonhorseback.ca; 7476 Prospect St; rides from $60) for a trot around the valley, or consider an even better look over the area by heading to the Pemberton Soaring Centre (☎ 604-894-5776, 800-831-2611; www.permbertonsoaring.com; Pemberton Airport; gliding sessions from $85; Apr-Oct). Climb into a two-person glider for a breathtaking swoop around the mountains – make sure you tell the pilot you like roller coasters and see what they do. You can regale the locals with your lofty tales at the town's chatty Pony Espresso (☎ 604-894-5700; 1392 Portage Rd; mains $8-14; 8am-10pm), a neighborhood hangout with hearty grub and good beer. The pizzas are especially recommended here.

5:30pm- midnight Sun) High-end comfort food such as steak, chops and seafood. Check out the great attic bar, a locals' favorite.

Trattoria di Umberto (☎ 604-932-5858; 4417 Sundial Pl; mains $20-35; 11:30am-2pm & 5pm-midnight) Classic high-end Italian cuisine in stylish trattoria setting.

Beet Root Café (☎ 604-932-1163; Unit 129, 4340 Lorimer Rd; light mains $4-8; 7:30am-6pm) This is Whistler's best home-style hangout, with bulging breakfast burritos, huge packed sandwiches and a rolling cavalcade of baked goodies. Yum.

Sachi Sushi (☎ 604-935-5649; Unit 106, 4359 Main St; mains $8-18; 11:30am-10pm Tue-Fri, 5-10pm Sat-Mon) Serving everything from good sushi to crispy popcorn shrimp to stomach-warming udon noodles, this is a relaxing après-ski hangout.

Citta' Bistro (☎ 604-932-4177; 4217 Village Stroll; mains $8-22; 10am-1am Mon-Fri, 9am-1am Sat & Sun) Citta' hugs the edge of Village Sq. Head to the patio for creative twists on comfort-food classics – think wild salmon club sandwich.

Elements Urban Tapas Lounge (☎ 604-932-5569; 4359 Main St; mains $12-18; 8am-11pm) Elements serves an array of small plates and mains, ranging from smoked-salmon tarts to beef tenderloin medallions.

Mogul's Coffee (☎ 604-932-4845; Village Sq; sandwiches under $6; 6:30am-9pm) Fulfill your caffeine needs and watch the bustle of the square.

DRINKING & NIGHTLIFE

Check *The Pique* and *Whistler Question* (both free) for listings.

Garibaldi Lift Company (☎ 604-905-2220; Whistler Village Gondola) The closest bar to the slopes – you can watch the powder geeks on Whistler Mountain slide to a halt from the patio – the GLC is the ultimate après-ski hangout.

Whistler Brewhouse (☎ 604-905-2739; 4355 Blackcomb Way) A lodge-like resto-bar crafting its own beer (try the Twin Peaks Pale Ale), this is also an ideal spot to catch the game on TV.

Dubh Linn Gate (☎ 604-905-4047; 4320 Sundial Cres) A celtic-themed bar with an impressive whiskey menu, well-poured Guinness and a large pub-grub menu.

Amsterdam Café Pub (☎ 604-932-8334; Village Sq) This boozy, brick-lined party joint is in the heart of the village. You can treat your hangover the next day by coming back for breakfast.

Moe Joe's (☎ 604-935-1152; 4155 Golfer's Approach) More intimate than Garfinkel's, this is the best place in town if you like dancing yourself into a drooling heap. It's always crowded on Friday night; Monday's drum-and-bass night is also popular.

Garfinkel's (☎ 604-932-2323; Unit 1, 4308 Main St) Mixing mainstream dance grooves with Monday-night live bands, Whistler's biggest club is a local legend. Thursday is the best night of the week, with indie and funk tunes.

SLEEPING

During the winter peak, you'll be hard-pressed to find a room for less than $150; book well in advance and note that many places have minimum stay requirements. The summer season is also becoming popular (and pricey) here, so your best bet for a deal is fall's shoulder season. Most hotels extort parking fees ($10 to $20 daily) and some also slap on resort fees ($12 to $25 daily) – confirm these before you book. Try the village's accommodation reservation service (☎ 604-932-0606, 800-944-7853; www.whistler .com) if you can't find anything yourself.

Adara Hotel (☎ 604-905-4009, 866-502-3272; www.ada rahotel.com; 4122 Village Green; r from $160; wi-fi

Sophisticated and quirky, this top-end joint offers art-lined interiors and dramatic mod rooms where the fireplaces look like TVs and faux-fur throws abound.

Edgewater Lodge (☎ 604-932-0688, 888-870-9065; www.edgewater-lodge.com; 8020 Alpine Way; r from $150; wi-fi) A few minutes' drive past Whistler on Hwy 99, this 12-room lakeside lodge is a nature-lover's haven and has a great on-site restaurant.

Fairmont Chateau Whistler (☎ 604-938-8000, 800-441-1414; www.fairmont.com/whistler; 4599 Chateau Blvd; r from $400; 🐾) A modern-day baronial castle where the rooms are adorned in rich hues and tastefully furnished with classic West Coast elegance.

Chalet Luise B&B Inn (☎ 604-932-4187, 800-665-1998; www.chaletluise.com; 7461 Ambassador Cres; r from $135) A Bavarian-look pension with eight sunny rooms – think pine furnishings and white duvets – plus a flower garden and outdoor hot tub.

Le Chamois Whistler Resort Hotel (☎ 604-932-8700, 888-560-9453; www.lechamoiswhistlerhotel.com; 4557 Blackcomb Way; ste from $160; 🐾) There's a French heraldic theme at this well-maintained older property, where the large rooms have kitchens and separate bedrooms. Near the base of Blackcomb.

Blackcomb Lodge (☎ 604-935-1177, 888-621-1117; www.blackcomblodge.com; 4220 Gateway Dr; r/ste from $109/139; 🐾 💻 🐾) With an excellent Village Sq location, the top rooms here have deep leather sofas, darkwood furnishings and full kitchens, while the standard rooms without kitchens are almost as comfortable.

Crystal Lodge (☎ 604-932-2221, 800-667-3363; www.crystal-lodge.com; 4154 Village Stroll; d/ste from $130/175; 🐾 🐾) Crystal Lodge combines chic loungey rooms and motel-style rooms; there's something to suit most budgets here. You're also in the heart of the action, less than 100m from the main ski lift.

Alpine Lodge (☎ 604-932-5966; www.alpinelodge.com; 8135 Alpine Way; dm/r/ste $50/125/175; wi-fi) This is a colorful, wood-lined lodge with private rooms and some dorms, most with private bathrooms and mountain views. There's a handy shuttle bus to and from the lifts.

HI Whistler Hostel (☎ 604-932-5492; whistler@hihostels.ca; 5678 Alta Lake Rd; dm/r $30/68) A 15-minute drive from the village overlooking Alta Lake, this secluded hostel has fairly institutional dorms and some private rooms. Bike rentals and a sauna are available. Book ahead.

SQUAMISH

Midway between Vancouver and Whistler on Hwy 99, Squamish enjoys an incredible natural setting at the fingertips of Howe Sound. Once little more than a rough-and-ready logging town, it's undergone an Olympics-driven boom in recent years and is a popular base for outdoor activities, especially in summer. Pull over at the slick Squamish Adventure Centre (☎ 604-815-4994, 866-333-2010; www.adventurecentre.ca; 38551 Loggers Lane; 🕒 8am-8pm Jun-Sep, 9am-6pm Oct-May) to find out what's on offer in and around the region.

Just before the town on Hwy 99, the BC Museum of Mining (☎ 604-896-2233, 800-896-4044; www.bcmuseumofmining.org; adult/child $15/11.75; 🕒 9am-4:30pm daily mid-May–mid-Oct, Mon-Fri mid-Oct–mid-May) is a popular stop. Once the British Empire's largest copper mine, it's been preserved with an impressive restoration. Its underground train tour (May to October) into the pitch-black mine tunnels is a highlight and there are plenty of additional kid-friendly exhibits, as well as a large artsy gift store.

Continuing your drive, you'll soon see a sheer, 652m granite rock face looming ahead. Attracting climbers from across the region, Stawamus Chief Provincial Park (www.bcparks.ca) dominates

TRANSPORTATION: SQUAMISH

Distance from Vancouver 67km
Direction North
Travel time One to 1½ hours by vehicle
Bus Services operated by Greyhound (☎ 800-661-8747; www.greyhound.ca) arrive from Vancouver (1½ hours, $8.35, eight daily) and Whistler (one hour, $8.35, eight daily). The slightly more salubrious Perimeter Squamish Shuttle (☎ 604-266-5386, 877-317-7788; www.perimeterbus.com) also arrives here from Vancouver International Airport (1½ hours, $40, three to seven daily) and downtown Vancouver hotels (one hour, $40, one to three daily).
Car See the driving directions for Whistler (p211) for instructions on how to reach Hwy 99 from Vancouver. Around 55km along the highway, turn left onto Cleveland Ave to reach downtown Squamish.

the Squamish approach. But you don't have to be geared-up to experience its breathtaking vistas: there are hiking routes up the back for anyone who wants to have a go. Consider calling Squamish Rock Guides (☎ 604-815-1750; www .squamishrockguides.com; guided climbs half-/full-day from $175/230) for climbing assistance or lessons.

The 100 or so cycle trails centered on the town draw plenty of mountain bikers. The Cheekeye Fan trail near the village of Brackendale (a five-minute drive from the town center) offers easy terrain, while downhill thrill-seekers prefer the Diamond Head/Power Smart area. Drop in to Corsa Cycles (☎ 604-892-3331; www.corsacycles.com; 1200 Hunter Pl; rentals per day $45; ☷ 9:30am-6:30pm) for rentals and a trail guide.

If you're in Brackendale in January, drop by the quirky Brackendale Art Gallery (☎ 604-898-3333; www.brackendaleartgallery.com; 41950 Government Rd), the center of the area's biggest wildlife claim to fame. The winter feeding ground for thousands of salmon-scoffing bald eagles, the village lures legions of binocular-clad visitors who flock around the gallery's eccentric owner Thor Froslev as he coordinates the winter bird count. Thor's rustic gallery is lined with eagle-inspired paintings and photos and has a cozy café that could double as a hobbit hole.

Back in Squamish, the West Coast Railway Heritage Park (☎ 604-898-9336; www.wcra.org; 39645 Government Rd; adult/child $10/8.50; ☷ 10am-5pm) draws fans of another type. This giant open-air museum is the final resting place of BC's legendary *Royal Hudson* steam engine and has around 90 historic railcars, including 10 working engines and the original prototype SkyTrain car from Vancouver. Weekend train trips are offered around the park and there's a main street of pioneer buildings that recalls pioneer-town BC.

If you prefer to travel under your own steam, Squamish Spit is a popular kiteboarding (and windsurfing) hotspot; the season runs from May to October. The Squamish Windsports Society (☎ 604-892-2235; www.squamishwindsurfing.org; day pass $15) is your first point of contact for weather and water conditions and information on access to the spit; it has change rooms and day storage, plus staffers with first-aid skills if you take a bloody tumble.

EATING & SLEEPING

Sunflower Bakery Café (☎ 604-892-2231; 38086 Cleveland Ave; mains $4-7; ☷ 8am-5:30pm Mon-Sat) This place serves fresh wraps and bagel sandwiches plus an array of chunky cakes and bulging fruit pies that will have you committing to some heavy exercise.

Naked Lunch (☎ 604-892-5552; 1307 Pemberton Ave; mains $6-11; ☷ 8am-5pm Mon-Fri, 8am-4pm Sat) A chatty diner where the menu leans toward gourmet comfort food – check the halibut burger or hearty soups.

Howe Sound Inn & Brewing Company (☎ 604-892-2603, 800-919-2537; www.howesound.com; 37801 Cleveland Ave; r $109; wi-fi) This place has warm and inviting rooms with plenty of woodsy touches. The brewpub is also worth a visit – try the Whitecap Ale.

Squamish Inn on the Water (☎ 604-892-9240, 800-449-8614; www.innonthewater.com; dm/r/ste from $27.50/70/80; wi-fi) Convivial lodge-style hotel with standard two-bedded rooms that are ideal for families, plus larger suites and a couple of dorms. There's also a riverfront sun deck out back.

Sunwolf Outdoor Centre (☎ 604-898-1537, 877-806-8046; www.sunwolf.net; 70002 Squamish Valley Rd; cabins from $90) Here you'll find good-value, rustic riverside cabins, plus guided eagle-viewing and rafting trips.

BUNTZEN LAKE

If you've been fighting the peak-season crowds at Vancouver's main tourist attractions and all you need is a restorative day-long commune with the natural world, this dramatic, sigh-inducing area will remind you just what Mother Nature (and 'Beautiful BC') is supposed to be all about. It's also ideal if you're itching for some calf-stretching hikes away from the shuffling shoppers of Robson St.

An expansive, naturally occurring reservoir hidden on the fringes of suburban Coquitlam, Buntzen Lake (☎ 604-469-9679) is embraced on three sides by steep, tree-covered mountains

---

TRANSPORTATION: BUNTZEN LAKE

Distance from Vancouver 30km
Direction East
Travel time One hour
Car From Vancouver, follow Hastings St (Hwy 7A) east through the city to Burnaby and then Coquitlam, where it becomes Barnet Hwy. Take the loco Rd exit and follow loco to the left. Turn right on 1st Ave and continue to Sunnyside Rd. Turn right again and continue to the Buntzen Lake entrance.

and on its fourth side by a shaded, gently curving beach, complete with picnic tables, old-growth trees and those ambling, beady-eyed Canada geese.

Originally named Lake Beautiful – it's not hard to understand why – it was the first hydroelectric power system to serve Vancouver, coming online to supplement an old steam plant in 1903. Renamed after BC Electric Company manager Johannes Buntzen, the lake sends water flowing through penstocks down the steep mountain slope to two power plants located on the banks of Indian Arm. Not that you'd notice any of that when you visit. In fact, it's the all-enveloping quietude that strikes most first-time visitors here as they sit back and drink in the scenery.

If watching the natural world go by only appeals for a minute or two, there are plenty of well-marked, multihour hiking and mountain-bike trails through the forest. Most of the routes are fairly challenging and are not aimed at first-timers. The **Buntzen Lake Trail** (8km) is the area's signature hike. It encircles the water, weaves through mature forest and takes you over several bridges, some of them of the swaying suspension variety. An alternative is the **Diez Vistas Trail** (7km one way), which appeals to fit hikers with its steep climbs that open onto some spectacular views of the mountains and waterways surrounding the entire Vancouver region. Among the area's dedicated biking trails, the **Academy Trail** (4km one way) is a popular trek.

If you'd prefer to hit the water but can't find that canoe you packed in your suitcase, there's a handy **rental store** (☎ 604-469-9928; Sunnyside Rd) near the park entrance. Don't paddle out too far – the lake is bigger than it looks.

Whatever you decide to do here, make sure you bring a picnic. Buntzen is an ideal spot to unfurl a blanket (or grab one of the tables, if they haven't all gone), munch on some sandwiches and let the city disappear from your mind. It'll be one of the most memorable green-hued highlights of your entire trip.

BOWEN ISLAND

So you want to visit some of the islands winking at you on the horizon, but you just don't have the time? Actually, you do. Bowen is a brief saunter across the water via ferry from West Vancouver's Horseshoe Bay terminal. Known as the 'Happy Isle,' Bowen hit its stride as a picnickers' paradise in the 1920s when the Union Steamship Company arrived,

TRANSPORTATION: BOWEN ISLAND

Distance from Vancouver 19km
Direction Northwest
Travel time One hour (including ferry) by vehicle
Bus Island-spanning public transportation is available via the Bowen Island Community Shuttle (☎ 604-947-0229) for $2.25.
Car From Vancouver, follow Hwy 1 west to Horseshoe Bay and take the Bowen Island ferry to Snug Cove.
Ferry Services operated by BC Ferries (☎ 250-386-3431, 888-223-3779; www.bcferries.com) from Horseshoe Bay (adult/child/vehicle $7.10/3.55/22.40, 20 minutes, 16 daily) arrive at Snug Cove throughout the day between 6am and 9:35pm.

providing a regular service from the mainland. Today, you can stroll the waterfront boardwalks near Snug Cove, the small village where the ferry docks. Most of the village, with its early-20th-century heritage buildings housing restaurants, pubs, galleries and shops, straddles Government Rd, which runs straight up from the ferry terminal. The **Visitor Centre** (☎ 604-947-9024; www.bowenisland.org; 432 Cardena Rd; 🕑 9:30am-4pm mid-May–mid-Oct, 10am-3pm Tue-Sat mid-Oct–mid-May) is also nearby.

Good swimming beaches are found at **Mannion Bay**, next to Snug Cove, and **Bowen Bay**, at the west end of the island. There are numerous walking trails, which range from a five-minute stroll toward the picnic tables at Snug Cove to a 45-minute trek from the ferry dock to **Crippen Regional Park**. Inside the park an easy 4km loop around **Killarney Lake** is favored by bird-watchers; the more difficult 10km **Mt Gardner Trail** reaches the island's highest point (719m). Many other trails are accessible to cyclists and horseback riders. If you fancy something more adventurous, **Bowen Island Sea Kayaking** (☎ 604-947-9266, 800-605-2925; www.bowenislandkayaking.com; rentals per 3hr/5hr/day $45/55/65, tours from $65), located by the ferry dock, offers rentals and short kayaking tours, including a recommended sunset paddle.

EATING & SLEEPING

Doc Morgan's Inn (☎ 604-947-0808; mains $8-12) This pub and restaurant has a couple of inviting patios overlooking the park and the harbor – a good spot to scoff your fish-and-chips.

Snug Café (☎ 604-947-0402; light meals around $5; 🕑 5am-4pm Mon-Fri, 7am-5pm Sat & Sun) This cozy little coffeehouse serves breakfast, plus lunches such as chili and shepherd's pie.

Lodge at the Old Dorm (☎ 604-947-0947; www .lodgeattheolddorm.com; 460 Melmore Rd; r $90-140) A five-minute stroll from the ferry dock, this heritage building has six rooms with Art Deco accents. Continental breakfast included.

SOUTHERN GULF ISLANDS

When Canadians refer to BC as 'lotusland,' the Gulf Islands are really what they're thinking about. Languidly strung between the mainland and Vancouver Island, Salt Spring, Galiano, Mayne, Saturna and the North and South Penders are the natural retreat of choice for locals and in-the-know visitors. Combining a mild climate, gentle natural beauty and an infectious, laid-back ambiance, these small communities seem remote but are generally easy to access from the mainland by ferry. The most popular destination for visitors is Salt Spring, but Galiano is also ideal if you want a rustic retreat without sacrificing too many comforts.

INFORMATION

Galiano Island www.galianoisland.com

Mayne Island www.mayneislandchamber.ca

North & South Pender Islands www.penderisland chamber.com

Salt Spring Island www.saltspringtoday.com

Saturna Island Tourism Association www.saturnatourism .com

SALT SPRING ISLAND

A former hippie enclave that's now the site of many rich vacation homes, pretty Salt Spring justifiably receives the majority of Gulf Island visitors. The heart of the community is Ganges, also the location of the Visitor Centre (☎ 250-537-5252, 866-216-2936; www.saltspringtoday.com; 121 Lower Ganges Rd; ☾ 11am-3pm).

If you arrive on a summer weekend, the best way to dive into the community is at the thriving Saturday Market (☎ 250-537-4448; www.saltspring market.com; Centennial Park, Ganges; ☾ 8:30am-3:30pm Sat Apr-Oct), where you can tuck into luscious island-grown fruit and piquant cheeses and peruse locally produced arts and crafts. You can visit some of these artisans with a downloadable self-guided Studio Tour Map (☎ 250-537-9476; www.saltspringstudiotour.com). Among the best is the rustic Blue Horse Folk Art Gallery (☎ 250-537-0754; www.bluehorse.ca; 175 North View Dr; ☾ 10am-5pm Sun-Fri Apr-Oct), complete with funky carvings of leaping wooden hares.

If food seems more of an art form to you, drop by Salt Spring Island Cheese (☎ 250-653-2300; 285 Reynolds Rd), where you can take a self-guided tour of the facilities – be sure to check out the miniature ponies – then sample up to 10 curdy treats in the winery-style tasting room.

TRANSPORTATION: SOUTHERN GULF ISLANDS

Direction Southwest

Travel time One to three hours by ferry; 20 minutes by plane

Air Services from Seair Seaplanes (☎ 604-273-8900, 800-447-3247; www.seairseaplanes.com) arrive from Vancouver International Airport's South Terminal at Salt Spring ($77, 20 minutes, three daily), North Pender ($82, 20 minutes, three daily), Saturna ($82, 20 minutes, three daily), Mayne ($82, 20 minutes, two daily) and Galiano ($82, 20 minutes, two daily).

Bus Not all the islands have bus or taxi services. If you're on Salt Spring, Ganges Faerie (☎ 250-537-6758; www .gangesfaerie.com; fares $8-14) shuttles between the island's three ferry terminals and the Ganges, Ruckle Park and Fernwood areas. On Galiano, Fly'n Riun's Taxi (☎ 250-539-0202; www.taxigaliano.com) provides shuttle-bus and cab services.

Ferry Services from BC Ferries (☎ 250-386-3431, 888-223-3779; www.bcferries.com) arrive from Tsawwassen terminal at Galiano, with connections from there to North Pender. There are also direct weekend services to Mayne (Sunday only) and Salt Spring (Friday to Sunday). For more frequent services to these and the other islands, you will need to travel from Tsawwassen to Vancouver Island's Swartz Bay terminal, then board a connecting ferry. Fares from Tsawwassen to the Gulf Islands are adult/child/vehicle $11.75/5.90/43.35. Gulf Islands Water Taxi (☎ 250-537-2510; www.saltspring.com/watertaxi) provides private speedboat services between Salt Spring, North Pender and Saturna (one-way/return $15/25, two daily September to June, daily July and August) and between Salt Spring, Galiano and Mayne (per leg/return $15/25, two daily September to June, daily July and August).

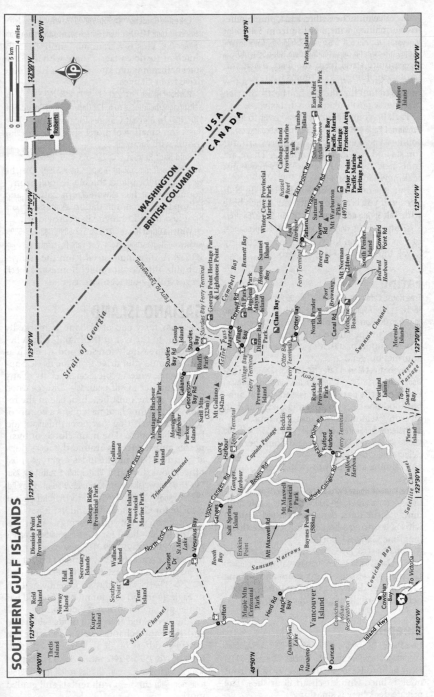

SOUTHERN GULF ISLANDS

5 km
4 miles

49°00'W   123°40'W   123°30'W   123°20'W   123°10'W   123°00'W

Strait of Georgia

Point Roberts

WASHINGTON
BRITISH COLUMBIA

USA
CANADA

Patos Island

Waldron Island

East Point Regional Park

Cabbage Island Provincial Marine Park

Tumbo Island

Saturna Island Indian Reserve

Russell Reef

Narvaez Bay Rd

Taylor Point Pacific Marine Heritage Park

Pacific Marine Heritage Protected Area

Winter Cove Provincial Marine Park

Lyall Harbour

Saturna Island

East Point Rd

Payne Rd

Mt Warburton Pike (497m)

Samuel Island

Bennett Bay

Campbell Bay

Fernhill Rd

Mt Parke Regional Park

Horton Bay

Mayne Island

Georgia Point Heritage Park & Lighthouse Point

Sturdies Bay Ferry Terminal

Active Pass

Village Bay

Dinner Bay Park

Mayne

Village Bay Ferry Terminal

Clam Bay

Otter Bay

Otter Bay Ferry Terminal

Breezy Bay

Port Browning

Mt Norman (244m)

South Pender Island

Gowlland Point Rd

Bedwell Harbour

Medicine Beach

Canal Rd

North Pender Island

Swanson Channel

Moresby Island

Sturdies Bay

Gossip Island

Sturdies Bay Rd

Bluffs Park

Galiano Island

Georgeson Bay Rd

Sutil Mtn (322m)

Mt Galiano (342m)

Parker Island

Montague Harbour Marine Provincial Park

Porlier Pass Rd

Wise Island

Bodega Ridge Provincial Park

Dionisio Point Provincial Park

Long Harbour

Trincomali Channel

Prevost Island

Ferry Terminal

Portland Island

To Swartz Bay

Prevost Passage

Piers Island

Ruckle Provincial Park

Beddis Beach

Beddis Rd

Captain Passage

Upper Ganges Rd

Ganges Harbour

Ganges

Salt Spring Island

Booth Bay

Vesuvius Bay

Sunset Dr

St Mary Lake

North End Rd

Southey Point

Wallace Island Provincial Marine Park

Secretary Islands

Reid Island

Hall Island

Norway Island

Kuper Island

Thetis Island

Tent Island

Willy Island

Stuart Channel

Crofton

Quamichan Lake

To Nanaimo

Duncan

Cowichan Indian Reservation 1

Vancouver Island

Maple Mtn Centennial Park

Head Rd

Maple Bay

Mt Maxwell Rd

Mt Maxwell Provincial Park

Baynes Peak (588m)

Fulford-Ganges Rd

Fulford Harbour

Erskine Point

Sansum Narrows

Fulford Harbour

Satellite Channel

Cowichan Bay

Cowichan Bay

Island Hwy

To Victoria

Beaver Point Rd

Fulford Harbour Ferry Terminal

49°00'N   48°50'N   48°50'N   48°50'N

Pick a favorite cheese then add to your picnic-in-the-making with a bottle from **Salt Spring Vineyards** (☎ 250-653-9463; www.saltspringvineyards.com; 151 Lee Rd; ☺ 11am-5pm mid-Jun–Aug, noon-5pm Fri-Sun Sep & May–mid-Jun, noon-5pm Sat Oct, Nov & Mar, noon-5pm Sat & Sun Apr), where you can sample a few tipples to find the one you like best – the rich blackberry port is dangerously tasty.

Pack up your picnic and head over to **Ruckle Provincial Park** (☎ 250-539-2115; www.bcparks.ca), a southeast gem with ragged seashores, arbutus forests and sun-kissed farmlands. There are trails here for all skill levels, with Yeo Point making an ideal pit stop.

But it's not all about hedonism on Salt Spring. If you crave some activity, touch base with **Salt Spring Adventure Co** (☎ 250-537-2764, 877-537-2764; www.saltspringadventures.com; 124 Upper Ganges Rd; tours $45). It can kit you out for a bobbling kayak tour around Ganges Harbour.

Eating

Tree House Café (☎ 250-537-5379; 106 Purvis Lane; mains $8-14; ☺ 8am-9pm Mon-Fri, 9am-9pm Sat & Sun May-Sep, 8am-3pm Oct-Apr) This magical outdoor spot in Ganges, in the shade of a large plum tree, serves comfort pastas, Mexican specialties and gourmet burgers.

Raven Street Market Café (☎ 250-537-2273; 321 Fernwood Rd; mains $8-14; ☺ 9am-8pm Tue-Sun, 9am-5pm Mon) On the north part of the island, this neighborhood nook serves gourmet pizzas and an awesome seafood-and-sausage gumbo.

Oystercatcher Seafood Bar & Grill (☎ 250-537-5041; 100 Manson Rd; mains $8-16; ☺ 10am-dusk) Come here for delectable local seafood, especially the oysters and salmon, and enjoy the waterfront Ganges views.

Restaurant House Piccolo (☎ 250-537-1844; 108 Hereford Ave; mains $20-28; ☺ 5-11pm) White-tablecloth dining – the duck is recommended – along with Salt Spring's best wine list make this a longtime Ganges favorite.

Barb's Buns (☎ 250-537-4491; 121 McPhillips Ave; mains $6-9; ☺ 7am-5pm Mon, 7am-10pm Tue-Sat, 10am-2pm Sun) Heaping pizza slices, hearty soups and bulging sandwiches draw the Ganges lunch crowd here, many of them grateful vegetarians.

Sleeping

Love Shack (☎ 250-653-0007, 866-341-0007; www.oceansidecottages.com/love.htm; 521 Isabella Rd; cabins $135) Near Fulford Harbour, this groovy waterfront nook is lined with kitsch-art flourishes. The private deck here is smashing.

Lakeside Gardens (☎ 250-537-5773; www.lakesidegardensresort.com; 1450 North End Rd; cabanas/cottages $75/135; ☺ Apr-Oct) This is a tranquil, family-friendly clutch of rustic cottages, some with TVs, en suite bathrooms and kitchens. It's a 10-minute drive from Ganges.

Harbour House (☎ 250-537-5571, 888-799-5571; www.saltspringharbourhouse.com; 121 Upper Ganges Rd; s/d from $104/109) In a great Ganges location, this place has a combination of motel-style and superior rooms with Jacuzzis.

Bold Bluff Retreat (☎ 250-653-4377, 866-666-4377; www.boldbluff.com; cabins & tepees from $190) On the west side of the island, this old-school, nature-bound retreat has a waterfront cottage and hilltop tepee accommodation. Accessed via a boat taxi from Burgoyne Bay (provided).

Wisteria Guest House (☎ 250-537-5899, 888-537-5899; www.wisteriaguesthouse.com; 268 Park Dr; r/cottages from $99/139) A 10-minute stroll from the Ganges hubbub, this comfortable, homestyle B&B serves truly gourmet breakfasts.

GALIANO ISLAND

The busy ferry end of Galiano is markedly different to the rest of the island, which becomes increasingly forested and tranquil as you continue your drive from the dock. Supporting the widest ecological diversity of any of the Southern Gulf Islands – and regarded by some as the most beautiful isle in the region – this skinny landmass offers a bounty of activities for visiting marine enthusiasts and landlubbers alike. The main clutch of businesses and services is around the ferry dock at Sturdies Bay and includes a garage, post office, bookstore and **Visitor Info Booth** (☎ 250-539-2507; www.galianoisland.com; 2590 Sturdies Bay Rd; ☺ Jul & Aug). Check the island's official visitor website for Galiano maps and listings.

Once you've got your bearings – ie driven off the ferry – head for **Montague Harbour Marine Provincial Park** (☎ 250-539-2115; www.bcparks.ca) for trails to beaches, meadows and a cliff carved by glaciers. In contrast, **Bodega Ridge Provincial Park** (☎ 250-539-2115; www.bcparks.ca) is renowned for its eagle, loon and cormorant bird life and has some spectacular drop-off viewpoints.

The protected waters of **Trincomali Channel** and the more chaotic waters of **Active Pass** satisfy paddlers of all skill levels. **Gulf Island Kayaking** (☎ 250-539-2442; www.seakayak.ca; Montague Marina, Montague Harbour; 3hr/day rental from $28/50, tours from $40) can help with rentals and guided tours.

If you're without a car or you just want to stretch your legs, you can explore the island with a bike from **Galiano Bicycle** (☎ 250-539-9906; 36 Burrill Rd, Sturdies Bay; 4hr/day $23/28).

Eating & Sleeping

La Berengerie (☎ 250-539-5392; 2806 Montague Rd; mains $12-24; ☯ 5-11pm) This charming wooded restaurant near Montague Harbour fuses rustic French bistro approaches with whatever is available locally.

Daystar Market Café (☎ 250-539-2505; 96 Georgeson Bay Rd; mains $4-8; ☯ 10am-5pm Mon-Thu, 9am-6pm Fri, 10am-6pm Sat, 9:30am-5pm Sun) A 3km drive from the Sturdies Bay ferry dock, this convivial locals' hangout serves hearty salads, thick sandwiches and fruit smoothies.

Hummingbird Pub (☎ 250-539-5472; 47 Sturdies Bay Rd; mains $8-12; ☯ 11am-midnight Sun-Thu, 11am-1am Fri & Sat) Sup ale with the locals on the patio here or try the bar-grub menu for sustenance. It's 2km from Sturdies Bay.

Bodega Ridge Lodge & Cabins (☎ 250-539-2677; www.bodegaridge.com; 120 Manastee Rd; cabins $125-150; wi-fi) A peaceful retreat of seven north island cabins, each with three bedrooms and furnished in a rustic country fashion.

Galiano Inn (☎ 250-539-3388, 877-530-3939; www.galianoinn.com; 134 Madrona Dr; r $249-299; wi-fi) This immaculate Tuscan-style villa has 10 elegant rooms, each with a fireplace and romantic oceanfront terrace. Adult, sophisticated and soothing, it's close to the Sturdies Bay ferry dock.

Island Time B&B (☎ 250-539-3506, 877-588-3506; www.islandtimebc.com; 952 Sticks Allison Rd; d $135-185) On the south side of the north island, this charming, old-school B&B has a wonderful waterfront location.

TRANSPORTATION

TRANSPORTATION AIR

Vancouver is easily accessible from major international destinations, via air or sea, and is also a short drive from the US border. Cross-Canada train, bus and flight operations also service the city, which is the main gateway for accessing destinations throughout British Columbia. Within the city, the transit system – bus, light rail and commuter vessels – is extensive, although the downtown core and its environs are highly foot-friendly. Flights, tours and rail tickets can be booked online at www.lonelyplanet.com/bookings.

AIR
Airlines
International and domestic airlines serving Vancouver International Airport include the following:

Air Canada & Air Canada Jazz (code AC; ☎ 514-393-3333, 888-247-2262; www.aircanada.ca)

Air New Zealand (code NZ; ☎ 800-663-5494; www.airnewzealand.com)

Air North (code 4N; ☎ 800-661-0407; www.flyairnorth.com)

Air Transat (code TS; ☎ 866-847-1112; www.airtransat.com)

THINGS CHANGE...
The information in this chapter is particularly vulnerable to change. Check directly with the airline or a travel agent to make sure you understand how a fare (and ticket you may buy) works and be aware of the security requirements for international travel. Shop carefully. The details given in this chapter should be regarded as pointers and are not a substitute for your own careful, up-to-date research.

Alaska Airlines (code AS; ☎ 800-252-7522; www.alaskaair.com)

American Airlines (code AA; ☎ 800-433-7300; www.aa.com)

British Airways (code BA; ☎ 800-247-9297; www.britishairways.com)

Cathay Pacific (code CX; ☎ 604-606-8888, 888-338-1668; www.cathaypacific.com)

China Airlines (code CI; ☎ 604-682-6777; www.china-airlines.com)

Continental Airlines (code CO; ☎ 800-523-3273; www.continental.com)

Delta Air Lines (code DL; ☎ 800-221-1212; www.delta.com)

CLIMATE CHANGE & TRAVEL
Climate change is a serious threat to the ecosystems that humans rely upon, and air travel is the fastest-growing contributor to the problem. Lonely Planet regards travel, overall, as a global benefit, but believes we all have a responsibility to limit our personal impact on global warming.

Flying & Climate Change
Pretty much every form of motorized travel generates CO2 (the main cause of human-induced climate change) but planes are far and away the worst offenders, not just because of the sheer distances they allow us to travel, but because they release greenhouse gases high into the atmosphere. The statistics are frightening: two people taking a return flight between Europe and the US will contribute as much to climate change as an average household's gas and electricity consumption over a whole year.

Carbon-Offset Schemes
Climatecare.org and other websites use 'carbon calculators' that allow travellers to offset the level of greenhouse gases they are responsible for with financial contributions to sustainable travel schemes that reduce global warming – including projects in India, Honduras, Kazakhstan and Uganda.

Lonely Planet, together with Rough Guides and other concerned partners in the travel industry, supports the carbon offset scheme run by climatecare.org. Lonely Planet offsets all of its staff and author travel.

For more information check out our website: www.lonelyplanet.com.

FLOATPLANES & 'COPTERS

Several handy floatplane operators can deliver you directly to the Vancouver waterfront. These include frequent **Harbour Air Seaplanes** (☎ 604-274-1277, 800-665-0212; www.harbour-air.com) and **West Coast Air** (☎ 604-606-6888, 800-347-2222; www.westcoastair.com) services from Victoria's Inner Harbour ($120, 35 minutes). These companies also serve additional BC locations and fly in and out of Vancouver International Airport (South Terminal) on some routes.

For a different type of ride, **Helijet** (☎ 604-273-4688, 800-665-4354; www.helijet.com) helicopter services arrive on the waterfront, just east of Canada Place, from Victoria (from $140, 35 minutes, four to 13 daily). This operator offers bargain $75 summer standby tickets if you want to gamble on getting on – its website can advise you of the chances on any given day.

See below for more information on the location of helicopter and floatplane terminals.

Horizon Air (code QX; ☎ 800-547-9308; www.horizonair .com)

Japan Airlines (code JL; ☎ 800-525-3663; www.jal.co .jp/en)

Lufthansa (code LH; ☎ 800-563-5954; www.lufthansa.com)

Northwest Airlines (code NW; ☎ 800-225-2525; www .nwa.com)

Pacific Coastal Airlines Ltd (code 8P; ☎ 604-273-8666, 800-663-2872; www.pacific-coastal.com)

Qantas Airways (code QF; ☎ 800-227-4566; www .qantas.com)

Singapore Airlines (code SQ; ☎ 604-689-1223; www .singaporeair.com)

Thai Airways International (code TG; ☎ 800-426-5204; www.thaiair.com)

United Airlines (code UA; ☎ 800-241-6522; www .united.ca)

WestJet (code WS; ☎ 800-538-5696; www.westjet.com)

Zoom Airlines (code Z4; ☎ 866-359-9666; www.flyzoom .com)

Ticketing Websites

In addition to airline companies' own websites, which often offer internet-only deals, a number of travel agents and third-party online operators are helpful in finding flight discounts. Try the following:

www.cheaptickets.ca

www.expedia.ca

www.flightcentre.ca

www.lowestfare.com

www.orbitz.com

www.priceline.com

www.statravel.com

www.travelcuts.ca

www.travelocity.ca

Airports

Canada's second-busiest airport, Vancouver International Airport (YVR; Map pp44–5; ☎ 604-207-7077; www.yvr.ca) is about 13km south of the city on Sea Island in Richmond. There are two main terminals – international (including flights to the US) and domestic. The additional South Terminal is for floatplanes and smaller aircraft, and it's linked to the main airport via a free shuttle bus.

Each of the main terminals has food courts, convenience shops, a spa, baggage storage facilities, ATMs, currency exchange booths and tourist information desks. The international terminal has a new shopping and dining plaza with its own stream and aquarium. In addition, the domestic terminal has a medical clinic, a dental clinic and a pharmacy. Baggage carts are free (ie no deposit required) throughout the airport.

In downtown Vancouver, there is a floatplane terminal (Map pp66–7) in Coal Harbour just west of Canada Place and a helicopter terminal (Map pp48–9) on the other side of Canada Place near Waterfront Station.

BICYCLE

Vancouver is a relatively good cycling city, with almost 240km of designated routes crisscrossing the region. Cyclists can take their bikes for free on SkyTrain and SeaBus services, as well as on the many bike-rack-fitted buses. You can also take your wheels on BC Ferries services and some Aquabus miniferry routes. Although the rule is often flouted, cyclists are required by law to wear helmets here.

Pick up a *Greater Vancouver Cycling Map & Guide* ($3.95) from a convenience store or bookshop for details on area routes and bike-friendly resources. You can view and download the map for free on the TransLink (www.translink.bc.ca) website.

GETTING INTO TOWN

Mint-green Vancouver Airporter (☎ 604-946-8866, 800-668-3141; www.yvrairporter.com; adult/child one way $13.50/6.25, return $21/12.50) buses ply the route between Vancouver International Airport and 24 downtown hotels from approximately 5.30am to 11.45pm. The service is reduced in winter. Buses depart every 20 to 30 minutes and the trip takes about 35 minutes, depending on traffic. Tickets can be purchased from the Airporter ticket office on level 2 of the airport, or from the driver once you're on board. Some area hotels can also sell you a ticket.

With the new SkyTrain Canada Line between the airport, Richmond and downtown not expected to open until late 2009, you'll have to lug your bags on a bus if you want to use public transportation. Take bus 424 from the airport, change at Airport Station and take the 98 B-Line express bus into the city (adult/child $5/3.50).

If you'd prefer to cab it, budget up to $35 for the 30-minute taxi ride from the airport to most downtown hotels.

If you're driving, proceed east after leaving the airport on Grant McConachie Way, and follow the Vancouver signs – including the big 2010 Olympics one – over the Arthur Laing Bridge. Take the Granville St exit and travel north along Granville St, continuing over the bridge into downtown.

If you're in transit or want to stay at a hotel close to (or in) the airport, check the options on p199.

Touch base with the **Vancouver Area Cycling Coalition** (www.vacc.bc.ca) for additional tips and resources. If you're traveling sans bike, you can rent one from businesses around the city (see p178).

BOAT

Vessels large and small sail Vancouver's waterways. Cruise ships are big business from May to September, generating $500 million from 330 sailings annually. Ships dock at Canada Place (Map pp48–9) downtown or Ballantyne Pier (Map pp44–5) to the east. A free shuttle runs between the two terminals.

Ferries

BC Ferries (☎ 250-386-3431, 888-223-3779; www.bcferries .com) services arrive at Tsawwassen, an hour south of Vancouver, and Horseshoe Bay, 30 minutes from downtown in West Vancouver.

Main services to Tsawwassen arrive from Vancouver Island's Swartz Bay, near Victoria (adult/child/vehicle $10.30/5.15/34.20, 90 minutes), and Duke Point, near Nanaimo (adult/child/vehicle $10.30/5.15/34.20, two hours). Some services also arrive here from the Southern Gulf Islands (see p218).

Services to Horseshoe Bay arrive from Nanaimo's Departure Bay (adult/child/vehicle $10.30/5.15/34.20, 90 minutes). Services also arrive here from Bowen Island (adult/child/vehicle $6.80/3.40/21.45, 20 minutes) and from Langdale (adult/child/vehicle $9.15/4.60/32.65, 40 minutes), the only ferry route to and from the Sunshine Coast.

You can buy passenger-only tickets at the ferry terminals (no reservations required). You can also make vehicle reservations for a $15 fee –

definitely recommended if you're traveling on weekends or anytime in July or August.

To reach Tsawwassen by transit bus (adult/child $5/3.50, 1¼ hours), catch southbound bus 601 (South Delta) to the Ladner Exchange and transfer to bus 620.

To reach Horseshoe Bay (adult/child $3.75/2.50, 45 minutes), take bus 257 or 250 from Georgia St near Granville St in downtown Vancouver.

A pricier but more convenient bus option is the Pacific Coach Lines service (opposite), which runs between Victoria and Vancouver via the ferry. You can also buy a ticket once you're on board the ferry for onward bus travel into either city.

Miniferries

Running minivessels (some big enough to carry bikes) between the foot of Hornby St and Granville Island, **Aquabus Ferries** (☎ 604-689-5858; www.theaquabus.com; adult/child from $2.50/1.25) services several spots along the False Creek waterfront as far as Science World. Its rival is **False Creek Ferries** (☎ 604-684-7781; www.granville islandferries.bc.ca; adult/child from $2.50/1.25), which operates a similar Granville Island service from the Vancouver Aquatic Centre at Sunset Beach, plus additional ports of call around False Creek. Both operators offer day passes at the same prices (adult/child $12/8).

See p226 for information on TransLink's SeaBus service from Waterfront Station to Lonsdale Quay.

BUS

Most out-of-town buses trundle to a halt at Vancouver's heritage, neon-signed Pacific

Central Station (Map p77; ☎ 604-661-0325; 1150 Station St, Chinatown). The station has a ticket office and left-luggage lockers, and is also the area's main train terminal (see p226).

Vancouver-bound bus and coach operators and services include the following:

Greyhound (☎ 800-661-8747; www.greyhound.ca) Services arrive from Whistler ($18.80, 2½ hours, eight daily), Kelowna (from $30, six hours, seven daily) and Calgary (from $70, 14 to 17 hours, six daily), among others.

Malaspina Coach Lines (☎ 877-227-0207) Serving the Sunshine Coast, twice-daily buses arrive from Gibsons ($24, two hours), Sechelt ($30, three hours) and Powell River ($51, five to six hours).

Pacific Coach Lines (☎ 250-385-4411, 800-661-1725; www.pacificcoach.com) Traveling via the BC Ferries Swartz Bay–Tsawwassen route, frequent services arrive from downtown Victoria ($37.50, 3½ hours).

Perimeter Tours (☎ 604-266-5386, 877-317-7788; www.perimeterbus.com). Popular year-round bus service to and from Whistler ($67, 2½ hours, seven to 11 daily).

Quick Coach Lines (☎ 604-940-4428, 800-665-2122; www.quickcoach.com) Express shuttle between Seattle and Vancouver, departing from downtown Seattle (US$35, four hours, six daily) and the city's Sea-Tac International Airport (US$47, 4½ hours, seven daily).

Snowbus (☎ 604-685-7669, 866-766-9287; www.snowbus.ca) Popular winter-only ski-bus service from Whistler ($21, 2½ hours, two daily).

See p226 for information on city transit buses.

CAR & MOTORCYCLE

For sightseeing around town, you'll be fine without a car. However, for visits that incorporate the wider region's mountains and suburbs, a car makes life much simpler.

Driving

With a few exceptions, you can legally drive in Canada for up to six months with a valid driver's license issued by your home country. You may be required to show an international driving permit if your license isn't written in English (or French). If you've rented a car in the US and you are driving it into Canada, bring a copy of the rental agreement to save any possible hassle by border officials. Seat belts are mandatory here.

Vancouver doesn't have any expressways going through its core, which can lead to some major congestion issues. Evening rush-hour traffic can be a nightmare, with enormous lines of cars snaking along Georgia St waiting to cross the Lions Gate Bridge. Try the Second Narrows Ironworkers Memorial Bridge (known simply as the Second Narrows Bridge to most locals) if you need to get across to the North Shore in a hurry. Other peak-time hotspots to avoid are the George Massey Tunnel and Hwy 1 to Surrey.

Parking

Parking is at a premium downtown: there are very few free spots on residential side streets (parking permits are often required), and traffic wardens are predictably predatory. Some streets have metered parking but pay-parking lots (from $4 per hour) are a better proposition – arrive before 9am at some for early-bird, day-rate discounts.

If you're going to be in town for more than a few days and you're driving a hybrid vehicle, consider registering your car with **EasyPark** (☎ 604-682-6744; www.easyparkvancouver.com), the city's main lot operator, for a half-price discount on parking rates. Check its website for information on the program, as well as regular parking fees and lot location maps.

Rental

Major car-rental agencies that have reservation desks at Vancouver International Airport, as well as multiple offices around the city, include the following:

Alamo (☎ 604-684-1401, 800-462-5266; www.alamo.ca)

Budget (☎ 604-668-7000, 800-268-8900; www.budgetbc.com)

Discount (☎ 604-310-2277, 866-310-2277; www.discountcar.com)

Enterprise (☎ 604-688-5500, 800-736-8222; www.enterprise.com)

Hertz (☎ 604-606-4711, 800-263-0600; www.hertz.com)

Thrifty (☎ 604-681-4869, 800-847-4389; www.thrifty.com)

For a cool, greener alternative, check out **Zipcar** (☎ 866-494-7227; www.zipcar.com), a company that owns a fleet of smaller, often hybrid vehicles, which it leaves at parking spots around town. Members reserve a car online anytime of the day or night, then stroll to where their nearest vehicle is waiting. Generally cheaper than regular car-rental agencies – there are no offices or staff to service – it can be a handy option if you're staying in town for more than a few days.

TAXI

Vancouver taxi meters start at $2.70 and add $1.58 per kilometre. Flagging a downtown cab shouldn't take too long, but it's easiest to get your hotel to call you one. If you're wandering the downtown streets and can't find a cab to flag down, head to one of the area's big hotels, where they tend to congregate. A 10% tip is the norm.

Reliable operators around the city include the following:

Black Top & Checker Cabs (☎ 604-731-1111)

Vancouver Taxi (☎ 604-871-1111) Has a fleet of wheelchair-accessible vehicles.

Yellow Cab (☎ 604-681-1111, 800-898-8294) Has a large fleet of hybrid vehicles.

TRAIN

Most trains arrive from across Canada and the US at Pacific Central Station (Map p77; ☎ 604-661-0325; 1150 Station St, Chinatown). The station has a ticket office and left-luggage lockers and is also the area's main bus terminal (see p224) for out-of-town services.

Operators and services here include the following:

Amtrak (☎ 800-872-7245; www.amtrak.com) US Cascades services arrives from Eugene (US$56, 13½ hours, two daily), Portland (US$42, eight hours, three daily) and Seattle (from US$28, 3½ hours, five daily).

Via Rail (☎ 888-842-7245; www.viarail.com) Trains on the Canadian service arrive from Kamloops North ($115, nine hours, three weekly), Jasper ($240, 17½ hours, three weekly) and Edmonton ($325, 24 hours, three weekly), among others.

Other city train services:

West Coast Express (☎ 604-683-7245; www.westcoast express.com) Commuter service arriving six times daily Monday to Friday at downtown's Waterfront Station from Mission City ($10.25, 70 minutes), Pitt Meadows ($7.50, 45 minutes), Port Coquitlam ($6, 35 minutes) and Port Moody ($6, 35 minutes), among others.

Whistler Mountaineer (☎ 604-606-8460, 888-687-7245; www.whistlermountaineer.com) Rocky Mountaineer runs this popular Whistler excursion (from $105, three hours, daily May to mid-October), arriving at and departing from a small North Vancouver station. The company also runs additional multiday trundles through the wider BC wilderness from its main Rocky Mountaineer Station (off Map p81). Check www.rockymountaineervacations.com for information on these package tours.

See opposite for information on Vancouver's SkyTrain.

TRANSLINK

TransLink (☎ 604-953-3333; www.translink.bc.ca) oversees public bus, SkyTrain light rail and Sea-Bus commuter boat services. Its website has a useful trip-planning tool or you can buy the handy *Getting Around* route map ($1.95) from most convenience stores.

A ticket bought on any of the three services is valid for 90 minutes of travel on the entire network, depending on the zone you intend to travel in. The three zones become progressively more expensive the further you journey. One-zone tickets are $2.50/1.75 (adult/child), two-zone tickets are $3.75/2.50 and three-zone tickets are $5/3.50. An all-day, all-zone pass costs $9/7. If you're travelling after 6.30pm or on weekends or holidays, all trips are classed as one-zone fares and cost $2.50/1.75. Books of 10 FareSaver tickets for one/two/three zones cost $19/28.50/38 for adults and $15 for children (all zones). They are sold at convenience and drug stores throughout the city.

Bus

The bus network is extensive in central areas – especially along Granville St, Broadway, Hastings St, Main St and Burrard St. Many buses have bike racks and are wheelchair accessible. Exact change (or more) is required since all buses use fare machines and change is not given.

B-Line express buses operate between Richmond and downtown Vancouver (98 B-Line), and between UBC and the Broadway and Commercial Dr SkyTrain stations (99 B-Line). These buses have their own limited arrival and departure points and do not use the regular bus stops.

There is also a 12-route night-bus system that runs every 30 minutes between 1.30am and 4am across the Lower Mainland. The last bus leaves downtown Vancouver at 3.10am. Look for the night-bus signs at designated stops.

SeaBus

This aquatic shuttle operates every 15 to 30 minutes throughout the day, taking 12 minutes to cross Burrard Inlet between Waterfront Station and Lonsdale Quay. At Lonsdale there's a bus terminal servicing routes throughout North Vancouver and West Vancouver – this is where the transit bus to Capilano Suspension Bridge departs. Services depart from Waterfront Station between 6.15am and 12.45am Monday to Saturday (8.15am to 11.15pm Sunday). Vessels are wheelchair accessible and bike-friendly.

SkyTrain

At time of research for this book, the Sky-Train network consisted of two routes, with a third Canada Line route from downtown to Richmond and the airport due to open in late 2009. For updates on this new line visit www.canadaline.ca.

The original 35-minute Expo Line takes passengers to and from downtown Vancouver and Surrey, via stops throughout Burnaby and New Westminster. The newer Millennium Line alights near shopping malls and suburban residential districts in Coquitlam and Burnaby.

Trains depart every two to eight minutes between 5am and 1.30am weekdays (6am to 12.30am Saturday, 7am to 11.30pm Sunday). All services are wheelchair accessible.

Tickets must be purchased from station vending machines (change is given for bills up to $20) prior to boarding. Spot checks by fare inspectors are frequent and they can issue an on-the-spot fine if you don't have the correct ticket. Avoid buying transfers from the 'scalpers' at some stations, since they are usually expired or close to expiration (the transfers, not the scalpers).

DIRECTORY

BUSINESS HOURS

Standard business hours are 9am to 5pm weekdays. Some postal outlets may stay open later and on weekends. Most banks adhere to standard hours but some branches keep shorter hours and others also open on Saturday mornings. Typical retail shopping hours are 10am to 6pm Monday to Saturday, and noon to 5pm on Sunday (although some shops are closed on Sunday). Shopping malls often stay open later than regular stores. Restaurants are usually open for lunch on weekdays from 11:30am until 2:30pm and serve dinner from 5pm until 9pm or 10pm daily, later on weekends. A few serve breakfast, and many serve weekend brunch. If they take a day off, it's usually Monday.

Pubs and bars that also serve lunch open before midday, with some lounge bars waiting it out until 5pm before opening their doors. Clubs may open in the evening around 9pm, but most don't get busy before 11pm. Bars and clubs can serve liquor until 3am. Twenty-four-hour supermarkets, pharmacies and convenience stores are dotted around the city, particularly in the West End.

Tourist attractions often keep longer hours in summer and reduced hours during winter.

CHILDREN

Family-friendly Vancouver is stuffed with things to do with vacationing kids. Pick up a copy of the free *Kids' Guide Vancouver* flyer from the Touristinfo Centre (p236) and visit www.findfamilyfun.com or www.kidsvancouver.com for tips, resources and events. See p88 for a list of top children's attractions, and check p170 for a selection of artsy activities aimed at families. Kid-friendly businesses and operators are also marked with the 👶 symbol throughout the book.

Children can usually stay with their parents at motels and hotels for no extra charge. Some B&Bs may refuse to accept pint-sized patrons – often preferring to keep themselves adult-oriented – while others charge full price for tots. Some hostels have family rooms.

Car-rental companies rent car seats, which are legally required for young children, for a few dollars per day, but you'll need to reserve them in advance. If you're traveling around the city without a car, make sure you hop on the SkyTrain, SeaBus or miniferry to Granville Island: kids love 'em – especially the new SkyTrain cars, where they can sit up front and pretend they're driving. Under-5s travel free on all transit.

Childcare equipment – including strollers, booster seats, cribs, baby monitors and toys – can be rented from the friendly folk at **Wee Travel** (☎ 604-222-4722; www.weetravel.ca). Your hotel can usually recommend a licensed and bonded babysitting service. If not, try **Kid Scenes** (☎ 604-688-8309), a reputable agency charging $60 minimum for four hours.

Make sure children coming to Canada from other countries (including the USA) have a passport or birth certificate with them. Divorced parents with a child should carry a copy of their custody agreement. Children traveling with a nonparent should have a letter of permission from the parent or legal guardian.

For more on holidaying with children, check out Lonely Planet's *Travel With Children,* by Cathy Lanigan.

CLIMATE

Vancouver's climate is the mildest in Canada, averaging 20°C in summer and 2°C in winter. But you don't hear much about that accolade. Instead you hear about the rain. Yes, bucketloads of it fall, especially in winter (January, February and March). In the mountains, a mere 20 minutes away, this translates into snow for excellent skiing. The official wetstuff number is 116cm (46in) annually. July through September are the best bets for sunshine. Check www.weatheroffice.pyr.ec.gc.ca for online forecasts and see p12 for general information on the best times to visit.

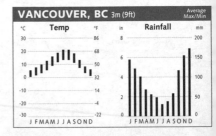

COURSES

Arts & Crafts

Vancouver's community centers offer inexpensive classes in everything from life drawing to flower arranging to knitting:

Coal Harbour Community Centre (Map pp66–7; ☎ 604-718-8222; www.coalharbourcc.ca; 480 Broughton St, West End; ☒ 19)

Roundhouse Community Arts & Recreation Centre (Map p71; ☎ 604-713-1800; www.roundhouse.ca; 181 Roundhouse Mews, cnr Davie St & Pacific Blvd, Yaletown; ☒ C23)

West End Community Centre (Map pp66–7; ☎ 604-257-8333; www.westendcc.ca; 870 Denman St, West End; ☒ 5)

Cooking

The city's top chefs and foodie types often teach short classes at the following places:

Barbara-Jo's Books to Cooks (Map pp94–5; (☎ 604-688-6755; www.bookstocooks.com; 1740 W 2nd Ave, Kitsilano; ☒ 2)

Cookshop & Cookschool (Map p91; ☎ 604-873-5683; www.cookshop.ca; 555 W 12th Ave, Fairview; ☒ 15)

Dance

Skip the light fantastic on a fun dance course at these local favorites:

Broadway Ballroom (Map p91; ☎ 604-733-1779; www .broadwayballroom.ca; 1050 W Broadway, Fairview; ☒ 9) Hit the dance floor in style and take a course in waltz, tango, cha-cha and more.

Salsa Vancouver (www.salsavancouver.net) Energetic workshops in Cuban, mambo, tango etc at locations around the city.

Language

ESL schools are rampant, and are popular with students from Asia. For other languages, try the following:

Berlitz (Map pp48–9; ☎ 604-685-9331; www.berlitz.ca; 808 W Hastings St, downtown; Ⓜ Waterfront)

Le Centre Culturel Francophone de Vancouver (Map p91; ☎ 604-736-9806; www.lecentreculturel.com; 1551 W 7th Ave, South Granville; ☒ 9)

Outdoors

Canada West Mountain School (Map p81; ☎ 604-878-7007, 888-892-2266; www.themountainschool.com; 47 W Broadway, SoMa; ☒ 9) is a long-established and well-respected institution, offering dozens of training and guided-excursion programs in Vancouver's spectacular outdoor backyard. Courses on offer include snow camping and rock climbing.

CUSTOMS REGULATIONS

Adults aged 19 and older can bring in 1.14L of liquor or wine, 8.5L of beer, 200 cigarettes, 50 cigars and 200g of tobacco. You can also bring in gifts valued up to $60 plus a 'reasonable amount' of personal effects, including cars, computers and outdoors equipment. Dispose of any perishable items, such as fruit, vegetables or plants, before crossing the border. Mace, pepper spray and many firearms are also prohibited. For the latest regulations, contact the **Canada Customs and Revenue Agency** (☎ 204-983-3500, 800-461-9999; www.ccra-adrc.gc.ca).

DISCOUNT CARDS

Aside from the free attractions (see p47), there are other ways to stretch your visitor dollars here. If you're planning to take in lots of sights in a few days, the **See Vancouver Card** (☎ 877-295-1157; www.seevancouvercard.com; 2/3/5 days adult $109/139/207, child $59/75/125) can be a good idea. It covers entry to dozens of regional attractions and activities and is especially good value if you include big-ticket items like harbor cruises, whale watching and the Capilano Suspension Bridge.

It's also a good idea to drop by the city's Touristinfo Centre (p236) to pick up a free Visitor Guide – it has pages of coupons in the back. Check out the annual 100 Days of Summer promotion, when discounts and two-for-one deals are offered on the center's website.

You can save on entry to the triumvirate of museums in Vanier Park (see p95) with a combined **Explore Pass** (adult/youth $30/24) covering the Vancouver Museum, Vancouver Maritime Museum and HR MacMillan Space Centre. Passes are available at any of the three attractions or at the helpful Touristinfo Centre downtown.

ELECTRICITY

Canada, like the USA, operates on 110V, 60-cycle electric power. Gadgets built for higher voltage and cycles (such as 220/240V, 50-cycle appliances from Europe) will function poorly. North American electrical goods have plugs with two (flat) or three (two flat, one round) pins. Overseas visitors should bring an adapter, or buy one, if they wish to use their own razors, hair dryers or other appliances. Visit www .kropla.com for useful information on electricity and adapters around the world.

EMBASSIES & CONSULATES

Most countries maintain embassies in Ottawa in the province of Ontario. Vancouver consulates are generally open only on weekday mornings, although a few are also open after lunch until 4pm.

Australia (Map pp48–9; ☎ 604-684-1177; Suite 1225, 888 Dunsmuir St, downtown; Ⓜ Burrard)

China (Map p91; ☎ 604-734-7492; www.vancouver.china -consulate.org; 3380 Granville St, South Granville; 🚌 10)

Denmark (Map pp44–5; ☎ 604-982-8892; Suite 101, 245 Fell Ave, North Vancouver; 🚌 236 from Lonsdale Quay)

France (Map pp66–7; ☎ 604-681-4345; www.consul france-vancouver.org; Suite 1100, 1130 W Pender St, West End; Ⓜ Burrard)

Germany (Map pp48–9; ☎ 604-684-8377; www .vancouver.diplo.de; Suite 704, 999 Canada Pl, downtown; Ⓜ Waterfront)

India (Map pp48–9; ☎ 604-662-8811; Suite 201, 325 Howe St, downtown; Ⓜ Waterfront)

Ireland (Map p77; ☎ 604-683-9233; Suite 1000, 100 W Pender St, Chinatown; Ⓜ Stadium)

Italy (Map pp48–9; ☎ 604-684-7288; Suite 1100, 510 W Hastings St, downtown; Ⓜ Waterfront)

Japan (Map pp66–7; ☎ 604-684-5868; Suite 900, 1177 W Hastings St, West End; Ⓜ Burrard)

Korea (Map pp66–7; ☎ 604-681-9581; Suite 1600, 1090 W Georgia St, West End; Ⓜ Burrard)

Mexico (Map pp66–7; ☎ 604-684-3547; Suite 710, 1177 W Hastings St, West End; Ⓜ Burrard)

Netherlands (Map pp48–9; ☎ 604-684-6448; www.mfa .nl/van; Suite 883, 595 Burrard St, downtown; Ⓜ Burrard)

New Zealand (Map pp48–9; ☎ 604-684-7388; Suite 1200, 888 Dunsmuir St, downtown; Ⓜ Burrard)

UK (Map pp66–7; ☎ 604-683-4421; Suite 800, 1111 Melville St, West End; Ⓜ Burrard)

USA (Map pp66–7; ☎ 604-685-4311; 1095 W Pender St, West End; Ⓜ Burrard)

EMERGENCY

See opposite for hospital emergency rooms and clinics.

Crisis Centre (☎ 604-872-3311; ⏱ 24hr) Provides counselors who can help with all types of emotional crises.

Poison Control Centre (☎ 604-682-5050)

Police, fire and ambulance (☎ 911)

Police – non-emergency (☎ 604-717-3321)

Rape Crisis Centre (☎ 604-255-6344; ⏱ 24hr)

GAY & LESBIAN TRAVELERS

Vancouver's gay and lesbian scene is part of the city's culture rather than a subsection of it. The legalization of same-sex marriages in BC has resulted in a huge number of couples using Vancouver as a kind of gay Vegas. For more information on tying the knot, visit www.vs.gov.bc.ca/marriage/howto.html.

Vancouver's West End district (p68), complete with pink-painted bus shelters, houses western Canada's largest 'gayborhood,' while the city's lesbian contingent is centered more on Commercial Dr (p83).

Pick up a free copy of *Xtra! West* for a crash course on the local scene, and check www.gay vancouver.net and www.superdyke.com for pertinent listings and resources. For nightlife options see p160. Don't miss the giant annual Pride Week (p15) in August.

For support and resources of all kinds, The Centre (Map pp66–7; ☎ 604-684-5307; www.lgtbcentrevan couver.com; 1170 Bute St, West End; 🚌 6) provides discussion groups, a health clinic and advice for lesbians, gays, bisexuals and the transgendered. These friendly folk also staff the Prideline (☎ 604-684-6869; ⏱ 7-10pm), a peer-support service.

Check the online directory of the Gay & Lesbian Business Association of BC (☎ 604-739-4522; www .glba.org) or pick up its glossy free brochure for listings on all manner of local businesses, from dentists to spas and hotels. You can also hang out with the locals at the popular Little Sister's Book & Art Emporium (p113).

HOLIDAYS

During national public holidays, all banks, schools and government offices (including post offices) are closed, and transportation, museums and other services are on a Sunday schedule. Holidays falling on weekends are usually observed the following Monday.

Public Holidays

Major public holidays in Vancouver:

New Year's Day January 1

Good Friday & Easter Monday Late March to mid-April

Victoria Day Third Monday in May

Canada Day July 1

BC Day First Monday in August

Labour Day First Monday in September

Thanksgiving Second Monday in October

Remembrance Day November 11

Christmas Day December 25

Boxing Day December 26

INTERNET ACCESS

Vancouver hotels often provide in-room high-speed internet services requiring an ethernet connection, although increasingly this is being supplemented or replaced with wi-fi access (see the boxed text, below). If you're not toting a laptop, some hotels have internet-enabled computers for guest use: these are denoted by the 🖳 symbol in Sleeping listings. You can also hit the computers and get online at these locations:

Electric Internet Café (Map pp48–9; ☎ 604-681-0667; 605 W Pender St, downtown; per 30min $1.50; ☺ 7am-3am Mon-Fri, 8am-3am Sat & Sun; Ⓜ Granville)

Star Internet Café (Map pp66–7; ☎ 604-685-4645; 1690 Robson St, West End; per hr $2; ☺ 10am-11pm; 🚍 5)

Vancouver Public Library (Map pp48–9; ☎ 604-331-3600; 350 W Georgia St, downtown; ☺ 10am-9pm Mon-Thu, 10am-6pm Fri & Sat, 1-5pm Sun; Ⓜ Stadium) Free internet access.

MAPS

The Touristinfo Centre (p236) provides a handy free map of the city's gridlike downtown core. The more comprehensive *Greater Vancouver Streetwise Map Book* ($5.95) has an easy A–Z format and is available at local bookshops and convenience stores. For handy online maps of the region, check out the City of Vancouver's free VanMap (www.vancouver.ca/vanmap) system.

MEDICAL SERVICES

There are no reciprocal healthcare arrangements between Canada and other countries. Non-Canadians usually pay cash up front for treatment, so taking out travel insurance with a medical-cover component is strongly advised. Medical treatment in Canada is expensive: the standard rate for a hospital bed is around $500 and up to $2500 a day for nonresidents.

Clinics

The following walk-in clinics will cater to visitors:

Care Point Medical Centre Commercial Dr (Map p84; ☎ 604-254-5554; 1623 Commercial Dr; 🚍 20); Kitsilano (Map pp94–5; ☎ 604-678-0598; 1861 W Broadway; 🚍 9); West End (Map pp66–7; ☎ 604-681-5338; 1175 Denman St; 🚍 5) All are open 9am to 8pm or 9pm.

Stein Medical Clinic (Map pp48–9; ☎ 604-688-5924; Bentall 5, Suite 188, 550 Burrard St, downtown; ☺ 8:30am-5pm Mon-Fri; Ⓜ Burrard) Appointments not necessary.

Travel Medicine & Vaccination Centre (Map pp66–7; ☎ 604-681-5656; Suite 314, 1030 W Georgia St, West End; Ⓜ Burrard) Specializing in travel shots; appointments necessary.

Ultima Medicentre Plus (Map pp48–9; ☎ 604-683-8138; Bentall Centre Plaza Level, 1055 Dunsmuir St, downtown; ☺ 8am-5pm Mon-Fri; Ⓜ Burrard) Appointments not necessary.

Emergency Rooms

Vancouver's emergency rooms include the following:

BC Children's Hospital (Map p91; ☎ 604-875-2345; 4480 Oak St, Fairview; 🚍 17)

St Paul's Hospital (Map pp48–9; ☎ 604-682-2344; 1081 Burrard St, downtown; 🚍 22)

Vancouver General Hospital (Map p91; ☎ 604-875-4111; 855 W 12th Ave, Fairview; 🚍 9)

WI-FI ACCESS

Vancouver has a patchy wi-fi network, with pocket of access at some hotels, cafés and businesses around the city – look for 'wi-fi' in individual listings throughout the book for those places where you can crack open your laptop. While some provide access for free, others – particularly hotels – may charge up to $10 per day. FatPort (☎ 604-608-6781, 866-328-7678; www.fatport.com) provides roaming access at around 100 local businesses for fees ranging from $9.95 for two hours to $34.95 for a month. Student discounts are available. Check the website for a directory of hotspots around the city – they're increasing all the time. For a list of Vancouver business offering free wi-fi access, visit www.wififreespot.com/can.html.

Pharmacies

Vancouver is well stocked with pharmacies, including the following:

Pharmasave (Map pp48–9; ☎ 604-801-6991; 499 Granville St, downtown; ⊗ 7:30am-7:30pm Mon-Fri, 9am-5:30pm Sat; Ⓜ Granville)

Shoppers Drug Mart (Map pp66–7; ☎ 604-669-2424; 1125 Davie St, West End; ⊗ 24hr; 🚌 6)

MONEY

Prices in this book are given in Canadian dollars, unless otherwise stated. See p235 for information on the taxes that may be added to your bill, p17 for general information on costs, and the inside front cover for exchange-rate info.

Paper bills most often come in $5 (blue), $10 (purple), $20 (green) and $50 (red) denominations. Coins include the penny (1¢), nickel (5¢), dime (10¢), quarter (25¢), 'loonie' ($1) and 'toonie' ($2). Most Canadians do not carry large amounts of cash for everyday use, relying instead on electronic transactions: credit cards, ATMs and direct-debit cards.

ATMs

Interbank ATM exchange rates usually beat the rates offered for traveler's checks or foreign currency. Canadian ATM fees are low (usually $1 to $1.50 per transaction), but your home bank may charge another fee on top of that. Some machines also dispense US currency, if you're planning a trip across the border. ATMs abound in Vancouver, with bank branches congregating around the business district bordered by Burrard, Georgia, Pender and Granville Sts.

Changing Money

It's best to change your money at a recognized bank or other financial institution. Some hotels, many downtown shops and some tourist offices exchange money, but rates are unlikely to be favorable. Aside from banks, try the following currency exchanges:

American Express (Map pp48–9; ☎ 604-669-2813; 666 Burrard St, downtown; ⊗ 8:30am-5:30pm Mon-Fri, 10am-4pm Sat; Ⓜ Burrard)

Custom House Currency Exchange (Map p74; ☎ 604-482-6006; 375 Water St, Gastown; ⊗ 10am-6pm; Ⓜ Waterfront)

Travelex Currency Services (Map pp48–9; ☎ 604-641-1229; www.travelexca.com; Pan Pacific Hotel, 999 Canada

Pl, downtown; ⊗ 9am-5pm Mon-Sat, 10am-3pm Sun; Ⓜ Waterfront)

Vancouver Bullion & Currency Exchange (Map pp48–9; ☎ 604-685-1008; 800 W Pender St, downtown; ⊗ 9am-5pm Mon-Fri; Ⓜ Granville)

Credit Cards

Visa, MasterCard, American Express and JCB cards are widely accepted in Canada. Credit cards can get you cash advances at bank ATMs, generally for a 3% surcharge. Be aware that many US-based credit cards now convert foreign charges using highly unfavorable exchange rates and fees.

NEWSPAPERS & MAGAZINES

24 Hours (www.vancouver.24hrs.ca) Weekday free commuter paper.

City Food Magazine (www.cityfood.com) A free primer on the regional culinary scene; available at restaurants and bookstores.

Eat Magazine (www.eatmagazine.ca) Another, even glossier local food mag.

Georgia Straight (www.straight.com) Alternative weekly providing Vancouver's best entertainment listings; free every Thursday.

Province (www.theprovince.com) Vancouver's 'tabloid' daily.

Tyee (www.thetyee.ca) Only online but possibly Vancouver's best news source.

Vancouver Magazine (www.vanmag.com) Upscale lifestyle, dining and entertainment monthly.

Vancouver Sun (www.vancouversun.com) Main city daily, with Thursday listings pull-out.

Westender (www.westender.com) Free, quirky downtown listings newspaper.

Xtra! West (www.xtra.ca) Free, gay-oriented, alternative paper, distributed biweekly on Wednesday.

ORGANIZED TOURS

Each of these operators offers at least a couple of tour options, so make sure you check out the full selection before choosing.

Boat Tours

Accent Cruises (Map p87; ☎ 604-688-6625; www.dinnercruises.com; 1676 Duranleau St, Granville Island; 2½hr cruise $25, with dinner $60; ⊗ 5:45pm May–mid-Oct; 🚌 50) Accent's five yachts provide an optional all-you-can-eat salmon buffet dinner during its cruise along the coastlines of English Bay, Stanley Park and Ambleside Beach in West Vancouver. Departures are from Granville Island and it's a relaxing way to spend your evening after a long day spent trawling around the city sights. One-hour sightseeing cruises ($15) are also on offer.

Harbour Cruises (Map pp66–7; ☎ 604-688-7246, 800-663-1500; www.boatcruises.com; north foot of Denman St, West End; adult/child/youth & senior $25/10/21; ✷ mid-Apr–mid-Oct; 🚍 19) View the city – and some unexpected wildlife – from the water on a 75-minute narrated harbour tour, often on board the company's signature paddlewheel boat. The tours churn past Stanley Park, Lions Gate Bridge and the North Shore mountains. There's also a 2½-hour sunset dinner cruise (adult/child $70/60), with West Coast cuisine (ie salmon) and live music, and a longer and lovelier lunch trek to stunning Indian Arm ($62).

Bus Tours

Big Bus (☎ 604-299-0700, 877-299-0701; www.bigbus .ca; adult/child/youth & senior $35/17/30; ✷ year-round) If it's cold and a little rainy in Vancouver, you're still guaranteed to see passengers huddling together for warmth on the open outer decks of these colorful tour buses – luckily you can also shelter inside if it rains too much. Stay on for the full 90-minute narrated loop or use your ticket as a two-day hop-on-hop-off pass to get to 20 attractions around the city. Departures are every 15 to 20 minutes during peak season, and good-value family tickets are $75.

Landsea Tours (☎ 604-662-7591, 800-558-4955; www .vancouvertours.com; adult/child from $59/35; ✷ year-round) Landsea's comfortable tours in 24-passenger stretch minibuses attract an older crowd. Treks include a three-hour city highlights tour (adult/child $59/35), departing 9am and 2pm; and a five-hour North Shore and Grouse Mountain tour (adult/child including admission $109/75) that runs at 11am daily with an extra 2pm tour between April and October. Additional guided tours to Victoria or Whistler are offered if you fancy traveling further afield.

North Van Green Tours (☎ 604-290-0145; www .northvangreentours.com; adult/child/senior $35/20/30; ✷ year-round) Departing from North Van's Lonsdale Quay (p104), this green-themed tour company is taking the emissions out of bus tours with its biofuel mini vans. The excellent, locals-led four-hour trek ambles through the mountain-fringed forests of the North Shore, including highlights such as Deep Cove, Grouse Mountain (entry not included) and Lynn Canyon (with its free suspension bridge). Tours to Whistler are also offered.

Vancouver Trolley Company (☎ 604-801-5515, 888-451-5581; www.vancouvertrolley.com; adult/child/student & senior $35/18.50/32; ✷ year-round) This company operates jolly replicas of San Francisco trolley cars (without the tracks), providing a hop-on-hop-off service to 26 main attractions. The circuit takes two hours and you buy your

tickets from the driver – attraction tickets are also sold on board. If you're here in late October, the buses are decorated in spooky Halloween garb, while Christmastime sees a karaoke theme adopted for those who like to ride and sing at the same time.

Walking & Cycling Tours

Vancouver offers a good range of guided walking tours, including specific themed treks like Sins of the City (p73), Edible BC (p131) and the free ambles around UBC (p101). There are also a few intriguing behind-the-scenes tours (p46) that are well worth checking out. The following offer a roster of more general tours around the city. Departure points vary for all tours.

Architectural Institute of British Columbia (☎ 604-683-8588 ext 333; www.aibc.ca; tours $5; ✷ 1pm Tue-Sat Jul & Aug) Local architectural students conduct these excellent one- to two-hour tours, focusing on the buildings, history and heritage of several key Vancouver neighborhoods. There are six tours in all and areas covered include Gastown, Strathcona, Yaletown, Chinatown, the West End and the downtown business district. It's a great way to find out about the city's past and walk off a big lunch.

City By Cycle Tours (☎ 604-730-1032, 888-599-6800; www.citybycycle.com; adult/child from $69/59; ✷ 9am & 2pm) Offering good-value four-hour guided rides around the city's highlights, including Stanley Park, English Bay, Chinatown and Granville Island, City Cycle Tours is a new addition to Vancouver's tour offerings. Rates include bikes and helmets. Check out the UBC and Pacific Spirit Park tour for a pedal among the trees.

Walkabout Historic Vancouver (☎ 604-720-0006; www .walkabouthistoricvancouver.com; tours $25; ✷ 10am & 2pm) Informative and lively guides in period dress lead these entertaining, two-hour tours that explore the architecture, characters and history of downtown and Gastown, Chinatown and Gastown, or Granville Island, depending on which trek you choose. Call ahead for reservations.

Specialty Tours

Harbour Air Seaplanes (☎ 604-233-3505, 800-665-0212; www.harbourair.com; tours from $99; ✷ year-round) Vancouver is home to the world's largest fleet of floatplane operators and, along with their regular scheduled services (see p223), some offer soaring sightseeing tours. Taking off and landing (you'll dive-bomb the water at a rate of knots) is thrilling in itself, but the scenery while you're up there will make you realize just how beautiful this region is. Harbour Air's 20-minute panoramic flight ($99) is great fun – there are additional longer flights depending on your budget – and you can carbon-offset your tour when you book.

Sewell's Sea Safari (Map pp44–5; ☎ 604-921-3474; www.sewellsmarina.com; West Vancouver, 6409 Bay St, Horseshoe Bay; adult/child/youth, student & senior $67/37/59; ☒ Apr-Oct; ☐ 250) Head to the marina near Horseshoe Bay to book a seat on a rigid-hulled inflatable for your two-hour, high-speed ride out to sea. With the spray in your face and the wind rattling your sunglasses, keep your eyes open for possible whale-pod sightings – barking seals and soaring eagles are almost guaranteed. It can be a cold and bouncy ride, but visitors are suited up in cushiony red coveralls to absorb some of the bite.

Stanley Park Horse-Drawn Carriages (Map p54; ☎ 604-681-5115; www.stanleypark.com; adult/child/youth & senior $25/14.50/23; ☒ Mar-Oct; ☐ 19) These narrated, one-hour tours are a leisurely – actually, extremely slow – and informative way to see the park without having to walk. Lumbering Clydesdale and grey shire horses pull the 20-passenger carriages past all the usual park highlights and you'll hear some fascinating tales about the area's history and development. Tours depart from near the information booth, just off the Georgia St entrance to the park. A free shuttle bus runs from select downtown and West End hotels to the departure point six times a day.

Takaya Tours (☎ 604-904-7410; www.takayatours.com; tours from $55; ☒ May-early Oct; ☐ 212) Operated by North Van's Tsleil-Waututh First Nation, Takaya Tours offers fascinating eco-treks that highlight the history and culture of the Coast Salish peoples. Most departures are from Deep Cove in North Vancouver. One of the most popular tours is the two-hour trip in a traditional canoe through the gorgeous, glassy waters of Indian Arm ($55). Takaya also offers traditional dance performances, a nature walk, a full-moon paddle, kayaking lessons and overnight kayaking trips. Tours require a minimum of three or four participants.

PASSPORTS

At time of research, citizens or permanent residents of the United States required a US birth certificate, US passport or US green card to enter Canada. However, all US citizens traveling by air or sea need a passport to get back into their own country, a rule that is likely to be extended to land travel in the near future. The bottom line is that having a passport is increasingly the best way to move across the border for US citizens. All other international visitors to Canada must hold a valid passport and present it at the point of entry. See p236 for information on visa requirements.

POST

Canada Post (☎ 416-979-8822, 866-607-6301; www.canadapost.ca) may not be remarkably quick, but it is reliable. The standard (up to 30g) letter and postcard rate to destinations within Canada is 52¢. Postcards and standard letters to the US cost 93¢. International airmail postcards and standard letters cost $1.55.

Postal outlets are dotted around the city, many of them at the back of drugstores – look for the blue-and-red window signs. Handy branches:

Canada Post Main Outlet (Map pp48–9; ☎ 604-662-5723; 349 W Georgia St, downtown; ☒ 8am-5:30pm Mon-Fri; Ⓜ Stadium)

Georgia Post Plus (Map pp66–7; ☎ 604-632-4226; 1358 W Georgia St, West End; ☒ 9:30am-6pm Mon-Fri, 10am-4pm Sat; ☐ 19)

Howe St Postal Outlet (Map pp48–9; ☎ 604-688-2068; 732 Davie St, downtown; ☒ 7am-8pm Mon-Fri, 8am-7pm Sat; ☐ 6)

Poste restante letters and packages should be addressed as follows:

FAMILY NAME, First Name

c/o General Delivery

349 W Georgia St

Vancouver, BC

V6B 3P7

Poste restante mail will be held for 15 days before being returned. Pick up your mail at downtown's Canada Post Main Outlet. Packages sent to you in Canada will be ruthlessly inspected by customs officials, who will then assess duties payable by you on collection.

RADIO

Around Vancouver, flip the dial to these stations or listen in online before you arrive:

Beat (94.5FM; www.thebeat.com) Urban music station.

CBC Radio One (690AM; www.cbc.ca/bc) Canadian Broadcasting Corporation's commercial-free news and talk by day, classical by night.

CFRO (102.7FM; www.cooopradio.org) Community co-op station where anything goes: storytelling, poetry and contemporary First Nations.

CITR (101.9FM; www.citr.ca) UBC's station for indie music, news, spoken word and arts.

CKNW (980AM; www.cknw.com) News, traffic and talk radio.

Fox (99.3FM; www.cfox.com) New rock and chatter.

JACK-FM (96.9FM; www.jackfm.com) Groovy retro rock station.

News 1130 (1130AM; www.news1130.com) News 24/7.

Team 1040 (1040AM; www.team1040.ca) Sports and talk 24/7.

Z95 (95.3FM; www.z95.com) Poptastic music station.

SAFETY

Vancouver is relatively safe for visitors. Purse-snatching and pickpocketing does occur, however, so you should be vigilant with your personal possessions. Theft from unattended cars is not uncommon, so never leave valuables in vehicles where they can be seen.

Panhandling has become an increasing issue for visitors; just say 'Sorry' and pass on if you're not interested and want to be polite. The more enterprising 'squeegee kids' might try to wash your windshield for a couple of dollars when you stop at a red light; tell them 'No thanks' before they get to your car. They often operate at the intersection of W Georgia and Thurlow Sts.

The city's Downtown Eastside area is a depressing ghetto of lives wasted by drugs and prostitution. Crime against visitors is not common in this area but you are advised to be vigilant and stick to the main streets, especially at night. The area around Pacific Central Station (Map p77) is dodgy late in the evening, as is Stanley Park in the wee hours.

Many Downtown Eastsiders panhandle in the abutting Gastown and Chinatown areas or on Granville St (especially between Pender and Davie). You will likely be discreetly offered drugs by a small-fry pusher or two at some point here – just walk on and they won't bother you again.

TAXES & REFUNDS

The federal goods and services tax (GST), variously known as the 'Gouge and Screw' or 'Grab and Steal,' adds 5% to nearly every product, service or transaction, on top of which is usually a 7% BC provincial sales tax (PST). Accommodation and alcohol have additional taxes of their own; see p190 and p148 for rates.

Visitors are eligible for refunds on GST, although the refund process is inconvenient. To wit: your purchase amounts (before taxes) must total at least $200, and each individual receipt must show a minimum amount of $50 before taxes. You must have original receipts (credit-card slips and photocopies are not accepted), and the receipts are not returned. Receipts for goods must be stamped

by Canadian customs to be refund-eligible (at the airport go to the Refund Office; at land borders go to the customs office or a refund-designated duty-free shop). Visitors departing Canada by commercial carrier (including air, rail, noncharter bus or ferry) must also include their original boarding pass or carrier ticket with the refund claim.

Once you've met all the above criteria, it's time to fill out and mail in the rebate form, widely available at tourist shops, hotels and tourist offices around the city. You can also contact the Canada Customs and Revenue Agency's Visitor Rebate Program (☎ 800-668-4748 in Canada, 902-432-5608 outside Canada; www.ccra.gc.ca/visitors; Suite 104, 275 Pope Rd, Summerside, PE C1N 6C6). Expect to wait four to six weeks for your check, which is paid in Canadian dollars, unless issued to a US address, in which case it will be in US dollars.

TELEPHONE

Local calls cost 25¢ from public pay phones, which are either coin or card operated. If calling from a private phone, local calls are free – a freebie that usually doesn't apply to calls made from hotel rooms.

Most Vancouver-area phone numbers, as well as Whistler and the Sunshine Coast, take the 604 area code, although 778 is increasingly being introduced for new numbers. Dial all 10 digits of a given phone number, including the three-digit area code and seven-digit number, even for local calls. In some instances (eg between Vancouver and Whistler), numbers will have the same area code but be long-distance; at such times you need to dial 1 before the area code.

Always dial 1 before other domestic long-distance and toll-free (800, 888, 877 etc) numbers. Some toll-free numbers are good anywhere in North America, others within Canada only. International rates apply for calls to the US, even though the dialing code (+1) is the same as for Canadian long-distance calls. Dial 011 followed by the country code for all other overseas direct-dial calls.

Cell Phones

North America uses a variety of cell (mobile) phone systems, most of which are incompatible with the GSM 900/1800 standard used throughout Europe, Asia and Africa. Check with your cellular service provider about using your phone in Canada. Calls may be routed internationally, and US travelers should beware of roaming surcharges (it can become very expensive for a 'local' call).

Phonecards

Prepaid phonecards for long-distance and international calls can be purchased at convenience stores and some post offices. Beware those phonecards that advertise the cheapest per-minute rates, as they may also charge hefty connection fees for each call. Leading local phone company **Telus** (www.telus.com) offers a range of reliable phonecards available in retail outlets around the city.

TIME

Vancouver is in the Pacific time zone (PST/PDT), the same as the US West Coast. At noon in Vancouver it's the following:

11am in Anchorage

3pm in Toronto

2pm in Chicago

8pm in London

9pm in Paris

6am (the next day) in Sydney

8am (the next day) in Auckland

During Daylight Saving Time (from the second Sunday in March to the first Sunday in November), the clock moves ahead one hour.

TOURIST INFORMATION

Tourism Vancouver's **Touristinfo Centre** (Map pp48–9; ☎ 604-683-2000; www.tourismvancouver.com; 200 Burrard St, downtown; ☒ 8:30am-6pm daily Jun-Aug, 8:30am-5pm Mon-Sat Sep-May; Ⓜ Waterfront) is a large repository of resources for visitors, with a staff of helpful advisors ready to assist in planning your trip. Services and info available here include free maps, automated currency exchange, visitor guides, half-price theater tickets, accommodation and tour bookings, plus a host of glossy brochures on the city and the wider BC region. Two **branches** (☒ 8am-10pm) also operate at the domestic and international terminals of Vancouver International Airport.

TRAVELERS WITH DISABILITIES

Vancouver is a good city in terms of accessibility. On arrival at the airport, vehicle-rental agencies can provide prearranged cars with hand controls, while the Vancouver Airporter shuttle-bus service (p224) can arrange transportation to Vancouver's major hotels. Accessible cabs are also available here and throughout the city, on request.

Guide dogs may legally be brought into restaurants, hotels and other businesses in Vancouver. Many public-service phone numbers and some pay phones are adapted for the hearing impaired. About 90% of downtown's sidewalks have sloping ramps, and most public buildings and attractions are wheelchair accessible.

All **TransLink** (www.translink.bc.ca) SkyTrain and SeaBus services and most transit bus services are wheelchair accessible. Check the website for a wide range of information on accessible transport around the region. If you're driving yourself, apply for a disabled parking permit ($18) via **Sparc BC** (☎ 604-718-7744; www.sparc.bc.ca). Check for other accessible transport options in Vancouver or throughout Canada at www.accesstotravel.gc.ca online.

Other helpful resources:

BC Coalition of People with Disabilities (☎ 604-875-0188; www.bccpd.bc.ca) Programs and support for people with disabilities.

BC Disability Sports (☎ 604-598-7890; www.disabilitysport.org) Connecting locals and visitors to sports and recreation opportunities around the region.

British Columbia Paraplegic Association (☎ 604-324-3611; www.bcpara.org) Support and service organization for the physically disabled.

Canadian National Institute for the Blind (☎ 604-431-2121; www.cnib.ca) Support and services for the visually impaired.

Society for Accessible Travel & Hospitality (☎ 212-447-7284; www.sath.org)

Western Institute for the Deaf and Hard of Hearing (☎ 604-736-7391; www.widhh.com) Interpreter services and resources for the hearing impaired.

VISAS

Travelers from Scandinavia, European Community countries and Commonwealth nations like Australia and New Zealand do not need a visa to visit Canada, but citizens of more than 100 other nations do. Check the website of **Citizenship & Immigration Canada** (www.cic.gc.ca) or contact the Canadian embassy or consulate in your home country for the latest visa requirements.

A passport and/or visa does not guarantee entry. Proof of sufficient funds or possibly a return ticket out of the country may be required. Visitors with medical conditions may only be refused if they 'might reasonably be expected to cause excessive demand on health and social services' (ie they admit to needing treatment during their stay in Canada).

If you are refused entry but have a visa, you have the right of appeal at the port of entry. If you're arriving by land, the best course is simply to try again later (after a shift change) or at a different border crossing.

WOMEN TRAVELERS

Vancouver is generally quite safe for women travelers. On the main streets, busy foot traffic continues past 11pm, though there are certainly areas to avoid – see p235. Note it is illegal to carry pepper spray or mace in Canada. The **Vancouver Women's Health Collective information line** (☎ 604-736-5262; www.womenshealthcollective.ca) provides advice and referrals for health issues. See p230 for other helpful resources, including sexual-assault crisis lines.

WORK

It is difficult to get a work permit because employment opportunities go to Canadians first. In most cases, you'll need to take a validated job offer from a specific employer to a Canadian consulate or embassy abroad. However, there is a shortage of workers in the hotel and hospitality industries in BC – a situation that may become serious in the run-up to the 2010 Olympics – so employers are increasingly looking overseas to fill the gap. Contact potential employers and see if they can help you with the paperwork.

Each year several thousand one-year working holiday visas are available to New Zealanders and Australians between the age of 18 and 30. Competition is stiff, so apply as early as possible. Applications are available through Sydney's **Canadian Consulate General** (☎ 02-9364-3082; www.whpcanada.org.au) or Wellington's **Canadian High Commission** (☎ 04-473-9577; www.dfait-maeci.gc.ca/newzealand).

Run by the Canadian Federation of Students, the popular **SWAP Canada** (www.swap.ca) program facilitates working holidays for US and overseas students and people under 30 (sometimes 35). Participants come to Canada from nearly 20 countries, including Australia, France, Germany, New Zealand, the UK and the USA.

Doing Business

Vancouver does brisk business in conventions and trade shows, with the **Vancouver Convention & Exhibition Centre** (Map pp48–9; ☎ 604-689-8232, 866-785-8232; www.vcec.ca; Canada Pl, downtown; Ⓜ Waterfront) hosting more than 350 events annually. At time of research, the facility was tripling its exhibition space with a large expansion project. **Tourism Vancouver** (www.tourismvancouver.com) assists business travelers and provides a useful list of suppliers (copying, printing etc) on its website.

Volunteering

If you're interested in volunteering during your visit, contact one of the following local organizations:

Charity Village (www.charityvillage.ca)

Go Volunteer (www.govolunteer.ca)

Vancouver Foundation (www.vancouverfoundation.ca)

Volunteer Canada (www.volunteer.ca)

GLOSSARY

Canada Line – New SkyTrain transit line, opening in 2009

double-double – popular Tim Hortons coffee order: two sugars and two creams

Downtown Eastside –Vancouver's poorest neighborhood, centered on the intersection of Main and Hastings Sts

First Nations – denotes Canada's indigenous peoples; often used instead of Native Indians or Native people

Granville Strip – Granville St nightlife area, between Robson and Davie Sts

GST – 6% goods and services tax levied on most purchases

Hollywood North – denoting Vancouver's large film and TV industry

ice wine – Canadian dessert wine

Ilanaaq – Inuit mascot for 2010 Olympic and Paralympic Winter Games

loonie – slang term for Canada's one-dollar coin, with a loon bird on one side

Lower Mainland – area covering southwestern BC, including Vancouver

Mounties – Royal Canadian Mounted Police (RCMP); cross-Canada law-enforcement agency

North Shore – geographic area encompassing North Vancouver and West Vancouver

panhandlers – local street beggars

PST – provincial sales tax, currently 7% in BC; when coupled with GST, it can add 13% tax to many purchases

SkyTrain – regional rapid-transit train system

toonie – slang term for a Canadian two-dollar coin

BEHIND THE SCENES

THIS BOOK

This 4th edition of *Vancouver* was researched and written by John Lee. The 3rd edition was written by Karla Zimmerman. The guide was commissioned in Lonely Planet's Oakland office and produced by the following:

Commissioning Editor Emily K Wolman

Coordinating Editors Stephanie Pearson, Carolyn Bain

Coordinating Cartographer Julie Sheridan

Coordinating Layout Designers Barry Cooke, Jim Hsu

Senior Editors Sasha Baskett, Helen Christinis

Managing Cartographer Alison Lyall

Managing Layout Designers Adam McCrow, Celia Wood

Assisting Editors Michelle Bennett, Kate James

Assisting Cartographer Hunor Csutoros

Assisting Layout Designers Wibowo Rusli, Cara Smith

Cover Designer Marika Mercer

Color Designer Tamsin Wilson

Project Manager Sarah Sloane

Thanks to Erin Corrigan, Heather Dickson, Jennifer Garrett, Suki Gear, Vivek Wagle, Josh Geoghegan, Indra Kilfoyle, Wayne Murphy, Paul Piaia

Cover photographs Second Narrows Bridge at Burrard Inlet in Vancouver Harbour, Manfred Gottschalk/Lonely Planet Images (top); City skyline and North Shore mountains at sunset, Vancouver, Greg Vaughn/Alamy (bottom).

Internal photographs p64, Rich Frishman/Getty; p61, Megapress/Alamy; p59, Jeff J Mitchell/Getty; p59, Kevin Miller/Getty; p61, Mario Tama/Getty. All other photographs by Lonely Planet Images, and by Lawrence Worcester except p59 (#2) Ross Barnett; p8 (#2) Chris Cheadle; p61 (#1) Eoin Clarke; p7 (#3), p8 (#1), p58, p63 (#1) Richard Cummins; p6 (#3) Lee Foster; p2, p8 (#3), p60 (#2) Ryan Fox; p7 (#1) Manfred Gottschalk; p60 (#1) Kevin Levesque; p5 (#5), Aaron McCoy; p6 (#2) Doug McKinlay; and p6 (#1) Glenn van der Knijff.

All images are copyright of the photographer unless otherwise indicated. Many of the images in this guide are available for licensing from Lonely Planet Images: www .lonelyplanetimages.com.

THANKS
JOHN LEE

Hearty thanks to my sister Angela for first bringing me out to Vancouver from England in 1986. Thanks also to Emily at Tourism Vancouver for her assistance on this and other projects. As ever, thanks are also due to my friends in Canada who were given the unenviable task of trying to remember what I looked like while I was in full hibernation mode during the write-up period, my fingers permanently stapled to the keyboard. And thanks also to my brother Michael in the UK for planning to come out for another visit sometime soon – whenever that might be.

THE LONELY PLANET STORY

Fresh from an epic journey across Europe, Asia and Australia in 1972, Tony and Maureen Wheeler sat at their kitchen table stapling together notes. The first Lonely Planet guidebook, *Across Asia on the Cheap*, was born.

Travelers snapped up the guides. Inspired by their success, the Wheelers began publishing books to Southeast Asia, India and beyond. Demand was prodigious, and the Wheelers expanded the business rapidly to keep up. Over the years, Lonely Planet extended its coverage to every country and into the virtual world via lonelyplanet.com and the Thorn Tree message board.

As Lonely Planet became a globally loved brand, Tony and Maureen received several offers for the company. But it wasn't until 2007 that they found a partner whom they trusted to remain true to the company's principles of traveling widely, treading lightly and giving sustainably. In October of that year, BBC Worldwide acquired a 75% share in the company, pledging to uphold Lonely Planet's commitment to independent travel, trustworthy advice and editorial independence.

Today, Lonely Planet has offices in Melbourne, London and Oakland, with over 500 staff members and 300 authors. Tony and Maureen are still actively involved with Lonely Planet. They're traveling more often than ever, and they're devoting their spare time to charitable projects. And the company is still driven by the philosophy of *Across Asia on the Cheap*: 'All you've got to do is decide to go and the hardest part is over. So go!'

OUR READERS

Many thanks to the travelers who used the last edition and wrote to us with helpful hints, useful advice and interesting anecdotes:

Annie Boyer, Thatcher Collins, Alison Course, Delisse Crawford, Steve Dolinsky, Olivier Dunant, Olivia Elieff, Jon Evans, Paul Falvo, Joy Glibbery, Mikelow Grosky, Pippa Kerby, Shirley Low, Rich Maywhort, Eva Mellert-Hartling, Marc Mentzer, Roxanne Robles, Ignacio Rozada, Rebecca Sharp, Rose-Marie Tonk, Alina Tuerk

ACKNOWLEDGMENTS

Many thanks to the following for the use of their content:

Vancouver Translink Map © Translink 2007

SEND US YOUR FEEDBACK

We love to hear from travelers – your comments keep us on our toes and help make our books better. Our well-traveled team reads every word on what you loved or loathed about this book. Although we cannot reply individually to postal submissions, we always guarantee that your feedback goes straight to the appropriate authors, in time for the next edition. Each person who sends us information is thanked in the next edition – and the most useful submissions are rewarded with a free book.

To send us your updates – and find out about Lonely Planet events, newsletters and travel news – visit our award-winning website: www.lonelyplanet.com/contact.

Note: We may edit, reproduce and incorporate your comments in Lonely Planet products such as guidebooks, websites and digital products, so let us know if you don't want your comments reproduced or your name acknowledged. For a copy of our privacy policy visit www.lonelyplanet.com/privacy.

Notes

Notes

INDEX

A

Abbotsford International Air Show 15
accommodations 189-200, *see also* Sleeping *subindex*
  airport hotels 199
  B&Bs 190
  costs 191
  Downtown 191-3
  Fairview & South Granville 196-8
  Granville Island 196-8
  Greater Vancouver 199-200
  Kitsilano 198-9
  SoMa 196
  tipping 190-1
  University of British Columbia 198-9
  Victoria 210-11
  West End 193-5
  Whistler 214-15
  Yaletown 195-6
activities 177-88, 202, 229, *see also individual activities*, Sports & Activities *subindex*
  outdoor activity courses 229
air travel
  airlines 222
  airports 223
  floatplanes 223

000 map pages
000 photographs

  helicopters 223
  to/from airport 224
Alcan Dragon Boat Festival 14
ambulance 230
antiques, *see* Shopping *subindex*
aquariums 52, 53
architecture 33-5
area codes, *see inside front cover*
art galleries, *see* Shopping & Sights *subindexes*
arts 26-33, *see also* Arts *subindex*, cinema, dance, literature, music, theater, TV, visual arts
  courses 229
ATMs 232

B

B&Bs 190, *see also* Sleeping *subindex*
Bare Buns Fun Run 15
bars 147-55, **4**, *see also* Drinking *subindex*
  Commercial Drive 153-4
  Downtown 149
  Gastown 152, **5**
  Granville Island 154
  Kitsilano 155
  SoMa 153
  West End 150-1
  Yaletown 151-2
baseball 187
BC Place Stadium 70
BC Sports Hall of Fame & Museum 70-1
beaches, *see* Sights *subindex*
beer 148
begging 235
bicycling, *see* cycling
bird sanctuaries, *see* Sights *subindex*
Bishop, John 130, 141
blogs 38, 113, 138, 197
boat travel **8**
  SeaBus 226-7
  tours 232-3, 234

  in Vancouver 226-7
  to/from Vancouver 224
books, *see also* literature, Shopping *subindex*
  cookbooks 135
  environment 58
  history 22
  local authors 30
Bowen Island 217-18
breweries, *see* Sights *subindex*
bridges 35, *see also* Sights *subindex*
Buddhist temple 106
Buntzen Lake 216-17
bus travel
  tours 233
  in Vancouver 226
  to/from Vancouver 224-5
business hours 228, *see also inside front cover*
  bars 148
  coffeehouses 148
  nightlife 158
  pubs 148
  restaurants 126
  shops 110

C

Campbell, Larry 37
campuses, *see* Sights *subindex*
Canada Day 14
Capilano Suspension Bridge 103, 104
car travel
  parking 225
  rental 225-6
Caribbean Days Festival 14
Carr, Emily 26-7
castles, *see* Sights *subindex*
cathedrals, *see* Sights *subindex*
Celebration of Light 15
cell phones 235-6
Celticfest Vancouver 13
cheese factories, *see* Sights *subindex*
chefs 130
  cookbooks 135
chemists 232

children, travel with 228
  activities 180
  arts 170
  attractions 88
  Vancouver International Children's Festival 13
Chinatown 76-9, **77**, **5**
  food 135-6, **5**
  Night Market 115, **5**
  shopping 115-16
  walking tour 78-9, **78**
Chinese New Year 12
choral music 171-2, *see also* Arts *subindex*
Choy, Wayson 29
Christ Church Cathedral 47
Christmas Carolship Parade 17
cinema 31-2, *see also* film
City Farm Boy 61
Clark, Rob 130
classical music 28, 166-7, *see also* Arts *subindex*
climate 12, 228
clothes, *see* Shopping *subindex*
  sizes 114
clubs 159-61, *see also* Nightlife *subindex*
Coal Harbour Seawalk 68
coffeehouses 147-55, *see also* Drinking *subindex*
  Commercial Drive 154, **4**
  Downtown 149-50
  SoMa 153
  West End 151
comedy 158-9, *see also* Nightlife *subindex*
  Global Comedy Fest 16
  Vancouver International Fringe Festival 16
Commercial Drive 83-5, **84**, **4**
  bars 153-4
  coffeehouses 154, **4**
  food 137-8
  pubs 153-4
  shopping 118-19
  walking tour 83-5, **85**
Commercial Drive Festival 14

INDEX

INDEX

251

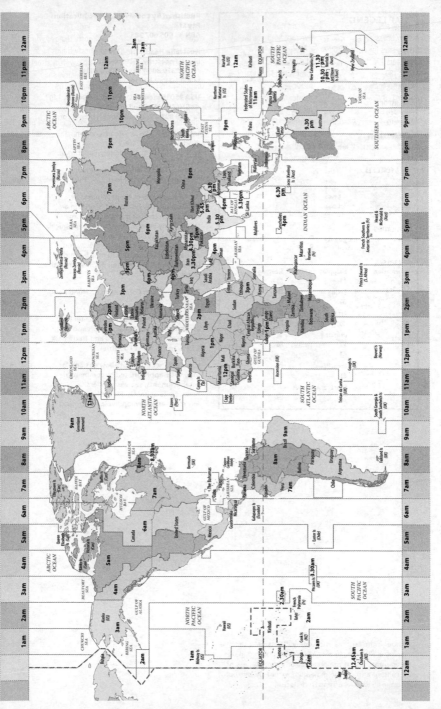

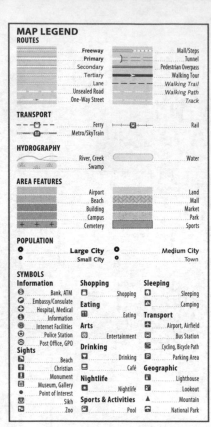

MAP LEGEND
ROUTES
Freeway
Primary
Secondary
Tertiary
Lane
Unsealed Road
One-Way Street

Mall/Steps
Tunnel
Pedestrian Overpass
Walking Tour
Walking Trail
Walking Path
Track

TRANSPORT
Ferry
Metro/SkyTrain

Rail

HYDROGRAPHY
River, Creek
Swamp

Water

AREA FEATURES
Airport
Beach
Building
Campus
Cemetery

Land
Mall
Market
Park
Sports

POPULATION
● **Large City**
● Small City
○ Medium City
○ Town

SYMBOLS
Information
Ⓢ Bank, ATM
Ⓞ Embassy/Consulate
✚ Hospital, Medical
ⓘ Information
ⓔ Internet Facilities
Ⓟ Police Station
⊗ Post Office, GPO

Sights
◪ Beach
✝ Christian
◨ Monument
▥ Museum, Gallery
● Point of Interest
◪ Sikh
◪ Zoo

Shopping
◨ Shopping

Eating
◨ Eating

Arts
◨ Entertainment

Drinking
◨ Drinking
◨ Café

Nightlife
◨ Nightlife

Sports & Activities
◨ Pool

Sleeping
◪ Sleeping
◪ Camping

Transport
➕ Airport, Airfield
◨ Bus Station
◨ Cycling, Bicycle Path
Ⓟ Parking Area

Geographic
◨ Lighthouse
◨ Lookout
▲ Mountain
◨ National Park

Published by Lonely Planet Publications Pty Ltd
ABN 36 005 607 983

Australia Head Office, Locked Bag 1, Footscray, Victoria 3011, ☎ 03 8379 8000, fax 03 8379 8111, talk2us@lonelyplanet.com.au

USA 150 Linden St, Oakland, CA 94607, ☎ 510 893 8555, toll free 800 275 8555, fax 510 893 8572, info@lonelyplanet.com

UK 2nd Floor, 186 City Road, London, ECV1 2NT, ☎ 020 7106 2100, fax 020 7106 2101, go@lonelyplanet.co.uk

Printed through Colorcraft Ltd, Hong Kong. Printed in China.